Free Association

An Autobiography

by the same author

STEVEN BERKOFF: PLAYS ONE
(East, West, Greek, Sink the Belgrano!, Massage, Lunch)

STEVEN BERKOFF: PLAYS TWO
(Decadence, Kvetch, Acapulco, Harry's Christmas, Brighton Beach
Scumbags, Dahling You Were Marvellous, Dog, Actor)

I AM HAMLET

OVERVIEW

MEDITATIONS ON *METAMORPHOSIS*

STEVEN BERKOFF

Free Association

An Autobiography

ff

faber and faber

LONDON · BOSTON

First published in 1996
by Faber and Faber Limited
3 Queen Square London WC1N 3AU
This paperback edition first published in 1997

Photoset by RefineCatch Limited, Bungay, Suffolk
Printed in England by Mackays of Chatham PLC

A CIP record for this book is available from the British Library

ISBN 0-571-19269-6

2 4 6 8 10 9 7 5 3 1

For Polly and Al
who gave me life

ILLUSTRATIONS

1 Eva and Louis, Berkoff's maternal grandparents
2 Berkoff, aged 3
3 Polly, Berkoff's mother
4 Abraham (Al), Berkoff's father
5 Berkoff (aged 8) and his sister
6 Berkoff at 17, in his Tony Curtis phase (Presto Photo Ltd)
7 Berkoff, 18, with his parents at a Jewish wedding (Michael Silver, London)
8 Berkoff, 18, a budding salesman with Sandersons
9 As Henry VIII in Robert Bolt's *A Man for All Seasons*, Bournemouth, 1962
10 As Bamforth in Willis Hall's *The Long and the Short and the Tall*, Liverpool Playhouse, 1965 (Alan G. Swerdlow, Liverpool)
11 Berkoff with Lee Montague in *Semi-Detached* at Cardiff Rep, 1963
12 Berkoff in *Write Me a Murder* at Canterbury Rep, 1963 (© *Kentish Gazette*)
13 Berkoff in *Zoo Story*, Theatre Royal, Stratford East, 1965 (David Sim, © *Observer*)
14 For a televised *Hamlet*, Berkoff in costume as Lucianus
15 Steven Berkoff, Actor/Manager, or The Nureyev period, *c.* 1971
16 Berkoff in *Knock at the Manor Gate*, 1972 (© Cordelia Weedon)
17 One of the first of Berkoff's companies, on a tour of Holland with *The Trial*, *c.* 1971
18 Another Berkoff company outside the Round House, London, 1969
19 *The Trial* at the Round House, London, 1973 (© Roger Morton)
20 Linda Marlowe in *The Trial* (© Roger Morton)
21 The horses in *Agamemnon,* Round House, 1973 (© Roger Morton)
22 *Agamemnon*, Greenwich Theatre, 1976 (© Roger Morton)

23 Berkoff and Shelley Lee in *The Fall of the House of Usher*, Hampstead Theatre Club, 1975 (© Roger Morton)

24 Berkoff as Usher (© Roger Morton)

25 Shelley Lee as Madeleine Usher (© Roger Morton)

26 Berkoff as Mike, *East*, Greenwich Theatre, 1976 (© Roger Morton)

27 Matthew Scurfield as Dad, *East* (© Roger Morton)

28 With Anna Nygh (© Roger Morton)

29 Matthew Scurfield as Dad, Barry Philips as Les, Anna Nygh as Sylv and Berkoff as Mike, *East* (© Roger Morton)

30 Les and Mike, *East* (© Roger Morton)

31 Berkoff in his Houdini period: *Metamorphosis* with Petra Markham and Jeannie James at the Round House, London, 1969 (© Cordelia Weedon)

All photographs not otherwise credited are courtesy of the author.

PREFACE

When I started to write these memoirs I had in mind all those I had waded through in the past and my impatience with their order of events. I was keen to get to the personality I knew, to bite into the mature fruit rather than be made to wait. It seems that everyone is born, has parents, goes to school, and it's not too much of a generalization to say that everyone resembles one another but for a few interesting details here and there. It is when the struggle begins and one is released from a life that has been organized that the aspects of personality begin to emerge, and one makes certain choices as to how to deal with the chaos that is the stimulus of life and how to give it some form and interpretation. I did not wish to leave out my early years, but rather to try to put them in an order that would show a causal effect within the later years. So I free-associated, as one does in conversation, letting one thought spark off another, so that my life unravelled in this way rather than in a sequential order. A chronological order of events may be clearer and certainly would have been less of a headache to write but the more spontaneous method produced unexpected links and the development of certain themes. If this is sometimes frustrating I apologize in advance and hope the reader with a dash of patience will be rewarded for it. This is the first volume and this is my life as I remember it.

INTRODUCTION

Breakfast at Ma's

The flat she eventually moved to was in Rowley Gardens, which sounded nice and bucolic, as if it was a sleepy village estate buzzing with wasps nuzzling their noses into butter-yellow daffodils, while actually it was a council estate abutting Harringay stadium dog track. But it did overlook Finsbury Park and joy of joys there was a balcony. I'd drive over on my motorbike on Sunday mornings and if it was sunny I'd sit on the balcony.

We had this tray with legs that would unfold, and she'd set this down with a little cloth napkin, which apart from a few egg stains and tea drips was still acceptable. I'd look into the middle distance, where the sky would dissolve into the horizon and shimmer with a bluish opacity. I used to wonder at the mysteries of horizons and what lay in and beyond those distant hills, which looked like countryside from Mum's eyrie on the eighth floor. Ma would be heating the beigels under the grill and meanwhile a cup of dark brown tea would arrive and a bit of natter would ensue. But Ma would never sit with me – she would stand, as if she were a slave of my desires and wanted to be standing, so as always to be ready to fulfil them.

She'd be wearing that funny apron and it had on the shoulder strap a little fluffy bit as if to soften the image of the apron, the cloth of motherhood, servitude and provider. She'd stand, as I remember, with an elbow on the balcony, ready to refill the cup and jump back inside to get another half beigel kept in readiness. She'd buy them in Stamford Hill and sometimes she would walk back to save the bus fare, although I never dreamed things were that tight. There would be a smear of cream cheese and a sliver of smoked salmon and the crispy warmed beigel and my teeth would crunch into the quadruple taste of bread, butter, cream cheese and salmon, plus a slice of pickled cucumber on top, and so you had all the flavours of the small world we inhabited in one go. Then another tea would be on its way. I might look swiftly at the paper – I would never read the *Daily Mirror* normally, but I was brought up with it and it seemed part of our lives, as we read the exploits of Jane and Andy Capp. Andy Capp lived next door and Jane was the delicious tarty girl we all drooled over and hoped to win. 'Live letters' were the simpering thoughts of idiots like ourselves. But now I condemned it and implored Ma to read a better paper; she too was dissatisfied, but couldn't change the habits of a lifetime. And so the *Daily Mirror* and the *Herald* were our morning fare: good, socialist reading. There might also be a dish of olives, that might have been in the fridge a mite too long and be a bit shrivelled.

She'd watch me eat as if I was a miracle, an angel who had flown in over the balcony at Manor House, a chimera, a long-lost son she hadn't seen for years who had returned from the war. But I had only seen her this time last week. 'Bing bong' as I pressed the bell and heard her patting down the corridor. When she opened the door, it was always the same huge melon smile of unadulterated joy, and so I would fool around a bit, and sometimes ring the bell and hide behind the door, or nip into the washing-machine room which they kept on every floor; I heard her say, 'Where the hell is he?' but enjoying the game too since we were playing with the sensation of how pleased we were to be seeing each other.

So, if it was sunny, I would sit on the balcony, and if not, in the little kitchen by the little yellow formica table, and I could look out of the window on my right which, while still a view, wasn't so nice. Then would begin the liturgy of how everything was in my kingdom of Islington, which usually began with how is . . .? – my current lady – and is all well, and then how is the cat, called Pottle, a tortoiseshell creature for whom I bought cat food for sixteen years, and then how is the house, and then work. The work would receive the most curses, as if there was some kind of conspiracy working against her angel son, simply because he was so angelic and wonderful and talented in her eyes. Then the son receiving all the adulation from the mum would become convinced of its truth; it would be Mum's truth, but it didn't matter. And then the son would get enraged on behalf of the mum and so both of them fumed, inveighed and seethed against the drab world which had no time for Mum's angelic son, who in the meantime was scoffing down beigels with cream cheese and salmon, washed down with abundant cups of tea.

And then it was over. When the breakfast was well and truly reconstituted and happily ensconced inside his tummy, he was too heavy to fly off, but would leave by the lift and hoped it did not stink too much of piss, which is performed less for relief than because of the working-class kid's atavistic desire to leave his mark. Like a cat. I had stayed a respectable time and cheered Mum up, as she did me, and we had had a few laughs together. I heard the moans and groans devoted each week to what an unfeeling monster my dad was, but on the other hand he couldn't help it, she added, as if she felt that perhaps it wasn't healthy to poison the son against the father, but I already knew about him anyway. There had been no love lost between Dad and me for years. So Ma seethed for a while, resembling a chimney gushing out smoke, until the fire of her rage subsided. But she needed to talk about it, and then we were happy again and stared at the horizon.

My favourite bit at the end, just before I left, was to impersonate the big man of the world and take out my wallet and bung her a few quid; the more I could give the better I felt. She had always helped me out as a teenager and had lent me some money to go and live abroad when I was nineteen. So that would be the last ritual after talking and eating and confessing and laughing and looking and more eating and more tea and please I've had enough, and there's just one half beigel left and you might as well eat that, and then the crisp notes and then the goodbyes. She'd stand at the door until the lift came and then I would get into the lift and wave while the door was closing and I would stick my hand outside the slowly closing door and pull it in just in time. Then I would walk out to the courtyard and see her waving from the lounge window. In later years, when I had a motorbike, I would ring sometimes when I got home to Islington, to show her how amazingly fast I had got there. And in one piece.

Brighton, 1990

It's a cold winter morning in Brighton as I stare out of the window contemplating the icy sea which is merging with a grey, rain-filled sky. I'm not working, and by that I mean in the full, large sense of the word when I am physically expressing the few gifts that I have brought to some degree of skill and illumination. I stare at the brochure for an acting company that is touring the world with *Coriolanus* and one other play and I twist inside with envy for lost opportunities. I worked out my definitive *Coriolanus* in New York in 1988; it was well received. For once the critics agreed with each other. It was exciting to unravel the world of Shakespeare, an opportunity I seldom get. Chris Walken played the lead and did well, but it was the conception and movement of the whole beast that helped him release his power, besides his own unique abilities.

I like to create each production as a piece of theatre in a way that has never been conceived or imagined before, as if there had never been a theatre. I attempt to approach each piece with the avowed intention of making this the goal and salvation of my life, as if my very sanity lies in solving the puzzle. This can make for a certain amount of strain, because I risk much of my peace of mind, but if I persevere I may enter another area of my imagination which is not programmed by what has gone before and that can be quite exciting. I bring areas of my unconscious into play, rather than letting them lie dormant like some fetid lake in the base of my skull.

I risk less now and do not face such torture, but when in May 1988 Joe Papp asked me to direct *Coriolanus* at New York's celebrated Public Theater, my mind was heavy with doubt and fear. I am not one of those directors who sit down and work out the set and the costumes and submit nice transparent drawings for the carpenters and wardrobe department – if I did the show would have little chance of organic growth since it would have been conceived in a conscious if not superficial way sans the involvement of the actors. The stars would flash their skills while they were 'on', but when they left the stage the whole thing would wait in a kind of ghastly limbo until they returned and the reviews would refer to the lead actor and little else as if Shakespeare had written a one-man show. On the page each scene reads with some vitality and you do not get impatient while reading 'lesser' scenes, since these are the plot-builders and warm-up acts, getting you ready to involve yourself and suspend disbelief. On stage these scenes are usually played by bored wrecks of civilization who have been chosen to support the star, a Dustin or an Ian to liven up the action.

The invitation to direct *Coriolanus* came at the time I was playing the Dad figure in my play *Greek*. I would be acting Dad on stage and suddenly I would be thinking of beginnings for *Coriolanus*. Dad was a part I didn't care for much, although I thought I had conceived a well-written piece of senile, patriarchal flatulence. I identified with Eddy, the central role, the reborn Oedipus, iconoclast rebel and lover; I felt I would be the role since I *was* Eddy and I wrote the play as a mask for my own feelings and ambitions.

On *Greek*'s first outing in 1980 Barry Philips played Eddy and was awfully good. I sometimes resented the fact that it was him and not me who was playing the part, but he did it so well that it was a pleasure to watch him using all the marvellous vocabulary of working-class body language to instil the play with such humour and vitality. We started off with a try-out in Croydon, then moved to the Half Moon Theatre in Alie Street, and it was a sensational evening.

I staged the play in a kind of white-walled box and whitened the actors' faces, which exaggerated the shape of their skulls and gave a feeling of the Greek mask. The movements were simple and dynamic, with much profile work, a burning away of simple, naturalistic 'fussy movement' and a strong use of gesture, close to dance but nearer to drama. Stillness was vital to the opening and the long speeches were performed in an almost statuesque manner. The family became the environment and the chorus when needed, supporting the action as a real family does. A table surrounded by four chairs became the centre-piece and the play sometimes had a feeling of oratorio. The large arias, as I call them, were supported by the other actors' vocal music and the whole production was an invention. It resembled nothing else I had ever done, since this is my mandate to myself, that nothing I do should resemble anything I have done before.

The play was generally shot down in flames, but it received a review from Marina Warner, a writer I have a lot of time for, which vindicated everything I had tried to say. I cared so much that this distinguished writer should so immediately understand and respond to my words while the zipped-up blokes with all their blocked-up repressions were having fits. Irving Wardle at least rewarded me with a review that said, 'A Berkoff production announces itself in letters a mile high.'

When we revived *Greek* in 1988 at the Wyndham's I was getting a bit long in the tooth to play Eddy, so I let a younger man take the part. As I said, I played Dad and got through it by fits and starts. It was successful and played to cheering audiences each night. My dear ally, the sadly departed Georgia Brown, happened to be in London, as did Gillian Eaton, who had played in it in LA in 1982, and so with Bruce Payne as Eddy we sailed forth on a whim and it worked. It was one of those things which you never have to plan, it just falls into your lap.

It was painful working with Bruce since he had been off the stage for a number of years and at first lacked the special sparkling edge of unpredictability he had when he appeared in my play *West* at the Donmar Theatre in 1983. Perhaps he had developed a kind of self-consciousness which I believe suppurating agents and unctuous PRs give you, inflating what was a raw young blast of energy into a career-mover. But when he kept chipping away he found what was the real human underneath all the lacquer. Eventually he gave a vital and dynamic performance and trod the edge of danger, even if I was exhausted in the process.

Georgia was a fountain of pure, undiluted energy; she and Gillian were both dynamic and comic. I played the old man, in the words of *Time Out* critic Steve Grant, as an 'East End samurai', which pleased me no end. Gerald Scarfe gave his considerable gifts to painting a backdrop which was to be a mass of heads and grimaces, suggesting a football mob or a group of alienated, disenfranchised mortals that stalk this city. The fresco became so fascinating that I was afraid the audience would keep looking at it and not at us, so I carefully lit the stage with overhead and side lights to soften its impact.

Of course I was excited to have engaged such a 'star' as Gerald. I recall coming in one day to rehearse, seeing him still working away and feeling distinctly proud that this famous artist was doing the backdrop for my little piece of scatological spleen. I had the star dressing room at Wyndham's and Chris Malcolm, my producer and friend, was the first to encourage me to stride forth into the great West End arenas, since he had none of the reservations I had. I thought maybe we should revive it in some flea-pit or worthy fringe hole, but Chris insisted we go for it, throwing ourselves on to the marketplace and testing our real worth.

Our ten-week revival worked. The reviews were now altogether more positive than they had been in 1980 and we were spared the snide and self-important cant of critics like Robert Cushman and James Fenton, whose one word after our 1980 première – 'Yuk' – was left the way a dog leaves behind a turd. It always surprises me that a critic who is himself a writer can be so cruelly sarcastic, even if he dislikes what he sees. However, *Greek* was written in the language of the people, a demotic tongue, with a working-class poet in the character of Eddy, showing that the middle classes are not the only ones who are allowed poetic flights of imagination. The language is raw, as befits the subject, which is love and passion in the time of the plague, and takes as its theme the Oedipus legend. The plague symbolized the gross acts of violence being perpetrated the length and breadth of Britain, which for me meant a fairly bitter, strife-ridden society that could make neither good sandwiches nor good love and that solved its differences with bombs in pubs and massive displays of frustration at the weekly ritual called football. Of course I am being a touch ironic here, since *Greek* was also in part inspired by the pain of a bitter relationship I was going through . . . The agony of it left me raw enough to use myself as the guineapig for the play. The love letters that were unsent were recycled into the text.

Even so, I enjoyed writing *Greek*; it flowed out of me easily once the theme had entangled itself in my craw. My love became Eddy's love, my hate Eddy's hate, my bile and pity Eddy's and so on. I very rarely need to 'research' to find my themes or seek for 'subjects', since take it or leave it the subject has been myself. The one exception was when I wrote *Sink the Belgrano!*, when I learned about duplicity and Exocet missiles.

Martha Graham, I believe, once said that we are unique in the

4

world as each one of us was born with a different face, soul and life, and we are the professors of that life. I tend to agree and side with Elia Kazan, who writes in his fascinating autobiography that what is most personal is most universal. I have seen plays written here that give me not the slightest inkling of the real *voice* of the author, let alone his or her sex. The plays are dissertations proclaiming their values and academic research, worthy little theses with little heat but much rant. Perhaps I do not give my contemporaries a fair examination, but I have seen too many plays which left me frozen and unmoved, the characters merely mouthpieces for certain correctly held attitudes. There is little daring or experiment with form, just a massive concern with themes, as if theatre were a kind of forum reflecting political and social events run by decent, well-meaning people who poke their moral thermometer into the world's cesspits from time to time and give their weather forecasts. I have always imagined theatre to be the last resort of an overburdened imagination, a hothouse of profanity, an opening of Pandora's box, but most of all an examination of us in all our warts, wounds and blemishes. Closer to Freud than to the political columns of the *Daily Rant*. However, there is room for all, so let the decent chaps with their socially conscious plays and decent actors keep on producing their worthy scenarios.

Zoot Suit – Childhood, 1950

The first production of *Greek* at the little Half Moon Theatre in Alie Street in 1979 took me back to my youth there. It was an eerie sensation strolling through the back streets of the East End, since years before, my father's tailor's shop stood just round the corner in Leman Street. It was a small hole in the wall catering almost exclusively for West Indians; on Saturday the place was full of 'coloured people' ordering zoot suits. There was a betting shop upstairs, and much of the profit from the old man's hard-earned calluses, produced over forty years of cutting with the huge shears, was frittered away on the nags, the dogs and anything else from poker to bridge.

I used to go down Leman Street while I was still at school, just to look proudly at a real shop; somehow I couldn't quite believe we owned one. I'd take the 653 bus from Manor House and disembark at Gardners Corner, walk down the few yards and gladly run across the road to refill the large tin teapot or do anything to be useful, but mostly I just wanted to look and stare at the empty shelves in the display cabinet and wonder why they weren't stuffed full of shirts and ties.

This was because Dad mostly did tailoring for 'schwartzers' – Yiddish slang for black immigrants – who wanted the jackets to their fingertips and trousers that swelled out at the knee and tapered at the cuff like a giant leaf. The pleats had to be reversed and the loops dropped so that the belt did not ride over the waist. The lining had to be satin and the jacket was invariably single-breasted with a long, narrow lapel that swept down to the hips and would be done up by one button. All these ramifications would be gone into in great detail and with much debate. I knew then that my dad made a unique suit called a zoot suit, and that nobody in London could make a suit for West Indians like he did and I was justly proud. His fame grew far and wide and yet he was never very keen to have me around the premises, as if my being there hampered his freedom. Being young I took all this for granted, believed that I was a nuisance and shouldn't hang around the father who had sired and fed me. I was happy just to pop in and be a nuisance for a while, to try on the beautiful satin-lined jackets that were waiting to be picked up and stare at the photos around the wall from so and so to 'Al' – my dad. He made suits for boxers who had their photos taken with him while they were choosing some cloth. I seem to remember a picture of Gus Lesnevitch, who was world heavyweight champion in the late forties, hanging on the wall. Boxers were part of East End life when Dad was a child, and the family knew the Jewish fighters Ted Kid Lewis and Kid Berg, who were both world champions. Uncle Alf, my mother's brother, was a flyweight and fought Jimmy Wilde, who was known as 'the hammer' and also as 'the ghost with the hammer in his fists', because he was so thin! Alf Mansfield went blind after his exertions in the ring and the many operations he had to remove cataracts which kept growing; he eventually lost his sight when he was twenty-eight.

After the war, when I was ten years old, my family – my parents, sister Beryl and I – were reduced by an American adventure that didn't work out to sharing two rooms and an outside loo in Anthony Street (off Commercial Road, E1), but fresh eggs were guaranteed by

6

the chickens in the backyard. I didn't mind it so much, since the street had a varied social life and there was the Troxy Cinema a mile up the road in Poplar for my Saturday morning treat and the Palaseum at the end of the road for the Sunday afternoon film. I'd take a bottle of Tizer and a basket of sandwiches, since I seemed to be perpetually hungry, and we'd sit through the double feature well satisfied and hang out on the doorstep in the evening for the ritual natter. I'd do my homework in the kitchen to be ready for school at Raine's Foundation, which was then considered a first-class grammar school; for exercise I would take a solitary swim in the giant lido in Victoria Park, which kept me healthy and out of trouble in those years, but I notice that the local authorities with their traditional myopia have since seen fit to shut it down. That pool was my salvation. In the winter I would swim at the indoor Betts Street Baths off Cable Street, where I was so determined and indomitable that the pool attendant, a grizzly old bloke, gave me half a crown after I swam a mile one afternoon. I got a certificate for doing seventy-three lengths and was terribly proud.

I was passionate about swimming and would escape into the cool, sublime and weightless world and be happy for an hour and then make my way back to our two rooms and the six cats I had adopted. I seemed to be a solitary child, a bit of a lone wolf even in those days, and felt compassionate towards strays, with whom I identified strongly. I would pick up off the street any animal that looked forlorn or sad, drag it home, give it milk and be contented that we had saved something. My mother also suffered a degree of loneliness. Dad was not much to be seen since the flat wasn't big enough for all of us – so he said. I'd walk to school and get a bus back. For lunch, there could be nothing more enticing than a meal at one of Joe Lyons's famous cafeterias in Commercial Road; my particular fave was tomato soup with a generous dollop of mashed potatoes plonked in it.

I was at Raine's Foundation for two years and formed a special liaison with a teacher called Mr Shivas; he became my favourite, as he seemed to respond to me. Since he was an English teacher he encouraged the budding of my youthful talent. He had a gentleness that I missed at home from my often absent dad. I bonded very easily with teachers and older men generally – I felt at ease with them and wanted them to be my 'friends'. The TV producer Mark Shivas, who became Head of Film at the BBC, is Mr Shivas's son; when I first found this out I sought him out; and he continued his dad's interest, actually producing a play of mine called *West* on Channel Four in 1983.

When we were rehoused through my mother's constant battering at the door of the LCC, we moved to council flats in Manor House, N4, called the Woodberry Down Estate which sounded rather posh for subsidized housing. We now had a bathroom, of course, and I had my own bedroom for the first time in years. It was wintry and dreary and I was totally disorientated. I was sent to Hackney Downs Grammar, where the young Harold Pinter was just finishing. Hackney Downs School, known to generations of North Londoners as 'Grocers', was founded in 1873 by the Worshipful Company of Grocers and was originally intended to fill a gap in secondary school education for children up to the age of fourteen or thereabouts. A scheme was devised with defunct charities to raise money for the school. The school was opened in 1876. On 18 March 1963 it was burned to the ground. The cause ironically lay in the desire to have drama in the theatre. Apparently a 'dimmer' used to raise and lower lighting levels overheated; the old building caught fire and most of it was destroyed.

However, I had achieved one of its early objectives by leaving before my fifteenth birthday. It was a ghastly school and I was put into a C grade for no reason that I could see, since in Raine's I had been in the A stream and nowhere near the bottom of that. The headmaster said that it was to test me and that he would grade me properly when he could see my capabilities, but my spirit was mightily crushed. The shock of downgrading was so severe that I never really recovered, since even at twelve I had great pride in myself and what I felt to be my goals – which were to be famous as either 'a writer', 'a priest' or 'a film star'. Kids always seem to have headline definitions of their goals. Now all was shattered. I went home the first day weeping as I crossed Hackney Downs under a grey, leaden sky, and fell red-eyed into the arms of my mother, who told me to get right back to school.

The grading was the beginning of my downfall since it corroded that little battery of pride which kept me committed to whatever I did and filled each day with a sublime sense of purpose. No one extracted more from a day than I did; boredom was unknown to me.

My exploration of my East End environment had been a never-ending source of fulfilment, and my energy still sought adventures in the four corners of the world.

Petticoat Lane

In the summer in those days, I and my mate Cornelius from across the road would get our swimsuits (cozzies), beetle down to the Tower of London and swim by a little strand of beach there that was a kind of watering hole for the East Enders. I would happily swim out into the filthy, polluted Thames since we knew not of such things as pollution in those days, but joined the rats and stray dogs out to cool off. Sometimes I would go with Ma, who happily sat in a deck chair, calmly watching me swim out to the middle and back.

On Sundays came the biggest event of all, when Petticoat Lane was in full swing and there was no bigger adventure in the world. I was a bit of a philatelist and there was a corner of the Lane for all the stamp collectors who gathered together like old crows, peering through magnifying glasses at the shreds of our stamps. What an album I had, what a feast of colours with great flag-like stamps of all nations, and how curious they all were! I loved the triangle-shaped stamps and the large ones that became larger the more puny and insignificant the country. I wondered at the Nazi stamps and stamps with a million Deutschmarks printed across.

I'd stop at the animal market first, at Club Row, and make my round of all the pups and kittens, annoying the traders with my expressions of concern at the sight of a glue-eyed creature. Then I would climb over a wall to save myself from being crushed in the river of flesh that wedged itself down there each week; it was the one escape, the one fantasy for the East End; it was like a fair and a carnival, a place of wonder and an Aladdin's cave. There was no telling what strange things might be for sale, what bizarre possessions might not be unloaded into the maelstrom. Weird and wonderful coins and medals, ancient watches, bits of machinery that seemed torn out of some instrument of torture, but your East Ender knew what to do with these bits of junk cannibalized from some old motor. After we moved away from the East End the Lane became my weekly pilgrimage, my dip into the old bath.

In later years I got rid of my beautiful stamp collection at the same place. Got rid of it hurriedly and without thinking to have it valued. Just to put some money in my pocket. As my biological needs changed in those spotty teenage years of turbulence, I swopped my stamps for another kind of collecting, an obsessive and relentless quest for girls. It became the goal of my life, occupying each waking moment and crowding my dreams. It was the search for the Holy Grail, as if in the pursuit some indefinable secrets would be revealed to me. However, for some time my contact with girls consisted of no more than restless stirrings in my mind and prolonged stares at these objects of desire. But now I was content to purge my energy in a swim each day, come rain or shine, and to fulfil my ambition to be a Channel swimmer, no less.

The evenings were no less charged with longing and wonderment at the possibilities that existed, since benevolent philanthropists and wise heads of communities had decreed that there should be a boys' and girls' club on nearly every street corner of the East End, so that our youth would not be prone to the evil temptations of slum life and fall into bad ways. I would go to the Bernard Baron Settlement in Berner Street, which was a nest of activities, and play a mean game of pingpong, do some PT on the roof or some painting in the art class. One day I was scrawling some impulsive doodles but they must have looked like the incipient stirrings of a great abstract artist, since the teacher, a very benign and cultured gentleman, came up to me and praised me highly, begging me to continue the classes and eventually go to art school. He wanted to see Mum, but she was bemused at the idea of my being an 'artist' – I'm never quite sure what she had in mind for me but I think she saw me as some budding salesman. The praise never left my head, though; it was to act as confirmation that I had talent, which I never doubted. I now started to see myself as some kind of artist and this was further developed once a week in art class at school.

On the way home from a hectic round of pingpong my thirst would drive me to a little hole in the wall at the top of Cannon Street Road, where a man sold coloured sugary juices that he'd mix with soda water. In later years the poor man was murdered, but the killers never found his stash of money wrapped in bits of paper – something like £20,000, including, no doubt, all my twopences.

Friday was bath night and at Betts Street Baths, just off Cable

Street, you would take your sixpence and wallow in the luxury of a huge tub and like a sultan shout out commands like 'More hot water, number 5!' Around this time Mum thought it wise to get me a Meccano set, which filled in any extra hours or rainy days during long school holidays. I loved to pore over the booklet and work out simple constructions; the complex ones fazed me and I knew my mind was not capable of retaining logical plans or thinking in a linear fashion. It was a freewheeling, scattered mind that worked on intuition and spontaneity. At school it was French that I adored, since I found the mystery of conquering another tongue fascinating and I invariably returned top marks.

Raine's Foundation in Arbour Square was not much given to the idea of freewheeling and talkative boys. The archaic form of punishment was to be given an 'entry' in the teacher's book for some alleged misconduct. After three pencil entries you would have an *ink entry*, which was getting serious, and after three ink entries, which could have been accumulated for nothing more than chatting in class, you would be thrashed with a cane by the PT master. I was the first in my class to suffer this humiliation. I was taken in front of the others and told to bend down. I could not believe the ferocity of the first strike across my tender cheeks. My breath was sucked out of me and I burst into a wail, but suffered two more and then sat down on my three stripes. The stripes became quite severe wheals on my backside. Mum was shocked, but thought it was something to do with grammar school discipline. You accepted your punishment since you always did what you were told. When we moved to Manor House I was not subject to the same abuse since I was getting bigger, although I did taste the cane a couple more times; on the third occasion I politely declined. 'No . . . my father doesn't hit me,' I lied, 'and neither shall you.' By then a favourite sport was to hit back at the teachers, which I must confess I did with a certain satisfaction when they tried to enforce their will physically. I was growing tired of adults attempting to communicate through the use of violence. A bit of a tearaway, I was, in the absence of paternal influence, accessible to bad influence elsewhere.

Now I became quite wicked, since the downgrading meant I had lost all I had worked for. There was no Mr Shivas at Hackney Downs, but he was replaced by Mr Brearley, who had made such an impression on the young Harold Pinter and was to take me under his wing and try to understand me as he rambled on in his sing-song Welsh accent. He was determined to have me master the intricacies of grammar, although I begged him to give me essays for homework. For the first time I sensed boredom. However, I found a club.

There is always a club for Jewish youth and this one was at Stamford Hill, which was a kind of crossroads of the immigrant's life. From the East End where the great Russian influx poured in there would be a gradual march up Hackney Road to Stoke Newington and then the wide open plains of Stamford Hill. N.16. Fresh air and greenery. Springfield Park and Clapton Pond. The Stamford Hill Boys' Club was a bit of a run-down shack, but at least you could play billiards and pingpong and once a year go to summer camp where you would tent out for two weeks in the Isle of Wight and be out of your mum's hair for a while.

I recall the tent life well. I became a victim. Perhaps I always felt this and I was being bullied rather appallingly, though for what reason I could never quite work out. Perhaps the potential victim gives out signals of insecurity or need, and this reinforces the other boys' sense of power. Frankly, I was desperately lonely at school. It must have started at Hackney Downs, where I felt a terrible sense of isolation. I found I was not so popular in class as I had been at Raine's and had few good mates. When a new boy arrived I would make a point of befriending him before all the others so that I might 'win' the 'best friend' I so desperately needed. But after a while the new boy would be absorbed by the others and I would take second place again. It wasn't really anything to do with me at all. That sort of need for friendship and affection makes schoolboys turn from you. So the year's summer outings were part torture, as the same thing would happen – the sense of isolation, shyness and eventually bullying. One summer I struck back at a bully and damaged his jaw with a whack I didn't know I was capable of. It was the moment of truth. I would not easily be bullied again. I had found myself.

The club at Stamford Hill was crawling with females of every possible variety and type, since the flow of immigrants out of Europe decades ago had created an interesting mixture of sweet, sensual maidens. Crowning the area was Stamford Hill itself, a large crossroads where each corner had its vital landmark. On one corner was the giant Regent Cinema, into whose vast caverns we'd all flop on Monday nights, while on the other corner was the huge tobacco shop with the barber's at the rear and an all-night café. On 'our' side was the E and A Milk Bar and the amusement arcade where you could play the machines. A few hundred yards down the road was a small common where you could take 'birds' for a walk – if you were so lucky, of course.

This area became my university for the next half a dozen years and spawned many of the thoughts and ideas that were to become useful to me later on. I spent many evenings drifting around Stamford Hill or I might even go back to the East End to visit my old youth club, a place off Myrdle Street, which had a dance once a week in its basement. (I 'changed clubs' as if they were the Garrick or the Savage.) This weekly hop was quite an event and we'd bowl down to give the girls the once-over; we would have no more idea of what to do with them than drive a car, but we would look and admire and stare with utter wonderment. If we were extremely fortunate we might gain access to violently passionate kisses, since that was the style of kissing, as if the prohibition on other parts caused you to throw all that rapture into the lingual embrace with much teeth-clashing, tongue-chewing, neck-biting and other arcane practices to demonstrate that you had style. I think the girls were influenced by the weekly movies at the Regent and would tear out your hair while ripping out your tongue and so such sessions were invariably succeeded by battle scars and red blotches on the neck. Stamford Hill girls were very demonstrative.

The Shtipp House

A middle-aged man called Bill ran the amusement arcade, which became the meeting place for 'the boys', our OK Corral. We called the place the shtipp house because *shtipp* is a Yiddish word for push and that was how we played the machines. The bus stop just opposite provided immediate transportation to whereverland. The West End was an uncharted territory that one day we had to conquer, but in the meantime there was plenty to occupy a young man with curiosity.

The arcade was like any other pinball arcade, but it seemed to gather around it the youth of the area. You would slide the pennies in the slot and await the comforting rumble of steel balls tumbling out and into your 'alley', where, one at a time, you would press the button to release the silver ball and then pull back another handle which acted like a cannon and sent the projectile careering all over the table, striking little spring-like pylons that would briefly light up and make the wonderful sound of a 'hit'. Then as the ball tore down the ramp you had the opportunity to try and whack it up again with a pair of flipper-like devices. You might play for a penny a point and so win or lose quite a bit of pocket money in one night. But the thrill was there and you'd grip the machine for dear life, gently nudging but not too much in case you registered 'tilt', which would be disaster and have the aged assistant Bill in his white coat rushing up and kicking you out for potentially damaging the machine. Then you'd be exiled and would have to stand outside in the twilight zone enviously hearing the rumble of the steel balls and awaiting the time when Bill decided you had served your sentence and allowed you to return.

A jukebox stood at the far end and for twopence you could play 'Jezebel', sung by Frankie Laine, over and over again and in a fairly spontaneous moment might perform a mini-jive with Anita, the uncrowned princess of Stamford Hill, a bold, beautiful blonde goddess who wore suits cut in men's styling, which was the fashion then.

School was by now invariably dull and boring. I had lost the will to study which had once been my obsessive goal. If the kids in the class played up, so did I. As the C grade we were regarded as less than useless, and the energies of the teachers went into the A and B streams. Beware of downgrading and demoting children, since it does not take much to poison their confidence. I started smoking, neglected my swimming as a sport and just did it in the summer at the Tottenham Lido, sadly lost interest in French, paid lip service to homework, and fooled about in class.

My friend in the class was Morris Hope, whose father was a furrier, and thus Morris always had more pocket money than anyone else and wore smart suits to school; he even wore aftershave and smelled terribly elegant. He was rather a handsome and prepossessing youth, blond with strong, healthy teeth and a kind of Kirk Douglas look. I found in him a kind of role model; I was full of admiration, even more so when he took a Charles Atlas course and visibly swelled up before my eyes. We played truant a few times and wandered around Hackney Marshes and he gave me advice about

14

what to do when you decide to get married – this is when he was fourteen. He eventually became a multi-millionaire, which was no surprise to me, and he is with the same wife he married when he was eighteen.

In the early days of 'Grocers', school was my only means of contact with the human race, as I had not yet made friends in Manor House and the weekends were full of a dread loneliness which affected me so much that it became a psychological trait: I have never lost the sensation of long and bitter loneliness with just Mum at home and the infrequent burst on the horizon of the father figure, who on very rare occasions actually took us to the pictures. Discovering the Stamford Hill Boys' Club made a dent in my loneliness and gave me a way of making a role for myself in society.

The Hill was the melting pot and training ground for what we would all be in later life. It was a school of hard knocks which encouraged you to defend yourself in the frequent skirmishes which would suddenly erupt as if from nowhere; you learned not to whinge or complain if you got a minor pasting. You also learned the ability to strut your gear and have a talent to amuse by being the joker or clown by your obsession with fashion, since you would always have your suits tailor-made even if it took a year of saving and many months of privation. A suit was your armour and your colours and further defined your sense of aesthetics. A talent to make money was much lauded and you would seek all means, some foul and some fair. By any definition it was a rough school, but a school which gave you the idea that it was down to *you* and not your dad, the state or any other charity that would bail you out. It was you. You had to give your all to whatever endeavour, since there was no one and nothing to fall back on except your own wits and ability to improvise. Some, like Morris Hope, had comfortably off parents and homes where smoked salmon would be on the table and the air smelt of their mothers' perfumed furs and thick carpets lined the hallways, but for most of us it was the pungent air of the council-house lift with its invariable odour of some youth's micturition.

Language was curiously very important; I see now retrospectively that my friend 'ginger Paul' was the funniest man alive. He wore a quiff that stood out from his head and defied the laws of gravity, was an ace dancer in the cool jive style of the period and would have us all doubled up in laughter at his ability to play with words. Ginger Paul was very handsome with a perfect profile and blue eyes set in scabby skin, which seemed to add to his attraction – or he would have been too perfect. Unfortunately he desperately wanted to be a 'shtarker', which is a tearaway, since he looked like James Cagney, but he didn't have the will and was a touch cowardly. However, he had such a demeanour that he was allowed to bluff and be accepted by the leaders and strut around with them, while I remained on the fringes with the second division. But for a while, Paul was a 'best friend'.

Paul was among the first to make that sortie into the rarer regions of the West End, which was at that time akin to venturing into Hades or the Elysian Fields: it was a territory filled with wild imaginings that gossip had inflamed. We would listen to stories of wild adventures in Soho and of girls who worked at the Windmill Theatre who were somehow known by friends of friends. We would hear of villains whose exploits had us gasping in breathless admiration and the great dance halls 'up West' where we longed to tread – those places where you wore suits and stiff collars pinned to your shirt by studs and links and your shoes were polished like jet. I would syphon all this out in later years in two plays, called *East* and *West*.

LES: I fancy going down to the Lyceum tonight. I double fancy that. Being as it's Sunday we'll have Mr Ted Heath the famous band leader, not the acid bath murderer or notorious political impersonator-cum-weekend transvestite – and Dicky Valentine in a blue gaberdine, button two, flap pockets, hip-length whistle and flute. I'll wear a roll-away collar, a Johnny Ray collar, that sails out of your neck and a skinny tie – a slim Jim. French cuffs on the trouser with a fifteen-inch bottom. What about that handsome Donegal tweed with DB lapels? Button one, patch pockets, dropped loops, cross pockets on the trousers, satin lined, eighteen-inch slit up the arse on the jacket, skirted waist. What that one? Er – yeah – it's beautiful – finger tip length, velvet collar, plenty of pad in the chest ('Come on Morry, I said, more padding').

[from *East*]

So, when I walked down Leman Street on the way to rehearsal in the little ex-synagogue in Alie Street, I saw the ghost of Dad's shop still there and the photos of the West Indians in the window and then sat and saw *Greek* being expertly played by my company of actors. The play worked like an electric current through the audience and the Half Moon was packed for five weeks. That was when we decided to look for a West End venue, but in the meantime to keep the play alive and play it when we could. It was spring 1980 and I had just returned from Israel, where I had been directing my version of *Agamemnon* in Hebrew and had also performed *Hamlet* with my own company for the Jerusalem Festival which toured round the kibbutzes. So that year had already been a fruitful time.

Greek did eventually make it to the Arts Theatre in Newport Street but didn't stand up as well as we expected.

It did OK, but didn't make enough to pay the rent and wages. Yet so determined was I to make a go of it and so thrilled to have my powerhouse play in the West End that I felt we should adopt a more revolutionary stance and work even for sandwiches and coffee! But after a few weeks I notice that actors start looking forward to the end and doing something different. To my utter astonishment, the actors, although they had no other work to go to, did not wish to sacrifice some of their wages, which might have extended the play, and so the most exciting play in the West End closed.

For several years I had been closely identified with my own plays, through performing in them, and the punters may have found it odd and unacceptable that in this case I wasn't. In fact I was a touch in my cowardly vein. I didn't know if I could tackle anything so personal in front of an audience, while in a more fictional character I could be as naked and candid as I wished. Another reason was that I had written such an unwieldy play with huge arias pouring out of Eddy's mouth and I had not the slightest idea how I would stage it if I was in it. But then I never do know until I am doing it. My small team read the play and they all liked it and praised it so much and warned me very gently that the play might 'suffer' if I was in it and that I would have a better 'overview' if I stayed outside it for a change and what a good visual director I was and how much they would love me to be out there keeping an eye on them, etc., etc. I had heard this before, but this time I heeded their advice and the play closed after the guaranteed six-week run.

1975

When I was staging *East*, I remember my close colleague Barry Philips saying how marvellous the play was and perhaps I would be better on the outside keeping an eye on it. In my uncertainty – since just before you begin you are at your most raw and suggestible – I actually auditioned many actors to play Mike, a part I was tailor-made to play, and I had to suffer the indignity of listening to them reading my lines without a clue about how to deal with the bizarre combo of verse and Cockney slang. Instead of giving it a light whiplash quality, like comic actors satirizing the macho stance, those of the heavy-duty realist school bashed it as if they were Hoxton thugs.

So I patiently listened to all these rather awkward actors coming into our rehearsal place in Marylebone Road, later occupied by the intrepid Debbie Moore's dance/fashion house 'Pineapple'. But I was keeping faith with Barry Philips, a marvellously inventive actor, who had made the suggestion that this time I stay outside, but who knows what motives lie behind our conscious decisions? Of course I had a better grip on the play if I wasn't in it, but then the play didn't have *me* and then it would be a different kind of animal without the Berkoff animal. So I pondered and felt, oh well, I mustn't be in everything . . . '*Why the hell not?*' I now think. '*I had been out of work for most of my young professional life*', but I didn't think clearly then. So for a while I listened to Barry and saw more and more actors whose training in the theatre had rendered them totally incapable of putting one foot in front of the other. Their bodies were some kind of stiff, useless adornment they carried around with them since the directors of the time, whoever they were, seemed uninterested in the multiplicity of purpose of which the human body is capable. Yet for *East* in 1975 I found two of the most plastic, adaptable, fluent and skilled physical actors – everyone else who came into the group would look wooden in comparison. Not only were they skilled in the use and rhythms of their body, but they possessed powerful and lyrical vocal qualities and could be at home in the classics and modern; in playing *East* they gave the text humour and strong delivery.

Eventually I offered the part of Mike to a dreary actor who gave a modestly fair reading, but in the end he swallowed it, which in my jargon means he hadn't the guts to perform it. So eureka! I was in! It is a bit of a heavy-duty play and has one speech in it which would daunt the best of us and did me in the beginning, when I describe in somewhat exotic and anatomical detail the genital equipment of the opposite sex. These were the days of openness and candour, the dropping of the veil, the revealing of all thoughts and the baring of the soul.

So gratefully I dived in and played Mike. It was such a fabulous role that only the fearful, armed with all the repressions of his life and his prior work in the theatre, could turn it down. Barry was miffed, but we struck on and I cast the beautiful, leggy Anna Nygh as Mike's tart 'Sylv'. She gave a fabulous reading and was nothing less than totally supportive the whole time, although she could get her moods if ever I dared to demonstrate a lack of faith on stage. The virago could give me a verbal thrashing, but it would pull me up. Barry Stanton, who had already appeared in my production of *The Trial* at the Round House in 1973, played Dad in the first production, before Matthew Scurfield took over. Stanton was as stalwart an ally as one could ever wish for and whenever I had doubts, which were many and often, like a great bull he would bash on regardless.

As I said, my credo was that each show should be a new concept of theatre and style and form, so I often straitjacketed myself by refusing to have anything to do with realism. I believed that somehow we would find some 'magic' solution, but it never came. We engaged a pianist to play throughout as counterpoint to the speeches and to cover stage action, and had Mum played by Robert Longden. It was a theory of mine that women in the East End, when they lost their charms, became more like men, but what I really meant was that the hardship and practical needs of day-to-day existence caused them to worry less about their femininity and thus diminish it. I considered the play to be a kind of Beckettian oratorio with little movement, relying on the ubiquitous chairs that were to become a syndrome of 'experimental' theatre; but with Stanton we soon loosened it up. When we came to a family scene I was loth to use a table and props like a teapot and toast since this was contra to my anti-naturalist stance – I felt it corroded our mimetic and imaginative resources. In the past this had been largely true, when I saw all around me stages cluttered with every kind of 'real' prop to suggest to the audience that this was reality and the people were as real as you and me. I loathed the cluttered theatre with its endless scene changes during which the audience would sit there like lemons and pretend that there weren't some silly farts on stage changing the set and taking ages about it because the director couldn't relinquish all the junk he had been used to all his life.

So we came to this scene with the family at the table, and all my natural proclivities had been to 'face front' and suggest we were speaking to each other in this rather stilted way, but Stanton raised his huge Falstaffian frame, grabbed a table and smashed it down on the floor, grabbed a few cups we had our morning tea in and some other bits, and played the scene. Well, it was the funniest scene I had ever done and it jelled with all of us around the East End table and Mum pouring the tea. It felt as right as a Donald McGill cartoon; so right, in fact, that we dared not rehearse it again until we arrived for our midnight première at the tiny Traverse Theatre at the 1975 Edinburgh Festival.

I was overwhelmed by the use of a real table for the first time in my directing career. I saw it as being less a table than an extension of the stage, another platform on which to perform, but basically it *was* a table, an old-fashioned but very real table that we brought on for some very funny scenes which people talk about to this day. I felt it was a Cockney Marx Brothers brought to life. I became real for a change and learned that you can borrow from all styles without being doctrinaire.

I also learned to listen to actors as good as Barry Stanton, for the big man had a heart to match his size and his inventions were full-blooded. He became the pivot for all of us, his huge energy overwhelming us. His wallet was a mass of bank cards, something we scarcely knew of in those days. He always gave encouragement to all of us and was a brilliant combination of all the Alf Garnetts in the world. In certain scenes, such as the dinner scene with the family, he tended to improvise and so the scene grew and acquired different characteristics. His inventions became more and more weirdly monstrous until the audience was screaming with laughter. I used many of his contributions when I published the final text. So I *was* glad I played Mike.

Why and How I Wrote *East* – the Sixties

East started years ago. The ingredients were mixed into the pot and had been stewing for decades and had never really been tapped. I changed my life when I studied to be an actor and altered everything about myself until I was no longer what I had been; my metamorphosis between old and new Berkoff was no less a change than that which separates Jekyll from Hyde. In consequence I may have lost certain of the defence mechanisms that had served me in my youth and, being in a new world, was glad to accept the new 'laws'. I plodded on happy just to be a working actor, no matter what garbage I did – at least I was functioning, and as an artist that is a whole lot better than hanging around in a meaningless limbo; for someone like me that 'hanging around' was akin to being in hell. And I was in hell many times. Many times I had, like innumerable other aspiring actors, written endless letters, made endless calls, begged endless casting directors: I remember chasing poor Gillian Diamond, then casting director of the RSC, down the street.

I went to the YMCA nearly every day to work out and play handball with the taxi drivers who came each lunchtime year in and year out. Handball is a fast, dynamic game and after two or three bouts I had shed a couple of pounds and was on a high; when I left and hit the cold air of Tottenham Court Road I was fit to play Othello, but I had nothing to play and so I made my way home. I used to feel the most powerful sense of regret that I was keeping myself fit and had nothing to do with all that fitness and energy I had just summoned. What could I not have done had someone had the wit and perception to employ me? I was a storm of energy and for the life of me I could not understand why I was getting so little work. What was wrong? True, I did not have the pearly sweet vowels of my heroes Ian Richardson or Alec McCowen, but I did not speak like Alf Garnett either.

I sat and sweated it out sometimes for months, and as the days went by, like leaves torn off the precious tree of my life, I was making profound changes that were to affect me later. All those rejections were to become fuel to me; all those discarded weeks and months were turning to coal inside my soul and that coal would burn and let out a fire in future years. I came to realize that each pain and each rejection was not part of a conspiracy against me, but a lack of understanding on the part of the establishment. Maybe I came across too keen and too desperate. I would trawl the depths of my talents trying to please, trying to be different. If I had an audition I'd stay home for a week and work and work on the speeches, hour after hour like some demented maniac from an Edgar Allan Poe story, until they no longer yielded meaning. And then the day of reckoning would arrive and I had to appear in the right light, so I wore a pair of close-fitting grey flannel trousers with a roll-necked black sweater tucked into them. Would that do? Should I leave the sweater outside the trousers? Were the shoes all right and not big clodhoppers? I dashed into Joe Lyons's Corner House in Coventry Street and checked myself in the mirror. I looked too bunched up in the midriff, so I pulled the sweater out, but then I looked a bit top heavy, so I put the sweater back in, and now I was getting into a state.

I crossed the road and entered the stage door, feeling out of balance but quietly confident. I came on the stage and tore into Hotspur's 'My liege, I did deny no prisoners . . .' and I thought I was marvellous, bloody sodding marvellous . . . Halfway through I felt my voice start to hit the back wall and bounce back like those funfair 'try your strength' machines where you hit the target with a hammer and the bell rings. I heard my inner bell ring . . . silence for a few seconds and 'What are you doing for your modern piece, Mr . . . er Berkoff . . .?'

I had a string of them; my only sense of purpose came from working away like a beaver and tearing all the best speeches out of plays to become my launching pads to fame and success. 'I would like to do' and it would either be a play by Sartre, *Crime Passionnel*, or a sweet piece of comedy by William Saroyan called *The Time of Your Life* in which I played a love-mad character called Dudley Bostwick. It was a very funny piece of stand-up comedy with this poor Jerry Lewis-like geek on a phone trying to arrange to meet someone. There were a couple of small titters from the dark womb, but then a few days later the inevitable reply, 'Thank you but no thank you.' How could this be? Like Henry Irving's crazy Mathias I had heard bells. Even if they didn't want me I knew it was OK and that they were looking for other types and already had many like me. Young men were not in short supply – everyone left drama school at more or less the same age, young, vibrant, talented, but not unique.

I auditioned for Chichester in 1963 when the great Laurence Olivier, who was for me Zeus on Mount Olympus and my guiding light, was casting his new season. It was the time when he was setting up the National Theatre and Chichester and actors were falling over themselves to join him. Eureka, I got an audition. Once the great Zeus had seen his acolyte offering his divine light one great genius would, I thought, recognize the incipient stirrings of another and yes, the great and noble beast would gather me in his arms and say, 'Come.' And so I worked and sweated my balls off in my usual ritual of a week of preparation and duly performed my new piece – not, alas, in front of my idol, but for some poor harassed underlings of Sir, who had the painful job of sifting the wheat from the chaff.

The piece was from a little-known play by Ionesco called *The Killer*. This play, unbelievably, still has had no London production. It is a macabre study of a society that appears to be perfect on the surface but has a killer stalking the streets and picking off the satisfied and complaisant residents of the city. As an allegory it works on many levels and the character Berenger, the architect, appears, as he does in *Rhinoceros* and several other plays. I chose a speech which lasts a whole act and cut it down to about ten minutes, which of course is still far too much for an audition. In my enthusiasm I imagined that the very uniqueness of the piece would engage them and that they would be amazed and aghast at the material, having had to sit through yards of Osbornes, Pinters and Rattigans. They would see my blistering performance as a heroic stab into the belly of placid British theatre. But halfway through it the poor man conducting the cattle market got up and said in a high-pitched whine, 'Really, Mr Berkoff, we have already given you too much time and we have too many people to see. I'm very sorry, but we must stop you!'

I was flabbergasted by this wretch, who had the effrontery to assault my carefully honed piece of expressionistic drama. Surely points for effort if nothing else. I said nought, and walked off the stage. I was cold with a dull anger that this hopeless underling had thrown away my chance of working with my great mentor, and I knew that if Larry had been there the outcome would have been different. On the bus home I imagined all the scenarios that would have taken place had the noble one felt the blast of my talents. And so as soon as I got home I wrote a long letter of complaint to Sir at the Old Vic. It was almost a love letter, outlining how I had been stopped in full stream and – what was worst of all – prevented from being united with *him*!

Many months later, I was taking a leak in the interval of some play, and it might have been at one of my many journeys to the Old Vic to see Sir perform there, and the same underling was in the next trough. 'Hello, Mr Berkoff,' he said, 'you know Sir Larry was really disturbed at your letter,' and he went on to explain how little time they had had that day, but all I could think of was that Sir had had contact from me. That he had actually read my missive and, like the actor he was, been disturbed that I had been ill-treated. I was over-whelmed to think that my hero, who was Irving, Kean and Garrick rolled into one, should respond to me.

I was by this time getting the idea that to be independent might be my only route to salvation. I had gathered a group of actors round me and we were doing work that was exciting and, for my own part, totally original, but so brainwashed was I with the idea that accept-ance into the mainstream was a kind of membership of the theatrical society, that I still hankered after one of those jobs with a spear and a few lines in a major company. Well, Larry was different and I would have given up my hard-earned dreams of my own group for the chance of a brief encounter with the master. Again, I may have held myself back by hankering for what was after all conventional and traditional when I was standing at the edge of a total revolution in my own thinking. I sometimes imagined that what we were doing was stimulated by being out of work and was a substitute for the real thing, and yet what we were achieving was more exciting than any-thing on the 'outside'. I envied some of my cast who had left the group to join Larry. Modestly talented actors who could just about play small roles in my company were relating stories of, how they auditioned for Sir. I paled in envy, not being fully conscious of the fact that it would prove to be my good fortune *not* to be accepted and become a happy little actor with no say in my own creation. The events of these years were creating this minefield within me and I was in danger of defusing it.

This danger besets me now, even as I write these words. The du-bious thrill of being accepted when with acceptance comes the need for conformity, restraint, adjustment, always to another. Do it yourself and rely on nothing but your own imagination and the goodwill of your fellow players. Risk all, since you will not die when it is over.

So when one of my actors, an imaginative bloke who has since sacrificed himself into the maw of one of those many encounter groups that were burgeoning in the seventies, came and told of his audition for Sir, I was green with envy and felt not a mite of rage at the arsehole who had weeded me out at the first stage – although now I thank him from the bottom of my heart, for he hardened me for the tasks ahead.

'What did he say?' I asked.

'He asked me to insult him!'

'Insult him?' I responded. Insult the great Sir, I thought, when I would have gone down on my knees and kissed the hem of his jacket and felt not the slightest diminution of pride.

'Yes, he asked me to insult him' – he beamed, so proud of his temporary sniff at the abattoirs of fame – 'So I said, How can I, a mere actor in front of the world's best, insult you, you old cunt!'

We all fell about at his story, uncertain whether to believe it, and carried on rehearsals for *Macbeth* in the church hall opposite my house in Islington. No matter how long we rehearsed or how many actors found work and left, I would not stop until the production was on. I remembered too well the long years of unemployment and frustration, frittering my teenage life away in Stamford Hill.

Stamford Hill Days – 1950

Stamford Hill saw me grow from a callow youth of twelve into a spotty, gaberdined and Brylcreemed young blade who occasionally wore a pinstripe button three with a slash up the behind called a vent. I would, as I have said, save and slave for months: Dad wisely refused to make me a suit for free since he wished to instil in me a sense of values, so I would beg, cajole, plead for a suit to be made and when I had saved the twelve quid he would oblige. While still at Hackney Downs School I had to rely on pocket money and an occasional job on a stall in Whitechapel to make up the funds that I needed as a man of the world who was dating girls and looked a young gallant, but had the humiliating sum of fifteen shillings a week pocket money to sustain his lifestyle.

My first job, at the age of twelve, was a Saturday job for a character called the Pen King who had a stall in the East End outside Whitechapel Station next to a Joe Lyons tea shop. In these early days Biros were still rather special and the Pen King had all sorts of colours and varieties. He possessed a huge hooked conk for a nose and also had a limp, but he had a kind of broken-down, debonair and rather louche way of conducting himself. He was a part-time singer and seemed totally fascinated by my stories, so he allowed me to try and flog a few pens when he took his tea break in Joe Lyons. Desperately as I tried, I could never attract the huge crowd that he could summon up in minutes with a loud demonstration to grab attention. He would whack the pen down on a formica plate and show that it couldn't break, that it was somehow invincible, and the crowd of East Enders would be impressed by these glittering toys in their coloured sheaths. Then at the end of the day in the market called 'the Waste' he would gather up the profits, bung me my five bob, very nice thank you, give me a few pens to flog at school, and we would head to his home in Holloway where he lived with two elderly sisters. I surmised in later years that he was gay, but in those days I was hardly aware of such things and always thought, in my constant search for a dad, that any man who took an interest in me was a good sport and made me feel whole.

I worked for the Pen King on and off for a couple of years until he retired and then one day, many years later, I saw him in Chapel Street Market in Islington, selling, or trying to sell, an old jacket. He looked terrible and at death's door, so I bunged him a few quid. He responded a bit feebly and asked me how I was getting on in 'show biz'. We exchanged a few saddened words and I didn't see him again. But I will never forget the astounding flair and energy of the Pen King. He was my guide into the realms of teasing an audience, and like it or not I was getting a taste from behind the stall of seeing the customers separated from me by a stage. Be it a stall at Whitechapel or the stage at a West End theatre, it's still a stall, where you must flog your goods with as much aplomb as your will can summon and all your heart has to go into those speeches, that patter, the spiel, the act, the legerdemain, the persuasive power of your personality plus the faith in your goods, and that is what the Pen King had in spades, even if he was to fade into a twilight world. How many stages are populated by the phony, the spiritless, the pretentious, people who would never sell anything to an audience which had not paid its money first? The same people, if they could be converted into street vendors, would sell sod all to anyone and be left at the end of the day without a crust.

However, I am not dumb enough, whatever my detractors may think, not to realize that my simple romanticism over the Pen King is hardly an analogy for the struggle to create *Hamlet*, whether playing it or directing, as I have done, let alone trying to do both at the same time, but did I have choice? Choice is something that doesn't always come your way. So you can sit at home and dream of playing Hamlet or whatever takes your fancy and wait for some benign director to offer you the chance, and in the meantime you pine and mourn over your lost hours and youth. Well, sitting at home and quoting the lines in your kitchen and purging some of your frustration may be one way of quieting the raging beast, but it will surface and eat at your heart until you have no heart left. As an actor you have little choice in the way your future is mapped out – you must take the roads offered you, if they are offered at all, and adjust your dreams on the way. It is like playing a game of chance at some remote place in your life, waiting for the throw of the dice that sets you marching again or instructs you to 'go back to the starting position'.

The most painful situation for an actor to be in is when his energy is in full flow, his mind and muscle co-ordinated to a fine degree and he has nothing to do with this combustible energy but look forward to the weekly visit to the Westminster Labour Exchange and exchange anecdotes with other players at the tea shop in Victoria Street. How many times did I queue up with my fellow actors consigned to the purgatory of the endless wait and the tip-off that so and so at the BBC was looking for actors for some epic, and how many times did I phone through leaving my credentials and a small prayer of hope with them? And how often did the poor agents, who could do nothing for me but wait and recommend, have to listen to my out-pourings of woe when I asked how there could be no work for such a superabundantly talented performer, and how often would I face each day with a dreary eye and a curdled spirit when I had nothing to do that day except go to the YMCA or take a singing class? Keep yourself for the time when Kafka says, 'When in this life that demands so mercilessly that we be ready at every moment can one find a moment to make oneself ready?'

Always be ready, just in case. Gaze in awe at those who, without seeming pain or great effort, swan from role to role, and they will always be your torturers, whipping you for every idle day and unfulfilled hour. You will watch those rehearsing and eat your grief privately and when you play your endless games of handball with the taxi drivers and work yourself into a fighting-fit machine to work and create, you will have to take that energy home with you and watch it dribble away.

A large company, it may have been the RSC, was rehearsing Shakespeare at the YMCA one year, perhaps in the mid-sixties, and I ached with the pain of what I was doing – playing handball – and what they were doing. Each performance of theirs was a grid that was placed over my efforts and revealed me wanting. Also I had inherited a guilt complex from my dad, who had instilled in me the idea that work was what you were born to do and who constantly belly-ached about the years he had toiled since he was a kid in the sweat shops of the East End, forced to leave school at fourteen at the height of his academic achievements. He had been a formidable maths pupil and forty years later he was able to do all my algebra homework without batting an eyelid; he could work it out in his head, so I never got the marks since he didn't show the process. He chanted out the number of years he had sweated and kept us all, and how many years he had supported me and what a bum I was turning out to be.

And how does a grown man feel about not fulfilling his role on earth but choosing to wait and hope and plead and cajole? How did it feel? Well, it felt as if I spent years in purgatory. A prison would have been heavenly by comparison, since then at least you have no choice. So I read and worked at my texts and trained and waited and went to classes and studied mime and took singing lessons from the kindly and most patient Mr Kuhn in Hanover Street, W1, and continued to fight with the dragon in my soul that was eating me alive. Then one day I said to myself that I would put a stop to all this once and for all. I would change the position I was in and be a guv'nor and be responsible for me. I would look for a play that I wished to do and call actors around me and ask them to join with me, at least to have a work-out and at most to put together our own work. So one day I did just that and for the first time I felt a rumbling deep down as I dug into the pit of my stomach for some courage to do it.

I return to the crossroads of Stamford Hill where the sensitive youth is struggling to assert his frail ego amidst the boisterous blades and tearaways; where he voyages from pillar to post, seeking at each station some clues to his identity. In those coal-fire days the fog would come down like a thick veil, muzzling the night. It was full of mysteries, since you improvised your night. You did not, like nice, decent, well brought-up people, know what you would be doing, like evening classes, pictures or the telly – and the telly in those days was very good. You would swan out into the night, not knowing or caring, but thinking that the mere presence of your mates would be enough to create a mix that would ignite into some wayward or bizarre plan. I even feel a guilt now, as I write these memoirs, as if by stepping into the quagmire of the past I am abnegating the assault on the future, as if by wrapping myself in the thoughts and experiences of the dead and departed I am warming myself at the bonfire of my own vanities. Well, it's something to do while I wait to direct *The Trial* at the National Theatre for the '91 season, and it's one of those times when you can't quite fit in something to fill the weeks usefully before you commence. The hunger is starting to gnaw again at your vitals and you haven't acted, you tell yourself, since last March and now it's November. Even if I have not grown desperate in recent years, I still have to work for my acting part by having to take on the role of director, actor and producer, let alone author. So what seems to have evolved over the years is that if I want to set foot on the stage I have to write the play and engage a company and then direct the piece while trying to make the role work at the same time. Who's complaining?! It's been extremely stimulating, but sometimes I grow weary of having to do all these things when I only want to act. But if I didn't I would have to suffer the iniquities of a director who would be less sympathetic than me to certain ways of directing and I might end up wearing what looks like a baby's diaper (which happened in a production of *Titus Andronicus* in 1971). On that occasion I was relieved of the burden and could merely act, but it turned out to be more painful than ever: it was the last time I walked out of someone's production. I walked and never looked back. I went quietly back to my basement room in Islington and continued working on my adaptation of *The Trial* by Kafka. As I sat at my long, beautiful, hand-crafted desk/workbench made by my mate Alistair Merry, I was so happy because I had found a thread that would guide me, I felt, into the book's mystery, its strange puzzles and dream-like logic.

The Hill – 1950–55

So at Stamford Hill I was learning to be part of the group, the maelstrom of human activity and the curious mixture and disparate types that made up our environment. Perhaps not really part, but on the edges. I reacted to and assumed a role and the group was as a chorus, sometimes furies, sometimes clowns, but always swimming around each other like a herd of jackals seeking out dead meat, roaming around for the carcasses left by lions and waiting for the answers that were never to come. So in the shtipp house we listened to 'Route 66' or Earl Bostic, Johnnie Ray of course, the wailing singer with whom I identified strongly, Kenton for 'Peanut Vendor' – these were the only 'popular' tunes we could get on the juke-box – while at home I would be happy and in a state akin to nirvana when listening to his more abstract concoctions like 'City of Glass' or 'Concerto To End All Concertos'. Or I'd beetle down to Oxford Street's HMV to listen in the cubicles to *musique concrète* and try action-writing, which was to try and put down whatever thoughts came into my head at the time. I was impressed by the abstract and arcane and even while stomping around the 'Hill' had time to mosey into the local library and devour books. In my fondness for the eclectic I would pick up on anything that had a good title, and so *Modern Man in Search of a Soul* by Jung was an eye-catcher, plus Aldous Huxley's *Brave New World* and *Ape and Essence*, but I was always seeking the touch of fantasy, the occult, 'unreal' world where my own imagination found liberation. I dived into horror and bewitched myself with Le Fanu and Poe, and when at eighteen I discovered the world of Henry Miller I was truly at home with a dictionary at my elbow and his reading list of the European writers from Blaise Cendrars to Céline.

At night, opposite the E and A Milk Bar, we would chat about such things, and there was a Stamford Hill philosopher called Ralph Levene who worked as a road cleaner during the day but would recite reams from the latest books he had read. We drank pints of tea while debating the meaning of life and other related conquests of the fairer kind and it all mixed in together. You see, we were of the café society and didn't go to pubs – in fact none of us ever went to a pub, for our heritage was rather more Continental and it was talk, talk and more talk that governed our lives. We lived to talk and tell and communicate and reveal and kibitz. It was from our grannies' heritage, from the ghettos of Poland and the cafés of Vienna, that we inherited the desire for human contact and fusion, whereas the British heritage was the pub as a refuge from grinding poverty and exploitation. The pub was the last resort to quell the chill in your heart and blast away at the hopelessness of your existence, as if you could stamp it out with alcohol since even your bosses could not quite remove the joy that was yours at the end of the pint. The working classes' sanctuary was the pub and although we were all working class, what separated us was not just race, colour, creed, food, habits, morality, or whatever else it might be. It was the need to communicate. That vital, overpowering need to be and to hear and to warm yourself by others' words and their adventures.

Of course, our compatriots from Tottenham, Hoxton and Bethnal Green felt the same, but the boozer was the sanctuary for the English working man and his missus. They were tough and hard and had weathered the most terrible conditions when the country was at its richest, and they had strived and scraped their pennies and fought for work at the docks, climbing over each other and breaking their bones to get it, and the Victorian imperialists, while resisting the unions' demands for even a dash more than a pittance, would build charitable institutions like Rowton House for the down-and-outs of the Whitechapel Road. So the generation after the war was a tough one; the lads were like Viking warriors with their blond crewcuts and blue eyes, and viewed us with disdain in our weekly jaunts to the Tottenham Royal for our dances. Their mums and dads had had the lowest wages to survive on and survive they did, by scraping each penny; while still in my little East End street I would watch the families get together when it came to hop-picking time and gather their belongings and their kettles and head down to the charabanc that would take them to the hop fields of southern England. I didn't do such things since Mum and I had no experience of that 'poor' culture and felt ourselves to be above it, even if for a short period we shared one bedroom and one kitchen with our six cats.

Fourteen/Fifteen Years Old

The jukebox blared out, 'Hey round the corner ooh ooh, beneath the cherry tree; hey round the corner, behind the bush, looking for Henry Lee . . .' It was one of those dark, grey, wintry nights and nobody ventured out to the shtipp house except ginger Paul and me. We were playing on the machine where two players, one at either end, would each man a steel hockey player. You had five balls and you flicked the wheel with the palm of your hand to make the little steel man whizz around and whack the ball into your opponent's goal. It got terribly exciting. You'd lean over the machine like a hairpin, bum out, pouring all your energy and concentration into that little steel man, and if we had twopence we might invest in a record to accompany our endeavours.

While we were playing I noticed Paul stand upright as some people came in and make a salutation as if he was greeting royalty. In my mind's eye I am aware of a presence that was as curious as it was satanic, since the man who had come in could only be described as charismatic with a touch of madness; his energy seemed to burst forth from him. I looked across to where Paul had addressed himself. I had never seen nor heard of this creature, and of course he cannot have been that old, but seemed to be without age, half pixie and half incubus. His hair was a luminous halo around his face and seemed to stand like electrified wire. His small, black, beady eyes fixed on me like a rat. His hugely broad face sat atop narrow shoulders, giving him an even more powerful demeanour since he was all face. Some people are a mixture of the two, body and face, and you read them through the contours of their being, but Curly King was all face, an animalism that devoured you. 'This is Curly King' Paul said to me as Curly watched the progress of the game, which we were able to continue now that Paul had made his genuflection and greeting. You couldn't just stand there and stare, and so it was permitted that you carried on with the life you had before he entered your hemisphere.

I look nonplussed as Paul went on, 'You heard of Curly King, aintcha?'

'I don't know,' I muttered, aware of some aura in the arcade, but not yet as afraid and awestruck as I was to become.

'He ain't heard of you, Curly,' as if this piece of information relegated me to the outer spaces of the universe or designated me as an idiot who drifted around the action of life in which they were the star players while I was like a flapping piece of old newspaper, carried along on the wind of their impetus.

'He doesn't get around much, does he?' Curly rejoined and I mentally retained the expression for future use when I too determined I would become a star player and the world would drift around me.

Curly had two or three friends with him and they wore smart suits even for a weekday and proper navy double-breasted coats. They looked as if this was a territory they had explored before and were paying a nostalgic visit to the old haunts, since they were now drifting around the corner to the E and A Milk Bar to check the scene. Paul and I decided to wander along when our game had finished, since while you were rightly in awe you mustn't be sycophantic, and as they marched around the old turf they were now gathering up a kid here and a young bloke there, like a magnet picking up filings, until they had a meteor tail of about ten of us. We were just glad to be near him. He was the first real 'shtarker' or villain I had ever seen. Curly turned as his friend drew attention to the fact that he had unwittingly grown this human tail.

We sauntered up Stamford Hill to the Boys' Club and picked up a few more and Curly visited the club and chatted like a king visiting his subjects. Then, as word must have got round the Hill, the local 'talents', the dignitaries and self-appointed stars and tearaways, came out to greet him with much laughing and chatting as if they were closer to being on an equal footing though they would never be Curly King. That was his real name by the way, and when you have a name ready-made, like King, you have a head start.

My admiration for him increased as I watched how everybody was drawn to him. I realized for the first time what a star was – not a great artist or a great actor, whose greatness is forged with endless painstaking work and repetition, but a natural star. Here in this strange beast with his fierce energy were the ingredients, the personal magnetic field that pulled you towards him. Certain people have this quality inherently, but it is forged and heated in the art they choose. By itself it will explode in all directions and eventually subside, but give it a patch and it will hone itself into a formidable power. I suppose Curly King had this natural charisma as a child, and in the struggle for dominance with his peer group and the need for assertion in the physical battles that characterize working-class and poor East End youth he would have honed his 'craft'. The poor and oppressed are closer to the call of nature than those whose middle-class veneer has domesticated their instincts, those tribal instincts which seek to throw up leaders who can protect the clan and ensure good bloodstock. They use each other as battering rams to test their power, for what is a tribe without its young defending warriors? Also, while not wishing to appear as if I am waxing romantic about a pride of yobs, there was one thing that was not tolerated and that was phoniness or pretentiousness, since that was not a key for survival and was like a corrupting, contaminating cell. Differences were solved as brute beasts solve them, toe-to-toe, in violent and Neanderthal conflict. Now we have lawyers to lie and cheat for us and it is not the strong who win but the ugly rich.

I recall in my youth the extreme beauty of some of the men and women, the sharply fierce eyes and beautiful peach-like skins and the men with their handsome Celtic faces. They would gather together like warring clans at the weekly stomp at the Tottenham Royal, which was run by Mecca. I was to write a short story about that dance hall called Mecca – it was published in my collection *Gross Intrusion*. What an apt title, Mecca Dance Halls, for it was indeed our Mecca and the weekly call to nature was as primitive as the herds of rutting deer that would gather on the Scottish moors for their mating, selecting and challenging. It was the golden time, the weekend, when the coarse and unsatisfying work had been shed and the day-to-day dose of humiliation was over, at least for me, and one could wash the week away in the 'neutral' environment of the Mecca. All men and women were equal there, since the humbling work you did during the week mattered not at the Mecca. Your schooling might be shabby and abrupt, your teachers callous and indifferent, your hopes no higher than to be cannon fodder for industry and factories if you were a native, and if you were a second-generation immigrant you might be absorbed into the skills the immigrants brought with them and be a worker in the garment industry, a cutter, tailor, presser, or as in my particular case, a salesman in a ghastly menswear shop. In the Royal, Tottenham, you were who you wished to be – warrior, lover, Jimmy Cagney, Tony Curtis, villain, spiv, leader, loner, heavy, Beau Brummell. A salesman. Ugh!

The gift of the gab, as they called it, tempted many of us into the 'easy' crafts of putting your case across, while braver men, like my friend Barry Wise, would go out into the street at Christmas time and sell 'three-string genu-ine di-a-manté pearls.' Like all good hustlers Barry would affect the 'demand' and look busy wrapping in tissue paper some tatty pearls that he had bought in the Houndsditch Warehouse while I kept watch for the law. That was my job. Keep an eye out and Barry paid me *a quid a day*! Even if he was lucky he'd make only three quid himself, but I got a quid since he needed a good spotter. If a policeman came by we'd dive into Woolworths and wait for the coast to clear and go out again. Guts and fortitude. While most kids of seventeen are playing with themselves or worrying what new pop shit to buy, Barry was out there grafting like a fiend. While still others are sitting back wondering whether to go to Oxford or Cambridge or whether to go into law or the BBC, Barry had no choice. Get out and struggle or go to the wall. I had secret wishes that I nursed and I knew that I wouldn't be walking the paths of limbo land forever, but for Barry this was to be his life. He had to be a merchant of some kind. At length he became a successful one, but for now he had to survive.

Mike describes it aptly in *West* and the speech is far too long for inclusion here, but I can't resist a sample:

… Bond Street where I was a managing director of a firm of wholesale jewellers/ flogging pearls out of a suitcase in Oxford Street for Xmas (genuine three-strung diamanté pearls/ a quid/ with beautiful engine-turned, bevelled edges)/ come on don't just stand there/ gentleman over there/ lady over there/ watch out there's a johnny/ nip into Woolie's or the ABC for a quick cup of bird vomit/ travelling salesmen swilling down some unidentified goo/ grins stitched to their unfortunate faces/ collapsed spine/ frayed cuffs and souls/ and breath to fell a dragon/ I saw a geezer shove his fork into a pie at one of these filling stations/ of garbage manufacturers/ but it was empty except for a mouse that was curled up inside with a happy look on his face/ sleeping/ and he didn't want to disturb the mouse like he thought it could have been a pet/ since a lot of these chain cafés have a lot of mice around/ so he took it back/ this mouse has eaten my pie miss/ he said/ this waitress who was slithering around in the dead grease/ with bunches of varicose like gnarled roots on her pins/ says: what and it's still alive!/ I'm glad something likes our pies/ …

[from *West*]

35

Barry had more guts than most young men of his age, but was always disturbed by his lack of achievement in his struggle to attain some purpose or goal in life. He was a good-looking young Jew, a lean, sleek face with very Spanish features, black hair and dark brown eyes that were both fierce and laughing, and he also had a good gift of the gab.

I like recalling Barry Wise since he was close to me for a while and we knocked about and were influenced by the same movies. He wore tailor-made suits and was unafraid in any conflict, yet had a gentle quality.

The first time I saw this young Samurai he was in the midst of a battle in a school playground with another runt who was trying to use his head as a nutting instrument. Both were fighting in a very strange way in that they were only using their feet and heads. The drama and adrenalin that pour through you at such moments is exhilarating. Both chaps flew across the asphalt yards like grey-hounds, but eventually Barry won since the poor opponent, in trying to nut him, cut open his own forehead and had to have stitches. However, you have to learn somehow and I gave him points for trying. Barry's dad was a communist, as were most of our dads, or at least strong Labourites; he was also a taxi driver and was eager to get Barry to do 'the knowledge', since then you would be your own governor.

MIKE: Why should I yoke myself to nine to five/ stand shoulder to shoulder with the dreary gang who sway together in the tube/ or get acquainted with parking meters/ be a good citizen in this vile state/ so I can buy an ultra-smart hi-fi and squander fortunes on pop singles/ what do you do at night between the sheets but dream of mortgages and oh dear the telly's on the blink/ we're going to Majorca again this year/ you who've never raped a virgin day/ with adrenalin assault upon your senses/ but aggravate your spine to warp/ while grovelling for a buck/ or two/ smiling at your boss/ and spend heart-wrenched hours at the boutique deciding what to wear/ ragged up like Chelsea poof-tahs/ or chase some poor mutt on Sundays/ mad keen to commit some GBH upon it/ and birds like screaming hyenas with teeth and scarves flying/ make your usual boring death-filled chat in smelly country pubs/ with assholes like yourself/ no that's not for me/ I'd rather be toad and live in the corner of a dungeon for other's uses.

[from *West*]

Barry tried, but for a long time he could not pass The Knowledge and was getting depressed. Then eventually he did pass and, like his dad, was happily driving a black taxi around. Yet he was cut out for greater things than this and did go on to better things. I always liked going to his flat in Lewis Trust in Hackney, a group of flats built for the Jewish working class at the beginning of the century; I liked his old man and what he had to say and the way Barry looked so much like him.

So on Saturday we could forget all these other struggles, the dead and stultifying world outside in which you had to assert yourself with the blunt instruments of a poor education and little guidance and the hope of becoming a taxi driver or the manager of Cecil Gee's Menswear. Now all that was behind you and in your drapes and rollaway Johnny Ray collar you spraunced into the Mecca with the expectation of a dream. Anything could and would and did happen, since the Mecca played into your hands: it was the greatest money-spinner of all time because it restated and restored the tribe and tore away the constraints of the civilized world of work and buses and factories. Here you could be who *you* thought you were. You created yourself. You were the master of your destiny. You entered quiffed and perfumed in the most expensive aftershave Boots had to offer. You entered and already the smell of the hall had a particular aroma of velvet and hairspray, Brylcreem and Silvikrin, lacquer, cigs, floor polish.

MIKE: Do you wanna dance/ I took her on the floor/ the crystal ball smashed the light into a million pieces/ a shattered lake at sunrise/ the music welled up/ and the lead guitarist/ plugged into ten thousand watts zonging in our ears/ callused thumb whipping chords/ down the floor we skate/ I push her thigh with mine/ and backwards she goes to the gentle signal/ no horse moved better/ and I move my left leg which for a second leaves me hanging on her thigh/ then she moves hers/ swish/ then she's hanging on mine/ like I am striding through the sea/ our thighs clashing and slicing past each other like huge cathedral bells/ whispering past flesh-encased nylon/ feeling/ all the time knees/

37

pelvis/ stomach/ hands/ fingertips/ grip smell/ moving inter-
locking fingers/ ice floes melting/ skin silk weft and warp/ blood-
red lips gleaming/ pouting/ stretching over her hard sharp and
wicked-looking Hampsteads/ words dripping out of her red
mouth gush like honey/ I lap it up/ odours rising from the planet
of the flesh/ gardens after light showers/ hawthorn and wild
mimosa/ Woolie's best/ crushed fag ends/ lipstick/ powder/ gin
and tonic/ all swarming together on one heavenly nerve-
numbing swill/ meanwhile huge mountains of aching fleshy
worlds are drifting past each other holding their moons/ col-
liding and drifting apart again/ the light stings/ the journey is
over/ the guitarist splattered in acne as the rude knife of light
stabs him crushes his final shattering chord/ the ball of fire
stops/ and I say thank you very much.

[from West]

First you go and deposit your coat and then jostle for a square inch
of mirror so as to adjust your phallic quiff, which has to protrude
enough for it to be stable, until your very arm aches and you have to
lower it to restore the blood supply. Many arms were crooked and
like birds we were preening and pecking. In the ladies' I imagine even
more complex rituals were going on, since this was the sea of flesh, a
virtual harvest of all the young, bright, beautiful, sweet, delicious
and not-so-beautiful and not-so-delectable, but at least the energy of
all that youth swarming together in the Mecca was formidable. All
those young, nubile maidens, those delectable cornucopias of sensual
delight. You were unaware of this then, of course, since it was all
taken for granted, but this was the mating game and the locking of
horns.

I would go with my mate Harold Harris, who was learning to play
the alto sax; the sound was most impressive, but it was like a cow in
heat and as I remember it drove his mother mad. Harold was a real
loony with a good heart and he discovered he could be very funny
and would adopt this bounce while he was talking, as if he were
listening to an unheard tune in his head and keeping time.

Harold actually introduced me to the Tottenham Royal, when I
was fourteen and still at school. I remember the awe I felt when first
entering this Mecca, my astonishment at the size of the place. The
first afternoon it was fairly empty, just a smattering of people, and

they played records. As luck would have it, I met a young girl who I arranged to meet later that night. I dropped round to her place, where they still had gas light. I had never been with a girl in any serious manner before and I had not the slightest idea what to do, but I had had the sense, even at fourteen, to bring a condom and when I got to the door, before I knocked, I fumbled around wondering how on earth you got the bloody thing on. So in the bleak dark streets of Tottenham on a cool spring night I was scrabbling about, but eventually had to leave it. I knocked and was welcomed by this terribly sweet young thing. Her mum and dad went to the pub to leave us alone, but it was a disaster for both of us since I had been brainwashed into the belief that this was what was expected and what you had to do. Neither of us benefited, but I was to learn.

In later times I did. But every night at the Royal was a dream time. You walked as if in slow motion and got there early so that you stood a good chance of pulling some sweet, delectable creature, had a good dance and swanned around. The dance was all-important since this was a way of demonstrating your skill as a mover, your grace, wit, balance and tricks. The jive was one of the greatest dance forms ever invented. And so all your arts were in some way fulfilled. You were the dandy, the mover and performer in your own drama, the roving hunter and lover, the actor adopting for the girl the mask of your choice. You wore your costume and walked the hall beneath the glittering ball and when you saw someone that you felt was about your stamp you asked her for a dance; if it was slow, when you took her on to the floor your heart started to increase its beat. She held your left hand with her right hand and you moved; if it was a slow, waltzy, shmoozy song you tried to be light and not tread all over her. Then that heavenly moment came when you could actually, by the laws of the ritual of the dance, put your arm around her waist ... eureka! ... and so I took her on to the floor and we moved to the music and she was acting the role of supreme indifference, which was only natural, but then as we danced it was inevitable that my leg might be a whisper ahead of hers and we would brush thighs before she swiftly pulled hers away. Sometimes the whisper of time would grow a whisper longer, until I was almost pushing her with my right leg leaning into her left thigh. I could tell, with senses alert as radar, that she felt pliant in my arms and not resistant, smelled her perfume and was aware, almost painfully, of the proximity of our parts and her stockinged thighs and my fingertips crawled further around her waist as if to protect her as we 'moved'. Her waist would feel so good and my thighs would be slicing between her thighs and her cheek would be awfully close to mine and I could feel its heat. The dance was coming to an end and I was getting mightily excited, but retained a slightly cool stance while not relaxing my grip; for one second as we turned, yes even for a second, I felt the contours and shapes of her body and read them with mine and then we pulled away again. All this was for the asking for the sake of the dance, and this ritual was enacted over and over again. You repeated in your best, most casual way the formal catechism, 'Do you come here often?'

'Sometimes, not always, sometimes me and my mate go to the Locarno, Streatham.'

'Where do you live?'

'Purley.'

'Oooh.'

The jive was a different kettle of fish.

I learned to jive at a formal session which a young teacher called Leslie taught at a small jazz club in Finsbury Park. I don't remember who took me there or how I heard about it. In one corner of the room (and I now remember the room was walled with mirrors – it must have been a small ballet school in more genteel times) was a record player and Leslie would show us the basic one-two-three-four. Once we had mastered this very simple rhythm, the next step was to guide the woman while in a kind of side-to-side locomotion our arms would spin her like a top. With the determination that was to be a hallmark of my youthful endeavours, I threw myself into the jive and practised night and day to work it out in mirrors, on door handles and on a current girlfriend, a flaring redhead who I met on the Hill. She was from the other side of the manor, which was bad news for both of us, but at that time we were mainly concerned with getting the jive together.

After a while I got into the swing of it and Greys Dance Hall became my weekly Tuesday night session. A kind of Finsbury Park clan would gather there. When you came in there was a little bar where you could buy sandies, tea, coffee and soft drinks. The place had a weird and pregnant atmosphere, not least because Curly King would turn up from time to time and it was also the time I first glimpsed the Kray twins. They were always immaculately turned out in dark suits and ties. There was something awfully macabre about these strange beasts, since their power over people was more than just the threat of violence. It was a willing subjugation to the will of the star, a kind of deification of the leader – you relinquish all pretence to any claims yourself and join the serfdom. Also they were East Enders from the other side. The other side meant, of course, the Gentiles, for whom the Jews had such a fascination since, 'they didn't wear coats in winter even' (*West*, 1983).

For us they were like the Goths, barbarians without any sense of fear or feelings, and somehow because of this they had a fascinating amorality. They were hardened like chisels. They weren't softened by too much mother love or gentle Friday night rituals of chicken soup, fish cakes and soft Sabbath candles. They had family love, of course, especially from what we know of the Krays, but their life was naturally harder. I watched them hawk-eyed and all they seemed to do when they visited the Royal was talk with their mates. They leaned against the wall and talked, and while Harold Harris and I chased around the place searching for the most delicious darlings, they would spend the entire time chatting. At length Harold had to confess that he couldn't imagine what they found to talk about.

When you entered the Royal, the band, usually Ray Ellington, would be up the far end. The Stamford Hill crowd would stand on the left-hand side and the crowd from Tottenham would stand on the right; there would be no mixing unless you felt cocky and wanted to fraternize; in that case you elected yourself to the position of leading luminary and went to pay your respects. Dancing was the thing and as the clock ticked away until the terrible hour of 11 p.m. when the band would stop, you became more and more desperate to find someone you could take home and crush for half an hour of fierce kissing and squeezing and creating sparks as your gaberdine rubbed against her taffeta. You became like a crazed fisherman trawling the remnants for those not claimed. You hunted the far corners of the room where the poor wallflowers leaned shamelessly against the wall, for they too needed some companionship. You blamed yourself for taking too long to make a selection, regretting that you had dawdled and tried too many samples and taken too many dances and now, God forbid, you would be left on Saturday night with no bird to escort home for a goodnight kiss or more. That was anathema, since your week was geared to this! Your foul week of suffering in some hideous, meaningless work had led to this moment of transcendence and it all had to fit. It had to have completion and she mustn't live at the end of the world. If she said Manor House or Finsbury Park that was heaven; Stamford Hill or Hackney, OK, but if she said Chingford for God's sake and if you went all that flaming way and there was nothing to show for it . . . You couldn't very well ask a bird from Kent or Chingford, 'Excuse me, but it's a hell of a way, would you be so kind as to give me some indication of the sexual delights I might expect . . .' So from her proximity in the dance you tried to gain some hints as to whether she was prepared to offer you at least the sanctuary of a little frottage, a little puffing and panting in the doorway. Much puffing and panting went on in my youth, as I remember, in summer and winter and in all weathers; when it was freezing the two of us would hurl ourselves at each other to keep warm. And if you were warmed up in such a way, then you didn't so much mind the five-mile walk home or the cab.

So the night was speeding away and you started to resemble one of those balls in a pinball machine, bouncing from one frock to another in the vain hope of a score. I had little ambition to be a tearaway, since I was too busy learning how to jive and being ruled by a rampant teenage libido. But for others skirmishes were frequent, especially towards the end of the evening, and it was a common occurrence to see a couple of Tottenham blokes fighting, sometimes still with a fag in their mouths. If there was no opportunity for me to hurl myself into the sanctuary of a take-away, I would traipse up the Hill and while away the last hour outside the E and A, discussing the events of the evening and maybe securing a couple of phone numbers for the future.

To be beaten up by the Kray twins was considered a kind of badge of honour and one Sunday I saw our own Ronnie Mitchell, considered no duff hand, sporting not one but two black eyes from the previous evening's encounter. Ronnie was a good-looking blade who had the most extraordinary walk the world had ever seen. He sort of bent at the waist as he walked and so he resembled a ship on the high seas, moving forward but swaying from side to side. It was remarkable in that, although vastly exaggerated, it made a kind of sense and went with his personality; before long it was adopted by others as a sign that you considered yourself to be a shtarker – this was your signal that you were not to be tampered with. So it was a provocation and at the same time an animalistic status symbol. Like a colour that warned others that you packed a sting, even when you didn't.

Ronnie's walk became very popular and was impersonated by Harry Lee, who was considered to be the Hill's hardest nutcase and feared nobody and nothing, plus Nigel, who couldn't quite make the walk from the waist, which gave it its windjammer grace, since he seemed to creak from the hip, making the walk top-heavy. Ginger Paul, of course, tried, but gave up, and a poor jerk called Mervyn who was so enamoured of the gang that they carried him around with them as a kind of slavish mascot. Mervyn would impersonate his betters and they would use him like a rabid dog to set on people. One day he had it in for me; I never fathomed why, but with Mervyn you didn't look for sense, since he was out of it. He wore glasses that he had to take off for the battles that he invariably lost. I had just come out of a little gym I went to in Tottenham, since it was the weightlifting craze then and I was just starting to develop some olives on my biceps, when I felt a tap on my shoulder. I turned around and Mervyn aimed a vicious kick in the direction of my pastime, but as I swung round the kick was prevented from doing what might have been serious damage by my gym bag which swung round with me and protected me. I was more amazed than angry and chased him down the road, but was held back by Moisher, one of the self-appointed guv'nors, a small, dapper, tough young man who sported a quasi-American outfit, an open grey shirt in all weathers with a white tee-shirt beneath, dark slacks rolled up at the bottom showing several inches of sock, and shiny black shoes. He had a broken nose, grey-blue eyes and also packed a star quality and looked like a wild cat or Popeye. He seemed to do nothing but stand at Stamford Hill with a rolled newspaper in one hand. He had a fearsome reputation. These three, Lee, Moisher and Mitchell, were the triumvirate that ruled the Hill and Moisher protected his impotent rottweiler, Mervyn.

They say that everyone had his barmitzvah with Mervyn, since the barmitzvah is your coming of age and Mervyn was the guy you had your first battle with to initiate you. The next day a small group assembled and it was decided that my first bout was to take place on the common, so we sauntered over there casually until as word got round quite a crowd was gathering; it felt a little bit like a crowd at a lunchtime theatre – not huge, but enough to make an event. Of course, nothing much happened, since after a couple of blows Mervyn went running around the car and Moisher stopped it by whacking me and blacking my eye, though he claimed he was just trying to break it up.

This was all a result of the boredom that these poor loonies faced each day with nothing much else to do but hang around and make trouble for people and occasionally put some poor guy in a hospital. It was because of the dreariness of their lives and the hopelessness many of them felt that they tried to whip up some excitement in a weekly monotony that they could not see beyond. Sometimes they would just stand there, day after day, out of work, often with no hope beyond the dole and nihilistic depression.

The pointlessness of this lifestyle and its aggression growing out of boredom culminated one afternoon in the Super Cinema when Harry Lee picked on my East End cousin Sidney Bennet. Sid was dating a girl called Barbara and the Super Cinema was where you went for the Sunday afternoon shows, which were different from the weekday ones. Harry was making some noise behind Sid and Barb, probably taking the piss out of the film with some choice epithets, while Sid felt the pride you have when with a woman. You can't back down and you'd kill not to show fear. Never confront anyone with his lady! But whatever sparked it off, Harry clobbered Sid from behind and did him serious injury; Sid had to leave the cinema with a swollen, but fortunately not broken, nose and make his way home. It was a brutal, unprovoked act and Sid was determined to avenge the crime.

Sid had a brother called Willy, who had been studying ju-jitsu and passed on the knowledge to Sid. Many weeks went by with no news, until one day we heard that Sid was coming to Stamford Hill to wipe Harry out. This was typically brave of Sid, since Harry was a tough young tike of nearly nineteen and Sid was only sixteen. (I was fourteen at this time.) Sid trained like a warrior each day and we all waited for the event to happen. It felt like something that would change everything, since this was a revenge battle between two of the toughest young men in North London – Harry, who feared no one and could take on anyone with his giant fists that he used to whack against doors to strengthen them – and Sid, who was a delicate, slim youth but strong and sinewy. I knew Sid to be gentle and playful, not a tearaway, although I knew too that he was brave. Willy I knew to be a bit of a tearaway. I feared for Sid and waited. And yet I felt that Sid would win.

One cold November night Sid came with Willy and waited in a shop doorway for Harry to pass, but he passed not. Then the next night and the next, and Sid said he would come here each night until Harry turned up, even if that meant he came for the next ten years. There was something almost mystical in his determination that Harry's crime must not be allowed to go unpunished. Sid had cut his hair and greased it so it could not be gripped and so he came and waited with his shorn head, and I waited and watched in awe for my noble warrior cousin.

And so, as it must be, Harry did come, but Harry's hair was not shorn. He came with his brother as his second and little was said but we all strolled round the back of the Super Cinema where traditionally the battles were staged. I remember Sid wearing a brown suit with the lapels turned inwards. They parried and sparred a bit, but Sid was not about to trade blows with Harry and so kept his distance, and then suddenly Sid threw his whole weight on Harry, gripping him round the body so that he could not use his arms, and threw him to the floor. Harry fell under Sid; Sid then pinned Harry's arm to the floor with his knees and, taking Harry's head by the hair, smashed it against the stones. Again and again he whacked Harry and punched from time to time. Ronnie Mitchell moved as if to stop them, but Willy said, 'Don't interfere, Ronnie' in a way that left no doubt as to Willy's intentions if he did. I'll always remember those words and the next I also will never forget, for as Sid was venting his rage for the vicious attack on him in the cinema and his violator was a bouncing thick skull being beaten into insensibility, Harry found the strength to say, 'You'd better finish me off,' implying, of course, that if Sid didn't kill him he would exact further revenge. I half admired the chutzpah in that sentence and also knew that he meant it in a half-animal, half-human way.

Sid walked away a conqueror and Willy, knowing that I would still be living in this patch, said, 'Let me know if they bother you.' I said I would. I was proud of Sid, proud in a way that was more than just pride in his strength and guts. I was proud of his amazing courage and dignity.

LES: So round the back we went that night. The fog was falling

45

fast, our coat collars were up, our breath like dragon's steam did belch forth from our violent mouths while at the self-same time we uttered uncouth curses thick with bloody and unholy violence of what we most would like to carve upon each other's skulls. The crowd of yobs that formed a ring of yellow faces in the lamplight hungry for the blood of creatures nobler and more daring than themselves, with dribble down their loathsome mouths they leered and lusted for our broken bottles and cold steel to start the channels gouging in our white and precious cheeks . . .

[*East*]

East and its Influences – 1975

The ogre or monster that plagued me for so long surfaces in *West* and *East*, where it is expunged and purged from my system. *East* and *West* dealt with prime basic elements; they were archaeological investigations into the twilight world of my youth, which provided much material for these first original plays. The plays, particularly *East*, were a game, a charade or masquerade, covering up emotions that must have been dormant in me for years. They were attempts to be bold, daring, outrageous, enabling me to confess my most secret thoughts, to say anything that came into my head, just as we did as teenagers. Scabrous and revolting language was manna to us and used for its shock value. We had no evasions or euphemisms, but spoke openly of the lubricious mechanics of the body, discussing them with true and spotty teenage wonderment. Most of our waking days were spent in a daze of priapic fantasizing, even if they tried to divert us by hearty games from which we played truant.

East was born of a wish simply to make each speech or scene a kind of confession of the characters' 'great moments' . . . times of real charge, the best experiences or the worst, but at least the speeches should be charged with an intensity which was bright and scored with energy. They were simple and profane. I wanted to write about a time when a sense of danger and adventure was always hanging in the air like a whiff of some illicit drug. Even youth itself is a dynamic universe to be in, the very act of being young and having your batteries charged up with testosterone. And so I tried to write a young play, to write it with the thoughts and emotions of a fifteen-year-old. At fifteen you have few qualms or reserves, but are an avaricious beast that can never be satisfied. You are in a constant state of need. Need for love and affection, need for approval, skill, excitement and suits. So I wrote a series of scenes of a working-class life that was a strange mixture of both sides of the Tottenham Royal. Mike and Les were from the 'good' side, Mum and Dad from the 'bad'.

For *East* I couldn't begin to create my real mum and dad, not in a million years, though they did surface in *West*. Dad in *East* is a raging amateur anti-semite who mourns the passing of Mosley and Mum reminds me of the old curlered and scarfed 'Dots' and 'Daisys' down Commercial Road. Since my mandate to myself was to omit nothing, to say whatever popped into my skull and confess everything, I went to work with a will, but the style?

> MIKE: I'll descend on thee like a moon probe thou planet of delights, fleshy ... Advance my antennae vibrating back to the lust computerizing cells the sanguine goodies that doth lie unmined ... I'll chart thy surfaces until thou criest from within thy depths, subterranean and murky and fetid swamps, 'Mike, oh Mike'; fluting gurgled falsettos from thy lips of coral ...
>
> [from *East*]

I wanted to take the act of sex, passion, lust, into the idea of mythic symbols so as to rid it of the tepid day-to-day realism or naturalism where everything is normal. 'Balls like the great cannon that Pompey used to subdue the Barbarian.' I could not render sex as an everyday encounter, but needed to treat it with comic humour and exaggeration so that it would never resemble the enforced nudity and simulated sex of the naturalistic stage. I had an aversion to the idea of real talk, real nudity, real crudity, since this could embarrass the audience. It had to be elevated and satirized until we saw it not personally but *socially* not intimately but objectively, and would read it as we see the cartoons of Gerald Scarfe – vast exaggerations which not only contain the inner life but show the 'drive' of that life, its slant and purpose.

From my past I may have learned to develop that taste for baring myself, living on the edge, telling it without restraint. Even on a teenage level. And so *East* excavated that little world and I found that it became a metaphor for struggle and joy. The joy of sex, battle, the boy's motorbike, seduction, mum's little playful Oedipal horror as she discovers that the dick she has in her hand in the dalliance in the dark East End cinema is her own son's. My fear of incest, perhaps, Dad's raging hatred for anything not in his own image. The desire, above all, to give us juicy parts – which they were, although the part of Les being more autobiographical was more fully rounded and his mournful dirge on the horrors of evil and boring work in the menswear shop was my attempt to extirpate it by vilifying that stultifying time of my life in a speech which is the definitive testimony to the agonies of 'bespoke' tailoring.

Everything in *East* had to be personal and observed, every incident in my life had to be in there, from the Kursaal Amusement Park in Southend to Mum sitting in front of the telly day after day. Every speech was to be an aria of woe or ecstasy or a mixture of both. I wrote the whole play out: it was pretty horrendous since I left out precisely *nothing*, and I put it in my drawer for a while. Then one day, for no reason that I can explain, I started to write the whole thing in verse and even to obey the pentameter in many places. I started to recreate the text, spicing it with metaphors and analogies, and my pen literally flew across the paper as if the structure of this style completely liberated me. It was no longer a struggle to write, it just poured out! I know not why I did it, just doodling perhaps and with a fondness for Shakespeare since I had never given up the hope of thespian glory and would incessantly practise the big soliloquies. It must have stemmed from that desire to be different, to be dangerous and entertaining, all of which came from my apprenticeship on the Hill. You must not be boring, that was for grown-ups; they were stultified and repressed, while we youth flew on the wind of our own imagination. I imagine that the success of rap is the fruit of street life in the USA.

East at this moment – 1990 – is into its sixth month in San Francisco, having taken over a decade to get to America, but America has embraced it. So I am not trying to say, 'Hey, what a significant play I wrote,' but rather that it seemed to work on many levels, including the performance, which was tight, light and crafty. Because it's 'Cockney' many groups play it 'heavy', but for me a lot of it is stand-up comedy and it should not be punched in the audience's face. On the night in 1975 when we opened in Edinburgh's Traverse Theatre we were the late late show; they knew we would get an audience even though we were starting at midnight, because we had already played there four times before.

East was a new departure for me. I think many people now identify me with *East* and *West* and perhaps *Greek*, although *Greek* is a different ballgame altogether and comes from my adult life.

However, my first fascination in the theatre was for the works of Kafka and Poe and by the time I wrote *East* I had made a reputation as an adapter of classic stories with a directing style that owed a great deal to my mime training.

The first night at the Traverse was a good night, but I had great trouble with one speech, the 'cunt' speech, if you will forgive the expression. In my early youthful enthusiasm (though to speak true I was no callow youth but in my late thirties), I wanted to break the taboo barrier; while stalwarts were breaking the space barrier and the endurance barrier in sports and the barriers of science, old Steve was breaking the four-letter-word barrier. Seems rather trite now, but in those days it was a formidable hurdle to say this word in front of a mixed audience and not just to say it, but to say it over and over again until the word is pummelled to death and the shock has worn off and by a process of overkill the taboo power is reduced. Then the audience have the power and do not have to be assaulted, the men throwing anxious glances over to their wives. Since the speech comes towards the end of a play whose language has already inured them to what is to follow, hearing the word at first was no big deal and there was no sense of 'This is too much'.

I was very nervous the first night and gritted my teeth and said it. During rehearsals even the cast would slip away as they couldn't bear the embarrassment and let me get on with it. Then I thought Barry Philips should play it as one of Les's speeches, but he wasn't having that, so I did it, though with a lack of real faith.

But on the next night, when I had got over the first fear of the première, I relaxed and there was a little giggling as I tried to endow each 'cunt' with a character and act it out. The third night I was a little more confident from the previous evening's response that they at least could find some humour in it, and I was emboldened on one of the many descriptions of that particular organ to look at the space in front of me as if standing before me was this gigantic pudendum from some lost world . . . I paused and looked up and then down and

49

there was a visible response from the audience, so I carried on. The next night, thus even more emboldened – and this goes to show you how the courage is added layer by layer and when you see it after a couple of months you are watching the accumulated courage of sixty or more performances – the following night at the same point I took my vertical glance up and down and then very gingerly I parted what looked like a pair of curtains, oh ever so little, and this of course grew until it became a monster whose giant maw I was parting to step inside with my flashlight and wander around. For a while this became one of the highlights of the evening's performance. The whole audience would crack up and be on the floor while I was trapped inside this enormous vulva, like a fly inside one of those insect-eating plants. Well, all this additional working out brought the show to a stop and I still had more 'cunts' to get through. I was able to take the word out of its offensive box of sexist curses, hurled as the worst kind of deprecation at your foe. I grew to enjoy the scene as long as I just jumped into the speech and when I came to 'amazing' went through my little mime routine. This took the sting out of the cunt speech and made it silly, farcical, astonishing and without offence.

The play went well at Edinburgh. My wife-to-be, Shelley, was up there with her dance company, also at the Traverse, and I had what I had always dreamed of, a partner in the same line of biz and one with whom I could actually act. When I'm rehearsing, like a lot of actors, I can't bear anyone from the 'outside' watching me, and while I don't mind strangers, the presence of someone close in the rehearsal room would be an occasion for extreme anxiety: I would sweat the night before trying to brace up courage to be seen by someone who *knew me*! Who knew the other side of me and knew my fears and therefore could *see right through me*! And the idea of someone who knew you in the other world could cause a dislocation of character, since while you're trying to enter the skin of your character and the spirit of your performance, there is someone out there unconsciously tearing the thin veil with which you are trying to cover yourself. So the first few times that I acted I had a little problem, both wanting my girlfriend to come up to the rep and see me, and fearing the pain of her witnessing 'Steve' on stage rather than my creation. But it got progressively better and then the dread came back again. If the visitor was a male, I could actually enjoy his presence and be stimulated, but when it wasn't going well I could still feel that Steve was sticking out of the character like a broken bone. I was too aware of women and didn't want to be seen to fail, but wanted to seem brave, unafraid and funny: when it went well and the house laughed, and I knew that my girl was out there, every laugh doubled the interest it earned in my ears.

Shelley and I met when I was trying to put together a production of *Agamemnon* from Aeschylus's *Oresteia* which I had rewritten, since the translations I found were stuffed full of stilted, over-respectful heroic verse with no resonance of human life. Staid, posy and archaic, except for a poet like Ted Hughes, whose *Oedipus* was such a powerful rendition from Seneca.

The Discovery of Agamemnon – RADA 1971

Now you may indeed ponder what on earth is the lout who sweats over how to make a speech about 'cunt' work on stage doing with *The Oresteia*. Yes, what indeed? Well, the story is brief. Hugh Cruttwell, the Principal at RADA, having seen or heard of my prowess with *The Trial* in its early stages and *Macbeth*, decided that I might be interested in teaching at RADA, or more precisely in directing *The Oresteia*. This is a play in three parts, but it's very much like three plays. I met this charming, snow-capped gentleman, who after talking to me became even more enthusiastic that I should do it, and so I agreed. On the first day I duly turned up at RADA and went into the rehearsal room to read the first part, *Agamemnon*, which deals with his return from Troy and his murder. That seemed to go OK and I talked vaguely about science fiction and the similarity between these powerful creatures obeying orders from the gods and representing archetypes and the Apollo space mission and how in some unconscious way the most advanced form of science, space travel, used the names of Greek gods, as if there were some mythic connection. All this went down well with the students and they thought, 'Oh well, we're going to do a spacy, weird and "experimental" show.' Then lunch came and I went upstairs to the staff canteen and I felt that I was in RADA, one of the bastions of the British tradition, and I was a slob from a little back-street drama school. In any case I was a sucker for an inferiority complex at the best of times and now I was teaching at the austere, revered and world-famous academy. I felt like a college professor on his first day. I went home at lunchtime and resolved never to go back.

In other words I funked it. All my old fears came back, the ill-educated boy who was tossed out of the Hackney Downs Grammar School at fifteen and spent the next five years of his life in insignificance and waste, and suddenly the fruit of the subsequent ten years vanished, the teaching I had done, the classes I had given and the productions I had put together all vanished in a cloud of angst. I jumped into a cab after sitting in that bleak canteen where no one spoke to me and beetled off to my Islington lair, my cosy basement, and stood in the cold, unlit kitchen while Pottle, my tortoiseshell cat, scratched at the window and demanded food. What on earth would I do now? This seemed even *more* bleak, so I rushed back to Gower Street. I apologized for being late and muttered something about getting the hour wrong.

So we sat and they read the second part of the trilogy, which deals with Orestes coming back to avenge his father's death at the hands of Clytemnestra and then this group went out and yet *another* group of thirteen young, keen, pink-cheeked middle-class youths was sitting in front of me to read the damned third part. It was like trying to direct three plays simultaneously, when the first part, *Agamemnon*, was a strong, dramatic play in itself. Also, I am the kind of person who works out a concept. I'm not like those fortunate directors who say, 'I'll plot the play in three days and then we'll fill in the detail', since you can only do this if your work is mainly naturalistic and you are copying life. Nothing wrong with this, but it means you cannot investigate other forms of communication. You cannot experiment with movement and rhythms. You cannot aspire to conceptions of anything but the norm; you certainly cannot investigate on an unconscious level. You can't 'play' with the material or create a sur-real imagery; you cannot change the modes of creation or develop choreographic themes, create an ensemble, work on a chorus as a multiple entity representing the mind of the protagonist, let alone as a malleable, moving environment reflecting the core of the play and sending out ripples from the centre with the chorus or lines of energy; you cannot even begin to say what are the themes or the coda and what are archetypal images; you cannot train a chorus until it's a polished mirror, moving sometimes as one beast and sometimes as many, sometimes on a split second and sometimes like lava, multifaceted, throbbing, a fighting machine, a choral group, an opera, sound effects, screams, moans, whines, wind, and silence – in other words *alive* and not a swaying group of masked faces dabbed with a little choreography and choral speaking, pulled together in the 'other room' with the hired lady who does 'movement' while the director works with the stars who are then fitted into the scheme. Aye, your British Greek chorus. Ensemble work is a tricky concept for the Brits, since it really comes from countries where people like and love each other and are free and liberal with each other. You have to be fond of experimenting since it means you desire to merge with your group. An ensemble is really a big family that does not feel uncomfortable, but in the class-ridden British society many directors feel a little awkward with the idea of ensemble work: they don't wish to get involved and hope somehow that it will come out all right 'on the night'.

I am fascinated by the patterns of human behaviour that can be made with a group and was encouraged to think like this when I first studied mime in London with the most inspiring mime teacher, Claude Chagrin, who had her little team of adoring acolytes in the City Literary Institute. This marvellous Institute for Adult Education was a sanctuary and it was saving grace that here there were these two classes per week. Here, the actor Edward Petherbridge and I would do our exercises and improvisations and then after a couple of years of this I went off with another couple of students to sit at the feet of the great Jacques Lecoq in Paris. Claude Chagrin and her husband were pupils of Jacques Lecoq and were two of the many of his students to turn pro and teach and perform.

From Jacques sprang the Moving Picture Mime Show, and the extraordinary protean Mummerschantz, whose work with masks is so brilliant and inventive, but I was determined to see how I could bring mime together with the spoken word as its opposite partner, using it to create the form and structure of the piece and thus ridding ourselves of the nineteenth-century Victoriana theatre with its cumbersome sets and décor, its fascination with toys and embellishments, which although eschewed in recent years is now making its wretched comeback as the imagination, what little there was, dries up. You've got to believe in what you're doing if you allow an audience into your theatre with nothing on the stage except *space*.

The naturalistic director's extraordinary addiction to settings creates the problem of a visually static environment, so to add fluidity the revolve has been in increasing use to shift scenery. However, revolves do tend to break down, resulting in the not infrequent sight of the administrator of some heavily subsidized theatre coming on to apologize to the audience and offer them their money back or tickets for another night. Of course one has to laugh. Loud!

I had all this behind me as I entered the portals of RADA. I had the mime and the teachings of Claude, whom I believed totally, gave me the possibility which mime does of creating *without text*. Creating from within and discovering your own spirit! Add this to the text and there could be a kind of fusion which I was to discover and to put into practice. I had nearly six terms of teaching at the Webber-Douglas, where of course I was not only teaching but learning. I was learning far more about the craft as a teacher than I had learned as a student actor nine years earlier. I was experimenting and making fascinating discoveries of which more anon; but suffice to say I was making steady scientific discoveries in the protean use of the human voice and body. Yet here I stood at RADA with the words gagged in my mouth and all my experience and all my training and classes seemed to go for nothing.

I had re-entered the room and listened to the drone of the actors, but what could I say about the third part, *The Furies*, when the rule of chaos must be brought to an end and the bloodletting stopped? Of course I could discuss the nature of each play, but I was much keener to concentrate on one theme and one piece. My mind worked in images and sound, not in intellectual 'debate' which would obstruct the natural flow of spontaneity and impede intuition. I could not go on all day picking my way like a tourist guide through the thickets of *The Oresteia*. It was all too much. I was the kind of person who would spend three months on one play and even then it might not be enough, though at other times it would flow with the speed of discovery, but every piece is its own master and makes its own demands. I had no problem with comprehension; the difficulty was how to get through so much material, given the way I work, which is by process of discovery and experiment. This would take forever, unless, of course, I did it naturalistically. Unless I said to the set designer, 'Work out a set that the actors have to weave themselves around,' a set that would be worked out before we had even begun rehearsal, so that the actors knew where they were to enter from. Also, and not least, sets have to be *made* and these take about four weeks and so you straitjacket whatever thin shoots of imagination are trying to take root and work to fit in with the set builders! Easier to let the actors get on with it. 'Enter down the steps, Trevor.'

So at the end of the day I went to Hugh Cruttwell and confessed that I couldn't work in this way and that it was all too much and how sorry I was and he'd better find someone else. Hugh went to his cabinet where he kept the Scotch and poured me a stiff whisky with soda and said not to worry, and why didn't I just take on the first part, *Agamemnon*; then another director whom he had had in mind originally would take on the second and third, and I could really do my stuff with the first and concentrate on one group of actors. He was so calm and so benign I could have wept. I decided to do just that and I even called in an assistant director, Chris Muncke, a young American I had taught at Webber-Douglas and who showed great promise and was most inventive.

And so we went to work. When I couldn't think what the hell to do I would sometimes engage in group exercises I had learned in Paris and the problem would be solved. This was because the problem was at the back of my mind and when I engaged in the exercise it would filter itself unconsciously into the way the exercise took shape. Chris said one morning, 'That was shrewd, you found the way through the impro', when in fact I had not even thought about the problem holding me up; I had merely wanted to warm up the class while I had nothing more to suggest and the answer popped in when I didn't push it. Zen and the Art of Theatre!

The rehearsals worked by fits and starts. The actors were not the cream I had been led to expect – as with many myths, live experience revealed the truth. They were an ordinary bunch of not very inspiring people, but two actors stood out. One was Jonathan Pryce, who played Agamemnon. He was a quiet, sallow, calm youth who had his big scene at the end of the play when Agamemnon returns with Cassandra. This meant that every day, with the slow, painstaking and often laborious way we had of rehearsing, he would be waiting until the bell went and it was too late. 'I say, oh I'm so sorry that you had to wait all this time and not be used,' but he looked calm and quiet within, said that it was quite OK and seemed totally unperturbed. Only after several weeks did the poor chap get on stage, since the text was so strangled and unwieldy that it took actors ages just to sound halfway natural and we were building the choreography as we went. The play was getting better and the movement was becoming more sinuous. We had composed certain choral structures as the actors entered with the story of the ten years' war. A slow march moving from side to side like an army seen from the distance and the drone as they begin.

Ten years since Agamemnon and Menelaus hard men/ iron might of Atreus/ equipped in deadly steel/ a thousand ships to the doom of Troy/ screaming like eagles/ maddened for the prey . . .

When we arrived at the scene of Agamemnon's triumphant return it was Jonathan's entrance and he started:

First I hail Argos and her Gods who know the right course from the wrong/ receive from me the conqueror's greeting on my safe return/ your wrath sent justice from my arms to break great Troy/ and doom her walls to dust/ and send to Hades those worshippers of pride, theft and lust . . .

When John came on he let out a vocal effect on the word 'Argos' that was a thrilling sound in such a young man – his voice was piercing and unexpected and coming at the end of the weeks of slog with the modest talents of the ensemble cast it was an oasis in a desert. He never let anything daunt him and was always 'on' whenever he entered the stage. I had a feeling that this young man would do well. Sometimes he would spare himself that great cry, since perhaps he thought the effect would lessen on repetition, but it never did and his performance was a big success.

The other actor who stood out was called Henry Goodman. He became a kind of ally in the beginning, but cooled off as the production got underway. He was inventive in the exercises, led the group and was totally responsive to my impros, which helped me to believe in them and their value. In later years he would perform nearly all my works in South Africa and applied to my agent for the rights to *Metamorphosis*, *East* and *Greek*; but in all that time I didn't hear one word of how the plays had gone. He even did *Decadence* and got into the RSC doing an audition piece of mine. I think he liked the plays more than he liked me. But in 1991, twenty years later, he worked with me in *Kvetch* with great success.

Many actors find that they can identify with my works and like to test themselves out in auditions. The irony is that the companies for whom they audition wouldn't dream of having a Berkoff play in their repertoire, but they have to listen to all those Berkovian speeches. Forced to. Oh bliss.

Of course by now even my worst detractors are force-fed my plays as they have to sit and listen to all these long speeches since when I wrote my earlier plays I, like the Elizabethans, had a passion to express an idea in a long speech – to get a run, if you like, to give the actor a chance to get up some speed and sum up the situation so far, a chance to unburden himself and confess his essential being to the audience. It's an aria, a personal observation of life that you don't wish to share with an actor but prefer to hog. It's also a means for a writer to demonstrate his technique, since the soliloquy is also a story and each speech an act in itself. It is the time when the heat lifts the lid off your socially acceptable being and you ultimately reveal *you*! Also it gives the writer a chance to flow and weave, to elaborate, to run with the ball all the way to the goal. It drives a harder bargain since you must not bore with your yards of text either in the writing or the performing and you have no one to bounce off, but it defines an essential theme that you wish to put across.

Perhaps the idea of these 'arias' came from the fact that I was always auditioning in my youth and looking for big speeches in order to demonstrate my frail talents, since that is what you're always asked to do . . . 'Do you have a piece you can do for us?' So I am not insensible to the fact that although the young like to perform me for auditions I am also very functional!

One day a friend of mine, Roger Morton, the photographer who took our pictures for years, reported to me that a lecturer at RADA who was also on the staff at the RSC advised young actors *not* to do Berkoff for their auditions! So we already had the banning of plays, if not the banning of books. But I can understand if you had to audition actors each season and all they did was come up with the hunting speech in *Decadence* over and over again and God forbid that some intrepid young thespian comes out with the cunt speech, oh no, I think I would ban me!

Roger, a Kiwi with a very wry wit and a shrewd eye, whom I met at the Round House, was asked to photograph our production of *The Trial* which I was presenting with *Agamemnon* in repertory in

1973. Roger did some of the best photos I have seen of our work and we became friends; and from then on he took most of the shows for the ten years. He came with us when we did a European tour of *Hamlet* and when we were short-staffed he came aboard as a driver and even ironed my one shirt in the interval: I did not or could not find one that matched, so Roger would iron the sweat out while I lay on the floor in ghastly pain with one of those duodenal ulcers which were going to haunt me all my life.

Agamemnon at RADA turned out to be quite a hit, but the chap who did the other two plays got a little too weird, I believe, and it didn't work out. It wasn't an easy task for me, either, but I did find a form for it and wanted to take it further, having put so much work into it already, thanks to the encouragement of the sweet and gentle Hugh Cruttwell and the occasional top-up in the office. I like a man I can run to and unburden my ills and be honest with. I can be rather trying, I imagine, but on the other hand I can't stand the cold, formal, distant relationship that so often characterizes men with men, scheming and afraid, jealous or bitter. I could sniff that resentment very quickly, those who wouldn't touch me with a ten-foot barge pole, but the ones who were willing to give me the time of day were generally paid back with interest. Rejection caused me grief and cold fury, and that too may have had its roots in the barking, endless criticism from old Dad. My life, my style, my friends, my this and that, my habits, even my pointy shoes (known as winkle-pickers) were the subjects of enormous screaming rages. So criticism or rejection became like a whip to a dog that has had plenty in the past.

Of course I don't have to interpret it as a threat to my being if someone doesn't want to employ me or do a play of mine or gives me a negative review, but years of conditioning take time to change. I recently looked back at some reviews from my early days which at the time I thought were negative and which almost made me want to defend myself in print. But reading them again I could see that some were rather favourable and took pains to discuss the play. So I hope that I have now achieved a degree more balance. I felt that I suffered because the vocabulary of my techniques was unfamiliar and was not given a good response, and I went through a period when play after play was condemned and I seriously thought that I had to be *less* inspired, *less* adventurous, more 'ordinary' and then I would succeed.

I became afraid to work, actually nervous of taking pains with what I did. This climaxed in a production of *Hamlet* which followed on a popular one, ironically led by my old pupil Jonathan Pryce, determined to take vengeance on me for making him wait at RADA. Following the determined huzzahs of the critics for his performance, which I have no doubt was remarkable, we came along at the Round House in the same season and it was my *production* that was, I believed, remarkable and the success didn't hinge, as it so often does, on the one player who bails out the director. I had done an investigation of *Hamlet* over a period of many months. What I received for it was the unanimous obloquy of the critics, which confounded me since it was the whole that I had worked on and not just me, and I had suffered for it. When I saw Nick de Jongh's review I was not too pleased, since I thought this critic had been using me as a whipping boy for years. Shortly after this review appeared, I met him in a London bar, leaned over and gave him a bit of my old Stamford Hill repertoire, implying some kind of speedy demise. Of course I was only acting, but he took it seriously – so my acting did convince him after all, which was the point I was trying to make.

After that encounter I returned to my table feeling the sense of elation you get when you have done something that explodes the bile that has been gathering on your chest for months, if not years. That sense of having burned away some terrible smell that you have been wearing on yourself. For once I felt good about myself and I didn't have to sit and gnaw my nether lip every time I saw Nick. Indeed over the years I have come to respect his views and we have become friends, which shows sometimes it needs conflict to bring people closer together.

The incident took place at a club called the Zanzibar, which was at the time a marvellously alive place beautifully designed by the architect Tchaik Chassay. It had a long, New York-style bar that swept down the room in a series of scalloped edges; in a raised area were tables and against the wall those long seats with high backs you could lean against. The atmosphere was always frisky and after a show you felt a sense of expectation just entering the place . . . the door from the street was large and promised by its weight and authority a pleasant evening; you were ushered in as if your membership was vital to them and at the bar you would be mixed a perfect Margarita, accompanied by as many olives and pretzels as you could eat. It was *the* place to go after a performance. This was at a time when I had rented the New London Theatre for a short season when it was considered 'off the beaten track'. So there I was in 1978, actor-manager of the New London before *Cats* took it over. We did our repertoire of plays that season – *East* and my adaptations of *The Fall of the House of Usher* and *Metamorphosis*.

I was playing in *East* one day when Philip Roth came by, having dropped off a card at the stage door asking for a chat with me, and of course I took him to the Zanzibar for a light snack at lunchtime – I felt good that at least I had somewhere decent to take my distinguished guest. Roth confessed that he was much taken with *East* and therefore, having enjoyed the candour of the whole play, and my performance, particularly with the 'cunt speech', oh dear here we go again, he asked if I would be interested in making an adaptation of *Portnoy's Complaint* . . . Well, to tell you the truth, I felt that while 'Portnoy' was a brave expanding of the boundaries of public taste, its message was not universal enough for me. I thanked him for the honour of seeking me out and I did remember certain scenes in 'Portnoy' with amusement, but whereas the sexuality in my plays was outward and demonstrative and shared, the pounding of meat in 'Portnoy' was too private and might appear to be sordid out of the privacy of the pages. He was very gracious and I said straightaway that I didn't want to do it rather than say 'give me time to think'. He came again with his wife, Claire Bloom, and Al Alvarez the writer, and they all had a good evening. We went to a little café afterwards with Claire and her daughter, who looked the spit of Rod Steiger. I never saw them again, although Alvarez would always turn up with marvellously encouraging words.

Little Wayne Sleep would always be at the Zanzibar, as would people like Lucian Freud and Harold Pinter. Since Harold and I had shared an English teacher I ventured to speak to him for the first time and acquainted him with our common experience, which was met with a distant 'I'm afraid Mr Brearley died four months ago'. End of chat, since to extend my bonhomie I had said that I had seen Joe Brearley just the other day; I actually meant several months ago, but wanted to imply that it was all fresh and recent. I was corrected. With Harold you must be accurate.

When we were invited to the opening of the Cottesloe Theatre I had *East* on at the Regent (now defunct) and *Metamorphosis* at the

Cottesloe running at the same time and for a few moments of my life thought I was reasonably successful. We had a party at the Zanzibar. The food was good and it stayed open. I wonder why these nice places go to the wall.

So having worked out a formula for the production of *Agamemnon*, I didn't want all those headaches and heartaches at RADA to go for nothing and just be a damp spot on the wall of my skull. I decided that one day when the opportunity came I would revive it and so I did, but not before I had rewritten the whole play.

I took it slowly, as a kind of hobby, since I was in no hurry and had no plans – during the day I would scribble a few lines in a relaxed way, especially if I was working at night and able to burn off my excess energy. That's always been the best way of writing for me, as a PS to the day, not like now when it is all I have and like a lifebuoy it sees me through and carries me another few miles up the river until I reach my destination. Now it gives me a reason to get up in the morning, no matter what God-forsaken hour. I can go into my front room in Brighton and survey the slate grey sea and matching sky, turn the gas fire on, get on to my typewriter and plug into my memory.

I liked the idea that I was an actor first and did a *real* job, going into the theatre and getting into a sweat, putting my guts on stage, fighting for my audiences or lack of them, getting the slap on and doing some wild thing in my acting, coming off the stage, my nerves on edge and stretched out, my heart pumping fast for the next two hours. Seeing a spectator who may have come backstage to say sweet words, mostly exaggerated, can be an awkward experience, since the ritual of going backstage and greeting someone who has just come off is like encountering a paranoid on speed. All actors are in or on a different planet when they come 'off' and no matter how sweetly calm and welcoming they seem it is deceptive – in truth they have the same relief and elegiacal calm as a murderer who has just claimed his victim. It is all over and the demon is stilled until the next night.

Knowing this, even in a distant way, the audience tends to pass verbal gifts and quieting compliments. It's only a job, after all. In your understated way you search their faces for traces of displeasure, your nerve endings are on stalks and you pick up on the phrasing, the rhythms and the use of words, their idiosyncrasies. It's hard to be an audience backstage without sounding fulsome and picking up on the dressing-room madness. After 'wonderful' comes 'really enjoyed it', 'stunning', 'I laughed so much people were turning round', 'superb', 'I loved the . . .' and so it goes on. 'But how was I tonight?' Do I actually say this? Of course not, but I might hint if it didn't go *so well*. 'It was a bit flat tonight?' 'Oh no, it was very good . . . aah, um, no, I didn't know it any other way . . .' And then the cynics determined to be true and unhypocritical but who hated it: 'How do *you* think it went?' '*Me*? Oh, it seemed OK.'

Of course you don't need to hear anything from a friend just in to say hello, you don't need any more than to see them and be glad they were in; your own relief and enthusiasm that you got through is enough and often you don't want to hear anything, least of all from some American students who say 'We did your play in the States and what made you play it like *that* . . .?!!'

'Like what?' I smilingly respond, while mentally getting my finger around the ignition button for blast off.

'Oh, in that *stylized* way. We thought of *Greek* as so *real* . . .'

'Where did you do it?' I ask in a vaguely bored way, and they chirp out some little flea-pit in the suburbs of Arkansas where they had a resounding success, an Equity-waiver where they work for nothing and play to thirty fans per night and think, as we used to in weekly rep, that '*ours*' was so much better than even the West End one, 'Mrs Twigg said so in the Buxton box office!' And so these youngsters had come all the way over to London barely to conceal their opinion that theirs was so much better, and of course in their eyes it was. They are so subjective, having spent months talking about it and months getting it on and running it from Thursday to Sunday for a month and then talking about it for the next five years when they do another 'show case' . . . And then they meet up at the weekends and endlessly discuss how it was and have reunions and parties (real Ayckbourn country). However, not all this is bad – I've done a couple of Equity-waiver shows in LA and some of the actors there are first class, full of determination and a grit I don't find so easily here. But, alas, there are the actors in that bleak theatrical desert who are still talking about the part they played when they got the 'notices' ten years ago.

So what I'm saying, in a circumambulatory way, is that writing didn't make me feel as if I was really working and, like Shakespeare, I did it to fuel my company and create my stock. You don't actually get up and sit in a room and shut the door and stare at a piece of paper . . . oh no . . . you're too smart for that. Writing is something that you do in bed after a blow-out at the Zanzibar when cooling down from a performance. I never thought I was working unless I produced sweat. Now I am just writing and doing nothing else, but waiting to start work in two months and I find it in a way very relaxing. I wrote my play *West* entirely in bed at night, since I thought if I ran out of ideas I'd just go to sleep, but if I sit at a desk and can't think there is no place to go – I just stare at the blank space inside my skull.

From *East* to *West* – 1978

I had problems with this play and it was indeed my 'bonus' play, since I had no desire or will to write it. It was my first and only commission from the BBC; an enlightened head of the Script Department, much taken with *East*, saw the possibility of me writing for television. I didn't want the commission since I felt it would force me to 'perform' – for me writing was at this time still an act akin to the act of love, something I did when in the mood and so disposed or even desperate. I could not turn on the inspiration at will. Writing is the result of an accumulation of events that have added layer upon layer of experience and you tap them out when you feel the pressure needs to be relieved, like tapping a rubber tree. There was no need inside me – I was well and therapeutically discharged with my three-play stint at the New London. When I discussed the commission with my agent I said, don't take the money, for that will surely block me, but say I'll write, since the temptation was too strong to resist. I would, when I had something, submit it to them, but I wouldn't take the money in advance. That way I would have no guilt if nothing came.

I thrashed around in my head for some weeks and doodled, since I never have started a play knowing where I was going. I write almost by process of free-association and that's the way I have directed, letting one idea fish out its friend and so on. I usually tease it out by the bait of the first line and once wrote a whole collection of short stories this way, each one totally different from the one before but all linked by the common theme of loneliness. I started with the most conventionally repellent image I could think of and then my pen would almost take off of its own accord and I never knew where it would lead me. I did not try to pull it back to a pre-worked-out conception with a series of headlines I had to fit into. No, my brain on auto is far smarter than I could ever be on manual.

I imagine that when you go the theatre you can see the works conceived on manual and those that were left to find themselves. Well, they never do just find themselves, of course, you have to guide them, but you follow your intuition to where it *leads* you. You don't go and make little models and little men and move them around the little model and come in and impose your will across the thousand and one possibilities that chance might have given you. But if you work intuitively, then you must allow for breakdowns and blockages when the current is broken and you have to say, 'I don't know what to do here' and not be afraid, since inspiration is a fickle beast and you must wait or do something else until it rises up again.

When Joe Papp in New York asked me to direct *Coriolanus* in 1988 I was thrown into a panic since I would never have wanted to direct that play. It has some fine scenes with Coriolanus and family and I used to do his stirring introductory harangue to the plebeians for my audition. I got to know Shakespeare more for the 'numbers' that I could pluck out, since most actors' favourite plays are favourites because of the roles in which they see themselves. But this experience was good for me since I learned a great new work and was able to put my mind into an unwieldy, sprawling masterpiece and give it form and, I hope, clarity: it was a learning experience in a large way. It was only the second Shakespeare I had directed in ten years. And so I am saying that commissions are sometimes good in that you don't have to wait for the moment when the psychic mechanism goes green – you might wait for ever, so sometimes you need a little prod.

So for *West* I lay in bed and thought and thought, but nothing entered my skull until one day I just jotted down the first line that came into my head. It was not an original line. It was stolen, or rather lifted, from a short story I'd written which had a chapter with a strange beginning, about a young man riding through the Highlands of Scotland on a motorbike. 'Breathless, I was aghast . . .' I jotted down this line that to me denoted exactly that, wonderment, amazement as the countryside majestically unpeeled itself before my hurtling eye as

I was thrust into its biting Scottish air on my machine. In the story the young man on his motorbike dies in a terrible crash and in death describes what he sees. I took the first line and spun it into another web. I took charge of the line and let it be a seed that created a completely different animal and it became *West*.

> Breathless I was aghast when I saw standing between the full moon
> and the blinking lamplight, this geezer, all armed, a certain aim he
> took and felled the swarthy git from Hoxton with a deft and subtle
> chop, I never witnessed Mike I swear such venom and gross form
> in leather stacked . . .
>
> [from *West*]

Yes, completely inspired to parody, or borrow, the lines from Oberon in *A Midsummer Night's Dream*. And so it went on and became what I called my modern *Beowulf*. Or a cross between *High Noon* and *Henry V*. It was my morality play about courage and the need to be unafraid and to use guts from time to time since it is better to get a black eye that will heal than a blackened spot on your soul that you will nurse until the day you die. Oh, how we would all like to live up to this impossible creed! Also, the play dealt with themes of fear, loyalty in friendship, the fear of standing by yourself and not giving a damn. The joys of pleasure and the bitterness of sexual decay. But apart from its serviceable qualities, which I seem to have sold here as if I was trying to sell a second-hand car, the play was also great fun and verbal fireworks and isn't that enough sometimes? Just to have fun and play?

I wrote in some mock-Shakespearian pastiche and some ironic observations on early life and once more went on a time trip to Stamford Hill. At times I am satirizing London past and present and the world of grown-ups here represented for the first time with pencil sketches of Ma and Pa! They didn't care since they were both dead by then. But my sister came along and shed a tear . . .

Thank you, oh thank you, dear David Benedictus of the Beeb, for giving me the opportunity to create *West*. Even if when I presented you, oh so proudly, with the finished product you didn't have a clue what to do with it and passed the script around and everyone shook their heads and didn't have a clue either and so it was mine again. Thus it went on the stage, where it was performed for sixteen long, summer weeks, thanks to the interest of Ian Albery, and then televised, thanks to Mark Shivas, who I think was a little desperate to find something for the relatively new Channel Four. And thanks most of all to John Frankel, who made such fascinating television. In the USA it was such a success that they showed it twice on their one non-commercial station . . . with subtitles!

For *West*, like most commissions, which don't come from divine inspiration, I borrowed certain themes to get started. In this case I borrowed from *East*, and that's why I called it *West*. *East* was meant to depict the east side of cities where the sun rises first and where the slums ooze together and out of the evil and desperate compost heap can create weird and exotic fruit. *East* was my mandate to express everything that I wished to without reserve. Almost as a battle against theatrical convention. *West* signified more of a developed concept and had a plot. The plot was pure *High Noon*. Hence *West*. Also going 'up west' was shorthand for doing something special and more elegant, of having a wonderful time and going on the town. You'd dress up to go 'up west'. It meant escape from the dreary slums or suburbs. Its very name gave a charge, as when Mum might say she was going shopping 'up west'. When you were in Stamford Hill going 'up west' still carried that aura of magic with it. As you stepped out of the Piccadilly Line at Leicester Square you might be leaving the railway station in Venice and watching the unbelievable panorama of undulating gondolas swimming past you. I suppose 'down town' in New York had the same connotations. The characters who were spawned in *East* now have a craving to go beyond their little world and see what mysteries lie beyond the Charing Cross Road. What adventures are to be had in those utterly mysterious enclaves and unknown streets. However, in *West* they talk of escape but seldom have it. They yearn for nirvana, for streets that don't stink of corner pubs and fish and chips. But it has got even ghastlier today. When I wrote *West* in 1978 I thought our working-class environment was fairly wretched but simple, with a couple of cafés and a few clubs and swimming pools, a few broken-down flea-pit cinemas, a sweaty old gym, a few parks in which to trot with your lady for a wintry squeeze. But now the same areas are positively gruesome and like wastelands. Grey deserts with the same bleak and dreary pubs except now they have machines that keep blinking at you which I find deeply offensive, but your average gorm pays no attention to a light show designed to induce epilepsy while the pub was originally meant to be a haven. The streets have been denuded of your little local cinemas or even the big emporiums, which have been replaced by these cineplexes; little viewing rooms so that there may be ten grotty little rooms in one building. On every corner the video shop has become the porn shop – the only things that seem to line the shelves are scenes of violence and sex or both together in a heap and it's usually run by some yobbo and his horror missus. The street or environment no longer nourishes in the way it once did, but is a place to get through as soon as possible. A few more Indian or Chinese cafés are open, but they soon fade into the same dreary predictability, as if they too had contracted the disease, so prevalent here, of total indifference. Well, I don't live in the West End, so I may have a jaundiced view, but I do love the markets and that pleasure of wandering through junk has never deserted me.

So *West* is Mike and Sylv's dream of escape after the initial crashing excitement of their desires. After this comes a squint at the environment that spawned them. Mike has to take revenge for the death of one of his tribe and the battle will be enormous given that the opponent is an admix of Curly King and Harry Lee, and Mike is a sensitive youth based more on my cousin Sidney Bennet, who, as we know, defeated the dragon for real in the epic battle of Stamford Hill! The desire and wishes are a compound of my own with Mum and Dad who rear their heads and one can hear Dad saying . . .

> I sit down by a bench all day/ machining trousers for five bob/ and dust choking my lungs/ and the noise of the machines/ you wouldn't believe it/ and fifty in a room/ ten pair of pants a day/ I slog to make/ cut and trim/ then throw them to Greek to finish off/ and put a fly in/ and at the end a Mick to press them/ I got callused hands already from the shears/ a spine that's curved forever/ and a cough that can't be cured by all the medicines in the world/ that's known to man/ to make a haven for my family/ which is a little heaven/ so don't get on my tits.
>
> [from *West*]

Of course the thoughts and desires of Mike are mine, since I cannot speak for Sid, but can only express his great courage.

Sylv makes her appearance as the spurned woman. The character bore a resemblance to a Sylvia I went out with. I took her name, and Anna Nygh in *East* and Sylvia Kyd in *West* played Sylv to perfection.

She had been a real person who did possess some of the thoughts and desires of her stage image. The rest of the characters bore only very fleeting resemblances to real people, but were more an amalgam of types and splinters of Mike.

I lay in bed and wrote with speed and mounting excitement. Having found my theme the speeches poured out: cowardice, compromise, fate, the Lyceum, although I do keep faith with the Tottenham Royal. I would have thought that having seen *East* they would have been prepared for *West*, but they hummed and aahed and paid me the second half of my fee and I had the play back and so thank you, Auntie!

I like *West* since it has the form that *East* lacks and a focus for Mike's energies and intents rather than a Bacchanalian shout of affirmation. Even in the staging this was reflected by the cooler style of dressing and the streamlined percussive movements. *East* was dressed as if we were some strange yobbos crossed with Anthony Burgess's book *A Clockwork Orange*, which I don't mind saying must have had some effect on me. *West* was free from that and I got back on to the job of telling a story. I was also influenced by the old English saga, *Beowulf*, and saw myself as the one man chosen to defeat the dragon. The one who must visit the lair in order to save the community from destruction, he who takes on the mantle of greatness and must take on the pain for the little people who are afraid. The sacrifice. The soldier who must go out and kill and yet a well-behaved boy at home. The rebel. The outlaw who yet acts with honour for his friends. I had many dragons to defeat and they were all out there snarling and slobbering at the mouth – but when you got close they turned into ordinary and harmless ogres that you had enlarged by the force of your overheated imagination. However, be that as it may, they still sat like fat gnomes in the seat of power, fearful lest you decided to step inside the temple, trying to thwart you at every step. You either had to kiss them or kill them – I believe the latter would have been preferable.

Rory Edwards played Mike and I couldn't have wished for a more splendid performance. He gave it a rare quality of sensitivity. I had chosen by this time to step down from my childhood heroic roles, although I had only played Mike, and I felt that now I was into my forties I should let the mantle fall on the young. I would have played it like a strutting peacock and been encouraged by the audience to play for laughs, as we did in *East*; I would have pranced around the stage doing neck movements like a pneumatic chicken and it would have been a caricature. Rory saved me from myself. His movements were like a dancer's and his body language conveyed Mike's thoughts all the time while his words conveyed something else. The whole team was excellent, especially the young Bruce Payne, who attracted a substantial amount of attention in a small role which he played like a virtuoso. In the end the play was compared by *Time* magazine to an inner-city basketball team, which I thought summed it up very well. It was also the second great role I lost as time overtook my desires. Because of the length of time it took me to get my plays on, I was too old to play the parts.

A Berkoff play is simultaneously avant-garde and déjà vu. Actors in whiteface mime extravagant gestures, confronting the audience with stylized, scatological invective. It is like being back in the rumble seat of '60s performance art, but with a raw poetic urgency. Other English playwrights may update Shaw; Berkoff wants to be an East End blend of Sam Shepard and Jean Genet. *West*, the first of his plays to infiltrate the West End, can be seen as a new *West Side Story*. Mike, leader of a quintet of Hackney toughs, challenges a rival gang boss to one-on-one combat and just barely lives to tell the tale. Berkoff's twist: Mike and every other character speak in iambic pentameter. Will the rival boss kick Mike in the crown? 'Balls! Were he Al Capone I'd pluck 'im down.'

This is the Theater of Too Much – a hothouse of voluptuous imagery where the adventurous playgoer can find weird refuge. As director, Berkoff has molded his performers until they are as mean and disciplined as an inner-city basketball team ready for the playground playoffs. Berkoff's work is not for everyone; but for audacious originality, he is the top boy in contemporary British theater.

Time magazine

1983

The little Donmar Theatre was a perfect venue for *West*, and it looked good. After my usual indecision about whether to go for a

69

setting for a change, we decided to keep to an empty space with a backdrop of old doors to suggest the street. Mark Glentworth scored the music, which was created live, and the whole thing had an almost movie feel to it. Mum and Dad were movingly played by John Joyce and the lovely and very warm-hearted Stella Tanner. On the first night some of the lads from the 'Hill' came to see it. I really wondered what they would make of our British *West Side Story*, but they were all well and truly chuffed. John McVicar has become a loyal supporter lately and he turned up, but he said he missed the scatology of *Greek*, which he had seen three years earlier. Strangely enough there is not one swear word in *West*! Not one single four-letter word, since it was written for the Beeb! My cousin Sid came, of course, since he was one of the inspirations, and it was very strange – as I introduced John McVicar to Sid I could see the contrast: Sid has become a successful businessman, while John still carries the colours of the tearaway and looks dangerous. Sid looked a little bovine and at ease; underneath John was still ready. Sid, as if sensing this, when I fulsomely introduced him as the inspiration, said something like, 'I don't keep as fit as I used to', to which John replied, as if in playful mocking, 'I can see that!'

Sid was happy to think that I had chosen to lionize him and to celebrate his victory so publicly. Ian Albery was happy with the response at the Donmar, although it did ease off and I was reviewed in that kind of respectful but guarded way – the consensus among critics was although it was exciting and different and well acted, there was something somehow suspect in the fact that it wasn't a treatise on one of those middle-class 'adult' themes that are so 'serious', as if the trials and tribulations of working-class youth are not of sufficient depth to demand any real creative exertion. The summer saw it through. I used to drive up from Brighton on my Moto Guzzi to check it out from time to time and it always played well.

East End Family Life – 1947

My cousin Sid was brought up in and around the East End and was eventually housed in a council estate off Berners Street. His mother Mary was my father's sister and they were part of a six-child family. On my mother's side there were eleven children, so I had fifteen aunts and uncles – always someone to visit or get to know or to receive letters from, and each was a character in a giant jigsaw puzzle that I was forever trying to put together. Each had distinct characteristics that were part of a mosaic of Eastern Europe or Russia and the most salient one was a gentle softness and craziness. An ever-moving mouthful of shrieks and cries. Loudly debating, often six at a time in different parts of the room on different subjects. They were afraid of silence and seemed to need to hear that chicken-pen of clucking and animated dialogue that felt as if it was the right tune. Always debating and arguing about people rather than themes of politics, except for my dad's brother Sam, who was the intellectual among them and an ex card-carrying staunch communist. Uncle Sam was the spiritual guru of the group; his photographic memory would transport us back in time to the early East End ghetto or to the streets of the Lower East Side, New York, where he emigrated and where he walked and walked, endlessly fascinated by the New World, and worked as a trouser cutter or machinist. Sam looked like Dad, but there the similarity ended, for Dad was a Don Juan, a ladies' man who wore wide-brimmed trilbies and was a mean hand at bridge or poker. He eventually played seriously enough to turn professional and haunted the West End clubs where he would sit most of the day 'earning his living'. At the same club would enter blind Uncle Alf, my mother's brother, the former boxer who, having been blinded in the ring, earned a living during the war selling bars of black-market chocolate or whatever else might have been in short supply. He would sit quietly in the club, looking smart and dapper with his polished shoes, and wait for someone to buy a bar of rare Cadbury's chocolate.

The temptation to gamble was in Dad's blood as it was in all East End families. Everybody gambled. The houses in Myrdle Street were lit until the early hours with the sound of shouts and murmurs and tea constantly being made as money went down the drain. Even my mother was a victim to this madness and would play for hours, as did Aunt Mary, but I think they would generally lose when playing with men. I once watched Mum putting her hand in her purse over and over again until I could bear it no longer and tried to drag her home, but like the hooked spieler she would only say, 'In five minutes', hoping against hope for the change in the tide. The game was usually pontoon or rummy and occasionally whist. Pontoon was easy since the cards went around fast and if you were the bank you had the chance of doing well and a ten in your hand was like a sweet caress and then for it to be followed by a picture card was sheer bliss. In years to come you'd have a Pavlovian response to cards whether you played any more or not.

The only cards I was interested in were cigarette cards in cigarette packets or bought in cellophane wrapping. They were always fascinating, especially the movie stars or the uniforms of all the soldiers who were part of the great sprawling British Empire. I was intrigued as to how we could be in control of all these far-flung nations and how they all had such smart uniforms. These cards really took my imagination to wander in some far-off dreamy locations, as did the foreign stamps. The cards of movie stars would encourage another form of day-dreaming, as the potted histories would be scanned, and we'd stare in fascination at these immortal beings. That is when I heard of this place called Hollywood, which was to be another haunting and magical word that sent me spinning off into fantasy land – not a hard thing to do. Movies did the same and as Mum and I climbed the steps to the Palaseum Cinema on Commercial Road we would be transported each week. I have only her to blame for encouraging a kind of rampant and secret day-dreaming that made ordinary life difficult to negotiate. At school break we'd flick playing cards up against the wall and the nearest to the wall scooped up the rest and so we had a big wad, if we won, of frayed and mixed cards that we could exchange if we wanted some homogeneity. I turned up one year when I was about eleven at Christian Street School, just off Cable Street, where Mum had gone to school as a girl, and I was nearly laughed off the street. The reason was quite simple. I was dressed to kill in a double-breasted check suit and long pants. Plus shirt and tie! I was dressed like a mini-Bogart. A small street hood, which was the style then in New York, where I had just been living for the last three months. I was an American! But more of that later.

In the Beginning: Evacuation to Luton – 1942

Dipping even further back into the quagmire of memory I recall a time when memory starts. Legs, the long legs of adults, trousered legs, table legs, Dad's legs. Then the small comforts of childhood: a red tricycle and the fire in the grate leaping like an inferno, and a fender and photos on the mantelpiece of an American cousin who was stationed in the army in England and who would come and visit and bring huge food parcels full of those strange American tastes for which I developed a craving. After the outbreak of war, my family had been evacuated to the small town of Luton, famous chiefly as a millinery centre. We lived in a little rented house, 25 Grantham Road, and I went to my first school, called Maidenhall Elementary School, just around the corner. I remember the first day when the plump yellow-haired lady who was my life and sanctuary, Mum, gradually disappeared from view while I was imprisoned behind a desk with another wailer. But soon we became obsessed with how to make an 'H' with our crayons and forgot our woe. Mum turned up at lunchtime and the world recovered as we strolled down the road to sanctuary.

The school was at first a friendly little place. During breaks we would gamble with marbles which we would roll down into a drain with a metal grate. The winner was the one to get the marble in the middle first. Sometimes a small marble would fall down the crack in the grate and I learned how to wait after school and put my arm into the foul-smelling mud and find the priceless gems. We did some exercises in the yard with a young female teacher. Each time she did astride together, astride together, her skirt would fly up, revealing to our curious eyes the first glimpses of those mysteries which lay under those billowing skirts. Those PT classes I found disturbing and could not put her flying skirts out of my mind; they led to strange stirrings in my six-year-old body and images that would not leave my over-fertile brain.

My first tentative stirrings were acted out in a fairly celibate relationship with Janet Ellis, who lived in the same street, Highfield Road. We would go over to the Frickers factory and, like young cave-dwellers drawn to the impulses of our early life on earth, would construct homes out of old petrol drums and cover them with corrugated-iron roofs. Then we would just sit in them, feeling most adventurous, and talk endlessly. Her brother John would come along and I designated him as my 'best friend' since I was so badly in need of a pal. He was indeed just the kind of mate I needed and would go most everywhere with me, collecting conkers from Wardown Park which we would string to play conkers in the season, often getting clipped on the knuckles when bringing a conker down with force on somebody else's. I learned to dip them in vinegar overnight and even reached a stage when my conker had made seven or eight 'kills' . . . There was no need to lie about the number of kills since you would only be deceiving yourself and that was silly.

The summer was spent by the open-air lido near the park and I learned to swim at an early age with the aid of a pair of yellow water-wings. I still recall the sensation when the wings came off and I floated of my own accord. It was astonishing and I never lost the thrill of floating. Each day I would go down to the pool with my sister and each day I would insist on going back. I admired certain blond-haired youths with short-cropped hair and sturdy un-English bodies. When I was told that these were German prisoners of war I became even more awestruck – they seemed so healthy and muscular compared to my scrawny body with my shoulder-blades sticking out like duck's wings. I was of course unaware at the time, as was the rest of the world, that while I was struggling to swim a full length, just a few hundred miles away under the same summer tens of thousands of young boys and girls were experiencing the hell on earth of Treblinka. That such things were going on while I was alive and collecting shiny brown conkers was chilling to me in later life. I thought back to those days and remembered that at times I found terrible and strange upheavals in my home life, periods of inexplicable sadness; mixed up with the normal joys of growing and discovery I seemed to recall profound confusion, unhappiness and misgivings. By some strange form of telepathy, some osmosis, could I have sensed some horrific happening – something of such barbarity that its scream touched my young soul? There seemed to be a lot of shouting going on in my family which I took for granted, as one does as a child, as if this was the lot of an adult and you were meant to shout and scream as you grew older.

In my street there was a scruffy kid called Baxter; we didn't play with him much as he was something of an outcast, but he always seemed to have bizarre information about the progress of the war and one day he confided to me that if Hitler arrived in England he would kill all the Jews. I listened to this information with a kind of detachment and wasn't too worried: I knew they would never get to England since we were 'good' and the good people always won. The films we saw confirmed these childlike thoughts. How could they come to Luton – the idea was preposterous. But I became aware, more and more, that I was selected for some different path which I could not readily comprehend but which I accepted as some prior knowledge without questioning the cause or reason. It was so in the fantasies of children.

I remember coming down the stairs in the morning and warming myself by the fire, hearing the wireless relay the news. We always seemed to be knocking those Messerschmitts out of the air, so I knew I was fully protected and could go about my life, but a seed had been sown and anxiety was never far away. When some small event occurred I could be thrown into a fit of worry and trembling far in excess of the incident that caused it. If my teacher made me stand up for some breach of conduct I would be scared shitless and quake in fear; if my sister said, for a joke when it became overcast one day, that the sky was falling down, I was seized with the most terrible fright. And so from being a fairly normal, venturesome child, I changed gradually into a ball of apprehension and doubt. I doubted everything and everyone and would accept nothing unless it was proven to me. The only things I was prepared to accept were the continual gift parcels from Cousin Morris and the American comics which thrilled me with their bright colours and surreal worlds of Batman, Captain Marvel and Superman. These were, of course, real to me and I expected that any day we would go to the USA where all our relatives were dwelling in luxuriant ease surrounded by comics and Hershey chocolate bars, and be happy ever after. And hopefully meet the caped Captain Marvel. America was Mum's constant dream. Even the stamps were fascinating and the games Cousin Morris sent were thrilling and different. The comics, once read, I would sell at school by converting the ten cents on the front page to fivepence, and thus supplemented my meagre pocket money. I did quite well for some time and entertained the idea that I would one day become a rich merchant. Most of our relatives on Mum's side had escaped the grinding poverty of the East End and emigrated to the States in the twenties, but Mum had stayed because she was the youngest of eleven and was still at school when they all disappeared over the waves. So she married Dad. They both went to America in the twenties and stayed four years – in fact they were married there. Mum adored it, but Dad had to return when his parents were old or needed him as a bread-winner, and so they went back to the East End. But Mum exchanged letters all those years with these strange relatives from far away and hoped for the day after the war when we all would be united again. It was all Mum talked about and it hung over everything like a shadow. 'Can I have a bike, Mum?' 'No, dear, we're going to live in America soon and you can get one there.' I was seemingly denied all requests on the ground that we were going to America. *Everything* was denied as if this was a normal thing. Even today I *expect* to be denied and frame myself into the defensive stance necessary to deal with the enemy. Again I pleaded for the bike as I saw we were not about to go to the States before a long time had passed and I could at least learn to ride, but this was met with a firm refusal. I became more pressing as I saw other kids with cheap second-hand bikes. Mum and Dad were of course worried that I might have an accident, but in their folly they didn't realize that when I borrowed a bike from a friend in the next street and rode it into the main road and wobbled about with no idea of road law, I came nearer to getting killed than at any other time in my life. I didn't know about rights of way, so I cycled down the road, braking at each side street that led into it, often inches short of collision. But I loved the idea of defying gravity – for that is how it seemed, that as you got faster your legs would take off and then you'd fly. It was an extraordinary experience and I borrowed the bike whenever I could, but still my pleas, daubed with tears from a screwed-up face, went for nothing. I persisted until they could bear it no longer and Dad made a bargain with me. If I wouldn't nag and would be a model of good behaviour for *forty days* I *would get a bike*. But I must be good and not whinge, cry or shout . . . for *forty days*!! It was like a biblical injunction.

The days crawled and I bit my tongue so as not to spoil my copy-book. I felt like Jacob in the Old Testament, having to wait seven years to attain the lady of his dreams, only to be told at the end of the seven years that he had to do another seven years. There are many great waits in history and mythology. In Kafka's *The Trial* there is the parable of the man who waits at the door of the law: he sits outside the door for years, waiting for what he believes will be his moment to be called and he never is called, and then one day he asks the doorkeeper why he has seen no one else enter the door of the law and the doorkeeper, seeing that the man is near his end and very old, says, 'The door was meant only for you. I am now going to shut it.' The story of our lives . . . Suddenly its meaning became clear to me: we tend to wait for years for that golden opportunity when we will enter the door and find salvation, but we wait and put it off with all sorts of excuses. Yet at the same time we demand the fruits of that knowledge and experience. Why don't we enter that door that we claim is ours? Because we don't know what is lurking on the other side and so we stay with what is safe. Kafka waited at the door for years pondering what was on the other side, deliberating, 'counting the fleas on the doorkeeper's collar', but unable to make the simplest decision about whether to travel to Berlin to see a woman he loved. He pondered what would happen 'if' and but, and perhaps it would not be, and the letters which are a form of insubstantial living, a body as a piece of paper, did the job for him, hundreds and hundreds of letters, flying through space subtracted from the physical being of Mr K.

So I began the long wait and became as one steeled for the task to resist every boyish and childish impulse to which I was hormonally and genetically programmed. I no longer rushed around and shouted or answered back or refused to eat food I found loathsome, like mushy, smelly greens, but gritted my teeth. I came in when I was told and went to bed when it was light and I was wide awake, but one day, for an infringement of a minor kind, I was punished and was made to go back to *day one* again. My dad thought he was doing the right thing and that his blackmail was having an effect as if he were training a horse or a dog.

Well, I can wait, and I did wait and wait and did what I was told, for I saw at the end of the rainbow a shiny bike that had the kind of workmanship that adult things have and I saw myself riding around the block and going to school on it. Saw many different kinds of visions that swam before my eyes as I waited and was calm and played in the recreation ground on the swings and roundabouts and always asked the old man in the shed, 'What time is it, mister?' so that I would not be late. The old man was a kind of Old Father Time who sat in the shed year in and year out and when you asked he quite happily put his gnarled old hand inside his waistcoat and took out a pocket watch and told us. Then ten minutes later I would be back asking, 'Please, what time is it, mister?' and he would repeat the gesture without the slightest sign of impatience. Therefore it seemed as if he was there just for us. One year he was not there. Another man appeared and we asked him the same question and he too took out his pocket watch and became our timekeeper. And the old man who had been there and to whom I asked the question which was the burning concern of my young life never returned. I knew then, for the first time, what death was, since he was the first person I truly missed.

I dashed home on the stroke of 5 p.m. so as not to be late for the ghastly compost heap of smelly food and wolfed it down so that I might at least spend a little time playing outside. I didn't do much, maybe sat on the garden wall, as each house had a small front garden – ours was full of weeds – and talked to my best friend John. While not really ashamed of how we lived I sensed only when I went visiting and saw gardens and flowerbeds and swings in the gardens and roses and lawns, that ours was a neglected dump. When I questioned anything about the garden I was met with the reply that it wasn't worth doing anything to it since we would be going to *America*!

When in school I was asked where or what I wanted to do when I grew older. I parroted, 'Go to America . . .' *America* became the total fantasy, excuse and hope. It prevented me from having music lessons when an inexplicable and overwhelming need to play the piano welled up in me. It was precipitated by the fact that in the first house we rented, in Grantham Road, Luton, there was a piano in the front room which was always kept locked. This room belonged to a sweet old Victorian lady called Mrs Everett and she kept huge aspidistras in the hall which got very dusty. When Mrs Everett came once a week to collect the rent she would open this secret room to air it and I would dash in and sit at the piano and play for all I was worth, even though it probably sounded like early Schoenberg. Mrs Everett seemed delighted to see a child whipping in and out and I surmised she was childless and didn't mind me plonking her old piano with its strange old woody smell. When we moved around the corner to a slightly bigger house where I had my own bedroom for the first time I had no piano and so wished to make up the difference. But we were going to *America*!

I believe it's possible to inherit certain proclivities or even inherit not exactly memory, but impulses that have been developed in a parent. So my reaction to a piano would have been natural, given the circumstances that my mother was bought a piano by my uncle Alf when he was a famous boxer and earning good money. My mother, who was very fond of Alf, used to tell me that after his matches at the Holborn Stadium or Blackfriars he would come home all bruised but triumphant, and the whole of Batty Street, E1, would come out to greet him. One day he bought her this piano and she practised hard; by the time she was eleven she was playing in front of the school assembly in Christian Street. When she was fifteen, so she told me, but I think she was inclined to self-dramatization, her heavy Russian father insisted that she go to work and sold the piano. Perhaps he associated the piano with childhood and thought she should now be grown up. I can scarcely believe that he could be such a brute when the whole family must have been so proud of her playing.

I think the real truth is that she met Dad when she was fifteen and they went out for four years and she married at nineteen. And of course her mind flew out of the window and made cartwheels in the sky when she met Dad, who was a dark, black curly-haired gypsy. 'How did you meet Dad, Mum?' 'One day,' she said, 'I was asked to deliver a message to the Berkowitz family who were friends of our family and when I went there I saw a young man outside the house covered in grease, who was fixing his *bike* and I fell for him there and then . . .' Ma liked to be romantic, for I am sure they must have met as they were growing up in the same warren of streets, but this was an image that she retained of Dad stripped down to his singlet like a young Brando fixing his bike.

Anyway, I never saw the piano and was not to see the bike. All the things that others took for granted were denied to me because we had plans. The piano was no sudden whim, since I talked about it for years. I believe if the parent suppresses natural inclinations and affordable desires there may grow some very strange blooms in their place. Lack of sex education, for example, in a puritanical household might sooner or later lead to a back-street abortion and possible death. Lack of love that's represented by constant denial will lead to getting what you want one way or another, which could lead to magistrates and prisons. Lack of creative outlet will lead to stomach ulcers, neurosis and sickness.

So the days dawdled and the dawn would see me up and about, listening to the wireless and eating tomatoes on toast. We won the war and millions died those most horrible deaths. The camps of Auschwitz revealed the bestial horrors to the world as the loathsome beast so admired by some of our English aristocracy was burned in the German chancellery. And I was obsessed to madness for a bike.

Did we know about these horrors? If we did, or suspected, I heard nothing, just felt this constant unease and wanted to be out of Luton and out of the little suburban street with its tiny, neglected front garden and our weed-strewn one at the back, and out of the school where boys fed on the myths of religious instruction would vent their 'war' games on you since you were now the 'bad guy' . . . the infamous and bizarre met the incredulous in that after the millions dead in the Holocaust, not to mention all the citizens of the world who gave their lives, after the opening up of the slimy pits of rotting bodies, there was still time to teach in school the old canard . . . the Jew killed Jesus!

So I waited in the gloom of restrained activity. One day I was out in the back garden and by now the 'training' I had received had rendered me a kind of nervous wreck who believed that nothing was coming easily and if I didn't get the bike I might anyway be bumped off when Hitler came to Luton. I always had the horrors of school, where I was beginning to feel like an exile or potential devil incarnate. And also hanging over me was this 'next year in New York' and the idea that nothing was worth planning for, nothing worth getting, nothing worth doing, buying, seeing, studying, wishing for, since the time would come. So out in the garden I remember my terrible and pathological fear of spiders and stayed close to the house. I saw my dad through the French windows. The windows were shut. I saw his face and even so, and with all the restrictions, I still felt a leap in my heart when I saw him, since he was the provider of those weird and wonderful deli tastes that he'd bring back from the East End. So there he was smiling at me through the window and his mouth opened and he framed the word which to me in my mind-set I read as *bicycle*. His lips pursed and his mouth opened and I am sure I heard the word I wished to hear and so I tore in, heart pounding and eyes ablaze; at last the moment had come. He stood there and even now I can hear him saying to my querying gaze, '*I've got beigels!*' He knew I liked beigels. Beigels I liked. But I preferred bicycles.

So the day came: the day of days for which all sacrifices would be justified, the event of a lifetime and the most extraordinary journey outside space travel I could have. A dream realized and as thrilling as my first trip to Brighton, when I saw the sea for the first time. Now it was serious, since Dad actually made me a new suit with short pants, which I was to wear only once in my life. But even in that I was deceived, since the tale I had to tell at school was that I was going for a short time to test the water, so to speak; then we would come back, pack up everything and return to America for good. What a cock and bull story: it confused even me. I didn't know whether to say goodbye for ever or 'See you after I come back.'

One morning we were wakened at the crack of dawn and driven down in a hired car to Southampton. Dad liked indulging in the odd hired car, like the time we went to Brighton and I was violently car sick. This time I don't recall being sick, but we stopped a few times to get some fresh air. When we got to Southampton I recall a huge building in front of me rising up and stretching out forever. It was the *Queen Elizabeth* looking resplendent, refitted after her war effort, when she was used for troop-carrying. This leviathan sat there in Southampton dock. It was beyond human belief, like those myths that childhood creates to deal with the impossible. I got on with Mum and Sis, but Dad stayed behind to 'clear things up'. We disappeared into the bowels of the ship, where I started to explore. I lost my way continually and saw little of Ma and my sister since I was in constant motion like a piece of meat in the stomach of a whale being shunted along the endless tunnels. Now was freedom in the strange steel cocoon that was to feed, house and sleep us and then after a week in the sea of infinity open us up into a new world. We were voyagers in space, and each day the never-ending adventure like Theseus in the maze, ever wandering through the passageways and decks. I vividly recall the small cabin which I shared with Mum in the tourist class and the trunk that opened out with its plywood drawers. The pretty labels on the side of the 'Queen' with its two funnels which showed it to be the *Elizabeth*, as opposed to the *Mary* with its three funnels or the late *Mauretania* with its four. The tiny wash-basin by the bunks. I was out first in the morning and on my travels. As usual, I lacked the funds for the kind of spending I thought would befit my station as a voyager and badly wanted to buy a pencil with a photo of the ship on the side plus other knick-knacks, and so I robbed my mum's purse of three heavy, plangent half-crowns, but stupidly left them on the sink so that when Mum returned from the outside loo she spied them. I went the deepest shade of purple for actually being caught as a thief for the first time and was slapped and told to ask in future. Fat chance of getting anything when you ask, that's why I thieved, although I didn't realize this at the time. What you are denied holds a certain fascination.

On deck in the sun they played games with little discs that you shoved around or people sat on deck chairs with blankets around their legs. Or you could throw those rubber rings which were the precursors of frisbees, except these were heavier and during one of my first throws the ring went smack in the eye of a lady spectator. I was most upset by my maladroitness. I spent much time in the first-class pool, a magnificent marble tomb with salt water, and nobody questioned my class since they thought only the rich would be so intrepid as to wander about nonchalantly. Then I would make the great journey back in time for supper, where Mum, Sis and I would congregate.

We were in a kind of heaven where time had no demands or meaning and the constant lack of land gave you the feeling of foreverness and all responsibility faded. This is truly the best way of leaving the Old World, for you have a chance to reflect on the past and to prepare your mind for the future in tranquillity and hope, which is impossible by plane. Also the ship is like a ritual cleansing of the past. It was 1947. I was ten. I wonder now who else was on that journey with me, since only the famous would travel on this great silver hotel. Through the port-hole I saw the sea rise and fall and wondered what would happen if we sank, since my mind was always programmed into viewing the worst possible scenario, but the five days flowed past pleasantly with only a moderate amount of seasickness and at last we arrived.

It was early dawn when we disembarked at Pier 93, New York City. I saw a huge city flow past my eyes. Unbelievable to all those European eyes, used to the modest human dimension, now floating past the Battery and seeing the giant peaks of Atlantis lit up in the cold October night. A city of glass. It was one of the wonders of the world to my young mind, brought up in a tight little street in Luton, where I could be transformed into a space traveller only through movies like *Sinbad*. Here was a real-life movie, a phantasmagoric science-fiction world which left me aghast and stunned, swept up and forgotten. I was transported. This was everything they had hinted at and more. I was high on being in the land of Captain Marvel.

The dawn slowly drained the ink out of the sky and it was light and then the long, long wait to disembark. Hours went past; it was at least 3 p.m. before I walked down to greet a host of strange, sweet-scented relatives whose breath smelled of cashews and American-type perfumes. I was thrown into a car which was a block long and, once in, thrust into my hand was a chocolate bar, a Hershey bar. My first taste of America. Hershey – sweet, almondy, crunchy, exotic, more-ish. My family looked strangely big and had large voices and Auntie Doris kept exclaiming about how I looked and kissed Polly, my mum, and cried with joy at being reunited with her long-lost sister whom she had not seen for eighteen years. We ended up in the Bronx for a feast and as we entered the building we saw Pearl, Doris's daughter, coming along the street clutching one of those huge brown paper bags that you see in a hundred movies. Upstairs we ate and ate and feasted on strangely flavoured strawberry ice-cream and I was sick, since I was not used to this variety and gluttony, and then the next day we were packed off to my auntie Ray, the eldest sister, who lived in Nyack, Upper New York. She had a small, white, wooden-frame house that was pure Norman Rockwell, as was the whole town. Cousin Morris had a drug store, as he was a pharmacist, and like all drug stores of the period there was a snack-bar on one side and a couple of girls served the best toasted sandwiches in the world. It was pure paradise . . . for a week.

The first day Morris took me into the men's shop next door. He got rid of that stilted navy short-trousered suit that was so funereal and formal, and turned me into a small American. First he bought me a brown check suit and then some long pants and a jacket for the winter, one of those waisted lumber jackets with a fur collar that you put up against your neck when it's windy back there, *plus* a top coat. The guy was a real champ and I think liked me a lot – perhaps I was a surrogate son for him since he was so bound to his mum's apron strings he never did get it together with anyone, though on the other hand he may not have wanted to.

The time in New York was like a lacuna in my chain of events, in that I was torn out of a real world and placed into an unreal one where my fantasies were fulfilled. No more the can't and always the can, but the needs had changed. I was constantly so bewildered and amazed that I had no time for the reflection and contemplation I needed in order to ascertain what it was I wanted out of life. Now it was shazam, kaboom, giant ice-creams, toasted sandwiches, trips in the car to the city to see the Empire State Building and Radio City and the ice rink. Eyes on stalks as I witnessed the Empire State, the crown of my fantasies and the symbol of all my dreams, the unattainable and marvellous, the stupendous and awesome seen from wherever we were. She rose majestically and no matter who was in the back seat, aged aunts and uncles, I would climb all over them for a *glimpse*.

After a week or so we were shunted back to the last port of call, to another brother, this time called Joe. Joe had miraculously put together an old Victorian rooming house which he rented at a low price. It was one of the few family houses left in the Bronx. It was approached by an outside staircase on both sides and then you would reach the first floor. We were put into an attic and it would be no exaggeration to compare the appearance of the house to the one Anthony Perkins resided in when doing his strange deeds in *Psycho*. Despite that, it was a friendly old house and typical for a guy who had saved some money, having worked on the waterfront all his life and reached a decent position. So after the pastoral dream time of Nyack, Middle America, cropped lawns, pine trees and the great American actress Helen Hayes living down the road, now came reality once more, flooding the senses with that old familiar sensation . . . *pain*!

As we crawled up the small narrow fire escape to the attic I could almost see Mum's despair and understood that the few days of pleasure and leisure had been put there to absorb the shock of what was to follow. Why they didn't get a proper flat I have no idea. It couldn't have been so unbelievably difficult – even if the post-war years were difficult for everyone, this was a joke. This was the kind of place you'd hide out if you were Anne Frank. It was a place to escape to.

We came breathlessly to the top and I saw what was to be our home. After Luton and my own bedroom plus weedy garden to play in, we were placed in a room with two beds, one double and one single for me with a window overlooking the yard and the next block. On the other side of the attic was an equal-sized area overlooking the street; it was let to a single man and between the two rooms were two curtains. There was a stove between us for light cooking and a toilet, but no bath. There were a couple of chairs and a dresser in front of the window. But of course we could use the living room of Uncle Joe and his wife Alice. We were part of the second great immigration, the first having been half a century earlier from Odessa and Bucharest. Fifty years to wait for a pair of red curtains to block off the bedroom from a hospital porter called Chris, a pale, poor, misbegotten shape of a man with watery blue eyes and flaxen hair. He'd keep an eye on us, he generously offered, and he seemed to be pleased to have some company.

Alice, with her high trill-like voice and swept-up hairdo, must have bowled Joe over, he being what you might call a rough diamond; he had served in the Australian cavalry when as a youth he had emigrated from England, and then worked his passage to the New World. Alice showed Mum around and introduced me to the school I was to attend. But first the school needed a clean bill of health, so I had to go to the doctor for a general examination. You can only hazard a guess at my utter shock, dismay and disgust when not only did the doctor present a bill for services which I had always assumed were mine as of right, but Alice proceeded to beat him down a few dollars, hinting that we didn't have too much money, being poor new immigrants! The idea of haggling was bad enough, but haggling with a *doctor* threw me into total confusion and I started to wonder what kind of society this was that allowed this to happen. I was used to our Luton values. Then came the first day at school and as we climbed the stairs to the headmaster's room I saw a policeman with a *gun in his belt*! To me, policemen were like something in comic books, funny with big hats and non-threatening except for a nasty truncheon if you misbehaved, but the idea of a cop who could kill you was totally foreign to me. I believe that the massive and gratuitous crime wave that sweeps America like the plague is rooted in childhood. From the very beginning unless you are sheltered from it and rich you are confronted at every turn with the inescapable idea that without money you are *shit*! Without money your ma can't get medical help unless she applies at the overcrowded, desperate, understaffed poor hospitals where you feel even more like a low-caste piece of trash. Money saves you from all that . . . without money you can't buy school books which I thought of as my right; at my schools in Luton we had paid for nothing except school lunches. We don't even think of it as children, but take it as normal that the dentist doesn't stand in the corridor being bargained down by a poor black and that you have to go to the dentist in England because the country *wants you to*. A certain caring and welfare naturally and easily given, especially at school, helps to prevent the poor from exposing their children, who are so very impressionable, to the contrast between them and a slightly better-off kid. So it was thrust down my throat very speedily that I needed and we all needed *money*! An ugly lesson.

I was welcomed into the class by the teacher, Mr Rich. It was a mixed class and I was already getting used to a strange grown-upness which was sweeping America in the late forties, or was it always so, with the girls of eleven and twelve wearing stockings and lipstick! Am I seeing right? Pulling their stockings up in class and checking their make-up in the mirror. I was not turned on since I was at that age when only the sweet freckled cheeks of Janet Ellis would have any effect on my incipient libido and the made-up tarts in the school only reminded me of grown-ups: they were certainly undesirable with their overdeveloped bodies and hairy armpits. No, I had, by the very unfortunate proximity of the female body or bodies in our cramped little room, been heavily put off adult females.

What I emphatically found a bonus was that since the education system was so behind ours in Britain and specifically mine in Luton, I was able to go over all those maths problems that had defeated me before. . . . Eureka!

I'd walk to school, which was round the corner from the gloomy house in 173rd Street. It was called PS70, Public School 70, and it had a huge playground with its fair quota of bullies. I was to find out pretty soon that the character of the kids was definitely different from what I was used to. They were more outspoken and articulate, but also more whingeing and petty. When they were friendly they were very friendly and curious about me, as if I was some kind of refugee from the camps. I started to make friends rapidly since they were so open to me and I started actually to count them, I was so proud to have made my mark in the Bronx. When I got to school I would still be pinching myself as if I was in a dream, telling myself that this was really America I was in and not Luton.

The first thing we did was go to assembly and sing a song which began very positively – 'I love life and I want to live!' – and we were told this was written by a Japanese POW who came to America and fell in love with it and out of her overflowing joy created this song. Then we'd all pledge allegiance to the flag. That done, we'd do a kind of thirty-minute gym routine to loosen us up for class. We'd go round the gym spending five minutes at each station. A few pull-ups. I could do four, but I liked doing that and watching the other kids pit their strength, straining their little guts out to pull up that extra inch or two. Then some passing the ball and other exercises. I can always remember standing there doing the breathing in and out, looking out of the window and seeing the Chrysler building misted up in the distance. It was very far away, but just its prominence was significant to me like an Aztec temple.

The skyscrapers were an object of profound veneration and worship to me; they seemed to tingle my imagination. They were America more than anything. I thought I would, like Ayn Rand's hero in *Fountainhead*, become an architect and for years afterwards I drew only futuristic buildings. If not a great concert pianist, then an architect. I ended up in a menswear shop in the Edgware Road, W2!

In *Fountainhead* the architect is so far ahead of his time that he causes angst among the minor artists whose idea of revolution is decoration. The pioneer is always ahead of his time since he has to show new methods of communication and like an archaeologist he might excavate old ones and find new values. He is always a step or two ahead and therefore generally viewed suspiciously by his colleagues and critics but adored by the public.

The public are usually ahead of the critics, since they are in the buying market and want new sensations and tastes, whereas the critic's taste has in a way been conditioned by what he has seen and had to review and can seldom stand the shock of something upsetting what he has always valued. Some critics do stand outside the system that educated them; they go about educating themselves and then demanding that the arts come up to their standard. Sounds a little familiar, but in *Fountainhead* the hero blows up a building that has been defiled by the interference of the small bourgeois clique who couldn't take his clean-lined purity. That film stayed in my mind a long time.

I did OK in class. Early in my schooling in New York I was asked something by teacher and replied with 'Yes, *sir.*' The whole class fell about because I had said 'Sir'. I find this now rather odd since Yankees are always saying 'Sirrr?', but in the school such a mark of respect for the teacher was unheard of and the kids would just say, 'Excuse me, Mr Rich.' I was profoundly embarrassed by my apparent solecism and never did it again.

I'd walk home to the house with one of my 'friends' and enter Uncle Joe's parlour and relate the events of the day, like how I'd write colour instead of color but still get a tick for my spelling from Mr Rich. It's strange how when diving down into the sea of memory, as you penetrate deeper into those dark areas, little motes of recollection come floating back. They are the images and instructions forever guiding us and influencing our decisions. In the warm parlour Uncle Joe would be very funny. He had an old record player and the big song then was 'Peg o' my heart', which appealed to me greatly for some obscure reason and I played it over and over again. I also learned how to use the phone.

Joe had a niece called Paula, who was the daughter of blind Uncle Alf. She had come to the States to work on the stage and she was forever doing the splits on the carpet or handstands and of course I was very impressed by her. (When I returned to New York thirty years later Paula took me to her gym, where she did splits and handstands.) My sister found a part-time job, I believe in a grocery store, and Dad was still 'winding up things' in Luton. The attic became oppressive and claustrophobic and I got stuck in there too much in spite of my 'friends'. . . I still had to return home. I got to staring out of the window.

Chris, the other lodger, started to get friendly in his clumsy but good-natured way and, as we stayed in nearly every night, offered to take Mum and me to the movies. 'Steve can sit in the middle,' he said, as if to allay any fears, but now I think he was probably joking. However, one night we did go out together and he took us to see *The Invisible Man*, which was a great treat, and what was even better was the show they had on before the movie as they did in those days. It was either a magic act or acrobats. Then we went to a Nathans or equivalent, where we ate hotdogs. These things were the greatest and most sublime taste that had ever exploded on my young taste buds and further reinforced this huge need I was developing for America and my obsession with diners, just as a place of comfort and sanctuary where all my childhood dreams would be realized. No meanness, no hostility or indifference and menus larger than your imagination. It was, as Mum always said, a 'country for the young'. She wasn't too happy hanging around and waiting for the man in her life to come and save her. I was sent down the road to get the 'dogs' – there was a place along the stretch of 174th Street lined with little shops and cafés, where you got great hotdogs for twelve cents. They have a special taste, no matter if you eat them in New York or Arkansas. It's a flavour that travels all over America. He puts the dog between the roll and 'You want sauerkraut and mustard?' which of course blended in and conjugated with the dog to make the most blissful union ever. You took the wrapped dogs home, getting a bit soggy by the time you got there but still redolent of all the flavours of youth. I missed the dog in future years. Thirty years later when I bought a hotdog I carried with me a pristine impression of a 1947 dog, and so I knew I would be able to tell, unlike the natives, all the changes that had taken place. I bit into it and the smell and 174th Street came flooding back. It had hardly changed!

I was doing OK in my fashion – like all kids, I was fairly malleable, cities were interchangeable and I had school to go to for social intercourse. But adults don't have such an easy time. They have little in the way of social structure unless they're working and often not then. When I went to school I'd see Mum hanging around the old house and waving to me from the attic window. I always remember her face at the window waving me off to school and after a while I wished she wouldn't, since it is something you do when you're parting for a long time, not just for the day until 4 p.m. But for her it was a parting, since she had no bloke there to comfort or to work for and support in his struggles. She was just marking time until Dad came and she could begin to function again. She had never worked outside the home in her life; she needed children to cook for and a home to look after and be creative in. Now she was just a lost face at the window and I felt sorry for her and for both of us. One day I saw Chris the porter pissing in the one toilet with the door open; it made me mad, as there were females on the premises, and I said to him, 'Don't ever do that again.' I was not only getting grown-up, I was replacing my dad and taking care of things.

Weekends Auntie Ray would take us for our weekly treat – a drive, a lunch in a deli downtown and then drop us off so she could get back to watch her favourite programme on TV. One day she made it so clear that we shouldn't be late that Ma got mad at her and started shouting and crying. That was the beginning of a lot of crying. We had no home, no Dad, little money, not many friends and no way to entertain friends except always to go to their house, no income from work, but we had hotdogs at twelve cents with sauerkraut. That helped sometimes. When things got too depressing for Ma Ray felt obliged to have her to stay in Nyack for a week or she would have a nervous breakdown. I had to go with her and my schooling was disrupted; I felt guilty going past the school after that and attended less and less. Mum and I would go downtown and see a movie on 42nd Street in the afternoon and rather than go back to the house we'd stay and see another movie and so I got to be a bit of a movie buff. We'd walk about Radio City and Rockefeller Center and look at the skaters and mingle with the pre-Christmas crowds. I had a new watch strap, one of those metal things that stretched, and I was very pleased with that, and my long pants and jacket that Cousin Morris gave me were keeping me warm as toast.

The snows came and covered the cigar-strewn street. Everything went white like a Christmas card and pure and there was once a visit to relatives in Long Island. The world out there looked like the magazines we used to get in Luton, of small towns and sleighs, wagging dogs, snow fights, turkey on the table and the smell of wood fires. Then it was back to the Bronx and by now the relationship with the family was souring up and sure, they didn't want to keep three people who had an able husband and father, who was too much of a bum to do it himself and would rather spend time trying to win a fortune in a sleazy card club off Piccadilly.

The axe was coming down on my fantasy world and the clock was ticking away the last minutes. We booked to return, this time on the *Queen Mary*, so at least I would have known two queens in my short life. It was February, a great time to travel the Atlantic! The snow was pelting down like the clappers and no one would even risk taking us to Pier 93. Eventually a taxi was bribed some incredible sum to do it. The snow was reaching blizzard conditions and I was torn out of the house practically screaming, hating the idea of returning to that damp, dreary and ghastly hole after my adventure playground.

Beryl, my sister, opted to stay. She had her job and was doing

OK, and so it was just Ma and me again. We had loads of trunks since we had intended to stay forever and Ma bought a huge box full of all those delicatessen goodies you couldn't get in post-war England. We got to the giant beast, which looked very like the other one. I immediately got on and while Beryl was weeping good-byes to Mum I was investigating the ship, but it was the roughest voyage on record and when the stewards were coming along the corridor towards you they'd be practically walking on the wall as the boat moved round them. I was terribly sick most of the time and spent most days in the sick room, only emerging on the last day or two when the storm settled. There were, of course, the usual celebrities who travelled by boat and this time I found a complete list of the people who were 'names'. It was shown to me by a friendly purser who pointed out that Henry Ford II was one of them. The list showed the cabin number. I made up my mind to go and have a chat with him before the end of the voyage, since I had no qualms about being with adults, whom I sought out as potential buddies.

As that night was the last of the voyage there was a big bingo game, then called 'housey-housey'; Mum and I sat down and I won a few bob. A radiantly beautiful woman was sitting near me and in the enthusiastic congratulations around my table she offered her 'Well done'. We got to chatting. I knew I had seen her before and I said, 'Didn't I see you in a film recently called *The Gangster*?' This was a movie that Mum and I had seen on 42nd Street on one of our outings when we would walk around and stare at the Great White Way and be amazed at the Camel cigarette sign which had a man blowing smoke out of his mouth on a giant screen. She modestly said that yes, she was 'Belita', the world-famous skating star, and it was really she. I was in seventh heaven, for now I had touched the hem of the famous, and Ma was really chuffed and hung on every word, since I was becoming Ma's way of getting to know the rich and famous. I naturally said that I too wanted to live in Beverly Hills, which I had recently been reading about, and could I look her up when I got there? She gave me her address and her autograph and just before she got up to go I ventured to add in my characteristically clumsy way, 'You don't get many stars travelling tourist class.' To which she responded that she was just 'slumming', which I failed to understand until Ma explained that she was travelling first class but probably was curious after five days and felt like seeing how the other half lived, since no doubt that is where she came from.

When we docked at Southampton I couldn't help but contrast the amazing bright world of the New York skyline and this collection of dreary low buildings. I made up my mind to catch Henry Ford just as we were entering Southampton. I beetled my way to his cabin, knocked on the door and as I expected he welcomed me in and asked about me and where I had been. I sat on the large state-room bed and felt quite at ease talking to one of the richest men on earth. There are certain things that kids can do if they are young and wilful enough. So I asked about him and what he was doing. He seemed perfectly happy for me to stay and when we docked I was still there as they were getting themselves ready. Just then there was much knocking on the door and the room was invaded by reporters who took flash pictures and asked me if I was their son! Well, I wouldn't have half minded if they had wanted to take me away with them. I had to get back to Mum and reluctantly left and prepared to disembark. Dad was there on the quay and gave Mum one of these sloshy, embarrassing kisses and then we got in the train for London. On the train he seemed concerned that Ma and I had spent so much money out of the funds we had arrived in New York with. I was again embarrassed for her and yet again when the ticket collector asked for our tickets, which were third class and we were sitting in first.

Auntie Betty was waiting at Victoria Station and we took a cab to her East End flat in Cannon Street where we would be staying until we found 'somewhere'. Cannon Street was just half a mile from Mother Levy's nursing home in Vallance Road, where I was born. I went to a little room where my cousin Barry was already asleep and climbed into his bed. I was back and it felt very strange. The snow was high here, too, and the next day they wasted no time in getting me to go to school. Up Christian Street I went with my double-breasted suit which had the kids looking aghast, so twice in four months I was to be a freakish traveller from other worlds.

The Return

America didn't relinquish its grip on my mind for years to come. I explored the postwar East End which I found while playing – it was the first time I had lived there when I was old enough to be aware of it. It was quite fascinating and a change from Luton. The streets were lively in those days, not so very different from the streets of the Bronx in that they were packed with second-generation immigrants from the Old World. The market in Hessel Street could have come right out of the Warsaw ghetto and probably many of the people had. Round the corner was Roggs the deli and beigels became a commonplace affair and no special treat from Dad, of whom I saw less and less since there was no room in Betty's flat for the whole family. Betty and Uncle Sam made us as welcome as they could and Sam never stopped talking – he was a constant and never-ending fund of stories, plus the energy and desire to tell them. As I write he is still there around the corner in Cannon Street, eager to buttonhole anyone ready and willing to listen to the ancient mariner over a cuppa. He will drink twenty cups a day and give you the names of all the silent screen heroes and heroines and the political villains at the time of the Wall Street crash. Lashings of quotations from Shakespeare and Homer and a run-down on the origins of the Communist Party. War and peace and the war in Burma in which he took part and a seemingly inexhaustible supply of information as if his brain was a computer that stored things and kept them permanently alive in his mind. He was a generous uncle and never failed to press two bob into my indigent hand, curiously always just when I needed it most.

Later we were ensconced in a room opposite with Mrs Speilberg, which wasn't too pleasant since there was an outside loo and in the freezing winter you hardly felt like traipsing out, so we had a slops bucket in the room like you have in prison, in case you needed to pee in the night. I sat for the Eleven Plus and passed. Mum was proud that I, like my sister Beryl, was a bright grammar-school kid. She took me for my interview at Raine's Foundation in Arbour Square, where I met the very genial headmaster, Mr Dagger I believe his name was. There was another exam that we sat as soon as I got into that school and I found that easy too and was placed in the A stream. I was always glad when I could show and be shown the results of my skills, when I was rewarded for them and praised. Here was visible evidence of my prowess and I excelled, glad to have such a palpable response.

My dreams of the gleaming spires of New York continued to haunt my mind and the same dream would recur. I'd dream I was in the streets downtown and so ecstatically happy that once more I was in the turbulence and smells I had come to love and I just had to find my way to the Bronx. I could never seem to locate the right street or the subway and would wander around, see familiar landmarks, nearly finding it but not quite and this dream would occur over and over again. I was lost but still happy to be there and then the lostness would start to unsettle me, but I had to find Joe's house to secure myself. I never found the damned place. Not Joe's nor 'Peg o' my Heart'.

Joe died in 1990. Bandy Joe from his years in the Australian cavalry. He was about ninety or more. He was a fighter to the end in that he never gave up and was also possessed of a magic tongue. The rest have all bitten the dust except for Uncle Sam and Betty, who sit in their attic eyrie in Cannon Street surveying the follies of the world. Sam is nearly blind now and so can no longer replenish his mental library, but he listens and watches the shapes moving on telly. Also Sid's mum, Mary, lived and thrived around the corner and still played the piano until her death in 1991. In 1980 Ma fell off the perch. She was seventy-seven. Not too bad an age, but when you're riddled with cancer it doesn't do your system much good. She got smaller and she was pretty tiny to begin with – five foot two. She died with millions of memories and left them to me in her will. When she died I happened to be in the middle of a tour of Israel with my production of *Hamlet*.

Israel, 1980

I walked down Dizengorf Street and everyone looked like my sister, Mum or Dad: a very strange sensation. It was a hot summer, and Avital Mossinson, the artistic director of the Jerusalem Festival, had seen our *Hamlet* at the Edinburgh Festival, where we had deliberately staged it in the round so as to have it ready for the Round House in 1980. I had discussed this with Thelma Holt, who was then running the ex-railway turning shed. It was the ambition of my life, since every schoolboy wants to be an engine driver and every actor wants to play Hamlet. I have already written a book about my methods, *I Am Hamlet*, so it would be superfluous to repeat them here; suffice it to say that our team put it together slowly as if we were creating a finely detailed mosaic. The cuts had to make sense and allow the through line of the play: don't cut into arteries and main lines, but trim away the adipose tissue. Some of the ideas of spacing came from the gym we were rehearsing in, since the floor was lined like a basketball court and these same lines became for us walls and corridors. I do like to define the spatial values in a work and so when the members of the palace made their way from one place to the next it became very important in my mind that we should see them walking along taped corridors or lines, turning at right angles on the bend. Rooms must be clearly demarcated, as must stairs and closets.

Anyway, we took the show to Edinburgh, which is a marketplace, and sold it for a tour of Belgium, Israel, and one of Germany and Europe for a Mr Jan de Bleik, the famous old impresario who worked out of The Hague. Wonderful, most wonderful. I was unlikely to be offered Hamlet in a month of Sundays and I made my *own* opportunities. I loved playing it in the round in Edinburgh and we also had to play it in one lighting state since our venue was a school lecture hall and the audience were lit as if for a lecture. The excitement is monumental, no cover, no lighting to disguise or dramatize, just plain, clear, naked, harsh, white light, the unvarnished truth, one hopes. I learned that when you are your own guv'nor, everything happens, and when you are waiting for something to happen out of the beneficence of others, then *nothing* happens.

Be your own master is a lesson I learned and had to relearn. When working for a large organization one naturally has to fit into the existing structure and that can be very comforting, for all the organizing and planning tours, casting, finding the dough and even deciding on the ads can be very tiring, but the down side is that you have no control over your product. If you want to tour you go cap in hand and beg and plead to overworked producers who have no time since they are busy with their own faves . . . whereas once I bestrode Europe like a Colossus and went from city to city like a bird of prey, from Basle to Düsseldorf, from Düsseldorf to The Hague, from The Hague to Vienna, and then to Paris, ending up in Jean-Louis Barrault's Théâtre du Rond-Point. And Paris really did come and cheer us and our team which was aided and abetted by our charming administrator Debbie Warner (now a respected theatre director).

No matter how hard the going was in the beginning of making my own work, and no matter who left, I would start all over again. Since I knew the other side. The desperate side. The months of heartaching unemployment. So some actors joined our troupe, stayed for a few weeks just to do something, but as soon as they got other work shot off like a light. Still, we soldiered on. *Hamlet*, at last my *Hamlet*, not a clotted, dry-iced, over-costumed, uncut, boring, deadly, miscast star-vehicle that everybody flies to see. For me the whole is as important as the individual since the whole is the whole book, each sentence as important as the one preceding it. It is my heritage or my conditioning that the gang are equal. The team is a family of equal merit and deserving. Some will play the larger roles, but all share a space at the table. All the actors were on the stage the whole time, which in 1979 was a rare event. I was to see more of it when the non-naturalistic directors sought to Brechtianize their works and put actors limply on the stage, but they did nothing while they were there except hang about like waiters in a quiet restaurant. The directors still clung to the antique idea of the star player surrounded by his prompters, who were the other actors.

My present spouse and I go to Europe or other more far-flung places and try to emulate some dish we particularly enjoyed and there is much excitement in the kitchen for several days after the return, as if we could hope to restore the memory of a trip through our taste buds. In the same way there is a virtuous attempt to redefine the complexities of staging, releasing the actors from the restraints of naturalism, i.e. stand there like a spare prick and try not to fidget while the lead has a go. And so many worthy attempts were made but what the directors lacked were the mechanics of rhythm and choreography, the complex skills of using the others as an ensemble, as a chorus, or as a group of living, breathing human beings. They had in fact created a unique style of making them even *less* human than they are. They wished to impart a sense of total life and ensemble but since few had been actors, they were incapable of doing so.

The kind of technique that I learned from the school of Jacques Lecoq had to be studied, sometimes for years. Lecoq would work on the group as a living entity. A group responds to the stimulus at its centre and he would give us exercises in balancing space and activity through improvisation. Dance, of course, does this naturally, since the dancers are always in training and don't sit around while the director gabs his mouth off, smoking themselves to death and asking 'pertinent' questions. Any idea of form or concept or desire to utilize the valuable energies of the actor was considered to be 'European'. European meant you tried to impart some sense of 'method' and psychology into the proceedings. It's not just another vehicle for Albert, Ian or John.

But British theatre tended to represent our old politics. We were an imperialist nation and worshipped and doffed our forelock to the guv'nor. Our ideas were and are based on a kind of economic supremacy and the quasi-religious belief in the colonial empire with its hierarchy and bosses. The rich were very rich and the poor were treated with decency and penny-pinching meanness when they were just on the edge of genteel starvation. Jack the Ripper was a product of this at a time when East End prostitution was rife and the streets unlit and you had to earn sixpence for a night's kip. The theatres were packed in the West End, and what could the theatre resemble but the country's social structure? The actor with the most lines was the richest and the rest just scumbags hanging around the dressing rooms, getting pissed and waiting to go on for their 'My liege . . .'

In America, the ensemble first emerged in the early experiments of Strasberg's and Elia Kazan's Group Theatre, but more intensely and profoundly later in the team work of La Mama, the Living Theatre and Joe Chaikin's Open Theatre and, of course, in East Germany in the work of the Berliner Ensemble.

I was affected deeply when I saw La Mama in *Futz*, the story of a man in love with his pig. I don't think I was ever so moved by anything in the theatre in my life. It was so simple. The men came on with large empty jugs, which they seemed to play as instruments, and told their story. They carried their women over their hillbilly shoulders and danced. They swayed and sang. They acted with their entire bodies, but still within the realms of realism, and gave the most electric piece of theatre I had yet seen. It was the energy of the whole, the untrammelled and unrestrained energy and imagination of the group.

The Living Theatre's *The Brig*, about life in a naval military prison, was the next most important and most profound conception in the theatre. It was tight, mean, threatening, scored almost like a ballet, an opera, a gymnastic exercise. It was dramatic, well-written and showed a day in the brig. In the underpopulated

Mermaid Theatre I revelled and sat in awe at the most moving display of human energy I had ever seen on a stage. I felt and of course knew that this was not just socialist theatre but the inevitable result of believing in the unique contribution of my fellow man. Predictably, it was dismally reviewed.

When we brought *Hamlet* to Israel in 1980 during Passover we opened in Haifa, where I was doubly nervous since they had only seen me as a director; now these same actors that I had cajoled, drilled and coerced would be seeing me on the other side of the stage while they sat comfortably in the stalls ready to judge. My production of *Agamemnon* in Hebrew was still running when we opened. The audience gave us a spontaneous explosion of applause at the end and all the actors came back and passed their usual benedictions on us and we repaired to the large Middle Eastern restaurant on the harbour to stuff our guts with falafel, hummus, tahina, aubergine dips, hot sauces, shish kebab and had a good time.

The producer of the Haifa Theatre, Amnon Meskin, was strangely subdued in his praise and I felt he didn't care too much for the show. He was a rotund, genial, sweet man who worshipped the 'Western' theatre and, like a lot of theatre groups in far-off places, talked about Gielgud and Olivier as if they were his neighbours; such people often seem devoted to the English theatre without necessarily exploring or developing their own lost arts. When I first arrived in Israel I imagined, perhaps naively, that I would be seeing the traditions of the Moscow Arts, and Habimah, the passing down of the total theatre ideas of Vakhtangov and Meyerhold. I expected to see ideas that stemmed from the rituals of the Hassidic Jews who exalted in the word until they sang and danced it, and this of course imbued itself into the Jewish theatre in the famous Moscow productions of the Jewish classics *The Dybbuk* and *The Golem*. Theatre as a celebration mixing gesture and dance with music and the text. Didn't we read about the great inventions of constructivism where theatre was part of the machine world and mankind inexorably linked to that? Instead the big hit at the Habimah was Neil Simon! The Haifa's big success was *The Lion in Winter* . . . it was the same dreary theatre with Hebrew titles! The Old World had gone.

I was determined in my first production there to revive the idea of total theatre, gesture, mime, music and story. I started in 1978 with my version of Kafka's *Metamorphosis* in Haifa. It was the success of the year and could not fail as it was Kafka, the Jews' hero of alienation, and his most extraordinary story. It worked as it had done in London and played all over the country. It went to every city and village and when they had run out of towns, they went into kibbutzes. I take some pride in thinking that I put back some of the old qualities of the Habimah in the strange blending of many arts to create the unique flavour of the old Russian theatre. But in a new and revitalized way. In the offices of the Haifa Municipal Theatre I saw on the walls behind the director's desk old pictures of the Habimah, they looked disturbingly old-fashioned, heavy make-ups and sorrowful. Dated into the times of angst and victimization. Lacking power but full of soulfulness. Something slightly decaying.

Our production of *Hamlet* played in kibbutzes and went to one near the Sea of Galilee where we played in a huge theatre so big it looked like an aircraft hangar. I wrote down some thoughts in my journal at the time.

When we returned to Jerusalem from Haifa I was put with some other members of the company in a flat in the rebuilt Jewish section of the city, but at night after the show we would wander around the old Arabic quarter with its musty, pungent smells and the twisting, winding old passageways of the souk which seemed to be honeycombed with stairs and tunnels leading in every possible direction. It was truly ancient and even if the wall was built by Sulamen in the sixteenth century, the actual city must have been there for many centuries before that, even if it is on a different spot from where Jesus is supposed to have trodden. Entering by the huge Damascus gate was like stepping into a time warp and although the city is now united its feel is Arabic and Moorish. As we walked into the tiny alleys and ate bread at an old bakery the past comforted us with its sense of continuity.

We played for two weeks in Jerusalem and our team of actors was touring and travelling in all directions like good tourists. It was on a Friday that my sister phoned from London to say that Mum had died. I heard the news with relief, for the burden of age and responsibility had gone and made way for another life. Ma had been ill for some time and each day I worried and felt the need to pay constant attention to the situation as it worsened; I also had the burden and the memories of my life with her. It's the date which, as a younger person, you dread with all the horror you can summon. As a child I pondered the disappearance of this being and quite literally thought I wouldn't survive it. As the years steel and toughen you, you get used to the idea of death as a passing into another world and I felt relief as I put the phone down, but the relief changed to grief within minutes and I was locked for a while in a weird no-man's land, unsure what to do, whether to eat breakfast, to tell any actors, to shout, scream or cry. Beryl, my sister, curiously advised that since by coincidence I was in Israel it would be an appropriate place to do something, but what? I think she thought that Israel and Jerusalem were like the HQ for God and that I was near to getting through. I didn't know what I could do there, but shared her feeling that since Mum had been more of a believer than I was I should do something that might accelerate her flight to the other world.

I wandered around the streets that Friday morning, relieved that I didn't have to perform that night and could dwell alone with my sorrow. Eventually I found myself by the Wailing Wall which, being the outer wall of Solomon's Temple, rebuilt by Herod, is the last remaining shrine of the Old World. I often wandered down there, fascinated by the naked and outward display of devotion and the many festivities that went on. The black-suited bearded orthodoxy from Poland and Germany dominated the scene and bus-loads of thin, pale ascetics would descend on the place from time to time. They seemed to my eyes to be possessed of some elusive mystery. When walking through the streets of Jerusalem looking neither left nor right but heading without distraction to the object of the journey, the old rabbis seemed possessed of certainty and of unquestioning beliefs. Now they gathered below like crows, their black coats flapping as they prayed with that peculiar and intriguing motion of the body, as if each swing forward was to hurl out of their bodies the chants of their mouths, as if to emphasize each word, each sentence said by the tongue confirmed in the trunk.

I wandered down and was confused as to what I could do for the departed spirit of Polly. Eventually I approached an old rabbi in an area of the wall to the left which led into a huge underground vault. The atmosphere was serene and sepulchral at the same time and old books were lying with their ancient and worn pages on tables for you to read and to pray from. I explained my problem. A death. What could I do? Something to redeem myself somehow and to take the

burden of a passing that lay on me and needed to be ritually sanctified. He asked me the names of my family and then proceeded to a
group of people who were on hand to help in such emergencies. They
said a prayer for me in Hebrew and through the utterances of the
language (it sounded like murmurs from another world, sounds that
rose and fell, guttural and yet familiar) I understood one word from
the rest. It stood out like one familiar object in an unfamiliar landscape. My mother's name, Polly. Out of the babble of the old
Hebrew tongue that word again bounced on the sea of their murmurs and Polly was being carried to we know not where. Then it was
over.

'That's it?' I said.

'That's it.' It had lasted a couple of minutes, maybe more. 'That is
the prayer for the dead and please give generously,' he answered.

I worked out that in all I had been there less than ten minutes. So I
gave a token couple of dollars. The man looked at my contribution
as if I had spat on his hand. I thought the performance a bit perfunctory and fast. I wouldn't have minded a little more projection and
some variety of pacing. They seemed to gabble it like a speed-run for
lines and I wasn't sure that it gave Ma the necessary impetus to make
it to the other side. 'No, that's enough.' I went outside into the sunlight, feeling let down and even a bit foolish. I hung around, bewildered and hopeless. I was distraught. Stood there in that big square
that was without meaning to me. A young man wearing a trilby came
up to me and asked if he could do anything, since I seemed lost and
forlorn. His very pleasantness drew me to him as if he was an angel
sent to rescue souls.

'I've just lost my mother.' He looked calm and understanding and
waited for me to continue. I asked, 'What can I do to make it right?'

He asked me what I was doing there and I explained that I was
playing *Hamlet* with a company of actors. He said there was one
thing I could do that would gladden her. Eager to have at least something that would allow me to purge whatever it was that needed
purging, I asked him. He said simply, 'Keep the Sabbath. Keep the
Sabbath to start with and that will be a blessing.'

I felt better already. It was a start. It meant much to her that I
should venerate something in my life other than the total and obsessive desire to pursue goals. To purify myself in some simple way. Like
an AA member he offered to give me the number of a family with

whom I could spend the Sabbath so that I might find relief. I didn't use it. I went back to the wall and made a simple prayer of my own. I felt the wall and poured out my private thoughts to it. I felt relieved. It was a good wail.

Origins of *Metamorphosis*

I staged *Metamorphosis* for the first time at the Round House in London in 1969. There were a number of productions after that, including one with Baryshnikov in New York, although the last and final one was a Japanese version.* It was a play that was to haunt me from time to time until I took it out of the cupboard again and dusted it off.

Why, some ask, do you repeat shows? Well, the simple answer is that for me a play is two different things, both of equal importance: the written text, and the production. I try to conceive a production as an entity with a choreographic and sometimes choral language that has to be forged out of many painstaking hours in rehearsal so that a show exists separately from any production which serves merely to reproduce naturalism and everyday life. There is some value to be had from this, but it is impossible if you are adapting a book or story like *Metamorphosis*. For this you have to invent a new style that will fit the story. You cannot do as many adaptations do, hunt out the 'dialogue', fish it out and tack it together and then take narrative, description and thought processes and lump them into a set. It does not work, since a play is not a novel. The novel carries speed and urgency and the interior of the person's mind. It conveys another world with many locations and leaps in time and space. How do you present a beetle? Do you see it through the eyes of the family and let the family be the chorus for it and see the creature reflected through their terror? No, since the protagonist is the bug and we must see the family more through his vision. I wrestled with the problem for several years before starting work on it and, like everything, you can think for years but it is on the 'site' that it begins to grow, from the first implanting of seed; you must take the risk and start planting. I did see in Oxford a clever version by students in

* See *Meditations on 'Metamorphosis'* for details of all productions.

which the bug was visible and crouched behind a wooden box with folded arms to suggest the forelegs of an insect. I was much impressed, but it didn't solve the problem of the play or its style or what we did with the family.

However, sometimes the simplest is the most effective. In Paris my mime teacher, Jacques Lecoq, often encouraged us to impersonate non-humans, either animals or insects, since we are so highly obsessed with the 'problems' of human beings that we take for granted the idea that the theatre is some form of therapy for middle-class problems and not, as it also should be, a manifestation of all forms of imagination. Can't one get a little tired of a diet of Chekhov? Don't we cling to him too much sometimes to express our little emotions and mannerisms? We're all so human with our pitiable and petty sorrows and the actor's bag of infernally dull tricks. Who gives a damn in the end?

Metamorphosis was to me the supreme analogy for human beings locked in the worst conditions imaginable. Imprisoned in the overwhelming sense of worthlessness so that if heat turns carbon into diamonds, then by a reverse process self-disgust turns you into a verminous insect. That suited me just fine. A bug. Loathsome, inferior, outsider, yet also magnificent, a fighting bug that, once transformed, can sink no further into obloquy. Once in the pit of self-abasement you know where you are. A most moving and terrible parable.

The story shook me when I first read it and it has clung to me ever since, as has most of Kafka's work. I identified strongly with his dream-like stories and his acute perception of detail, detail that is not ordinary and programmed, the detail of the life beneath the frustrations. The life within. Closer to dreams and closer to Freud and closer to the world of Grimm and Bunyan. The shiny beetle scurrying here and there with an apple on his back which festers.

First I got on the floor and tried to move like an insect. Short, staccato movements. Stillness. Then sudden scamperings. Crossed arms and legs. Opening and closing but not together. On my back in alternate movements. First arms snap shut, then legs, and as the legs close, arms open. Try and get the rhythm. Move alternately. You want to move together and it feels odd separating the limbs of your body like this, but after a while it comes. I roll backwards and forwards with arms and legs locked. An insect trying to get up.

Backwards and forwards . . . mustn't hurt my head. Backwards and forwards until you are perched in the upwards motion almost on your crossed feet. I have six legs only, but that will do. My crossed arms are one section, but I can alter the movement of my wrist to convey segmentations. Even the finger can join in my little army of separate parts. My knees help as I move them separately, and then the feet. The feet, to flex and point each one again in isolation if I wish. They move across the floor. Wrists, fingers, elbows, head. Jerking this way and that, left and right, up and down, but percussive and not soft, knees, then push with toes for locomotion. As I write I can feel myself doing it all those years ago.

Then the place. Where does it live? Not a house, but something resembling a house. The rhythm must be the guiding image. The rhythm of the insect is quick, staccato, sudden. I felt that the insect controlled the family as a huge spider in the corner of your room will control all your movements and you will react to it. A rat moves fast and you scurry out of the way. You keep your eyes fastened on it, unable to relinquish the sight or the vigilance of your eyes that, like sentries, keep the enemy in view. To lose it is to invite panic of the worst kind. Also the creature is a victim of habit, the same boring relentless getting up and working as a travelling salesman with no future and no joy. The surreal laziness of others where time has no respect for convention . . . 'The other travellers are still at breakfast while I've returned with the morning's orders.' The world moves like a clock, ticking away with certain functions to be achieved at certain times, the neglect of which brings immediate retaliation from those for whom time is God. Gregor is still in bed, only a little late before the chief clerk is at the door wondering where he is. The actions determined by time are disrupted and the forces of order attempt to restore control lest chaos and freedom break out. The freedom to dream.

I couldn't have the text staged naturalistically, of course, since this would merely be passing on information. I had the actors perform the opening scene in a rhythm that demonstrated that they were almost clockwork creatures ruled by the quotidian demands of time with the rules and habits that make you a good, automatic human. At the same time the rhythm reflected the insect's own moves. Immediately the actors looked more prepossessing and alive. They were performing their inner life as marionettes and yet they seemed more human than when they were real. They seemed greedier as they ate, and as their cheeks bulged in and out to the rhythm of the metronome they were like greedy little animals waiting for the breadwinner animal to get up and go out. Once we had established this opening, which felt strident, we could relax the style. Of course the audience found these motions funny and saw them, I suppose, in the way you view cartoons that pick out certain parts that give a person that characteristic 'look' ... You knew who they were from the beginning since their 'essence' was more obvious. It was flaunted at you.

When the insect Gregor wakes and says calmly, but with extreme curiosity, 'What has happened to me?' we stop the motion of the family and return to the stillness of Gregor on his back, arms and legs crossed over like an insect. Slowly, very slowly, in small, sharp moves, he discovers the enormous change that has come over him. He studies his body, very slowly. He has to be seen, but he spends time on the floor and will be masked by the large bodies of the family, and since the set must be functional and not just decorative we made a ramp behind the family so that the beetle could be seen above them. Now, since I wished Gregor to climb and hang from the ceiling, my architect friend, Martin Beaton, designed a frame based on an idea of my first wife, Alison Minto, who was a painter. We created a steel insect with six legs that dominated and engulfed the family. The back of the frame was like the body of the insect and this is where I lived. The body had bars of scaffolding rising up, so I could climb and fake being a trapeze artist though I was terrified of heights, but of course one doesn't mind dying for one's art!

In the great roof of the Round House the lights shone down as I lay on my back. I felt the comfort of steel in my hand and the canopy of the scaffolding set stretched above like a metal web. So much more powerful than canvas and size, that peculiar-smelling glue used to stiffen the canvas and characteristic of the smell of the *theatre*. 'The smell of the greasepaint, the roar of the crowd.' I liked our set of steel scaffolding which had to hold my weight as I climbed up and hung upside down like an insect on the ceiling. I made the actors stand under me for some time before I dared let my fingers relax their vice-like grip. My knees fastened over the bar as if they could melt it, but after a while I became braver and looked forward to that each night.

The play worked and was hailed as a triumph by the press. It was one of the very few times when I had unanimous approval, including that of the late Harold Hobson who, in a glowing review, compared the moment when I crawl on to the stage from my platform to the effect he imagined Irving had in *The Bells*, the Victorian melodrama in which Irving scored such a resounding success. Such a review was an actor's dream, let alone a director's, and I was champion for a week until the next week when I or the newspaper was relegated to catching the grease from an over-filled fish and chip bag.

Connoisseurs of horror, which is a legitimate aesthetic emotion, though perhaps not one to be indulged seven nights a week, should on no account miss Steven Berkoff's adaptation of Franz Kafka's *Metamorphosis*, which he also directs, at the Round House. The story is a parable, and a terrible one, revolting and pitiable at the same time. A young man, Gregor, played by Mr Berkoff himself, has been scurrying back and forth for years working for his family, getting food and money for them like a beetle collecting dung. One morning he does actually change into a dung beetle.

The dismay and pity of his father, mother and sister gradually develop into fear and hatred. The knowledge that upstairs, in a bedroom, is this loathsome insect that was once their son, crawling over the floorboards or clinging to the ceiling, becomes an intolerable burden to their nerves. The audience shares their emotion. So much so, in fact, that when Mr Berkoff, on elbows and knees, his forearms crossed like the legs of an insect, at one point emerges from his room, and seems about to explore the whole house, we instinctively shrink back in something that approaches terror. This is the sort of horrific effect which I imagine Irving used to achieve in *The Bells*, when he fell from his bed with his neck twisted like that of a man who has been hanged. It is very rare in the modern theatre.

Mr Berkoff brings it off without the use of any kind of disguise. At the beginning of the play he is a personable young man, and he remains so to the end. His power resides, not in the triumph of the make-up department of the theatre, but in the devastating grip he establishes over our imagination. This grip is by no means one of mere disgust and fear. Something nobler enters uneasily into it.

Nothing was as thrilling and perpetually exciting as to have audiences queuing to see *Metamorphosis* at the Round House when the rest of London was dying in a heat wave. Heat wave or not, nothing stopped them pouring in after Harold's wonderful review. The last night was sold out and we finished in triumph. It was us and no one else. Martin Beaton and I had raised the money with a moneylender in Charing Cross at forty-nine per cent interest per annum, but we had calculated that we would pay him back in a month as our run was limited. And we did. George Hoskins, the kindly old rascal running the Round House, was well and truly chuffed. Kafka sold out! When Franz Kafka was alive and visiting a bookshop to enquire how his latest collection of short stories had sold he was told they had sold four copies. Intrigued, Franz replied, 'I wonder who bought that one, since I myself bought the other three for friends.'

During the run at the Round House in 1969, I chose as a curtain-raiser another Kafka piece called *In the Penal Colony*, which I had tried out the year before at the Arts Lab in Drury Lane. That was my first professional production at Jim Haynes' stimulatingly wondrous and bizarre fringe theatre. *In the Penal Colony* was Kafka's indictment of the mindless cruelties of military and nationalistic obsession and acutely prophesied the horrors that were to come. A man wishes to retain his execution machine. He is an officer with total belief in the old order of things and when he sees that his ways are anachronistic he commits suicide in his own machine to demonstrate his duty to his beliefs. A more accurate prognosis of Nazism it would be difficult to find. I was totally fascinated by this fantastically gory and yet very strange story, a kind of modern Poe, and always thought of adapting it for the stage. It became the piece with which I would make my debut as director.

Drury Lane at this time was the sanctuary of many of the original artists and performers of the late sixties and seventies. Later it became a vipers' den crawling with middle-class hippies from all over the world who in the next decade became yuppies and furthermore denounced the previous era as if it were a manifestation of some ogre who had indecently assaulted them as they ran home to mum. They cut their hair short again and joined Channel Four.

The Arts Lab was a place to try out new works – you just had a chat with Jim Haynes and before you knew it you were booked. I think we earned about twenty quid per night at the box office, which we gladly shared out. Happy times! Tony Crerer, a marvellously inventive mime, worked the sandwich bar and if there was an actor short would hang up his apron and do his thing. Lindsay Kemp did his various pantomimes there, and so did the People Show. The Freehold, under Nancy Meckler, performed their celebrated production of *Antigone* with the young, stunning Stephen Rea and Dinah Stabb, and there was growing a definition of and care for the techniques of theatre not to be easily seen elsewhere. Also a desire to search for new material and not just keeping churning out the social realism so beloved of the time.

Theatre seemed to be polarizing into two definite camps. There was the Brechtian or Royal Court school dominated by hard drinkers and rabble-rousers in the shape of the talented Nicol Williamson and others, whose idea of a good night was a verbal punch-up followed by its physical equivalent. This school seemed to attract its fair quota of devotees who all shouted and drank in the Salisbury pub and were meaninglessly aggressive, for what reason I could not at the time fully fathom. While Nicol was a fountain of talent, his acolytes were by no means as richly endowed except in verbal abuse and were boring in the extreme. They were usually playing small roles in the latest misinterpretation of Brecht. After a while I deliberately avoided them. There were a lot of workmen's boots around the Court at that time and a heavy emphasis on a kind of school of realism. But much interesting work was done there.

We at the Lab were, if it doesn't sound too precious, into classes and group exercises. So I was becoming divided, half-drawn to the passivity and gentleness of the hippy culture while still being part of the fortnightly rep school and Play of the Week on TV, and now my occasional branching out on my own. That was of course the very best, but I suffered under a strange delusion. I thought, Oh, how lovely it would be to join some turgid large company and be the 'great' actor I still yearned to become, rather than see my fate deliberately pushing me to investigate my own creativity. While every young actor wanted to be Jimmy Porter I would much rather have been Joseph K.

I was drifting further and further away from the obsessively realistic, plausible, social and naturalistic theatre so beloved by the rational-thinking and logical Brits. My mind was more interested in states of mind than states of the economy or the problems of the class war. The ones involved in realism were also into booze, and the ones who were into Greek myths, mime or any ism you care to think about were starting a revolution in the theatre that was to invade the ground of the establishment without actually taking root, since the earth was far too acidic and sterile.

The revolution died, but there were some small echoes in the major companies, even if they were mere gestures. When one saw 'experiments' in companies hitherto devoted to dry-ice machines for atmosphere, one felt physically sick, and there was this nibbling at experiment while keeping well clear of the fully grown virus. The Living Theatre returned to the Round House, still very exciting in their version of *Frankenstein*, but to my horror I saw much of *The Brig* being reproduced and then, instead of so brilliantly conveying the brutality of the system by showing it, this time they chose to preach it at us and became silly; I lost all faith and respect.

For sheer daring most of the American groups would still excite and be monstrously liberated: I remember an inventive *Arden of Faversham* visiting the Royal Court, performed by La Mama, plus *Ubu Roi*. Sometimes directors sought to emulate these groups and fell on their faces since our methodology is quite different. Runts spewing out their drivel and often giving themselves names like 'La Mama, London Branch'! Imagine the Moscow Arts Theatre, 'London Branch'. They sat open-mouthed at the feet of the gurus but had not the past or the background.

Even established and famous directors could be seduced by this *physicality*, these psychological explorations, these games. No more the 'Move down right, ducky...' One director known for high-definition work of painstaking care was set to become a bumbling idiot in the most ridiculous recreation of a Shakespeare play I had ever seen. He was hopelessly in love with the rogue Yankees and their outlaw mentality. I think he later recovered his wits. This was the time of Experiment with a capital E and it was all so very, very serious and high tone. Artaud was the prophet for a while and then it might be Stanislavski or the next phase, perhaps Jan Kott. When you do not have the compost of your own life and your own pain and emotions you are prone to leap into the bed of any seducer who will show you a good time.

I loved the summer of 1968. The wild experiments at the Arts Lab with the cinema downstairs where you had to take off your shoes and the place stank of mouldy socks. The money left at the box office and the sheer unadulterated pleasure of thinking that I had done this myself. Nobody had handed it to me on a plate. I had ripped it out of the frustration of unemployment and when I took my share of the takings I felt just great. After the show I went to have a drink next door in the pub with an Israeli actor I had met at drama school, Asher Tsarfati, who was my partner on the stage and I was so happy to be out and working. It was a *tremendous* feeling. The place was an object of curiosity to many visitors: one night I saw my great hero, Jean-Louis Barrault, accompanied by Arnold Wesker. Peter Brook came by one Sunday afternoon at my invitation; we were amazed that he should visit us and held the curtain for him. He eventually turned up and watched politely. When we'd finished we all crowded round, keen to hear sweet words, but he was buttonholed by Jim Haynes and paid little attention to the man who had just performed for him for forty-five minutes. Mind you, I suspect he's wary of types like me, whose hunger or earnestness he would find debilitating. Or did he know I was the loony who screamed out 'Rubbish!' when I saw his *Oedipus*? It was an awful thing to do, but when they wheeled on this big gold cock I thought he was out of his tree. I have to admit I found the whole thing too eclectic for words since it made very good use of the class exercises of every American group, but didn't we all? Didn't we all dip into the pot and steal some recipes? Yet this man who I admired above all and through whose talents an evening in the theatre was an event had, I felt, let me down. Or had he disappointed me in a more profound way?

Webber-Douglas – 1958

I was a student at the Webber-Douglas Academy of Dramatic Art in 1958/59. It doesn't seem so long ago that I wandered in, nervous and timorous, and sniffed around. Since I had suffered until then six years of unrewarding, frustrating and soulless work, the dreariness of going from job to job from the ages of fifteen to twenty-one, I felt I had had my apprenticeship in the school of hard knocks. Perhaps that's why I feel impatient with people who, upon leaving the sanctified atmosphere of university, go into safe and subsidized jobs and then whine about not having enough cash. Perpetually whingeing, complaining about economics, forever begging for more money and threatening closures if they don't get it. Of course it's easy for me to say this on the outside of such responsibility, but my impatience is there nevertheless. I felt I had to have some experience of life *out there*. It had been a grim and often boring time, but full of incident and I had to earn my living. I could never demand. Never whine. I would be told, 'Get your walking papers.' If you can't do it, then scram. If you want a wage packet at the end of the week, you graft and there is no fine equation around this. This was what you did, and you had to do it. Good. Fine. You worked. I had *one hundred* jobs in six years and so it was becoming obvious to me that work of that nature was not quite suited to my temperament.

I had been attending evening classes at the renowned City Literary Institute for three terms and enjoying that; for the first time in my life I was finding a deep satisfaction in going to class and studying. I had missed it. Terribly. So after about a year at the City Lit I wanted to study full time. I auditioned at the Webber-Douglas, having become friendly with a young actor from Canada who said that if I auditioned there I could probably get in – and I did.

I first got to know about the logistics of receiving state money, a fact that many others seem to have known almost from birth, when I applied to join Webber-D. and was told to apply for a scholarship so that the school would receive some fees and I would receive money to live on. The idea of the state giving you money was somehow miraculous and I couldn't for the life of me imagine getting it, but I duly applied and the forms came to our Manor House flat. I looked at them and my heart sank. How many degrees or A-levels do you have? Other awards? Did you go to university or other schools to study? I had no levels of any kind since I had been propelled out of Hackney Downs with all the speed the headmaster and I could summon. I had no recommendations of any kind. I had no chance since the phrasing of the form made it clear they inclined towards studious, decent, certificate-bearing chaps. I wrote back that I had left school at fifteen and had been through the mill of a hundred different jobs and occupations, that I had been virtually turfed out of my school and had even brushed with the Juvenile Courts. I had joined the Navy at nineteen (very briefly) and was on a collision course with society. I pleaded with them to help. One morning I was summoned before the committee at Westminster to perform my pieces. I chose one Shakespeare and one modern. Nothing too original, but I did them and felt confident doing them. I thought that the committee was favourably disposed to me, having accepted the frank confessions in my letter. Behind a large desk six solemn faces sat quietly and looked and I made them somewhat uncomfortable by addressing my Richard III speech directly to them. A way of auditioning I dislike intensely, but in those days I thought that was the thing to do. A few days later I received news in the post that they had recommended me for a grant and for the first time in my life I was to feel what it was like to be a student and be paid for studying. Well done, GLC! I remember writing fulsomely to them and thanking them for the honour.

I was a bit emotional in those days. I had a grant and that meant I would have to have a bank account, and so for the first time I became a proper citizen of this society and could begin to rid myself of the foul taste accumulated over the years beginning with Hackney Downs Grammar School, when I walked across the park with tears in my eyes at my sense of worthlessness. Now I was somebody. Or thought I was.

I was put straight away into a play called *A Victorian Comedy*, directed by a Mrs Ellen O'Malley who remembered Henry Irving, as I now recall. She was about seventy-five, and when she directed us in *Macbeth* she recalled that when the murder of the king is discovered and Macbeth shouts out pretending great shock and alarm, Irving banged on all the shields that are fixed to the walls like ornaments. She was very fond of recalling this detail and was a very sweet, very charming old lady from the ancient school of theatre; a piece of history that we kids in our profound ignorance knew nothing of and cared nothing about.

I remember Webber-Douglas by fits and starts. There was a canteen in the centre room of the school where we would hang out and an old duffer called Bert would dole out the tea. But what bliss. I was *acting*. I was a student for the first time. I was no longer a member of the serving trades. No longer a piece of unmitigated scum scurrying around like a rat looking for a job and haunting the wanted ads of the *Evening Standard*. No longer going to the Youth Employment Bureau – all good experience, mind you. But now I was a proper being.

Pride shone out of me and I bought a long black scarf to make me look appropriately intellectual. It was about five feet long and would wrap round my neck several times. I was on my way to some glorious future. I carried books to work. I studied like a fiend and talked about Nietzsche in the make-up room to a rebellious student called Michael Coles who appeared to have read everything ever written. Terence Stamp would get our little group together and do some Brecht scenes. There was an Italian café called Dino's around the corner (still there) where we would sit and drink endless cappuccinos. We nattered like budding Sartres, since we were all so idealistic and brought up on American social realism.

Arthur Miller, Clifford Odets and Tennessee Williams had dominated the new way of perceiving actors and were the instruments of social change battering rams to smash down antiquated concepts. The actor was an instrument or ally to the writer to create the 'social hero' . . . not the wimp, not the Noël Coward neurotic narcissus, but the animal of instinct prowling the jungle of the cities. We had therefore to be conscious and would read and attend lectures and debates. We read the plays of Europeans such as Sartre and Ionesco, saw the plays of Behan, were fascinated with the productions of Joan Littlewood in which our theories were being tested out before our eyes. We saw actors as companies, ensembles with distinct individual characteristics. Going down the East End was a treat because you knew that when you saw Littlewood you would not be disappointed. Mike Coles eventually realized his dream and worked there.

Our heads were in the clouds, but that is where they should have been because when we looked down we were handed our scripts for the end-of-term production. Mine was a light thing called *Miranda*, an old hit about a chap who brings home a mermaid. However, it was at least acting and I went to it with a will and determination to find something to do with these flaming things at the ends of my arms called hands.

My favourite teacher was a Miss Fleming, our voice teacher, for whom I would do anything. She guided my voice and encouraged me and had herself the most beautiful velvet tones. It was a strange and somehow blissful time without too many cares.

I remember one day being directed by another Ellen, who was reputed to have been Shaw's mistress or at least as far as Shaw's definition of one went, which legend has it was more wish than fulfilment. Her name was Ellen Pollock, she was an actress who supplemented her income with a bit of teaching. Very old-fashioned, very arch, with great emphasis on articulation. She came festooned in bangles and beads and directed us in an old creaker called *The House by the Lake* . . . I remember a Raymond Bowers in it; he was a mature student and being so very good I expected him to be a serious contender for the classic roles. I always sensed who might make great actors and was always surprised when in later years they were making a reasonable living but not nearly fulfilling the great promise that they had. For this I blame directors. I think a lot of directors are seduced by the obvious a bit of flash and youth, and push these young flabby ingénues upwards until they are able to cling on to a bit of fame. The real talent is kept behind. I have seen this over and over again.

The terms flew past in a series of play extracts, mime classes, which chiefly consisted of getting into a tableau and us guessing what it was and dance classes where I would stand in the back row and find my nose pointing in the direction of Samantha Eggar's fishnet-stockinged bum as we performed our calisthenics. Fencing I really did enjoy and found it quite liberating and exciting. Sam, as Samantha Eggar was called, was to play opposite me for a couple of scenes in another old creaker called *The Young Elizabeth*. In one romantic scene I took her in my arms. She was young and red-haired with leaping freckles and blue-green eyes and I thought that I would not be in her proximity except in a play and was somehow grateful to the play. I think she was sweet on Terence Stamp, anyway, who was the beau and always had a white car waiting for him after school, with a young lady in it. As everyone knows Stamp was very handsome in those days, but he had a more serious and thoughtful side which he was to bring out only in later life when he became master of his own destiny and not the tool of others.

The students were friendly and everyone was somehow aware that we were in this game together and had to connect with each other and not be aloof or competitive. But I found the lack of discipline irksome. I had come to drama school to work and was not being driven. The school then was run sloppily and encouraged débutante tarts who had nothing to do during the day (with Penelope Keith an honourable exception to this stricture). This was humiliating to me and I thought was wasting the grant that I had fought for and won. Teachers were lazy and rehearsals cancelled or taken by other students. I rang up Westminster Hall one day and complained.

Student Becomes Teacher – 1967

Eight years later I was back in that little school off Brompton Road teaching a whole crop of keen eager faces and attempting to make my hours there not only worthwhile for them but constructive for me. It was ironic that I should have ended up back at Webber-D., but I had to try and earn some wages in my out-of-work state, which was becoming more of a habit than I would have liked. The truth is that it was to be the most profound upheaval of my life, for I was to learn more from teaching at the Webber-Douglas Academy of Drama than at any other time in my career. It was a laboratory full of human specimens dying to be experimented on and meeting me head on in my frustration. My need to be worthwhile and creative coincided with this period. I might have been satisfied getting a job four spears from the end and playing Scrabble in between entrances or being another small-part actor in a small-part series. I might have thought that this is a good place to be while waiting to fulfil greater dreams and ambitions. I thought, how can I use this valuable knowledge I've gleaned from both Claude Chagrin's illuminating mime classes and the experience in Paris with the grand master? So Ralph Jago, the principal of Webber-D., encouraged me to teach and then direct plays and it was in this period that I was forced to learn to use groups of people 'equally', to create within the class a pattern of working that would utilize the energies of all of them, not just the ones with the most lines. Each student would come into the room for my class with a kind of expectancy and uncertainty and I had to think, as all teachers do, *how do we get through the next hour and a half?*

I evolved a system of work that would bring the two areas of movement and text together. I went through the mime techniques that I had been taught and when I ran out of them I would adjust them slightly at first and bring in improvisation to complement the movement. While demonstrating the gestures to create an object, I would suggest that the students search for the verbal equivalent of the gesture, even if it was opposite to what they were creating with their bodies. We experimented constantly with this with some very interesting results and the actors were then forced to use their bodies for a scene in a way that would not have been thought of conventionally. The classes seemed to be popular and I found allies among the students who were to join me later when I was forming my own works. Sometimes we used music and created improvisations to whatever the music suggested and sometimes we used props and improvised round them. Ralph Jago seemed pleased with the way things were going and suggested that in the second year of my teaching there I should tackle some productions. This was a very large step for me to take but was to be the foundation of all my future work.

About this time Peter Brook was holding auditions for a forthcoming production of Seneca's *Oedipus*.

I stepped past the stage door of the Old Vic. No flies on me, mate. I had done a two-hour vocal and physical work-out before even entering the building for my audition. Peter Brook was auditioning actors and the casting department warned the agents that we should be prepared to do a 'workshop' . . . the others approached anxiously but not me, I was used to this and had been teaching these very exercises for over a year at Webber-D. I welcomed this opportunity to meet the master and while the other actors were all aquiver I felt supremely confident as if at last, at long last, I was in the waters of my youth like a salmon that has returned to its natural stream.

I had anyway admired this man and his work. Who could not be stunned at the *Marat-Sade*, *The Dream* or *The Physicists*? I also had plenty of time for his experiments at the Donmar, watching Genet's *The Screens* with the bizarre and talented Alexis Kanner, the young Canadian who was Orson Welles's prodigy and who played Hotspur in the Falstaff plays in Ireland, and then like a comet disappeared into the deep recesses of space. Brook stood for high art as far as I was concerned. Illumination and metaphysics. Not for him the trials and tribulations of the old kitchen sink. No, the great archetypal images. The white sets like operating theatres. The clarity of language polished like jewels. The space for King Lear to roam in, crowned with the magnificent Scofield. Great actors need not only space but great directors. See them with lesser directors and see the difference.

So here at last I was prepared for all experiments and was an experimentalist. I had heard from those who had been in his company and had enjoyed their proximity to Brook by proxy. 'What was he like? What did you do?' The idea of actually working with him was by now an awesome event in my mind and I was ready, primed to take my place in the disciples' queue. I was dressed casually and easily for work. The thought of being asked to share six hours or more a day with him was too much like Nirvana and I couldn't believe it was possible, and yet I had been chosen to audition. The first step!!!

We were ushered into the presence of Sir, who was sitting behind a desk along with assistants and casting. He calmly explained what he wished from us. I had no fear since I felt I already knew Peter. He was the kind of great man that a small man like me could approach. When I went to the Lamda Theatre to see the Artaud experiments I was told it was completely sold out. I saw Brook standing in the foyer being buttonholed by an eager groupie, Bernard Levin, but trusting Brook I went right up to him and said I couldn't get in but had to see it. With infinite patience he said, 'Just stand at the back, it will be all right,' and gave the ushers instructions to place me there. Why do I feel with some people the utmost confidence and with others not? Well, there is simply something in genius that is so powerfully human that it takes on transcendental qualities – rather like a priest, if you will. Its presence is so strong that the possessor of these qualities reaches beyond the merely human, the bourgeois, with its vanities, narcissism, power trips or arrogance. The true genius is usually truly sublime and vulnerable, approachable at the right time, beyond bourgeois definitions. I could go up to Brook, whom I had never met, and demand to be placed in his theatre and expect and get the very thing my instinct wished, while with others I would cross the road so as not to be made to feel discomfort. I approached Jean-Louis Barrault in Paris and received very nearly a similar response. Or perhaps the real reason is if you admire someone so much you radiate a certain amount of that feeling when you meet them.

So we were in and had received instructions. There was an actress I had worked with in rep, the charming and very pretty Anna Carteret, one other woman and two men including me. The other guy was not really an actor but had done martial arts of some kind for theatre groups. OK, let's go.

'First,' he said, 'you're playing tennis.'

'Right on,' I thought, 'let's take this easy. He wants to see how we move in space, how we are balanced.' So I whispered to my 'partner', 'Take it slow, since I did these very exercises in my classes.' While the others were smashing the ball all over the place in their keenness and looked awkward, we played like flying swans watching the ball sail through the air as if it were a small balloon. The other actors smiled in regret that they too hadn't thought of that. Then, of course, Peter asked us to do the same thing in slow motion . . . Oh, oh, I had anticipated him and we did the same thing again, but even slower and more gracefully, while the others still made a lot of noise and puffed.

Then he said, 'Pass not the ball but the sound.' OK, we passeth dulcet and sweet sound, but the other bloke with his one outstanding party trick kept doing high-pitched karate screams. Brook was much interested in this anomaly and asked him about this extraordinary cry and heard the story that he was a karate expert, etc.

At the end of the session we were all sweating and puffed but elated and the others said how lucky I was to have had this kind of 'training' and they wished they had. We waited at the end of the room while the desk conferred. Eventually the casting woman said, 'Thank you for your good work and Anna and this "screamer", would you stay?' I was dismissed. I couldn't believe what I was hearing. I was being dismissed while the others were asked to say. I was dumb. I knew I had done really well, far better than even I had expected, since this was in the realm of my art. Even the actors had passed comment. Also I do know when I'm bad. What was up? Did he suspect that I might be trouble and that I knew a little too much? Was my enthusiasm just too much to take? Did he feel a little caution and 'Oh, oh, we'd better watch out for this one?' It's possible for directors to feel threatened by a certain kind of performer and I admit that I have often felt an insecurity with some actors but have broken through this in the end. Sometimes the insecurity will drag other feelings with it, like self-consciousness, over-awareness, even timidity. You want to feel totally free and not that someone's watching you with that critical eye.

I don't know that Peter Brook felt any of these things, but there was something in his cold, clear, blue eyes when we parted that told me we might meet again. He did me a great favour, for when I went to see the production to see what I had missed I was not elated. I saw actors tied to pillars in the best Hollywood fashion and there was the 'screamer' on the stage, sitting on a box along with the other actors, passing the sounds from one to another, which was done well and highly polished. Then having had little to do the whole time he let out this huge scream, the party trick he did at the audition. By this time I was not only relieved not to have been chosen, I was getting angry with the self-consciousness of it all and the familiar group exercises.

At the end of the play, when Gielgud looked most uncomfortable in his suede shoes and not because of the shoes, the apotheosis was a giant piece of middle-class folly – this vast golden dick is wheeled on stage! And worse was the tune to go with it, 'When The Saints Go Marchin' In'. By this time all credibility had been shot to pieces and being the little stormer I was in those far-off days I wasn't averse to letting my feelings be known. So I stood up and in my most stentorian shout let out the unbeloved epithet . . . 'RUBBISH!' Well, it was pretty loud. The whole audience heard it as well as the cast, I am sure, and probably thought that it was that mad Berkoff again, jealous because he too couldn't be sitting on a box making sounds. The roles themselves were well played and fiercely spoken. Why scream it out . . . because I wasn't chosen? Because I was jealous? Because I hated the show? Because I thought it was phoney, but I should still have been chosen? Because I was a loony? Probably a bit of everything. It was like a primal scream of rage: rage for everything, rage for my utter frustration, rage for rejection when I came with my love and devotion, rage because it was the end of one particular dream. And rage because I knew that that ending was intellectual rubbish.

So it was no big deal and the worst thing about it was thinking how badly I might have felt during rehearsals. Yet with his consummate vision Brook must have remembered me, since the following year, when I was performing in my own production of *In The Penal Colony*, he came immediately upon my invitation to see the show. When he turned up I wondered if he 'enjoyed it' since he gave little intimation, and yet I felt somehow that he knew that I was the one who had brayed my disapproval that night. The cast would have told him, oh yes, it was the chap you didn't wish to have, the one who 'knew'.

Years later, reading an account of Olivier's life, I was struck by the story of Olivier's begging Brook not to put that big dick on the stage. Olivier was very concerned, and not just because he was an old-fashioned prude, since he very much wished to encourage the new and was well-known for putting his own neck on the line; it was the tatty, phoney vulgarity of it, the throwback to student rebellion and the possible need to be as outrageous as our American colleagues. The fact that Olivier hated it so much vindicated my own response, since actors are so much more intelligent than directors. They are like horses who can sniff danger ahead; it is an instinct that is as sure as the noses on their faces since they are out there and can test the water and do not do it by proxy. No, they are not well read as a whole, are not greatly intellectual, but can read into a line the mysteries of the thought that gave it birth. They can pitch a line to dive like a dart into the bull's-eye of the audience's sensibilities. They can tell when an audience is silent through joy or boredom. They can sniff out a laugh from a line the way a dog sniffs out dope from a suitcase. So they can tell when lines are working and when not. They know when plays are boring even when critics enthuse. They are there serving the food each night and know what tastes good, what is OK, what is exotic and what makes them sick. Olivier sensed that this would not be agreeable and he was right and more than right. He knew and pleaded for it to be stopped, according to the biography I read, and I was glad, years later, to have unwittingly given Larry some vocal support.

Every day for nearly a year I went into Webber-Douglas and tried to create plays that would involve all the actors who paid their large fees; as a previous student I knew what it was like to be uninvolved or always watching when you needed to be doing. I believe the desire for ensemble came from this. It came from a sense of guilt if I didn't feel that all the actors had been *worked on* during the three hours. I had a choice of what to do and so naturally I started with the obvious, but since I was teaching two different groups, one in the morning for three hours and then one in the afternoon, I had to do two plays. I chose those I knew and they were *Hamlet* and *Macbeth*. Later in my professional life I would do them both with my own company. So in another way these classes were enabling me to solve some of the problems in the plays and put the discoveries to one side, where they would become the ground plan for my own productions.

Macbeth got off the ground fairly quickly and was very animalistic, since I saw the play in this way. Primitive, earthy, mysterious. That is what I remember from *Macbeth*. For *Hamlet* I had problems since I was so determined to find a signature that linked the elements of the play together. It caused me a great deal of pain at the time – I was after all totally unfamiliar with staging and blocking and could not relax and let the actors find it. I was obsessed, like Jimmy Durante trying to find the 'lost chord'. Also my mind was divided between creating a *Macbeth* in the morning and a contrasting style for *Hamlet* in the afternoon. Thank goodness one day it all clicked and we were on our way.

I wanted to show the decadence of the Danish court and so we performed an entrance 'walk' based on a mime that was the key exercise of a Dutch mime called Will Spohr, who taught classes at the Drury Lane Arts Lab. These strange movements, which incidentally really came from the school of Etienne Decroux, were a way of seeing the body in terms of angles and hard shapes. The walk was a linear stride that was eerie and yet compelling to watch. I was fascinated by the physical aspects of the theatre and its gestural subtext and the plays were intensely theatrical, but I was aware that I was neglecting the text somewhat and fitting the actors into a 'pattern of events that exploded out from play'. I learned to match and mate in future years and not neglect one for the other.

The two plays were most successful at the time, although they were both cut down, but I do remember being intensely nervous when the curtain went up in the little Chanticleer Theatre on *my work*. In the middle of my Meyerholdian vision some chap burst in during 'I have done the deed, didst thou not hear a noise?' and in a very Sloaney voice, said ''scuse me, anyone here own an MG, it's blocking my gateway?'

The next term I decided to attempt a version of Kafka's *The Trial*, which had obsessed me for years and which seemed perfect material for some of the mime techniques I had used with Lecoq. We started on the book merely by reading a page and then improvising what we had read. It was an extraordinary way of working, but it yielded some intriguing results. Here I decided to blend more carefully the physical structure and the spoken text and to be as inventive with language as I was trying to be with the structure. To be faithful to the book and yet liberate it from the page. Since we did not have a long rehearsal period and we were adapting one of the great novels of the twentieth century to be part of a double bill, we were rather ambitious. Even so, we worked carefully and tried to keep the essence of each scene. Unbelievably it ran an hour. During the five weeks we experimented with each technique that we had learned in our mime/impro workshops. This was after all a drama school and not meant to be a Berkoff workshop, but that is what it turned into. Nevertheless I had to be aware that the actors must learn how to deliver speeches and use their powers of suggestion. Ralph Jago seemed to like using the school as a laboratory, since it would not be used like that again, at least not during my tenure.

My two years there were exhausting, particularly having to balance or juggle two shows at once, but these years became the school I had always wanted to be part of. I was stretched and now I was ripe for the outside world. My first production was to be *Metamorphosis*, based on Kafka's novella.

The Round House, Chalk Farm – 1969

The Living Theatre had just left the Round House with their version of *Frankenstein* and we were going in. We had the benefit of a try-out at LAMDA; I always like to try my plays out first and we performed it for a week there. When the one ad that the whole cast chipped in for came out in the *Guardian*, the phone did not stop ringing. *Metamorphosis*. How on earth do you do that? We were to show them, but somebody answer the bloody phone! The success at LAMDA encouraged us to go for bigger things, and the Round House had always been my choice.

It was a hot summer and the advance at the Round House was sluggish. I had to do *In the Penal Colony* first, wash the blood off and then get into my trousers and braces and don't forget to put cotton wool under my knees or the pain was terrible. One paper called it a 'triple triumph' and I was particularly partial to that since I had written, directed and performed and therefore used myself in every area over which I had control. It was my control over me and not somebody else's permission, or direction, or favour, or begging for an audition, or money from a reluctant producer. It was mine. The cost was not small, since I had been thinking about doing it for three years and had made two false starts. But there was the extreme satisfaction of exploiting your own being and not being in thrall to anyone. Even to demanding that the ads outside the Round House be gigantic, and they were.

Alison Minto and I designed the poster in the image of a playing card, my image in the stance of the bug cut in half and then joined up. Posters were made and plastered all over town, but it was the image on the wall of the Round House that I loved. You saw it a long way away as you came down the Chalk Farm Road, a great black and white monster. What satisfaction and what a reward for my efforts and years of unemployment, waiting and begging someone for work which in the majority of cases was fairly unnourishing anyway. Now while they (the other side) were still doing revivals of *Look Back in Anger* and *Little Malcolm and his Struggle against the Eunuchs* and still shouting and screaming in the pub, I had presented my own piece of total theatre. A piece of theatre that had what I wished to achieve. It was movement, light and text. Geometric, architectural and dramatic, and I could show off a bit by hanging upside down like Houdini.

Of course I was proud, but I didn't see it at the time as anything but a job I liked to do. If I was as proud then I would have done nothing else but sit back, but I had to work and the irony of it all, the dreadfully stupid, ridiculous and insane thing was that while I was creating my own theatre and style and drawing the audience, I was asking for work elsewhere. I even, at the time, wrote to the RSC, hoping that they might be able to see what I had achieved. Of course they were always too busy and 'in rehearsal' to come. I was too modest at the time to realize that I should just carry on in the same fashion and let the others stew in their own mess. What had they got to do with me? But I still harboured this old chimera of wanting to be the great classical actor. I wanted to see what I could do with Shakespeare, which was still, in my eyes, the ultimate test of an actor's range and interpretation. These conditioned reflexes from the arid years didn't allow me to appreciate fully what I had achieved; and my sense of needing to belong to a 'family' led me to neglect the beginnings of my own family.

The third week of our run we were sold out and could have played on, but I was exhausted with doing the two plays each night and so we put *Metamorphosis* to sleep for a few years. No producer came to offer it a further life, since they were never very bright, any of them; they would bewail the loss of business in that hot burning summer of 1969 without ever seeing what was under their very noses.

After *Metamorphosis* I was out of work. But not for long. During the run many 'faces' turned up and some came backstage, as is usual. One of these was Wolf Mankowitz, who was much taken with the show and asked me if I wished to join him on a project he was doing in Israel with Richard Harris, a film about a footballer; Wolf wanted someone to make a documentary while they were shooting. This I thought was good. I always overestimated the quality of the work I was offered since I was so overwhelmed to be offered anything by anyone. I leaped at the chance, this being at least a way of learning about film. It was to be my first time in Israel.

A Ghastly Film with Richard Harris – 1969

Wolf was an ebullient and jovial chap who, like many of his stamp, loved to hang around those Mayfair offices where all the film moguls seemed to be ensconced, especially in those days. Of course I was intimidated to be ushered into offices in lush surroundings where Wolf would introduce me to sallow-jowled and bored executives with the words, 'This is Berkoff' . . . they looked up uninterested . . . 'We'll all be working for *him* one day.' I liked the way Wolf would champion my talent and praise me in front of others, but this was just the honeymoon before the full horror unravelled. When you have a film script which is pure unadulterated crap no amount of gallantry and prestidigitation will make any difference.

It was called *Bloomfield* and it was one of the first times I would learn that what I possessed between my ears was more valuable than all their offices and dinners in Alvaro's and big talk and movie actors screaming and all the rest of that puerile parade that squandered its way through the sixties and seventies. Not that I wasn't very grateful to him, since Wolf was drawn to my work and even talked about a film of *In the Penal Colony* (which of course in those days meant nothing, since most of these guys he'd try to solicit money from were so full of wind they'd go into orbit).

The Israeli director came over for meetings and whatever it is they do. He was a very clever and funny comedian called Uri Zohar and was famous in Israel. A handsome man who combined low-budget, interesting Israeli movies with stand-up comedy in huge auditoria. Since we were all in 'showbiz' all meetings and greetings were in that forced, extroverted manner . . . 'Hello, Wolf, you *shmock*! You ugly bastard, let's go eat.' There was a way of conducting yourself that had to be relentlessly showbiz and provocative. 'Uri, you Israeli cunt, meet Berkoff, he's going to assist you and make this fucking documentary, and Steve take Uri to some "fringe theatre"' . . . I was the fringe expert who would take Uri round the underbelly of London's famed nightspots where the dangerous theatre revolutionaries were hanging about.

Bloomfield was a ghastly shlock piece of sentimental junk conceived by quite a talented writer, probably after a blow-out at Alvaro's plus other refreshments. It was the story of an Israeli footballer who gets involved with a little kid (ooh, how cute) who comes from the little town to see his hero and on the way has various adventures. It seemed a ridiculous idea since Harris had made the great British movie *This Sporting Life*, Lindsay Anderson's masterpiece based on David Storey's novel, which, for once, gave the film industry here some credibility. In this Harris played a tough rugby player, which also was a neat metaphor for his scrummage through life. Now he was to be a 'footballer' . . . anyone with half an eye and who was not stoned, as everyone seemed to be in those wild, heady days, would have read 'TURKEY' in bold, bright, capital letters. Everyone that is except Harris, the producers, Mankowitz, Romy Schneider (romantic interest) and Uri Zohar. I think Israel wanted to build up its film industry abroad, since its limited population made it impossible to get a showing of anything outside and so this was a contrivance. An Israeli/UK production.

I took Uri out. Fortunately there was a production of *Arturo Ui* on at the Saville which I had been in when it was at the Edinburgh Festival. I had played the small role of the club-footed Goebbels character, for Michael Blakemore. Sir Laurence Olivier came to see the show on the last matinée in Edinburgh, and lo and behold, Michael was chosen to be one of the seven samurai to run the emerging National Theatre. I think Michael staged *Ui* well, but he had seen the Berlin production and may have been influenced by that. The best Arturo for sheer menance has to be Nicol Williamson in Jack Gold's TV version.

Leonard Rossiter was the inspired choice for Arturo Ui and gave a simply brilliant performance. I loved being on the same stage with him, though that wasn't frequently since I was going through my 'nervous period' . . . it may have been a change of age or hormones or psychic disposition, but I had a terrifying fear of drying up on stage. I think it was partly due to the fact that the role had me off and on stage all night, a small scene here and another there, which I find difficult because I am slow to warm up, but once warmed up I really want to *go*. Now in this play I had to snatch a piece of the action and then go off. I became more and more crazy with fear as the week wore on and I was panicked that I would just dry stone dead and would repeat the first line of each scene over and over and *over* again before I went on. It's a wonder that this 'smash it into your brain' method didn't cause me to lose the lines. I got through it and even had a good review from the kindly Mr Wardle of *The Times*.

For my Kafka season at the Round House I had not the slightest shred of any nerve since I was on the stage the whole time in each of the one-act plays. Not the slightest suggestion of a quiver. In fact I enjoyed the sensation. However, I really believed in the text of Kafka, whereas I couldn't quite in the bubble-cartoon dialogue of Brecht. Funny and witty as the characters were, they were basically comic-strip personalities and everyone laughed at the tin-pot gangsters. The play is a brilliant pastiche and a clever satiric comment on the Third Reich, but thin on character. So I lost my nerve a little. I need to *believe*.

Now I was visiting my old chums and hoping to impress my guest, a real film director. We saw the show and I thought that Rossiter had lost the steel and softened the razor edge for cheapo gags. I was horribly disappointed, but know that without constant supervision an actor of invention is liable to go on inventing and inventing. I stepped backstage and saw all the guys and introduced Leonard Rossiter to Uri, who was overwhelmed by the sheer bravura of Leonard's performance. We passed compliments on his acting. Leonard was quite chuffed, more than I would have expected him to be, but by now they had played some time and mates had probably run out, so he was glad to see a couple of 'pros' step round the back of the Saville Theatre and pass comment on an exhausting demonstration of Hitler/Ui/Rossiter madness.

When Uri stopped effusing, Rossiter, to my disbelief, said, 'It was better this afternoon, they laughed a lot more this afternoon, this was a tough audience.' He seemed genuinely disappointed that we had not seen the afternoon's show. He said this as if he was confiding a simple truth. Actors are notorious for saying one night is better than another or preferring one matinée to another when to the outsider who might have seen both there was very little difference; to the actor and his overstretched antennae the difference can be thunderous. Actors on stage are like bats registering secret sonar signals that we in the audience cannot possibly be aware of. They have to concentrate with a force never needed off stage. To remember not only lines but motive, rhythms, and to have a contingency plan in the subconscious to go into play for emergencies. It is an *unnatural* life!

Wolf Mankowitz had had some West End runs and was doing OK. I believe he wrote the 'book' for *Oliver*, which had been running for years and the odd screenplay, but his most famous piece was still *The Bespoke Overcoat*, adapted from Gogol, which is a small masterpiece. Now he had scripted this vehicle for Richard Harris, who amazingly allowed himself to become involved in such a diabolical piece of cobblers. Perhaps it was the loot, perhaps it was Israel, which had just been in an heroic six-day war and whose own star was at a peak never to be seen again. So to go to Israel two years later and see the united Jerusalem was something difficult to resist. And then there was the country and the propaganda, and help Israel and let's do our bit for the arts, and so, lo and behold, Richard Harris is persuaded to act a Jewish Israeli footballer. A more bizarre concoction one cannot think of.

I arrived at night. It was a strange, warm atmosphere and the first time in a country I had heard of, read about, seen movies and books on. I had followed like the rest of the world the David and Goliath battle of 1967. How we cheered, how we exulted in the idea of Israel's deliverance from the jaws of death. And now I was in this soft, warm and exotic land. I was ensconced in a hotel in Hayarkon Street, facing the beach, and when I looked out of the window in the morning Tel Aviv looked like a jerry-built town that would not last. It seemed fragile, crumbling, and already the buildings were showing signs of dilapidation.

We started filming. I was assistant to the director, who was having trouble directing the film himself, since he seemed too much in awe of the legendary star. Richard appeared in the Dan Hotel on the first night, descending the stairs with a bandana around his head like a hippy or the Crimson Pirate.

I was asked to run the lines with the cute but uninspiring little homogenized Home Counties kid who was playing this tough, small Israeli. So I went over the lines and coached him as best I could, trying not to think for a second that this was the biggest piece of shit on earth and that I had just left a masterpiece to defile myself with this. I didn't think like that then. I thought, I hope I am up to the task and how important the film is and how important everybody connected with it is and think about all this money and these exotic stars and I let myself be flushed down the loo of my own lack of confidence in my own goals and work.

The longer I worked on crap the more crappy I would feel and the more lacking in confidence since I was marooned in a sea of something that polluted it when the sewers overflowed. I was pathetic, happy to be coaching a little jerk and being rudely dismissed by Harris . . . 'Don't interfere!' . . . when I tried to make the boy say a line that made sense. Mind you, he was probably getting pissed off with the whole thing too and hating each and every moment, and with each and every moment that he loathed, his bile started to overflow in my direction.

Wolf became more and more disgruntled and I became sadder and more depressed until I had to return to the valium that I had once given up. Now it was my only way to get through the grim, dreary days and stupid scenes.

My big relief was going into the small and enchanting port of Jaffa and walking around the old market stalls in the huge indoor market with my friend Asher Tsarfati, who had acted with me in *In the Penal Colony* in London and had now returned to Israel. At least with Israelis I felt safe. They were friendly, rough, honest and struggling.

I was working on the casting at first and then I took photos for a while, being a dab hand with a Pentax or Rollei, and eventually was asked to play a part, so whichever way the wind blew I would, like a piece of old rag, fly in that direction, aided by my green and black valium bombs. Uri Zohar was getting depressed with the obvious conflicts between his way of working, which was small and careful, and this way, which was much bigger and involved two stars, Richard and the beautiful Romy Schneider, with whom I had little to do but who seemed a very nice lady. The rushes were awful, though I am sure that given his head and encouragement Uri would have made an excellent piece of the folk art for which he was famous. As it was there was nothing but depression in the viewing theatre.

It might have been because the Irish Richard was not ideal casting to play the Israeli footballer. Not half he wasn't.

We gathered in the small bar in the basement of the hotel, the crew and I, and whined and hated each day; the film soured my experience of Israel, and I thought how terrible it was that my initiation to this great land should be via this piece of junk. Still, I rolled into Jerusalem at weekends and revelled in the sounds and sights and smells of the souk and felt cleansed by Sunday, when we returned to work. I started to meet theatre folk from the Cameri Theatre and the Habimah, but they showed little interest at the time in an Israeli *Metamorphosis*. This surprised me but when I saw the Western junk that so fascinated them I wasn't surprised any more.

Eventually things were going down the plughole and it looked like a wrap. Everybody hated everybody else and it was obviously a waste of time. Of course nobody blamed the real source of the disease . . . the stinking script! It was Israel, or the crew, or the bad phone service, or the actors, or the cameraman, or especially the director, the warm-hearted and passionate Uri, who now had the axe. So much easier to kill off human beings than the junk we had to perform. Richard now fancied himself as a director and since I was Uri's assistant there was no use for me. I was glad, for I was travelling down the route to self-destruction faster than anyone and all my achievements were as dust in my mouth. Then I was sacked and for the first time since I had been in Israel I felt liberated and *clean*.

I took off for Eilat and explored Israel. I wanted to save my money, so I worked on the land, even found myself digging roads with a drill. I collected rocks to build walls and heaved cement on my back until my neck was raw, but I loved it and felt real and human again. There was a lot of activity in Eilat in those days, since it was the sister town to Arab Aqaba on the Red Sea and there were always soldiers carrying Uzi machine-guns. I became quite fascinated with this frontier town. In the hot afternoons I would go and swim off the coral beach and see the most spectacular fish that almost defied description. I shared a room with four guys and we each had a strip about four feet wide, but that was home to me after the hotel and that film. My strip of floor was like a piece of heaven and I stayed until I got restless and decided it was time to investigate the London scene. I returned to my lady Alison, loaded down like Marco Polo with gifts from the markets of east Jerusalem.

I later learned that the shock to Uri had been so great that he left showbusiness completely and studied to be a rabbi. Now this once vulgar, loud, big-hearted, drinking, smoking, raving Israeli can be seen in Jerusalem striding through the Damascus Gate with his dreadlocks swinging by his ears and the Torah forever in his hand. Funny what a bad script can do.

London was cold when I returned and I missed the café life along Dizengorf Street and one particular place called Kassit where the writers and artistic crowd went. It was a ramshackle place with old paintings on the wall left by clients, and you could play chess. It reminded me of cafés in Vienna or Berlin or in a European city where the Jews had taken root and had created a particular culture. I was not to return to Israel until ten years had passed, and then I *was* to do *Metamorphosis*.

Back in Israel – 1980

On Saturday night after the Shabbat the crowds will stream along Dizengorf Street just walking, mother with kids, lovers holding hands, youth on the rampage for a good time, but all in peace and tranquillity. Cafés were jammed together one on top of the other and each group chose theirs. Mine tended to be Kassit in those days, the customers would get too maudlin and drunk but there was always someone there you knew. I thought of my mother stuck in her eighth-floor council flat in Manor House and how she would have loved the café life. The good thing about Israel is its community and its awareness of self. You need never really be alone and it is an eerie feeling at first to be in a land of Jews. You are used to small Jewish communities in Christian lands, but here is one huge Jewish community. The bus drivers, the street sweepers, the waiters and chefs. The beggars, even, and the prostitutes plying their trade on the outskirts of town, the no-man's land between Tel Aviv and Jaffa. Jew land. Sometimes a great surging warmth would come flooding into me when I sat at a favourite little café near the bus station after returning from Jerusalem. There was an old waitress there who reminded me of Ma.

1 Eva and Louis, Berkoff's maternal
grandparents

2 Berkoff, aged 3

3 Polly, Berkoff's mother

4 Abraham (Al), Berkoff's father

5 Berkoff (aged 8) and his sister Beryl
6 *Right*, Berkoff at 17, in his Tony Curtis phase

7 Berkoff, 18, with his parents at a Jewish wedding

8 Berkoff, 18, a budding salesman with Sandersons

9   As Henry VIII in Robert Bolt's *A Man for all Seasons*, Bournemouth, 1962

10   As Bamforth in Willis Hall's *The Long and the Short and the Tall*,
Liverpool Playhouse, 1965

11 Berkoff (*left*) with Lee Montague in *Semi-Detached* at Cardiff Rep, 1963

12 Berkoff (*right*) in *Write Me A Murder* at Canterbury Rep, 1963

13   Berkoff reaching for the stars in *Zoo Story*, Theatre Royal, Stratford East, 1965

14   For a televised *Hamlet*, Berkoff in costume as Lucianus
but posing as Hamlet, 1964

15   Steven Berkoff: Actor/Manager *or* The Nureyev period, *c.* 1971

16 Berkoff in *Knock at the Manor Gate*, adapted from Kafka and used as an
opener to a programme including *Metamorphosis*, 1972

Our family's origin was Russian and they, like many others, had decided to see what life was like in England in the 1890s, since things were a trifle too exciting in Russia under the Czar. But for him and his Cossacks I might have been a contented little Russian living happily in Moscow or Odessa and not been a pain in the arse to so many people here. However, now I saw where others had fled to and what a conglomeration of races and faces and features and accents and names had resulted. It was the most polyglot society on earth and the genetic pool was so varied that it also managed to get rid of, in a few generations, the signs of inbreeding and the unhealthy restrictions of ghetto life. I saw few exaggerated noses, few sunken, staring eyes, but I did see healthy, fit and strong Israelis, called *sabras* after the prickly cactus. Sabras were a new race of Jews, a very powerful and healthy race. Green eyes abounded in olive skin and the women were really beautiful.

Once on one of my trips after I had shaken the dreadful film off as you shake off a disease (although let me say I was grateful, for without the film I might not have seen Israel), I went to a small Arab hotel in the old city of Jerusalem; the old city was then still very Arabic and not so artificially mixed as it is now. Now Israelis are determined to live there to create again a strong Jewish population as there was at the turn of the century, but the city has that strong Arabic Middle Eastern smell. The souk with the sellers crouched in their fruit-perfumed caverns can only be Arabia.

So I was sleeping one night in this old hotel where the only sound was the hoarse spitting like a camel coughing up its guts, which you heard throughout the hotel. That part was not so edifying, but in the middle of the night when you'd just dropped off and were dreaming of the desert trip in the morning and the Dead Sea came the ear-piercing sound of the muezzin calling the faithful to prayer. It started suddenly like the long wail of an animal in the throes of sexual bliss. I lay there in the pitch black and felt the land of Israel tighten around me; I was mystified to be in this so ancient city and sleeping within its walls.

In the morning, tea with mint leaves. The next day the Dead Sea and Massada, where Herod built a fortress on top of a mountain. I walked to the top of Massada along the snake path which was the original path of the Zealots, and below stretched out the Dead Sea like a burnished mirror, and the desert. This is where, according to

Josephus, the last Jews committed mass suicide rather than submit to the Romans and God only knows what bestial atrocities they were capable of. At the top sometimes a guide will tell a group of tourists the story of how the leader of the escaped Jews, who had all been living there for some time, made a speech to the assembled people instructing them to die by their own hand. The speech has been handed down to us since, according to Josephus' account, two of the Jews didn't want to give up their lives but hid and decided to take their chances with the host. So they recounted the story to their captors. This story is now told by the guide to an assembled crowd of eager-faced tourists from Los Angeles or Manchester. It's terribly moving and very simple and its message is persuasive. One day I would be asked to read its message. It was in 1980, eleven years later, when I returned there at the end of our *Hamlet* tour. The guide showed us around and then came the story and this time she asked, 'Would anyone care to read the story since my English is not so perfect.' Everyone was silent but I could not resist. She gave me the speech of about twenty-five lines and above the mountains of Judaea in the crystal blue air of the Dead Sea I spoke Eleazar's words. I recalled my dead mother who lived for forty years in her small council flat in Manor House and wished she could have seen this wondrous land.

After all we were born to die, we and those we brought into the world: this even the luckiest must face. But outrage, slavery, and the sight of our wives led away to shame with our children – these are not evils to which man is subject by the laws of nature: men undergo them through their own cowardice if they have a chance to forestall them by death and will not take it. We were very proud of our courage, so we revolted from Rome: now in the final stages they have offered to spare our lives and we have turned the offer down. Is anyone too blind to see how furious they will be if they take us alive? Pity the young whose bodies are strong enough to survive prolonged torture; pity the not-so-young whose old frames would break under such ill-usage. A man will see his wife violently carried off; he will hear the voice of his child crying 'Daddy!' when his own hands are fettered. Come! while our hands are free and can hold a sword, let them do a noble service! Let us die unenslaved by our enemies, and leave this world as free men in company with our wives and children. That is what the Law ordains, that is what our wives and children demand of us, the necessity God has laid on us, the opposite of what the Romans wish – they are anxious none of us should die before the town is captured. So let us deny the enemy their hoped-for pleasure at our expense, and without more ado leave them to be dumbfounded by our death and awed by our courage.

Josephus, The Jewish War

Back to Manor House

In the 1950s Manor House was a strange area, a huge council estate abutting Finsbury Park and claiming to be the biggest housing estate in Europe, as well it may have been. Block after block of relentless conformity stared down at you. Like prison blocks with a single balcony wrapping itself around each block as a conveyor belt for everyone to pass your window as they made for the lift which doubled as a urinal if you couldn't hold it. We had eventually made it out of the East End and were housed in this bright, clean and new building where no one had lived before and I was over the moon. At eleven, I had my own bedroom and could furnish it in *my* style and have things like a bedside reading light. I rushed down to Stamford Hill to get one. It was thirty bob, which was a lot in those days, but Ma gave me carte blanche over the interior design. The piano bug kept recurring and I was again assured that now that we were ensconced the time would soon come when a piano would make its appearance. For now funds were short and was this piano business not just another one of those childish whims that once satisfied would soon pall?

Of course it was, they thought, and for now just get out and play. Do something. Amuse yourself.

So I joined the club at Stamford Hill and gazed longingly at young girls. Sometimes we'd go to the huge cinema called the Astoria, Finsbury Park, which had a roof like the night in an Arabian desert and a turret and dome with figures of people on them; when the light went down the stars came up. There were cinemas everywhere in those days, since few people had television, but when the little black and white screen first made its appearance we were stuck to it like flies to flypaper and my constant image of Pa and Ma after that is of two backs. After a while I forgot what they looked like, since I would be mainly addressing my remarks to two Magritte-like heads which at first turned slightly, but after a few more years just answered from that position.

The years oozed past via Stamford Hill, the Royal, Tottenham, and then the adventures of the West End and the great Lyceum. Sunday was Lyceum night, but you could always do some hopping at the 51 Club in Little Newport Street. That was good for jazz and they played the best records and you danced your feet off. If I did less and less exercise at school I made up for it by jiving, at which I was becoming a veritable Gene Kelly. I had perfected my jiving via Leslie at Grays, Finsbury Park, fine-tuned it at the Royal and let it go at the '51'. It was my sanctuary, a small dark room with some of the best dancing to be seen in the West End. I would come home some nights soaked to the skin and it was even better than sex. I evolved a style that was ultra cool. By this time the Johnnie Ray era had been replaced by Teddy Boys and you wore four-button suits, shirts with stiff collars and double cuffs. My collars were sent each week to 'Collars Ltd' for starching and laundering, and woe betide them if the collars came back soft or not stiff enough. I would go bananas. The style of dance was affected by the suit you wore and so you had to lift your arm keeping your elbow fairly well in to your side or your jacket would be pulled up and you would appear ungainly. No, you had to dance cool so as to keep the form intact.

It was a brief but unique period in English social and fashion history, since it twisted the jive away from its American cousins and adapted it to fit into an idiosyncratic London style. The chaps at the Lyceum became fops and Beau Brummels and the suit was more than ever your calling card or your source of esteem. You had to be immaculate and therefore it became even more incumbent on you to lay your hands on *funds*.

I didn't realize until some time later that the Lyceum had once been a theatre. That Henry Irving had played there many times in the 1890s and that the crowd that hung around outside after the dance . . . 'Wherejalive darlin'?' . . . had once been excited theatregoers among whom would have been Oscar Wilde, a great admirer of Irving. Aaah, so that's it, is it? I was drawn back through time through the spirit of Irving, in whose footsteps I would eventually impersonate an actor/manager. Perhaps Irving telepathically drew me to haunting his old palace! Perhaps spirits are drawn to some potential vehicle with whom they sense affinity and invade their souls and thus Irving took me to the Lyceum each Sunday night. Jesting, of course, but I do believe that when you become fascinated with great personages of the past, those same persons will come to you in other ways. But for now I was quite content to hear Oscar Rabin or Ted Heath play and to perform my weird and wonderful gyrations. Of course Curly King was always there too and the evening ended in the usual fracas.

Jobs and Jail – 1952

It was summer and I left school, glad to be free of the confines of that grim Victorian building to which for four years I had taken the 653 bus twice daily and watched from the top deck the same dreary streets stream past, the same grim houses, the boring stores, old churches, town hall, squalid suburbs and then the same deadly walk across Hackney Downs into a place that I was hating more and more. Now I was free. When you know nothing of the outside world you fantasize about what working will be like, and I saw myself in a suit with a smart briefcase jumping in the tube at Manor House and going to some elegant office. I had not the faintest idea in the world what I would be doing except working, but it was a mystery to me what work it could possibly be. I had no guidance and in those days nobody seemed to give a damn either at school or at home. You just looked in the 'Wanted' ads in the paper and went for the job.

So that's what I did and I took on the most improbable job, as an office clerk in an engineering firm in Baker Street. It was called Matthew Hall Ltd and what I had to do with it was beyond me. I found myself standing in front of a filing cabinet all day, having to perform some dreary filing. I soon demonstrated my lack of zeal and was out on the street again.

Then I met someone who was in advertising. This seemed rather more creative and romantic and I saw myself in my dream world again, sitting in a smart office in Gerrard Street writing copy and dreaming up witty ideas. They had other thoughts, however. I was to be used as a messenger boy at the very bottom of the deck, being sent to Fleet Street with the advertising blocks which were to be printed in the next day's papers. This I quite liked, since it got me out and about and I got to know every newspaper in Fleet Street. I could also watch the old tarts in Gerrard Street plying their soggy wares day after day. Luncheon vouchers meant a good dinner time in the Lyons Corner House where you got good value for three shillings and sixpence. Years ago this had been a favourite haunt of Ma's and mine, since they had the famous Salad Bowl where for four bob you could pile your plate up so high you could never finish it. Nevertheless you wouldn't learn and continued to pile it up, so delighted were you that such things were infinite. Now it was a fixed lunch and I went back to work for more running around.

I was quite happy in this friendly little firm, earning my two pounds ten a week and giving a pound of it to Mum for housekeeping. Now for the bad news. I have a not very interesting theory that what you are denied for no good reason will fester inside you until it comes out in unpleasant ways. Be it love, sex, certain forms of literature, or even something like a bike. Somehow this had crumbled along with all my other fantasies, but still germinated deep within. If I had saved I could have bought a bike. Instead I decided one day on my errands round Fleet Street to take off with a smart-looking machine. My heart was thumping like a maniac as I tore off. It was a mad impulse but part of my 'schooling' was that you took what you were denied.

I rode it around for a few days saying at home that I had borrowed it, but eventually my crime deepened as I sought to sell the thing and make some money. This led me to the bike stall in Kingsland Road. The man looked at the machine and at me and at the machine and said he'd give me a fiver for it. But, he said, he had just started and hadn't the cash; he would have it that evening if I'd care to call back. He told me to come to his house around the corner, because it was easier to do his business there. I should have been a little more of a pro and smelled a bad herring, but I was too enamoured of the idea of five pounds in my pocket.

I dressed up that night in a bright red shirt and black barathea pants that Dad had reluctantly given me since a customer had not turned up. I had a date later at the Tottenham Royal, I recall. I also had a houndstooth jacket on. As I headed out in the cold night, I heard a warning voice telling me not to go. But I was inexorably woven into a chain of events from which I could not seem to unravel myself. Nothing had meaning any more. My work was trivial and pointless and my prospects nil. I passed the time. I worked and lived for nothing more than the most agreeable way to fritter the hours away. My values, such as they were, had been shot to pieces and the dreams ground into the dust of day-to-day reality. I was heading for a fall. I was fifteen.

I knocked. The bloke answered and I expected my fiver. I went into the front room where two strangers approached me and questioned me about how I had got hold of the bike. The man had been alerted to the theft, as probably had every bike dealer in London, and I was nabbed. The policemen seemed hefty blokes. My stomach dropped out. I was under arrest. My one and only concern, which I repeated pathetically over and over again, was 'Please don't tell my dad.' The fear of this outweighed all other considerations. How one remembers the details at the time of arrest. Shock seems to freeze time and everything hangs motionless in one's mind. When Joseph K. is arrested he recalls a white blouse hanging from a window.

They took me to the police station and put me behind a large table. I wondered what my girlfriend would be thinking. That I had just stood her up? They phoned my parents. I expected the worst. Unfortunately Dad was home and came down to the station. They told me to get up since I would be going home on bail. Dad came into the room and predictably took a huge lunge at me as if to knock me out. He was prevented by the police, who warned him off. No beatings or reprisals. The court would deal with it. Of course, who was he beating but himself? He was ashamed. After all, he had trained me.

Dad drove me to Manor House and I don't remember what he said except that it was the familiar ritual of 'I'm sorry the day you were born' and 'You've given me nothing but pain and misery', 'You're worthless and disgusting' and various other such expressions which had become such a theme song that they no longer made the shocking imprint on my mind that evil words do on children. Mum was of course upset but understanding, and I went to bed early.

Next morning I was due to go to the Juvenile Court in Aldgate and Ma gave me breakfast in bed, as much, I now realize, to avoid my seeing Dad as to make my last breakfast a nice one. It was my fave, of course, tomatoes on toast. There was no chance of my being sent to Borstal or Young People's Correction Centre since it was my first offence. No chance in the world. There was even a first-offence leniency law designed to give a spontaneous offender another chance and not to ruin him. It wasn't a huge crime, but I reckoned without the old crust sitting on the Bench, an evil, vindictive old sod called Basil Henriques, who, rumour had it, thought it was a healthy thing for kids to be sent away. Here I realize I sound like an old lag – all villains call the magistrate some evil and vindictive sod since no one likes eating porridge every day. Anyway he decided to send me for evaluation at a remand home in Stamford House, Shepherd's Bush, for two weeks! A psychological and social evaluation before he passed sentence. I was delighted since it meant I didn't have to go home and might have a bit of fun; it was starting to feel like those gangster movies I was always seeing of the guys holed up in the Pen. Now I could see what was going on inside. Terrific.

Dad departed and I was driven off in a van to Shepherd's Bush. When I got there I was given some bread and fish paste, which tasted good since I hadn't eaten all day. I wore the grey uniform of the remand home and slept in a dorm with about fifty other kids. We were woken with the usual music-hall wit of 'Hands off cocks, pull up your socks' and we all traipsed in for showers. The two weeks went by quickly enough in my enforced schoolboys' camp and I recall little except the yard outside and films in the evening; though I did once get into a scrap and this was duly marked as an indication of my bad character.

I saw a visiting psychiatrist who seemed concerned about me and having this older and knowledgeable man take such an interest made me blurt out everything. He was perturbed that Dad didn't feature much in the story of my life and I told him I could count on my one hand how many times we had gone out as a family and never once just us two. Except to the Juvenile Court.

Perhaps there was something in my father's emotional make-up that made him feel ill-at-ease with me, for what reason I cannot at this stage tell. Maybe he thought I was someone else? Who knows what weird ramifications went on inside his head? He seemed cosy and affectionate for a few minutes, but that was all. He would never come out with us. When I was a child in Luton I remember constantly begging him to come to the outdoor pool, just once. And once when it was so hot that the tar melted, he did come. I wasn't saddened by his seeming indifference, but perhaps felt an extra need for a pal and that is why a pal is so important to me even now. Friends and, especially when I was younger, older friends. Support and encouragement, endorsement for achievements and help when things seem difficult. Without this a child loses his way and has no one to guide him apart from people he chances to meet, no matter where. If they are strong enough they become role models, whether they be saints or thieves. In my area there were a lot of thieves around.

I didn't feel sorry for myself since at that age you think that this is normal, and you believe that having elders who sometimes hate you is normal, since childhood is such a nuisance. Childhood is being naughty. Speaking in class is being wicked. In the end everything becomes wicked – laughter when you should be quiet is wicked; needing is very wicked; sexual feelings are terrible and the strange stirrings in your body are dirty. You wend your way through this minefield trying not to get hurt on the way through, but you do.

I spoke all this out to my shrink and he was happy that I did. He was very encouraging and told me frankly that many kids go my way who have had little support from a male figure. And particularly a male figure who is there – not absent or killed, but there and yet not there. There he was, my dad, a figurehead sitting in the armchair like an Indian chieftain smoking his Players cigs. Ma puts his slippers on. The telly is switched to the right channel. He comes home laden with fruit like a breadwinner on Sunday and we search for the goodies, but after a while I shudder when I hear the key in the door. After a while we no longer speak. I go into my room.

After some months or years we manage to make small chat and as he gets older the chat takes on some hues. He goes to see my shows, at least a couple, and is proud. Steadily going blind he continues to play bridge with a magnifying glass or read the paper the same way. He goes on holiday alone to give Ma a break. 'I need to go alone sometimes,' he says. He stays away from home because he goes to the Turkish baths and sleeps overnight 'talking to my pals'. After a hard day at the shop he goes to the Imperial Turkish Baths, Russell Square. Then he goes midweek too. Sometimes after dancing all night Barry and I went to the Imperial. I never saw Dad there. I liked the steam swirling around our bodies and the fierce heat and you'd sit there with your head low and then plunge into the pool. Afterwards you'd go to your cots or bed or sit up and order tea and thick slices of toast. It was like being in Imperial Russia or an Arabic palace. Carpeted and silent and burning hot rooms where fat old men melted and eyed the youths.

'Where have you been, Dad?'

'The baths . . . Working?' he asked me just to change the subject.

'He's got a job in a rep, Al, he's going to do some plays in rep.'

'Good . . . Anything on the telly?' Always telling me how Morrie's boy is going so that his achievements may be placed next to mine and mine seen to fall short. 'You're a bum . . . good for nothing.'

He comes in with a little whistle like he thinks this is the greeting of a saint, a lovely signature that will endear him to us. Ma's eyebrows go up and she mouths silently, looking like the comedian Les Dawson. 'Ask him how he is,' she mouths. It's hard. I sit in the kitchen behind the glass partition where I have been eating my breakfast on my Sunday visits in the future. She puts down toasted beigels and cream cheese and salmon. This is the Sunday tradition to wipe out the week's strife. That and endless teas. Then she wants to give me lunch, but I am stuffed and say why did you give me so many beigels if you made lunch . . .?

'So wait a while,' she says stoically and asks about all the women in my life. How is Yvette, a sweet French girl I once brought home when I was twenty-one. How was she? She really liked her. She had such a sweet face. And Blanche, another French girl, and how was she and do you hear from her and Ma so much liked Blanche, she was such a pretty girl and Ma wanted such a pretty French girl with soft, warm features to be a daughter-in-law to cure me of this reckless toing and froing. And does Shelley cook properly, my wife Shelley in future years who was away touring? Does she know how to cook? she'd ask, as she got smaller on each visit until she nearly disappeared and her hair went white and stuck up when she couldn't be bothered to comb it and her face became wizened and I hoped when I rang the doorbell every few weeks, hoped that the ravages of age would not have scarred her too much from the time before and that the flat would not start to smell of age and neglect. Then Dad would come in and we'd shrivel up in the kitchen and talk behind the glass partition. Anything on the telly?

But when I was fifteen Ma was middle-aged and I was telling the shrink all about it. He nodded sagely and with approbation, since this all fitted into a plan and theory of youth and its behaviour patterns. He reassured me that after the remand there was *no* chance that I would be refused probation since I fell almost into a classic syndrome. No chance at all and that combined with a first offence. No, I would probably be given a year's probation and I would be advised about what to do with my life. We enjoyed talking to each other; he was a gentle soul who seemed to find me interesting and was puzzled as to why I was there in the first place.

Each boy had a visit from a priest during his stay to give comfort in whatever denomination he was and one day I was called into a private office where I sat facing a young Jewish minister. I am not sure that he was a rabbi, but he was very sympathetic and of course reminded me how unusual it was for a young boy of the faith to be in such a place and what could I have done? When I told him the sheer heinousness of the offence he was quite taken aback that I should be here and thus reinforced my by now utter conviction that these two weeks were going to be the sum total of my punishment. A good shock it had been and never again, mate. That's for sure.

He asked about my habits and where I went and when I told him, it was he who informed me that the Lyceum had once been a theatre. For some reason this took me aback and even now I can clearly remember his saying it. I remember nothing more of the conversation, which might have lasted an hour, except that the Lyceum was once a *theatre* and of course the root which led to the flower.

Why do I remember this after all these years? Was there some synchronicity that made me aware of my life-to-be? Did I know at the age of fifteen that I would be in the theatre? I knew nothing of the theatre at that time. My ambition even then was to be an actor, but the only acting I was aware of was in movies. A movie star was what I had a yearning to be once, after having my hair styled at Maxie's barber in Stoke Newington High Street, where he actually used tongs and a hair-dryer and 'set' my wave on both sides of my forehead like the waves divided by the prow of a ship. When I saw at fifteen the miracle that had been performed on my hair I felt indeed the new man that Max had prophesied I would.

We all went to Max in those days and were transferred into clones, with waves that curled up from the skull, sometimes looking like birds' nests. So one day I felt transformed and stared hard in the glass and like Narcissus fell in love with myself and saw myself destined.

So I still remember the minister surprising me with talk of the Lyceum being at one time a theatre. It was as if he had said that the place, profane with music, noise and dance, was once a church. It stuck in my mind as so odd that this place which I thought was built as a Mecca dance hall was a temple to the theatrical arts. The circle upstairs where you sat with a Coke had once been the dress circle, the corridors where you might snog for a few minutes between numbers had once streamed with cultured, expectant theatregoers pouring in to see *Hamlet* or *The Bells*. It stayed in my mind and I have to believe there was a reason for it. There has to be an explanation, for he might have easily said it used to be a museum or bus station or palace or library and it would have drifted down the tubes of my mind and dissolved as an unimportant record in the cells of the brain where such things are stored in case they might be of use at some later stage. I knew nothing of the theatre, having only been once before with the school to some tedious show at the Old Vic when everybody fidgeted. Now, years later, I am fascinated by what play that might have been.

So did the sprite of the future land on my shoulder, and are past, present and future part of a seamless flow so that the word theatre knocked on some door that echoed into the future and echoed back? Yes. I can suppose no other explanation and so the thwarted desire for the piano would have met with compensation in the future; by not taking it up, my will merely changed itself like the trajectory of a spaceship thrown off course but still going forward. The moment when the nice man told me that my favourite dance place in the world was once a theatre set a train of thought going in my mind and I never forgot it. The next time I went to the Lyceum I would remember and look for artifacts and clues to its origin.

The day of the hearing arrived. This time I would be sentenced in the light of my psychiatric examination, and hadn't he told me there was no chance of my being put away? My behaviour in the remand home had been good, except for one provoked skirmish. So I attended with all confidence. I saw the magistrate, Henriques, spend two minutes on the report and there in front of my father he reported what should have remained utterly private; he read a sentence or two out loud in front of Dad standing there in the court, things that I had been assured were confidential. The swine cared not and puffed on, saying, 'You make some claims that your father neglected you etc., etc. . .' It was the most embarrassing moment of my life that these thoughts, uttered only with the knowledge that I would be protected in my deepest admissions, should be made public. The grotesque old monster humiliated me in front of everyone. My dad got up to defend himself futilely, but was cut off . . . it was a charade whereby everyone's feelings were as bits of junk and we were just part of the flotsam.

My school report was read out and the headmaster's slurs on my character rang out in the court – the magistrate was quite pleased to see how badly I had done in that wretched little school. Not how badly the school had done by me by stripping me of everything I believed in, like a form of rape. Not the desultory and grim methods of teaching that produced idiots, taking a child with high marks and achievements and lazily throwing him into the ash can to see if he crawls out.

Given all these *facts*, the ideas of psychiatry were obviously so much hogwash for this eminent Victorian anachronism who, though apparently childless himself, had no compunction about sending other people's children to borstals and other institutions. Three months! His voice rang out with the sentence.

'You are obviously in need of a short, sharp shock,' for this was the term for the newly invented detention centres that were the latest fashion in incarceration. You did a lesser sentence and did not ruin your life with a year in borstal, but could be returned to the community a chastened youth thanks to this new method whose discipline was so severe that doctors forbade sentences of more than six months, and in most cases recommended three or four. It was a centre based on hard, ruthless, physical work until you either dropped dead or became a new person, terrified of offending again. So it was for first or second offenders whom society might return to its bosom. But it was an evil régime. Or it might be that a fifteen-year-old locked inside the older body is asking for some kind of redress.

The train took us to Oxford, and then a car to the small town of Kidlington, where they had built a kind of concentration camp where wayward children could be coerced into being good citizens. Before I left the court I had to change my trousers, since the customer from whom I was the lucky recipient had decided after all to claim the black barathea pants with the cross loops for the belt. So Dad said, 'Get them off' and I changed in the loo. When we got to the centre it was on the double. You never walked but did whatever it was 'on the double' . . . It took a while to get used to it.

I had a nice chat with the detective who accompanied me on the train. When he escorted me into the office I was asked my name and when I replied without the necessary 'Sir' the loony behind the desk screamed, 'YOU ANSWER "SIR" WHEN YOU REPLY HERE!' His scream was so sudden and so bizarre that I shot a sidelong look at the detective as if to plead for some support, but he looked back with a slight shrug of regret, as if he too found it a bit over the top to talk to a fifteen-year-old as if he were a mass murderer, but was helpless to do anything except record my shock and send a small signal of sympathy.

I was put into a lukewarm bath and changed into a grey flannel uniform. Then, as it was teatime, I queued up with the other inmates and sat at a table feeling a sense of wonderment. This did fulfil some fantasy of sharing with those movie villains the scenes I had so admired. The yard with the guys hanging out and planning their escapes. Now it was for real and I resolved never to look at those movies again without a sense of complete empathy. After tea, where I was placed with some other fairly harmless-looking newcomers, we were told to change and get ready for PT. Oh well, PT can't be too bad, but I had not reckoned with a sadist called Leeson who with his cold blue eyes sought to victimize anyone who seemed vulnerable or weak. This was a PT I had never experienced before or since. It was a nightmare. After endless feet together, apart, together until we were ready to drop, he then asked us to collect our *logs*. We then had to hold these logs, weighing maybe four or five pounds, above our heads and run around the gym. Several of the boys collapsed in a heap and were screamed at to get up. If you survived that you did more legs apart, together, to recover some of your strength and the *pièce de résistance* was to hop around the room with the logs stretched out in front of you. I don't remember what the punishment was if you failed, or if we just feared a beating, or if it was ever given, but the fear was there.

Then we'd return for cocoa and listen to the 6 o'clock news. After the news we'd be asked questions and there were fears of reprisals if you did not remember something. You'd listen and recall one or two obscure bits and hope that when it came to your turn no one else had chosen the same bits. Fear of cuffing, slapping, beating always hung in the air, but I quite like the news and always managed to remember some item. Then bed. A single cell for the newcomers. Up at 6 a.m., lukewarm and quick showers and then cocoa, breakfast of bread and some spread and porridge, and off to work. For the first days I was assigned the pleasant duty of scrubbing the toilets while the other chaps might be working outside. It wasn't too cold yet and they built walls and chopped wood and dug the earth. I longed for lunch and prayed for tea, but it was always the same, thin slices of ham and bread which after a while became like manna.

For the first week or two the newcomers like myself found the staff hysterically funny and we would sit there at meal breaks pissing our heads off because they were so determined to be hard nuts and so obviously acting that their behaviour was a constant source of amusement. Our spirits were not yet crushed. We learned how to deal with the murderous PT, dropping the logs to our waists when the maniac Leeson wasn't looking our way or was bullying some poor small kid. A master or warder observing us giggling said that we wouldn't be doing that much longer, as if he detested the fact that even in this concentration camp we could retain enough of our human joy to let it out when we could relax.

The days grew shorter and colder and the boys who were working outside returned at night freezing with chapped and cracked hands; one or two tried to break their fingers with bricks to be let off the work. It seemed a ghastly thing to do and since I was still cleaning toilets I had no idea of what was so terrible outside except that it was freezing and a cold winter. The gym got worse when Leeson spied our little tricks. Eventually I developed a lump in my groin, in fact one on either side and I was let off outside work when it looked as if I had a hernia. No treatment was given. I was then put on to cleaning and polishing the dining room for the rest of my stay and became quite involved with getting a good shine on the parquet floors before the lunchtime mob came in.

Since the shock centre was still in its infancy there were few facilities to help the kids improve their minds. There was one small library from which you could borrow one book per week and that was all. Towards the end of our time they devised boxing and we all went in and had to smash each other about for five minutes, which was considered good for us. I found it quite strange at first, this organized violence, but got to enjoy it until my nose was put out of joint; thereupon I made my early retirement from the ring. Once a week we had, like all good prisons, our allowance of sweets and these were as nectar since we were starving most of the time. Because I cared less for sweets than bread and paste I would swop a bar of toffee for two slices of bread. This was the beginning of my 'sweet baron' days and they went on quite harmoniously until one day I wasn't paid my slices because the poor kid was so hungry on outside work he couldn't bear to part with them. Now to give up my precious sweets, my means of staving off hunger took a considerable amount of will-power on my part and I was somewhat miffed to be denied my slices. So one day I seized the boy concerned by the shirt and warned him to pay his debt. Unfortunately a nasty little guard was watching and I suspect had been already informed, since he stepped out of the shadows and 'arrested' me.

I explained that I was not a 'baron' but doing a fair exchange. It was no good since such exchanges were forbidden and the boy denied he owed me anything, so what with that and my giggling at breakfast I was in for the high jump. As if this centre were not already the last word in brutality, stupidity and plain ignorance, there existed a punishment block where unruly offenders were put into solitary, a real adult facsimile. I received seven days solitary. Now it is not good to put children into solitary confinement for twenty-three hours a day, since they have an unfortunate tendency to commit suicide. There was an assistant governor who was always very friendly and paternal to me and seemed to regret that I was in such a place. When he passed my cell for kit inspection he would always ask how I was and was I coping and this solicitude helped me. When I was continually at fault for small lapses in the regime's ritual I told him I was not as institutionalized as the others, most of whom were perpetual offenders or had some stone-wall experience. You see, nobody goes away for a first offence, only those unlucky enough to go before Henriques, for whose gifts to society they have renamed a street. The assistant governor, like everyone else, was slightly taken aback, but hoped I would try to get through. When I was sentenced to my seven days in solitary and loss of remission for my small experiment in bartering he was indeed sorry and came to see me.

The cell was small and cold and I was locked up the whole day. My lunch was shoved in on a tray. I mean, this is the treatment they give killers and bomb merchants! There was a small window and at night I could see the distant cars, so unaware of how free they were.

My daytime occupation was scraping rusty baking tins. They seemed to have a whole warehouse of these tins and I was given some kind of pumice stone and sat all day scraping my heart out. Just scrape and listen to my thoughts or the sounds of the boys in the next cells since there were two others sharing my fate. I once heard one of the fatter wardens, who with his bulging beady eyes looked like a child molester, come into the cell of the boy next door, a hard, spirited Hoxton lad. Beady eyes said, 'Take off your shoes', since when you beat anyone you don't want to risk a kicking with the prison-issue boots, which could leave a very nasty bump on your shin. The boy screamed back, 'I'm not taking off my fucking shoes.' This went on for some time until the coward gave up since he could not do something so illegal and report the boy for it. The greasy sod just slunk away. I realize that these poor men were just as much a part of the process as we were and I suppose the best the system could get for the money, which must have been very low.

In the morning I would be woken at six o'clock and, naked, rushed on the double to the showers. I would be put under ice-cold water which took my breath away, but I had to stay until I turned blue. Then I was told to get out of the shower, dry off quickly and run back upstairs. The cold morning air which had been so freezing when I went into the shower was now warm as toast by contrast. Then I was given my cocoa and bread, the treat of the day, and got started on my trays again. Once again the hours stretched out to infinity with the constant scrape, the shouts next door and sounds of beating, but mostly mad, infantile screaming from the warders.

I started to develop the idea that I would never get out and that they could do with me what they wanted. I might be in here for ever since who was to know? It seemed endless. The days would not budge, but got stuck like a closely observed minute hand. At night I watched the traffic and saw the lights spring into the Oxfordshire night sky when they went up a hill. I dreamed of Cadbury's chocolate bars and all those things you take for granted outside.

Christmas was coming and there was a flurry of activity and expectancy: the rumour was that kids were going to get a real meal and not the starvation rations that had led me into the punishment block. On Christmas Day I still had two days left to serve in solitary, but it was deemed heartless to keep me in and so I was let out into the prison community again. It was like the Savoy Hotel compared to where I had been. We had extra portions, nobody worked that day and group games had been organized, but I remember little else. We were all so hungry in anticipation that it seemed the overriding concern, although our dream of a feast was shattered by a dinner that was the same size as usual except with a bit of chicken. We were given loads of sweet, sickly pudding, which we could eat and eat, but we got tired of it. We all went into the large lounge and did the usual bashing of each other with boxing gloves. At night I said farewell to my brief moments of freedom and went back to solitary.

To my horror I was not let out the next day, since the Christmas Day was added to my seven-day sentence and I still had to serve the extra day. I was so upset I truly thought they would keep me in for ever. I started to pray aloud to God. I even swore I would do no more wrongs. I prayed over and over again and lo and behold the door opened and I was told to go. My sentence was up.

I changed into my street clothes. They seemed so soft and luxurious. I had a gaberdine raincoat in that stone colour that Mum had bought me. The screws stared at it and I suddenly looked like little Lord Fauntleroy. I still didn't trust these weird men and so I kept up my best behaviour until I was out. A wretched screw with a red face who was scruffy and a bully inside took me to the station. We exchanged no words. I was cold as ice since he now had no jurisdiction over me. I wanted to tell him what I thought of him, but thought better of it. He handed me my ticket.

During the three months I had had only one visit from Dad. Mum was hospitalized with a serious operation. Dad came with a bag of sweets. We had sat in the bleak room, but could not say too much. He handed over the bag of sweets and was told to take it back since this was not allowed. I think I might have cried. Dad gently tried to cuff me with his trilby, as if saying, 'Come on, keep your pecker up,' but found it difficult not to cry himself. He cared a lot, but could not always show it at home. I think the visit upset him greatly.

Now I was on the train and going to Paddington. Everyone seemed so normal and noisy, going to work and flapping newspapers, so alive and busy, smoking, drinking teas and coffees. I got to Paddington and walked up the moving stairs and quickly past the barrier. Dad was going to meet me, but I was obstinate and did not wish to wait. I made my way home and let myself in. The place seemed cold and bare. Ma was still in hospital having had peritonitis and been close to death's door. The place looked neglected. I took my coat off and started cleaning . . .

Oh, the shame of it! I wondered who knew of my accursed crime. Had word seeped out into the 'manor' and would I now be ostracized by my peers for such a petty little itsy-bitsy crime? Now if it had been a break-in on some big scale or some daring caper I could have had cause for pride, but a bike is hardly cause for having lost your virginity in the metaphoric sense. I stayed home for the first week and never peeped out of the door. I didn't yet know how to face the world outside and felt totally disorientated. My stomach was on fire from an ulcer which I had developed inside, but my hernia was healing. Apart from that I felt comparatively well, although the stomach would be a curse for the rest of my life, coming out like a weather vane to point to good and bad in my emotional weather pattern. However, it did save me going into the army when I was eighteen.

As eighteen came around to the lads of Stamford Hill there would be a rash of diseases as the guys who were the best actors on earth started to do their stunts. The doctors' common wisdom was 'build up a case' . . . So you would be jiving away happily at some Sunday function, when suddenly a guy collapsed in the middle of the floor. We all knew he was working his ticket and didn't pay too much attention, but he had to get the management to call a doctor or the ambulance and so it went on. After a while everybody started collapsing and that route went out of fashion. Barry Wise decided not to sleep for a week and each night he'd stay out, going to movies all day long until he looked like a wreck. That took a great deal of the kind of fortitude I knew he had and in due course he was Grade Four. Also he acted like a loony during the exams.

My card came and my medical was due in two weeks, but I wasn't committed to Barry's tactics. I had decided some months back to complain to my doctor of terrible nightmares and hallucinations. Before I knew where I was I was strapped down and wires placed all over my head. Well, I thought, that was good for a start, and then I attended a psychiatric clinic in Camden where you had to look at splashes on a sheet of paper and make up a story. My stories were very Kafkaesque and a preparation for future inventions in literature. Outside in the waiting room there was a young black chap with whom I exchanged experiences and we laughed so much tears were flowing down our cheeks. He had come to be shrunk because of depression, but when we laughed together we realized that much pain and depression come from having no relationship with people of like minds and temperament, that many people were perfectly healthy and alive and simply needed friendship and companions.

The day of my examination came and just to be on the safe side I tried to stay up all night and look wan. I applied liberal doses of talcum powder so that I would look as white as possible. The chaps examined me and said I seemed be healthy. Then they asked me to strip down and I had to reveal my body, deeply bronzed from weeks at the Serpentine Lido, while my face had this artificial white mask.

'You seem like a healthy specimen,' the doctor said, admiring my tan. 'Any problems apart from these dream disturbances?' (These seemed not to bother him a bit since mental stuff is always a bit vague and can be knocked out of you.)

'A duodenal ulcer,' I added hopefully.

He quickly searched for confirmation in the doctor's report and found it . . . 'Ah yes,' he added, as if he had hooked a good fish only to have to throw it back in the water.

Pushing my luck, I added, 'The doctor said if I stick to a careful diet it will go away . . . in a few years.'

'A few years, hmmmnn!' Not good news. You haven't time to make a special diet in the middle of the Korean war. Ulcer sufferers are a bloody nuisance. *Grade Four*!!! No dreary khaki uniform for me. The ulcer had saved me further incarceration.

When I was removed from polite society I was an avid fan of certain kinds of music and my tastes were becoming more and more eclectic. I would swing wildly from classical with a devotion to Chopin's piano études to Stan Kenton, Count Basie, Milt Jackson, Gerry Mulligan. Aaron Copland, whose marvellously atmospheric 'El Salon Mexico' inspired fantasies of distant lands. Darius Milhaud, whose 'Creation of the World' was the most marvellously haunting, exotic thing I had ever heard. Peggy Lee and Ella, Chet Baker, and of course Dave Brubeck. Now in those days there was much experimentation and by sixteen I was already an experimentalist, liking the bizarre, weird, surreal – what was called avant garde. Brubeck had made a record called 'Fugue on Bop Themes' which was a really clever evocation of Bach and quite thrilling to listen to. I would play it over and over again, but in later years it was deleted and I could never find it. Kenton's experiments made for good listening and 'City of Glass' was still my favourite meditation record, which would send me into a kind of trance and I would conjure up any variety of bizarre scenarios. I had a predilection for jazz played with cellos and violins – an interesting marriage that produced very stirring offspring.

Another fave was the music from the film *The Wild One* with Brando, who of course was our representative of youth, along with such older figures as Anthony Quinn, James Cagney, Bogart, Ladd, definitely Jack Palance in anything. We were fed a regular diet of gangster movies to keep our spirits up. Lesser figures we also liked as they gave good value, like Dan Duryea, Richard Widmark, Tony Curtis, but not James Dean. Adults seemed to like Dean as if he represented what they thought was youth, but his snivelling whine was not to our taste. We went for non-complaining, tough, wise-cracking, resolute, two-fisted, funny, but not 'problem child', oh no, we couldn't take that. Big on *Carmen Jones*; that Preminger adaptation of *Carmen* was the cleverest thing he ever did and brought opera to millions who might never have heard or understood it. We all revelled in it and thought it amazing. That was the general consensus in Stamford Hill, so it must have had an effect. 'Stand up and fight until you hear the bell, trade blow for blow, make those punches tell' – stirring words.

Johnnie Ray struck a particular dart in my heart and his eerie, high-pitched cry reached into my soul. I bought all his records and looked forward to the next one. Why did it touch me so much? The words were good, the music strange and the delivery a touch cute with hermaphroditic overtones. Yes, men can cry. That was good. I took my girlfriend to the Palladium to see him and we worshipped at the Ray shrine. He was somehow perfect. Slim, beautiful, flawed with a hearing aid and sexually dubious. We all felt protective, as if he was expressing some part of us.

Fast Forward to 1984

Many years later I happened to be in Los Angeles and noticed in the weekly listings Johnnie Ray singing at the Bar and Grill at the crossroads of Hollywood and Vine, and I just had to go and pay a visit. It proved to be a very moving experience, pulling me back over the years.*¹ It was Olympic Festival time and there was a huge arts festival; participants were asked to submit a production or work that in some way suggested and reflected the Olympic spirit. Of course, no one would create something for such an event, but the Japanese did bring a Greek play, their version of *Medea*, while I recreated my version of *Agamemnon* for a black company, since I felt that the American blacks were fitter, stronger, more physically alert and better-voiced than their white compatriots, who were used to doing plays where you had to have your ears on stalks to hear the crap they were saying, which wasn't very interesting when you did hear it. Also, the blacks were a community and had a camaraderie that I thought would make a great 'chorus'. I was proved right. They *were* a splendidly cohesive chorus and I could have cast the production two or three times over, there were so many actors, and so talented and eager.

It was a powerfully emotive experience for me to think that here I was in California, working with black actors who were alert in their bodies and minds and could move whichever way I wanted, and that I was teaching and choreographing them. They were watching me and my assistant, Barry Philips, who played the herald so brilliantly in the London production. Barry performed a mimed run-on-the-spot for five minutes before speaking, since we wished to suggest the journey the herald would have had to make – he is first spotted as 'a herald, running from the shore'. He ran with his chest pushed out, and hips locked in one position and legs moving like pumps behind him. This is very exciting when done well and Barry did it very well, accompanied by a drum. He was in the centre of the chorus, running his heart out, and the chorus were all around him, but gradually as he got nearer they retreated further back and on he went running, pounding the deck with bare feet, sweat spraying off him and the chorus chanting, 'Nearly there,' the drum beating to the rhythm of his feet and breaking up into every kind of rhythm possible. Then the drum stopped and you heard only his breath, his lungs, young and clear with their fierce emission of breath, no wail or fatigue in it, an optimistic breathing and then his feet steady, one two, one two, one two, one two, one two, one two. Now the drums came cracking back

* See *Overview* for the full story.

into time with his feet. It was as if he had been on the wrong side of the moon and lost radio contact, for the drum was now going at speed, whipping those muscles on to further feats of triumph. Full, personal, triumphal energy, the energy of youth, of life, of the desire to impart great news, of the *marathon*.

The herald finished his run and now breathed heavily, sweat releasing itself easily from his wide pores. The chorus, impressed, breathed with him as if they too could be part of the race and had vicariously shared it. Then in a voice which I can still hear and which reminded me of the effect of the young Jonathan Pryce as Agamemnon all those years ago, Barry let out a great tenor 'Ooooooh, this good soil of Argoooooos!' Whether the run had loosened up his voice box or diaphragm I would not know, but he was like a human organ and his lungs squeezed out of him an avalanche of power as he delivered one of the most enthralling speeches I have ever heard.

If anyone thinks this is nostalgic scratching for the old times, let me say that I have proof on tape and would be glad to let anyone hear this formidable and grandiose performance which was Barry at his best. He was Greek, heroic, sculptured, obsessively fit, like an athlete. Yet seldom would anyone give this gifted artist work. I did as much as I could – he created Les in *East* and Eddy in *Greek*; was Laertes in *Hamlet* and a marvellous one too, plus some unforgettable cameos. The strange thing was that since he 'created' the roles in our productions he always seemed tailor-made for the part.

After about seven or eight years Barry and I moved apart. He wished to score his own successes, but nothing came his way and I think he grew bitter. How could anyone ignore this man? But I was forgetting the system of British theatre. Barry was a working-class athlete who always felt put down when he went for jobs and watched as far lesser actors got the part. Also Brit theatre at that time tended to work from the neck up with plenty of room in your pockets to shove those useless appendages, your hands.

Barry went to Los Angeles to try his luck and became my assistant when I was there. He was very good at this too and very helpful to the cast. Roger Smith played the herald and also excelled, with some helpful coaching from Barry. But Roger also generated his own sense of power. The show gradually came together and was as exciting as the one I had done in Hebrew in Israel. The battle scenes worked well and the movement and choral work were as good as I could hope for. Susan Loewenberg was the producer, having produced *Greek* two years earlier when it won several critics' awards, including best play. So now we were competing with some of the best in world theatre. From England came *Cyrano de Bergerac* with the esteemed Derek Jacobi and *Much Ado About Nothing*, neither of which seemed to have too much Olympic theme unless you count Cyrano's record-breaking nose. We, on the other hand, were presenting exactly what the festival seemed to feel it needed.

The reviews came out and slaughtered the play and production as if the critics couldn't bear the idea that blacks could create something special and highly defined. They had seen blacks for so long as janitors and dope dealers and finger-clicking, tap-dancing coons that the idea of them as a colourless or colour-blind Greek chorus was more than they could stomach. That a black company should be dealing with the ideas of Aeschylus – even with my 'improvements' – was anathema to them and they condemned their very virtues. Their trained and beautiful bodies were called muscle-bound, and no or little credit was given to their standard of acting, which I felt was very high indeed. Diana Summerfield as Clytemnestra was a powerhouse of delightful, playful and erotic charm. She was both beautiful and talented, and the chorus was equal to the chorus in Israel, where the production, virtually the same except for improvements in LA, had been hailed. I had thought it would be the surprise winner in LA and take everybody off balance. It was well scored with immaculately staged battles and choral speaking. I couldn't have done it better. Most of my colleagues seemed to enjoy the play and it was fortunate that Nick de Jongh from the *Guardian* came and, without knowing any of the background of LA and black prejudice, wrote a hell of a great review. I had it copied and sent to each member of the cast to buck up their spirits after the insults and patronizing they had from the LA critics. Here is the Herald's speech that Barry and subsequently Roger did so well.

On this good soil of Argos/ I never dared to dream that I would see my blessed earth again/ Great Agamemnon's coming back/ render him the welcome he deserves/ Troy has toppled down/ her shrines dissolved in dust/ her seed exterminated by/ chattering machines of death that spit from iron mouths/ by the hot breath of napalm/ scorching the sins that stank to heaven/ while howitzers screeched arias in the streets/ Ack Ack/ Ack Ack/ and dumb-dumb shells explode/ their scattering claws of steel explore men's veins and arteries/ and spread confusion in flying brains/ and guts that fell like hail and slimed the roofs/ a panoply of armour ripped the sky apart/ as Zeus unleashed missile after missile/ and anti missile missile missile/ equal to the weight of ten thousand tons of hate/ ploughed the fields/ destroyed the crops/ forever/ lay waste even the waste/ bore holes the size of mountains/ while our brave boys/ burning under a monstrous sun/ and seizing what they had/ gleaming bazookas/ Patton/ tanks like Trojan horses made from heavy steel/ rasped deadly snorts into the walls/ which fell like flaking skin/ that's nuclear scorched/ and Zeus laughed and laughed and spat out deadly gasses from his guts/ and men collapsed like flies/ heaved out their entire wet insides/ we sloshed around a slaughter house of guts/ then in we marched/ with masks of death/ protected 'gainst that burning breath around us/ grasping in fists our automatics proudly cocked/ small fat grenades packed in our crutch/ and ricocheted around the town our tuneful whistling bullets/ smooth bore/ cannon/ trench/ mortar/ shrapnel/ tommy gun/ and blow pipe/ **RAT TAT TAT TAT/ RAT TAT TAT TAT/ KA BOOM/ KA BLAST/ KA BLAM/ SPLAT! PHUTT! SMASH! PHAM!!! WOW!** Watch! them! Watch them! Stampede of footless bodies/ trailing like snails/ their last remaining drops of bloody spore/ for target practice we took them/ and watched them as they clawed the walls/ and cried Ma Ma with lipless mouths/ then slid into their raw and running juices/ Meanwhile outside the town/ beneath the deep/ and surfacing like black and angry sharks/ a fleet of submarines/ torpedo boats with armour/ so intense/ it hurts to speak it/ gun boats too/ in skins of iron opened their deadly jaws/ and belched a hail of delayed action fission shells/ to mop up what we leave/ and soften little knots of fierce resistance/ huddled in the hills like scorpions/ and watched them fry alive in holes/ and then our king/ our Agamemnon/ in the front/ with only his bare hands/ and at his side ringing against their skulls like truth/ his sword and sabre/ rapier/ scimitar and cutlass/ dagger/ battle-axe and mace/ his trusted knuckle-duster that he likes/ just all good plain steel/ cold hard honest naked steel/ he kept on never tiring/ all alone except a regiment or two to keep him company/ deter annoying hands from bothering him/ with toys that spray at lightning speed fine strands of steel/ that slice to ribbons all unfortunates that go too near our king/ our beloved and holy Agamemnon/

It's over now/ the dead will never rise again/ no point in crying over life's unkindness/ pack up your troubles/ our losses do not balance out our gains/ give thanks to God for what he's won/ my speech is done.

When I was adapting *Agamemnon*, I found that there was something onomatopoeic about certain words which seemed to convey the essence of what was said and flowed into what I felt was a Greek sound, even if we were speaking English. They exploded off the tongue like the destructive power of the machines they described.

I remember writing this speech in a country cottage one morning and it flowed out of me without any hesitation. While this is not necessarily a guarantee of creative genius, it might suggest that you have hit a chord in your being. And everything flows. By introducing modern weaponry I intended to make the speech sound more Greek, since the weapons were so bizarrely christened with names like bazookas and napalm, nuclear and fission. They seemed not only to fit in but to express the brutal rage of war. I tried to weld the two together and for me it worked without that jarring modernism which I can't bear, when you see a classic dressed up in army togs and they're still using old references.

There is a second part to the Herald's speech which is altogether in a different key and again flowed from me with ease, as if it were writing itself. Of course I had a literal translation to work from and I enjoyed adapting it. I think it one of the most descriptive passages I have written. The Herald describes the catastrophe at sea:

Not quite so fortunate/ a storm did hit the fleet/ the first day out/ the last crap on the beach/ the sails repaired/ hoist up the rig/ release the hawsers/ a soft wind fills our sails/ like the giant cheeks of Cyclops' ass/ all's well/ the sea's as calm as thick as syrup/ today the sky a halcyon sheet of baby blue/ deceptive calm/ too quiet/ this smooth untroubled stillness/ eyes claw the skies/ same small puff of wind/ so gently pushing us out/ as if perhaps into the ring . . . then one black night/ we felt a team of elephants begin to move beneath our bows/ that sudden lurch which brings our supper foully back into our mouths/ *(Sound of ship's bell)* The sea began to boil and rage/ and waves the size of cliffs came roaring at us/ ship smashed ship like butting rams/ stampeding/ still it raged and foamed/ old Neptune's nightmares make him thrash around down deep/ in some infernal tortured sleep/ whilst up/ the sky fell down in chunks of hail like bullet spray/ and screamed and howled/ white veins of lightning twisted on its face/ and in each neon flash/ we saw our faces whiter than the scathing foam/ then suddenly it stopped/ old fishy Neptune turned around/ went back to sleep/ the stars peeked out again behind the scuddering clouds/ and blinked a bit/ as if not sure/ and as the dawn rose we saw the Aegean thick with bloated Greeks/ like flowers scattered by the wind/ and lazy sharks unbelieving their good luck/ were having breakfast/ the fleet was smashed except for us/ we sailed through that infernal nightmare/ with not one timber sprung.

I like an element of bathos, going from the sublime to the ridiculous and imagining after the destruction of most of Agamemnon's fleet the sound of 'ordinary', cosy household words like 'breakfast' and the image of fat, sleek sharks having a calm nibble. There is nothing more enjoyable than catching your mind in flight and tethering it to your will for the few moments or hours that it is so. I have never really sat down like an office-clerk writer with that discipline I so admire and said 'I am now going to write from nine till twelve, have lunch and then do two more hours.' I think what you then submit has that same rhythm to it, the same dreary linear routine sequence of events, but I may be proved wrong and I am sure that some works are written by writers who put themselves into a state of mind.

However, I think scheduled work is best used for interpretation and acting. There you must turn up, and you have the lines which always set up a chord of response, but inspiration will often come when it will and in a relaxed state when there is no commission; however, there is always an exception to the rule, since *West* was written under commission. Normally I write when I sit in some place which has nothing to do with writing but may be used for another function, like a café. I am one of that breed of café writers, difficult of course in Britain where our utilitarian habits see the café as a place to eat in and then get out. Not as a place for congregation, thought, camaraderie, study, as it is for our European cousins who seem to have a greater need than us for such pleasures as sitting and enjoying quiet contemplative moments. We need cafés to meet friends and talk without the constant badgering and bullying of the British sadist, who loves nothing better than a bit of power with his ritual of rules; minimum charge between this hour and that and you can't sit here; lunches only and you can't do that and no, we don't serve drinks between this time and that; and no, we have no food, we've stopped serving, and sorry but you *must* drink up and so on; the dreary litany continues and so this very lack of social opportunity creates a weird and sour Brit for whom the pub is either a battleground or a boozer.

I have a theory that the British pub has harmed more than it's helped. Since the young are banned from the grotty pub, they have little chance to model themselves on anyone. Instead they tend to have a pack attitude, hang around city street corners or crowd the plastic emporium of McDonald's until the age when they are allowed to booze, but the pub has not gone hand in hand with the idea of communication or fraternization. The boozers' absence of children, unknown in any French café, also coarsens the adult, so that the pub takes on the air of a 'drinking den' for blokes. Women must keep their own company rather than face sitting in one of these places. Heysel Stadium's riots are not far off.

So after this peregrination I come to the conclusion that you must write at home, but when the desire grabs you, and in this respect I have been lucky in having a career as an actor of some sort. As a result, writing has not been the prime moving factor upon which hung my fortunes or fame, and this has enabled me to see it as a mistress rather than a wife. A release rather than a task. I think writing should always be fun and I have treated it this way, as an adventure with language, not a chore. Eschewing naturalism, I had no need to reproduce slavishly the speech patterns of Joe Bloggs in Barnet, but could invent a language to fit the characters as I saw them; even if East Enders didn't use metaphor or occasionally lapse into verse, they could in my plays. My characters in *West* and *East* had limited ambitions, but my desire to write passages in verse was an attempt to expand their vision and let the emotions articulate themselves, to stylize and to reveal by exaggeration.

Also, there is the sheer joy of language itself which any wordsmith feels when soaring and exciting him or herself by the very intoxication with words. There is a power in the language that allows you to play like a kid with fireworks. There is a danger in juxtaposing ideas, placing words out of context, teasing convention, playing with form, stubbing the toe of conventions, cocking a snook at what passes for tradition, escaping from everyday representation. Language as a passion. Language as energy, exuberant, raucous, dirty, sexy, bestial, offensive, lyrical; language as a sexual drive, language fuelled by eroticism, words meant to tease, excite and throw, hurl into the air, smash into the ears; language as rage, revenge for the milky, toady junk that has infected your ears for years; language as a self-portrait, as a means of speaking who you are; language as an assault weapon and language to give vent to all the frustration in your life when the only thing you have left is the language in your skull. Eventually your last resort. Needing no job, no acceptance for audition, no partner, no money, just a pen and your brain. Your language untamed by coercion, unless you are writing with a partner – and what kind of language is that, that you can write with a partner? What individuality can be present in team work? Although they say Shakespeare finished off other authors' works. Language as graffiti, to say whatever you wish, to back yourself and not cringe afterwards when you see what you wrote in heat. Not to be fearful and censor yourself, for language is a weapon to hurt and maim and wound, and to expect back the same and worse; but language also to caress and stimulate, to make love with and to express. But no café to write in!

Los Angeles was good for this, since there were scores of the most wonderful diners to write in. I could sit in a booth with a high back, ensconced and cocooned in these opulent people's cafés. The USA makes the best environment for the working classes, like diners you bring the whole family to, where you are treated like a king and spend not much more than you would in England in your dirty, slovenly, greasy, tabloid-chewing workman's café, which is as palatable as a Victorian doss house. So I would sit there and write on a daily basis whatever popped into my head while drinking endless coffee and dreaming, since in America you have space to daydream.

So Agamemnon was caned in LA since the critics there weren't used to what I was giving them. Although they seemed to respond well to *Greek*, they resisted a branch of the same tree with an original Greek stance. This rather depleted our not very large theatre, but the actors soldiered on and loved the work. They were above all, and very much above all, glad not to be playing *blacks*. They were classical actors and warriors and performers and would seldom have the chance again to play in the theatre. LA is basically a two-horse town with a couple of big theatres and the rest a whole beehive of tiny ninety-nine-seat holes where actors showcase so as not to rot away. Equity turns a blind eye to this form of exploitation, figuring that it is better to work for nought than not exercise your art. However, there are some producers who will never step out of this free pool of actors, and whose theatres are built specially to cater for this free-fall; producers who with a tiny bit of will could legitimize their efforts but will not when all this talent is there for free. Very often good work is done, but basically it is bad to loathsome, since free acting is now a fact of life. Actors work to get their rocks off and when a job comes up the stage manager goes on, or an assistant sometimes with the book, and so the core of the rot is that it is actually *bad news* if an actor gets a job to support himself. The producer's welfare lies in the hope of the actor being *unemployed*. Now can you imagine in your wildest dreams the condition that makes it preferable for a player to be *out of work*? *It is mind boggling.*

The show wound up and on the last night we had a small party at the house of the producer, who must have lost so much money that we were reduced to take-away pizzas in cardboard boxes. The actors even had to give back the marvellous track pants we bought from the trendy LA store, Parachute. There was talk about the show going to London, since it did look and sound marvellous, and for a while there was a minor flirtation with a producer who liked the feel of it, but in the end he ducked out, like a lot of those cautious types who like to stick within the confines of their own limitations. The actors talk about it to this day and refer to it as the high point of their theatrical lives. I wish there was some way I could regroup them. They returned to playing blacks once more or dope fiends, tap dancers and muggers.

1954

The last time I had seen Johnnie Ray was in London when I was about seventeen. Then I was doing desultory and casual work while determining what mysteries I should unleash on the world. I went back to the Lyceum with thoughts of the theatre in my mind. I flirted with the possibility of becoming an actor, but had no idea how or where and felt there was something else I had to do first. I put it off, but still developed the yearning. I was drawing away from the simple Stamford Hill mob with their useless and usual obsessions. I even started meeting new people who had nothing to do with that area. I was still going from job to job, trading jobs as often as once a week and sometimes lasting one morning only. I hated and loathed work that didn't engage my mind and was manual, trivial and boring, but I also knew that I would lose my mind if I kept going from place to place like a yo-yo. I worked in a warehouse in the East End lifting and stocking rolls of cloth, thinking that one day I would be a wholesaler or merchant. I got to know what fabric shantung was and could identify colours like eau-de-Nil. Then in desperation I worked in a small button shop in Commercial Road which was old and charming and I lasted a few days; I did Smart and Weston menswear for a couple of months in Shaftesbury Avenue, now metamorphosed into a McDonald's. It was a grotty shop in my opinion, and I got to loathe the cheap merchandise. It helped when you liked what you were selling; still the staff were matey and I was becoming adept as an arse-licking salesman.

Then I spent a hideous time in a rotten flea-bag of a shop in Edgware Road which was as loathsome as it's possible to be. It was run by a dirty old sod who sat in a corner like a spider . . .

> LES: He'd sit there so greasy you could fry him, in that dirty little back room he'd be watching – having his crummy little tea break . . . ''ere, Les, go get us a cake will ya, son . . . a chocolate eclair or something' . . . 4.15 His looked-forward-to tea break in a day that poured down boredom like yellow piss . . . His frog's eyes bulging in case you didn't sell the shop-soiled crew neck six sizes too big to some innocent black cunt. 'Yeah, it fits you beeeauutiful! Lovely shade, it goes with anything' . . . He spits as he rushes out of the back room like a great huge dirty spider with bits of eclair sticking to his revolting fat lips . . . 'Fuck me! Les, we got to top yesterday's figure,' he squelched from the side of his mouth, a hiss like a rat's fart . . .

This extract from Les's soliloquy pays adequate testament to how one can pretend retrospectively that all these years were research. Edgware Road was like pus from a wound that ran off the West End.

I never liked it and I don't really know why. It was a no-man's land that drained Marble Arch and was oozed into by Paddington. That area always did seem strange and alien to me, and perhaps it was, whereas Baker Street and Marylebone and even Hampstead seemed OK. Although sometimes Hampstead was also awfully depressing in spite of the heath. There was something deadeningly middle class and terribly unnourishing about the whole area, but it was OK to visit, I suppose, if you wanted to have a coffee by the pond or go to the Everyman Cinema, where I first saw Kurasawa's films, and there was that wonderful café where everyone played chess; now *that's* a café.

The salesman routine was making me ill. My ulcer was screaming at me with all this standing around and hanging there like a corpse supported by the counter where were displayed the torture relics, shirts, ties, cufflinks, collar studs, socks, oh how many times did I straighten the ties and straighten the socks, do something quickly lest you lose hold of your life? Quickly put the sleeves neatly between the jackets while your brain rots and a little more crumbles off the mountain that is your mind. While others studied Latin or Greek, medicine or architecture, drama or music, ballet or science, chemistry or poetry, I was straightening sox, sox, sox and more sox. One day the filthy wretch 'let me go' and I washed myself clean for weeks. His ghastly little slum store stayed like it was for a few more years, then rotted into an ooze along with the guv'nor.

Then something in Dalston and quickly out of there to a special place which I found purely by a chance ad. It was a very exclusive shop called W. Bill, a rather elegant name in South Molton Street. As soon as I entered it I knew that I had definitely come up in the world. No more greasy, farty, cheapo menswear, but a famous shop full of the most expensive cashmere sweaters in the world. Mrs Shepherd, the elegant manageress, showed me around the sweet little store which had *no* counters but desks where the salesgirl and ladies sat. Here the customers examined these beautiful, silky, soft things that I had never seen or touched before. I was enchanted by it, and lo and behold after a few days they gave me a cashmere sweater of my own to wear in the shop. I wore it proudly and stood in front of the fire, which I would stoke up a bit and wait for customers. In the beginning I wasn't allowed to serve unless we were very busy, so I'd run errands to Savile Row, collecting patterns of cloth when a customer wanted to see tweeds or cheviots, worsteds or cashmere cloth, Donegals, Harrises, and all other homespun goods. I would take off at a trot to Savile Row, arrive with my intro from W. Bill; I would exchange the time of day and take my time coming back, stopping off for a cappuccino. Once back I would put the kettle on, throw some biscuits on a plate and serve the tea. Then I stood in front of the fire once more, admiring my quiff in the mirror and looking at the talent strolling past the shop.

It was an idyllic time and at last I liked and respected the people I was working with and their well-made and high-quality goods. I got to know all the best makes and could tell one from another. Cashmere is fine goat's wool which tends to come from India and Tibet and comes in various grades, but theirs in the shop was the finest and the touch of it was like silk across your hand. I had good conversations with all the staff except for one suburban yob I didn't care for, nor he for me. The salesladies, Mrs Shepherd and Miss Fitzgerald, were the epitome of English good taste and the likes of Ava Gardner would be popping in and pulling their sweaters off in front of you in the back room. People spent money like millionaires and it was common even then to take £200 from a customer. Sweaters were about £40 each since they were still a huge luxury after the war and may have had a heavy tax on them. I started to get to know the other salesgirls in the street and as they passed by the window I would dash out, saying, 'Oh, I'd better pick up some samples from Savile Row.' I'd wear my four-button pin-stripe suit for work with a stiff collar.

As all good things must come to an end, I was sacked for nothing more than some minor infringement of duty and calling Miss Fitzgerald 'Fitzy'. I did it because I felt very comfortable with these people, but they all thought I was getting too familiar. I also had personal problems at home which were getting to me. So one day my Mayfair idyll was over, but at least I had seen a better life.

From South Molton Street I deigned to go to Harry Fisher of Regent Street, who made shirts to measure and was at least in the class I was now used to: I became like one of those servants who works only for gentlefolk. While Harry Fisher was elegant and expensive it had not quite the class of W. Bill, but Harry himself was one of the nicest and most fatherly men I had met. He was at all times charming to me and even shared his home-made bortsch with me on occasions. I managed to survive for a while there, although I was thoroughly bored by the limited scope. Harry would always defer to me: when salesmen came in with their long boxes of silk ties he would ask me what I thought or he'd kid the sales rep and say that I was now the buyer.

However, there was a fly in that ointment, too – another salesman who had the terrible habit of interfering when I was making a sale if the customer happened to be a pretty girl, and we did get a lot of them buying ties for their boyfriends. This bothered me so much that I started, like Hamlet, keeping a journal and burying all my radio-active thoughts in there. It gave me some relief, but I think they saw me too often writing away furiously with a big scowl on my face. It reached such a pitch of animosity that Harry had to 'let me go', but he did it with tears in his eyes – I felt he truly loved me as a son, but couldn't bear the bad feeling in his charming little store.

Then a brief excursion to Hampstead, to a little shop belonging to an ex-boxer. It was unusually drab and very quiet. A fabric ware-house in Wigmore Street, a dose of travelling salesman for a Portland Street firm when I went from one dress manufacturer to another, and then a spate of selling space in an advertising magazine which was obviously a con. The governor showed you all the people who had advertised their wares, like Harrods and Fortnum and Mason and D. H. Evans, and you thought to yourself, 'Oh well, this is easy,' and off you went trying not to feel uncomfortable in the knowledge that the salesman got fifty per cent of the take. The first man I approached was a simple soul in Hackney who actually bought some space. I was over the moon and counting fortunes, but it was 'No' from then on. This experience came in very useful later for my play *Lunch*, whose hero was a space salesman.

> MAN: I'm different, I sell the promise of something – the intan-
> gible mystery of an empty space – pure white virgin, untouched,
> waiting for a buyer to claim – to insert his identity, his wares . . .
> his amazing declarations . . .
> WOMAN: A trade book . . . A trade book! You sell space in a
> trade book?
> MAN: I promise trade in a space book.
> WOMAN: How, promise?
> MAN: When the book is full – when the white spaces are bought
> – those infinite columns of expected wealth – I sell the book.

WOMAN: To whom?
MAN: To them – to the clients themselves, the space buyers, so they can gaze at themselves immortalized forever in block letters – electro-type on quarto double-weight.
WOMAN: Lovely!

From now on I was leaping from place to place, getting jobs that would last a day or two, then I would drift off at lunch and never come back. My will power and stamina were at their lowest ebb. I was mightily depressed and sitting in one of the many coffee bars, probably the Kaleidoscope in Gerrard Street, I decided I had had enough. I couldn't bear it any more. I was, not surprisingly, going out of my mind. Wally, a friend of mine in Stamford Hill, used to talk all the time about going abroad and it was one thing that I desired above everything. We would devise plans and think of living in Paris like bohemians; I had given up my stiff collars and taken to wearing black roll-neck sweaters on week nights.

Meanwhile I decided to go back into fabrics and joined Sanderson Wallpapers and Fabrics. It was like joining an old Dickensian company with its hierarchy of salesmen and a supervisor called Mr Budd, a bloated, red-faced cur who was nevertheless fair and only kept me in the warehouse for a short time. I had to learn the stocks, but one day I dressed to kill in my best French-tailored suit by Diamond Bros, who made the sharpest suits in London and it was designed to my style. I came in looking like a *Vogue* plate and they put me upstairs in the showroom with the clients. I felt a surge of pride again, was becoming a mini-expert in the field of fabric, design and colour, and would advise on all aspects, showing the clients Jacobean design over Regency and generally having not a bad time. It was a bit dead-endish since I would never take orders or really design, as they had trained people for that, but it was one of the most pleasant jobs I had had. I met the young John Oliver, who was to become the famous designer, and we became rather good friends – he often came over to Manor House. Mum liked him a lot since he was such a friendly and sensitive youth.

Just at this time I heard that Burberry's were taking on experienced salesmen in their PX stores in Europe – these were stores on the American army bases catering for soldiers and their families – and that many of the chaps were going out to work in Germany, France,

Italy, Iceland and other PX stores where Burberry's had a concession. Now Burberry was a very important name, but the clothes, in my opinion, were very crudely tailored and not befitting the name of Burberry. I dashed to the interview, was thought presentable and lo and behold I got the job. No more bouncing around like a demented flea, for now I was leaving England.

Discovering Europe – 1955

It was a great thrill when, after a couple of weeks' 'training' at Ruislip army base, I left Victoria for the boat-train to Wiesbaden. I was also very sad since it seemed like the end of an era. I had brought my notebook, which was becoming a regular feature, and as the train slid out of Victoria I wrote about Ma and Pa. The sea journey made me sick, but now I was excited all the time. I reached Wiesbaden and met Mr Collins, who had devised the way we would operate in Europe. He seemed to be the brains of the operation. We had supper in an old hotel, since Germany was still smouldering from the war, and I recall the huge bed with a big duvet, something I had never seen before. It was 1955. I was eighteen. Germany seemed weird and gloomy – I was really seeing what it was like before the war, since it hadn't changed much. There seemed little bomb damage but there was a strange atmosphere of being abroad in another time. I walked around in the morning amazed at everything, at the signs, the bars, the strange cafés. At the time I spoke not a word of German, but would soon be speaking like a native.

Burberry's decided that it needed a body in Bitburg, near Trier. It was a tiny hamlet in which there was a US army base. Mr Collins decided to drive us both there and we set off in the afternoon. We passed through Luxembourg and made the mandatory call in the local street of bars where the hookers operated; like all good tourists, we didn't partake but liked to be near the action. I was terribly enthralled by all this; it seemed as if I had taken a trip to another planet and I could never get bored or depressed – this was really the adventure of my life. We stayed overnight and the next day arrived in Bitburg, where I was shown a little room in a local house. I would sometimes eat with the family at night if I wished, since this was the style in those days.

The PX store is usually a huge area devoted to making the serv-icemen feel as if they are still at home and for me it was a double bliss since I could feel as if I was in America!! Oh my God, I could eat hamburgers again and smell all those wonderful Yankee smells that seem to permeate their stores, smells of soap and packaging and candy, sweet-sickly smells and plasticky artificial smells and smells of vanilla and bread and magazines and Hershey bars. It was all so American. In my lunch break I would sit in the canteen and absorb the atmosphere.

I was starting to become more sociable and more knowledgeable and I would take myself to the library at night and pack in some reading. Even the books seemed bigger and they had these thick covers protected with strong plastic and solid to touch. My col-leagues in the store were pleasant without being too friendly to me, which seemed usual; and after a couple of drinking nights in the town they soon took off without me and even let me spend Christmas on my own, which wasn't the greatest fun. I hated and still hate being alone and soon found a sweet young woman, a single parent called Analise. We would meet after work and have a frenzied cuddle and she'd make some coffee and I'd go home. In those days that was excitement enough. I was OK in my digs and could sit in and read or go to my local café where old German widows would sit drinking schnapps, but at least it wasn't a pub. I could also read or write there, but I didn't write so much in cafés then – only if I was lachrymose.

In the huge PX store the soldiers would come in for a suit and you'd measure them up carefully, or you'd have a suit with a sleeve four inches too long and a waist five inches too narrow, so don't squeeze the waist with the tape. I didn't like sticking the metal end of the tape between their sweaty legs and devised a way of asking them to place it in the appropriate spot. The chaps had to wait about four to six weeks for the crummy suit to come back and they had no fittings, which is not the really classy way of making a suit to meas-ure. In a way it was made to their proportions, but if it came back fitting it was a miracle. It always had to be altered.

I hung around and rapped more and more with the young Yan-kees. Like all youngsters we discussed things out of our depth in literature and art and the meaning of life and I would spend more time with the guys in the canteen. This pissed off my two colleagues, but they tolerated me. We were all being paid eighteen pounds per week, which in those days was a fortune, and I was saving half of it.

It was a cold winter and I crept in and out of my lonely state, becoming more and more like an eccentric recluse except for Analise. In the library one day I saw a book by a man with a strange name, Franz Kafka. I read *Metamorphosis* for the first time there in Germany and connected it with Germany, with the environment, the atmosphere and my state of mind. I thought it was the most marvellous story and I could at last really identify with something. The beetle.

Some evenings we would go to Trier and, like everybody else, just sit in the coffee house all night talking and eating cakes and drinking lemon tea. I bought a smart German raincoat and felt most distinguished. The days passed until the terrible Christmas, when I was inconsolably alone for three days and nearly went bananas. When I returned to work one of the thin, mean-faced staff, who looked prime Nazi material and constantly made remarks to undermine you, said, 'Did you pass a nice Christmas?' and because I was in a rotten and evil mood I asked what difference it made to him, or words to that effect. He turned on his heel and spun off. While I did not like him, he was my only ally in the PX store and I tried to make up, but to no avail. I bought a lighter with a tortoiseshell case, I remember, which I treasured for years after. You could buy strangely exotic things like lighters in the most beautiful cases.

One day Analise was passing my stand and an evil, thick-necked brute, who was a bullying bastard, started shouting at her to get back to her work and not talk to me. He was obviously used to authority and with his shaved head and cold, vicious eyes I could really see him in an SS uniform. I left my stand and told him in no uncertain way not to shout at a woman, since coward that I could be I knew moments of fearlessness when roused to anger and was prepared to act on them. Analise dashed off to her stand and he warned me and I warned him and the upshot of it was that I was shifted back to Wiesbaden! Which is a hell of a town with a marvellous café in Friedrichstrasse where Dostoievsky used to sit and write and I was happy once more. I found an old pre-war hotel which had a Victorian cosiness to it and downstairs you could eat the marvellously delicious oxtail soup. A veritable feast. I was happy in my room.

I went to work in the PX store the following day and got into the same routine I had in Bitburg. The people who worked there were of a fairly dreary variety and of course there was little I could say or do with them, but they were friendly enough and on the first night I was taken to the *Spielhaus*, the local gambling casino, where we walked around clutching our pfennigs and Deutschmarks and occasionally being rather daring and putting a mark on the red or the black. This was a new world, and something I had never seen, nor had I dared to imagine that such opulence and glitter with its shining crystal chandeliers and elegance could exist as a place to gamble in.

The days trudged their weary dreary way in the unspeakable little stall in the PX store but I gradually found amusements that had been absent in Bitburg. There was a great park in the middle of Wiesbaden and the long street of Friedrichstrasse where I could walk and be amazed at the amount of things in the German shops already, ten years after the war. I'd compare prices like any tourist and sit at a table in the great café and be served elegantly and watch the world and watch people and all in all find it most civilized. It's terrible how civilized countries are turned into mortuaries by people with ideologies. I am sure that Germany was once one of the most civilized places in the world to live. There was an opera house and theatre in the town next to the *Spielhaus*, which was opposite my favourite café, so you could say that all senses were taken care of. An old movie house would run early Ealing comedies which the German Anglophiles would shriek at and you'd discuss the film afterwards in the coffee house. All this was very different from Manor House and I could see why each time I went back I would get more and more depressed with London and its sheer lack of possibilities for a young person who wished simply to be a part of the world and not somehow stuck.

During one of my visits to the great café, I happened to meet a German lady who was the wife of a high-ranking officer in the American army. Her name was Fay. In those far-off days I had what I might dare to interpret as a romantic streak; in other words I would fall in love heavily once I got going. Is this a more feminine aspect of oneself, this ease of letting go and crumbling into the abyss? Anyway, I found myself becoming involved with this very pretty, slim woman, who at thirty was to my eighteen at a very tempting and knowing age. We would drive around in her huge Chevy and go to nightclubs and see acts. She would insist on treating me, although I wasn't getting badly paid; I felt very cosseted and feminine and a little spoiled. We saw each other more and more frequently and I was able to talk to her in the frankest possible way, in the way a teenager might about his desires and ambitions. She took all this to heart as if my quest or pain was hers.

In the meantime I had developed an unfortunate taste for the *Spielhaus* and went two or three times a week, becoming an old hand at the tables since I had developed my own simple double-up system. I would wait for the red or black to come up twice and then back the opposite. I worked out that it must come up red or black at least once in six throws, so if you backed the red after two blacks had come up and black came up a third time, you could double up four times. I noticed through constant observation that a run of six or more for black or red was very, very rare. So while I did not win any fortune I could earn the equivalent of my wages. It meant sitting for a long time, but it was safe so long as I stuck to the play-on-the-third-throw rule and as a safety measure if it did come up another four times, then *stop*. Then start again, because if it did go past six it could conceivably go ten times and wipe you out.

I would stroll in, leave my coat and buy my chips. I'd sit at the table and order cigarettes, the German ones, and an old retainer would come and break the packet for me and tap a couple out to ease my taking a fag while concentrating on the table. After winning the equivalent of thirty marks, three quid in those days, I would quite happily take myself off with all the will power of a good gambler and go into town for a snack before going to my little hotel and sleep.

The rooms in the hotel were small and I could hear a couple making love in the next one. It all seemed part of the German experience. Everything fitted in to my lifestyle and needs. A good and fascinating woman, a wonderful street to stroll in with great coffee houses and a *Spielhaus*. What more could I ask? The job was terribly dreary and we would find ourselves with many quiet periods. Fay would pass by and smile, but because we had to be clandestine I would give the smallest nod. The guys would go mad around the stall and say, 'Cor, did you see that one?' and generally remark on passing females the way chaps do when protected by each other's presence. I kept shtumm, and never revealed my marvellous secret about my dearest Fay. Fay and I lived in her car. We talked in it and cuddled in the back of it and listened to music in it since she was mortally afraid of being seen.

One day, since business in Wiesbaden was so slack, the firm decided to lay off a few of the slouchers and the ones who were in Europe just to escape from home, like me. Fairly, they gave me a couple of weeks' notice and I didn't mind, since I had saved well over a hundred pounds, which to me felt like a thousand. I was going to use this money well and prepare for my future life as an actor. Of course I had as yet no idea of how this metamorphosis was going to take place, but take place it would. One does not know until the fated time how one feels about anything: not until the moment of departure do you feel the real pain and anguish. I was never to know by forward thinking how certain situations would affect me. I would say I felt OK now and plan some change without an inkling of the sense of the shock to come. I didn't know how I would feel about leaving Fay, since at the time she only felt like a rather nice woman whom I had fallen for like all the others I kept falling for in England.

Since I was going to leave Wiesbaden I decided to play the tables with just a dash more frequency than my cautious thrice-weekly, when I would always stop after winning thirty marks. Now I felt my system was strong enough to withstand a little expansion. I read that Dostoievsky used to play the same tables and made himself broke doing so. I walked up the path past the Opera House and made my usual contented and optimistic entrance – gambling does buoy up the spirits and put you into a challenging situation. I sat and played and as usual it worked for the first hour, but I would be leaving this haven of opportunity and while I would never blow my stash, I decided I might be a tad more adventurous. The red came up twice. I put not my usual ten marks but what the hell, twenty on the black. Red! Forty on the black. Red! Eighty on the black. Red! A hundred and sixty on the black. Red for the sixth time! Three hundred and twenty on the black, stop now, stop, you must stop, you're down 640 marks. Stop. The table is looking at you as you sweat over the decision. Everybody is backing black since this is an unusual roll. I have some money left, but don't double, claw half back. Stop. But if it comes up now? Go for it. Red again. It came up nine times. I went grey. All my saving and suffering in Bitburg, all the standing around and the slavish hours and the long winter months and the loneliness in my room at Christmas, and all the time I was saying it doesn't matter since you are saving money for your future, all pissed away in twenty minutes!

I was sick. I tried to leave nonchalantly and ignored the shaking heads of condolence from others who must have seen it all happen before. I was distraught and so, as often in such circumstances I decided to eat a pizza, which is always good for relaxing your thoughts. Then, late as it was, I woke up a German girlfriend, a young intellectual called Edith. She was a very smart young lady and wore her hair like a pudding basin, later to be a Beatle style. She consoled me and we sat up until four a.m. trying to get me over the shock. We tried to laugh it out and listened to the music on the radio. I was so grateful to Edith, since alone I don't know what I might have done.

Now work seemed more fruitless and more repugnant than ever, and all I could think of was getting out. I was nearly broke but I had a return ticket and two weeks' wages. I even tried to get work in order to stay near Fay, but it was half-hearted. I turned up at the PX and complained of being seriously ill. I said I had a 'heart attack', since I was prone to extraordinary flights of exaggeration. They insisted that I come in at least for a few days, but I just couldn't face those grim faces in that ugly little stand.

I passed the last days in a state of drift and at the weekend took the train to London. Some of the other redundant ones were returning too. Fay took me to the station. We had spent the evening at our café in Friedrichstrasse and I was kind of looking forward to going home and seeing Mum and telling her my adventures and waiting in the way one does for the next chapter in life to start. It was a midnight train to the Channel ferry. The countdown began. Why are such matters, the break-ups and upheavals familiar to everyone on earth, the great emotional storms that are so important, such beacons in one's life? At every station and airport in the world such scenes are enacted. People pass by hurrying to duty-free while the universe is collapsing for you. Only to you are these moments of such dramatic importance and they will go on and on; the world will continue and you will pick yourself up amidst the flotsam and jetsam and continue your meander to the end of your time. But for now it was the entire world. Fay parked the car near the station. We had about twenty minutes left. We kissed each other and held on for dear life. Suddenly the dam broke and I became horribly aware of what was happening.

I had day dreamed for much of my life and now it was the cold and final ending. I felt most awfully alone and lost without her; and she became the only thing I valued in my life. I could not stop myself expressing the most terrible grief and wept inconsolably as it surged through me like an enormous tidal wave.

I eventually got out of the car and walked to the station. The guys were waiting and we got on the train and their company soon eased the isolation. We got down to some serious card-playing for the rest of the journey to London. Manor House looked very grim.

'There's a divinity that shapes our ends, rough-hew them how we will.' I don't know if destiny has a part in it so much as certain conditions, influences, environment, shapes of the streets we live in, the house, all pushing one way, forging, moulding, building, and adversity too having its effect in that you work against it, struggle or fight, at each step make a small conquest of your mind and plight. The long council block like a prison block with the lift at one end. No balcony to sit out in the summer and no garden and so I'd lean over the balcony which was the walkway for all the tenants. Or, when it was too wet to go out, idly stare out of the window at the block opposite. Nothing much going on there, so I'd go to the park, which was and is a big, open lung, Finsbury Park, and good to walk through, but it abuts the dreariest stretches in the world. Finsbury Park seems always to be in perpetual decay, full of pram shops and rotted cinemas that for some inexplicable reason stand for years behind hoardings. Where are the shining stars of the Astoria Cinema now? On the other side is Harringay with its grim dog track where the hordes of men file away after the races in the long walk to Manor House tube. Horrid Harringay and its mile upon mile of ribbon-developed streets which syphon off from the main artery and drift away into infinity. Miles and miles of death and then the anonymous areas of Wood Green, Bounds Green, Palmers Green, whose very names bespeak the dread conformity, more urban Amazons flowing away into the distance, served by corner pubs and the ubiquitous newsagent and off-licence, the triumvirate of the soulless British life.

On the other side it is not so bad, since Hackney is made more interesting by its population mix, its more ancient origins, Greek and Turkish cafés, weird pubs with weekend music, but in those days pubs were never my concern – the few times I might have strolled in they seemed like morgues and while life outside was deadly enough I didn't need to visit the actual graveyards. I never got pissed, either, except by accident at a party. I think I only got into the habit when I was an actor going into the pub after a performance. I was pretty TT before then. Then we used to get a bit smashed at parties on gin and tonic or gin and orange, and not being accustomed I'd heave my guts out, which was always an awful feeling. I felt as if my whole insides were exploding and I couldn't breathe. I never understood how people could make a joke about something so awful.

Once I was working in Golden Square in a textile house called Garrigue and Sons as a cutter of those pattern bunches that you see in tailors' everywhere. How pathetic were the shreds of my skills – oh, Dad, why didn't you teach me those mysteries of tailoring? I might have had a good trade today! So I had these pinking shears and spent all day cutting little patterns and nursing an ulcer which was now a daily whinge. We had the firm's Christmas party and we all traipsed downstairs and got stuck into the booze. This was fun and much better than the work upstairs where the glass roof let the sun beat down relentlessly. I do remember that they were a nice group of people and didn't say anything when I slipped off early to go to the Serpentine for an afternoon swim. So this party got underway and I got slowly more and more drunk until I passed out in my own sick in the gents. I lay there for some time and then it got dark. It was cold on the concrete floor, but I eventually got up and went home. I had a good time.

Booze seems to be something that is wished on to you – no matter how revolting you think it is and how little interest you have in it, after a while it just seems to creep up on you and you can't avoid it. There was a Christmas years back in Soho when a club called the Caves de France was still operating, a really wonderfully homely, charming French-style bar where you were always welcome. It was like a sanctuary in my Soho days and I would always make a bee-line for it. I had met some actors in the Salisbury and I decided to show them my wonderful club. Well, I had made the discovery that a beer called barley wine was a lethal drink that did not swamp your insides with rivers of liquid since it was a small wine-glassful. It detonates as soon as it hits your stomach and sends glorious waves of well-being around you. In the French pub a few doors down it was a French beer called Pelforth.

So here we all were, mates at Christmas, and I still had the bag with my shopping from my favourite market, Berwick Street, including the nice black bread from Grodzinski's. I sat and ordered barley wines, stingos as they were called, and consumed about five. As a result I felt an almost transcendental bliss, an openness and affection for my chums – I would never get violent when pissed, but terribly affectionate and sloppy. I never understood then how the grape or hop, those wonderful releasers, could turn others into violent lunatics, especially some actors. We were rapping away and quaffing back the booze, and I thought I'm so happy with my friends I wanted to introduce Liz Shaul, a young mother of two with whom I had been living, to some of my mates. So I made a telephone call. 'Hey, it's Christmas, come and have a tipple in Soho.'

Three more beers went down the hatch and no food. I excused myself and went downstairs and passed out. Liz came and nobody knew where I was. Nobody thought to look downstairs where I lay semi-conscious to the world. They carried on drinking and talking and laughing and eventually left, thinking I must have gone for a walk. I picked myself up and staggered home. It was terrible to be reduced to such a state. I don't know why I didn't know exactly when too much would cripple me or when one more would tip me into this wonderful and carefree land. I never did manage it. Eventually I stopped the bad habit of drinking in a pub at lunchtime as we out-of-work actors did at one time. It seemed quite normal to meet and get slightly wobbly and then fall into a Chinese restaurant in Charing Cross Road. At least we were convivial and keeping the doldrums at bay.

Booze in the Theatre – 1962

In Dundee rep for the delightful Piers Haggard, where Lynn Redgrave made her début as Portia, we would go for a pub lunch and have not one but two beers and wonder why it all seemed ragged in the afternoon's rehearsal. I was sucked into the booze world of the Brit theatre, which I must say seemed fuelled on drink at that time, and I was slowly but surely sliding along the vomity path to oblivion. Dundee was a deadly hole anyway; I remember it as always grey. As I was coming in to join the company the old company were leaving. I ventured into the green room and there was a chap playing the piano. He had a surly and sulky face, as if the world revolved around his emotional centre. There were these horrendous reppy photos outside for the previous week's production of *A Streetcar Named Desire* ... I didn't know anything about Nicol Williamson then, but as his reputation grew by leaps and bounds I remembered the face in Dundee. This was during my perambulatory years in rep when I would scour the country and basically learn my craft. It was great fun since you didn't get bored and you became a voyager traversing the entire British Isles from top to bottom.

My Dundee engagement started in March 1962 and one of the first chaps I met was a shy little assistant called Brian Cox. He was such a gentle and accessible person then and so warm-hearted. He invited me and another actress to his house for tea and made lots of sandwiches. He was the friendliest chap there, I remember, although it was altogether a friendly company. I was amazed to see the change that had come over him from Dundee days when I met him on the way to Spain about ten years later for a film called *Nicholas and Alexandra*: he had been to drama school and started to be another Albert Finney. He had become harder and liked his booze. He was much louder than before and I know that he has gone through yet another metamorphosis and has become a very successful actor. I will always remember him as that gentle, searching youth he once was.

I believe that deep in our hearts we do not change that radically from when we are small children, unless somewhere on the way we have been mightily impressed by someone in whose image we carve ourselves. I have been many people and changed like a chameleon. Sometimes I identify very strongly with Kafka and become absurdly withdrawn, cryptic, observing the world from deep within my private body which is not accessible. I become like the bug. An outsider, unloved, given to deep probings and guilt and yet with a sense somewhere of my superiority in pain. Other times I wish to be Kean or Irving, striding important stages and galvanizing the audience like Kean or making myself a sacrifice; being consumed by the flames of my own passion, like an Artaud; or like a Wilde, sensual, loving, pained by the world's abstruseness and predictability and sitting alone on my own pedestal of words with which I enchant the world. Other times I think of Norman Mailer, a literary pugilist stamping on and punching anything that criticizes. Or a Poe who is stripped bare to the nerves, skin pulled back and raw. And other times plain dull and ordinary me, gripped by indecision and loathing my quandary and lack of work. So if Cox has changed I can understand it only too well. Mailer had and has a way of making words dance and shaping them up to look good and probing into the netherland of his soul to come up with the knock-out phrase, but he is too transparently obvious in his desires and too keen to be an Aryan hero like Hemingway. Nevertheless, when he writes well it is just the most stunning thing to read.

The agent Vincent Shaw had said, 'Come in and meet Piers Haggard,' and asked me if I wanted to go to Dundee. Sure, why not, play some good parts I hope, but I think Mr Shaw recommended some other actor over me for the part of Gratiano in *The Merchant of Venice* and I was landed with trying to make something of the combination of the salads, as they are called in the biz ... Salarino and Solanio. I was playing one of them and actually scoring a huge amount of laughs since out of frustration I would attack the part furiously and demolish the poor thing. I even gave acting lessons to the chap who was playing Gratiano; to this day I say those lines to myself or out loud. I love the ring of Shakespeare and its strong message that allows you to feed it with energy, since it revitalizes you even in the speaking of it. Some words cannot just be read but must be tasted and resonated. It makes a lot of difference. 'Let me play the fool./With mirth and laughter let old wrinkles come;/And let my liver rather heat with wine/Than my heart cool with mortifying groans' ... wonderful sentiments. Let me play the fool! Certainly one of my commandments in life.

We plotted through the play in the mandatory two weeks and got into our costumes, which were made by a very pretty boy called Simon who was crippled and rather sadly deformed and yet his nature was continuously cheerful and he was gay in an obvious way, the way people can be in the theatre. He was a good friend and we had many chats, since again there were few there with whom I could exchange much noodle. The play was successful and Lynn made a good stab at Portia and we all went to the pub.

Since now Piers could see that I was such stuff as dreams are made of, he immediately re-engaged me to appear in *The French Mistress*, in which I played the young, sweet sixteen-year old (really) *convincingly* and scored a huge success. I fell in love or nearly with the

actress playing opposite me, but as luck would have it she went for
one of the company's pretty guys. Maybe I was already too intense
for her. She was so awfully pretty, but Bryan Stanyon (how we recall
names from the void when we go back) grabbed her and I think they
had a long and lasting relationship while I was out in the cold.
Luckily I scouted out a very acceptable older lady for some companionship. In rep the first thing the chaps do is search out what's
floating about in the way of female company, since there is nothing
worse than going back to empty digs with a bag of fish and chips.
But sharing that same bag of fish and chips and buying a bottle of
wine to wash it down and everything else that goes with that can be
this side of paradise.

So this lady, whose name I forget, was a part-time companion, but
went off me suddenly and strangely, and I got ready to rehearse
Mandragola by Machiavelli, very brave for Dundee. I was playing
some evil character and not getting anywhere. Simon had devised
these bright pastel colours for the whole cast to wear and I was to
wear these ghastly pink tights! 'No *way*, Piers,' I said. 'I am not
wearing those flaming pink tights.' I hate and loathe tights – they
wrinkle and you look really naff. I mean how could I go from Stamford Hill to pink tights? *Anathema*!! I would wear, I suggested, these
black wool dance tights which were now the fashion, but not *pink*
tights. Piers looked at me as if I were a weird younger brother whom
he had to contain somehow or lose face forever.

'Look,' he said, 'if you put a penny in the waist and roll it tight
they won't wrinkle,' and he patiently did it for me like a wardrobe
lady.

I looked, but I hated the sight of them. I had definite ideas about
my costume and make-up and would spend hours on Sunday practising my make-up for the next week's play while the rest of the cast
were getting over hangovers. My make-up was fine, but not this.
Piers patiently insisted – he was a bastard for getting his own way,
and that's why now he's a successful TV director. Eventually, seeing I
was getting precisely nowhere, I burst into tears, a ploy I had begun
using lately, now that I was a 'released' being in the theatre. He just
stood there and said that I and the costume looked wonderful and
that the audience would be watching me and not my tights. In the
end I wore the bloody pink tights. I forgot about them after a while . . .

After the affair with the tights Piers's patience with me waned and once more I was on the train heading down to St Pancras. But at least I was enjoying my life to the brim except for the deadly periods of unemployment. One day I would have to learn to deal with them, but as yet I had no firm idea how. My drinking habits were still on the whole moderate and I would refrain in the future from any daytime drinking while rehearsing, but wait until that magic hour when we'd all run into the pub afterwards, the way actors always do to replace that energy and psychic loss that nerves and adrenalin have extracted from them. After the show the first drink is always the best of the evening, but drinking before a performance was something I couldn't conceive of. I believed that the thousand and one details one had to remember and have at one's disposal demanded a clear head. I had heard of people drinking before going on and I wondered how they could retain the lines. It would horrify me to be on a stage and dry – forget my lines – and this very fear is one of the great stimulants for a performance, in that one gathers all one's energy and clarity to deal with whatever exigency should arise.

However, I was doing a summer season in Cheltenham in 1961 for David Giles. I remember meeting him for the audition, in January or February of that year, in a small room in Soho. He was alone. He had a soft, gentle face and was enormously sensitive to actors. He had bravely cast me to play Oberon in the *Dream* to start with. This was one of the most exciting things that had ever happened to me. At last I was going to 'quality repertory theatre', where you had two weeks' rehearsal, as opposed to one week which I had been doing; for the first play we were to open after *three whole weeks'* rehearsal. When I was told on the phone I had the job I was so overcome I remember throwing myself on the floor and howling with joy.

I went to work with a will and even researched fairies in the Reading Room at the British Museum. I had no idea how I should play Oberon; I sensed it had to be fey, fluid, elegant, but in those days I was still tentative about how far I could go and would be intimidated by the fact that it was Shakespeare and had to be beautifully spoken. A talented young actor and revue artist called Tony Tanner played Puck and the way he hurled himself into each role was to have an influence on me. We kept looking for ways of improving the bits we had together. I thought him extremely gifted and mercurial, and an excellent Puck. To the manner born, you might say.

David directed the play very cleverly, with masses of wonderful business for the lovers and great clowning and comic acts. It was a resounding success. The TV playwright Douglas Livingstone played Bottom and Windsor Davies played Snug the joiner. It was Windsor's first stage play and he was also stage-managing. I found him a completely charming man who told me he had left his old work, which I believe was teaching, and in his thirties was taking up acting. I thought him very brave. He was always terribly solicitous to me, full of compliments about my style of acting and paying me these in a full, round, rich Welsh accent.

Since I was a bit intense in those days I would always be wearing black and a bit stand-offish, though not for any reason except I would be utterly immersed in my role, which I would study night and day. I was very nervous the first few nights and didn't really get too much satisfaction out of it, but was glad to have played it and looked forward to the time when I would have another crack at it. I think that some roles, like music, need constant practice until they are part of your bloodstream, but in rep you're only just really conversant with your lines when you are taking the make-up off after the last performance. I had seen no other actor playing Oberon and so had no one with whom to compare myself. I could not see an image clearly in front of me, but did conceive a kind of strategy whereby he might appear like a weightless human, with shades of Marcel Marceau. David wanted something a little more 'King of the Fairies', more satanic and harder, and so I fell somewhere between the two stools. He resisted greatly my notion of making long, pointed nails out of film negative, which extended my fingers wonderfully and made me feel more feline. After a fair amount of pleading, I removed my two-inch painted strips of negative and my fingers, by contrast, looked stumpier than ever. In retrospect, I see that David Giles made an error in not letting an actor's creative juices flow; anyway, the nails would have made me more animalistic – correct for Oberon.

We followed the *Dream* with *The Matchmaker* by Thornton Wilder, in which I had a good role and played it well. Tony Tanner had the lead. After this I tried to sing in his musical adaptation of Jean Anouilh's *Thieves Carnival*, composed by Tony's partner, Neville McGrah, who was a rather enthusiastic and sensitive sort of chap. However, my singing flopped dismally and I was dissuaded from further forays into that field. Some short time later Neville committed suicide in the most awful way imaginable, by setting himself on fire. I never understood why he did this terrible act, but I knew he had formed a relationship with Liz Shaul, with whom I was living at the time, and used to spend time at our flat in Warwick Avenue. His sensitive way of teaching me to sing and helping my first warbles was a lesson to me in how people bring out their best when they are loved and not bullied. He was a remarkable man, and sadly missed.

Then we did *The Aspern Papers*, in which I was cast as Pasquale, the oily servant, and I scored a conspicuous hit. Not unaided, I must admit, by seeing the show in town and the role played to roguish perfection by Olaf Pooley, whose daughter, twenty-five years later, played Eva Braun to my Hitler on TV! Though I made the character my own, the modelling helped and I was always grateful to that very good actor for giving me some hints!

Summer in Cheltenham was beautiful. I had a gorgeous little flat overlooking a garden and my memory of it is full of summer smells and hyacinths, gladioli and roses in every garden. Long Sunday walks. I even hired a bike and went cycling into the local villages. It was a very innocent and bucolic time.

To my astonishment as I read the old programmes that I have so fortuitously kept, I see that the wonderful long summer I remember in Cheltenham was really a very warm spring and the entire duration of my golden memories was barely eight weeks of 1961. Yet in my mind it seemed to be so much longer, so you see how memories of happiness expand in your mind.

I had finished playing Cheltenham one Saturday night and decided, like many others, to go back to London for the weekend, but alas the last train went just before we brought the curtain down and nobody had room to give me a lift. So I walked from Cheltenham to Oxford and caught the early morning train. I must have walked about twenty-five miles and all the way I saw only country lanes and the sudden spear of light over the horizon as cars made their cosy night rides past the solitary figure trudging home like some weary Edmund Kean, who used to walk from engagement to engagement. The night seemed to go on for ever and when after two or three hours the cars thinned out the darkness covered me in black velvet and I could hardly see ten feet in front of me. There was no moon and I sensed only deep, dark shapes which in my mind grew into such strange ogres that I was glad beyond belief to reach Oxford and find there was a train. I arrived in Warwick Avenue with swollen feet and was never so glad to be anywhere in my life.

We took *The Aspern Papers* to Oxford as part of our touring circuit. During that week my colleague Peter Brett, who was playing the Michael Redgrave part (since lead parts in rep are seldom called by name but after the star who played the role in the West End), gave me a strange book which he thought 'a bit weird' but might interest me. It was called *The Theatre and its Double* by Antonin Artaud. I read it quickly and with great enthusiasm. Artaud seemed to be articulating everything I had ever felt about what the theatre could be. I was never to forget that book; for a while it became a kind of bible to me. I was fascinated by the life of this strange, theatrical hermit with his ideas of an explosive theatre full of wild cries and gestures. Reading him, I felt very similar to the way I had felt on first reading Kafka years before in Wiesbaden, that here was a man more interested in your mind's dreams and imagination than in reproducing reality, more interested in the stirring forces that art can provide than in the sympathetic identification with roles which in itself is us looking at ourselves, a form of narcissism. Certainly the latter approach creates wonderful stories and pictures of how sweet and strange we are, but it does not go so very deep. Literature can take you much farther, which is why fewer people *read* plays; they would much rather see them. With Artaud I felt there was no reproduction of the middle-class people with whom the theatre is so enamoured. Instead he expressed a concern for the movements of people rather than impersonating, of dissecting and not observing, a way of presenting *critically*, as would a Daumier, a Voltaire or a Swift, let alone a Kafka. We see the world more painfully and more sharply through parable. Who can deny the power of Orwell's *Animal Farm*?

So I kept Peter's book and kept on learning my craft in rep. I wanted to be a good actor and I knew that no matter which way I might eventually go, technique was paramount. I loved technique, exploring different ways of playing and walking and even making an entrance.

The next play we did was a ghastly pot-boiler directed by a trainee TV director who was offered for free to the theatre by the BBC. It was painfully awful. I was playing the Paul Scofield part and cannot for the life of me remember any of it except that the set was full of couches and chairs. I felt distinctly awkward in the role and hated every moment of my awkwardness on stage. One night towards the end of the run I was having a tomato juice in the pub opposite the theatre where we could have a snack before the show, when out of some bravura dared to drink a barley wine. I sipped it slowly and felt a buzz since I was hyper-alert before the show anyway and was tempting the devil; then I went on stage, a little fearful, but well in control. I did the show and felt none of the effects I feared I might; the lines flowed along and I was a mite more relaxed, perhaps because I had dared my mind to falter and, seeing that it was holding its own, felt emboldened.

The next night my pact with the devil continued and I slowly drank my magic brew. Seeing that I had another hour I risked a second and again went on a little concerned but feeling a lot more free, taking risks and now and then making abrupt changes of pace and eye-catching mood swings. I sensed I had broken through the discomfiture of the role's restrictions. I was teasing the role round to fit me, playing with it. Even the actress playing opposite seemed somewhat taken aback and impressed with my new-found confidence.

The following night I stuck to my formula and found it easier still and wondered if this was the 'answer' to difficult parts, as if the alcohol, once it had liberated you, wore off steadily but left you in full charge of the imp that it had loaned you for the night. I now understood actors who relied on the demon to extract some fire and that they couldn't seem to get going without it, either from wear and tear over the years or from brutal repetition. I have heard of one actor who shall be nameless who, while playing Macbeth, had shots of whisky lined up at various entrances and exits. I don't know if it generally improved his performance – the night I went to see him it certainly had not.

However, with only a couple of nights to go (we were playing for two weeks), I threw caution to the winds, drank four of the beasts and went on drunk as a lord. I seemed perfectly sober on stage but felt the rush of energy that takes place when you are taking the most awful risk and daring yourself on. It was an extraordinary performance, full of eccentric and wild changes of pace – the poor actress thought I had gone completely mad, but I felt and knew I was doing something I had never before dared on stage. I came off completely elated.

The next day when going to my butcher for my lamb chops he happened to remark that he had been in that mighty night and was most impressed; I thought myself vindicated, but I never did it again. During the evening I felt a slight vagueness in places which gave me ever so slight a shock, but it passed. The lines which by now had sunk into my deeper memory channels seemed secure, but I had seen the warning light.

Shortly after this David Giles decided to cut the company down as business was bad – although I had to learn this through one of the actors who was now his associate, David was in London that week and would not tell me himself! So once more I was trudging round the agents.

Booze was not to feature again in my working life, except for a brief stint at the Royal Court when I was playing the small role of Raymondo in Arnold Wesker's *The Kitchen*. John Dexter cast me at first reading for a production that I had seen and admired several weeks earlier; it was having a re-run and among the replacements were Jeremy Brett and myself. Jeremy had the daunting task of taking over from Robert Stephens. The show was based mainly on the daily rituals of the kitchen and its workers, toiling like a colony of ants and occasionally stopping for Weskerian philosophy about life. It was tremendous to watch and quite dizzying – probably the first time an English director has succeeded in creating a great physical theatre to compare with Brecht's.

The 'Court' was a swinging power-house in those days with each show creating some sensation or new pathways. Osborne's *Luther* was in performance at the Phoenix and I was able to see Finney once again, giving his big-grinned, huge, stentorian-voiced, big-hearted performance, and admire his robustness and nerve. Mind you, he had the great roles and he did Luther with a kind of visceral energy not often witnessed. Robert Stephens had been brilliant a few months before, again unleashing a power-house performance, the first of many. One felt then at the Court, even in my brief sojourn, that it was the place to be and working men's boots were a sartorial must. Albert Finney would eat in the working men's café which existed in those days halfway up the King's Road and where you would sit on benches in those high-backed wooden seats, like cubicles or booths. Lashings of mashed potatoes, peas and thin roast beef followed by a pudding was the order of the day. Yes, them were pioneer days. In those days the best theatre was to be found there and the most avant garde. While you had your working-class-hero drama, you also had a chance to see Max Frisch's *Fire Raisers*, Olivier in *Rhinoceros*, which I enjoyed all the more because Orson Welles was standing at the dress circle cueing the lights, Sartre's *Altona*, with Maximilian Schell, and a beautiful production of Wedekind directed by someone I never heard of again. There was a team of louche young men who stamped their mark on the place and their history has been well documented. For me it was just another job and I was not involved in the Court clique of actors or directors, but tried to do this one as best I could. Among our cast were Edward Fox, Harry Landis and Glenda Jackson, plus others who all stirred their bit of acid into the pot. It was a powerful production of a moving play and I was now in the same league as some of the leading actors and feeling good about working there. At the same time I felt an unease in that the slimness of my character gave me so little to do. The fuel I need in order to go into orbit is never given to the small-part players, so most of the time you're on the edge of your nerves and can never even get a remote sweat up. I have always hated playing small roles since I need to get right into the part or I skate perpetually on the edge and fail to tap those areas that small roles can sometimes reach.

I was locked into one area of the stage and had to create a cake that would take me the whole evening. I went about my task with assiduousness, learning the whole process of pastry-making, breaking the mimed eggs and whisking them with my real whisk – all utensils were real while the food was mimed, which made it very clear to the audience and gave an effective manipulation of props. So carefully did I pick out my little bits of egg shell and so carefully did I break my eggs and who noticed except it was part of the great tapestry of industry?

Harry Landis shared my little work bench and shoved me off stage as much as possible while I shoved the bench on – Harry was a good teacher in the theatre of combat. As I started to get into my mimed cake I would add little flourishes with the creamer and actually get a few laughs from the audience, who were beginning to appreciate this cake being made. I am sure the previous tenant of my role did not achieve this since Harry, who had been in the show before, with all the spirit of a good opponent would suddenly and furiously whisk his cake just as he knew the laugh was coming. He was protecting his terrain. Therefore I had to learn to adjust my cooking procedure and do my fine art work at different times in the play, when his attention was elsewhere, but he would wait for those moments and draw focus, as they say.

After a while I upbraided him for this unseemly and unsportsman-like behaviour, but he looked wide-eyed and innocent and swore he wasn't treading on my laughs. Rather he was following the biz, since he always did his after mine, but of course he did his during the key moment and snatched the laugh out of the air like a poacher. Eventually I found some delightful business with throwing the pastry in the air during one of his lines and then he stopped. But he was always stimulating to work with and had a stream of the funniest, filthiest wit I have ever heard. A born comic, Harry Landis. I don't think he was even that bothered about who got what laughs, but overall saw theatre as a means of confrontation and terrorism. An avowed and most articulate communist, he saw through the 'game' of theatre with its intensity sometimes bordering on preciousness. Harry was more of a street urchin. He wished always to deflate pomposity, and there was plenty of that around in those days.

One felt that the Court was not really a people's theatre like Joan Littlewood's, but a cabal or club. That it did good work was undeniable, but the prime moving force was a concern less for human issues than for careers and self-esteem, which I suppose is normal except one felt this overweening pioneer atmosphere and clubbiness. Who was in and who was out of the regular coterie that would hang around the pub. Who could go to the classes that were sometimes held and who couldn't. Rather precious experiments with masks and other gimmicks they had discovered that were exciting elements to work with, but here they were espoused like the dis-covery of the ark. They even put on a public performance, which was the last word in the theatre of embarrassment since these exercises only work in the safe confines of a private place. Here the poor actors were demonstrated on like performing monkeys and I do re-member squirming in my seat. A lot of things seemed like worthy but calculating gestures, artistic but vain. I did not feel very comfortable there, since it was not my idea of an all-embracing theatre. There was to be sure a craftsmanship and dedication to plays in the William Morris kind of school, earnest experimentation in the Arts and

Crafts style. People were slightly trendy but not obviously so and it was always winter and heavy coats.

Since I was not part of this club and did not remotely desire to be, it might be that I suffered some degree of alienation or paranoia, but it was a feeling others shared. Even when we went on the anti-nuclear march there was the 'gang' out there together and while we were all walking along Sloane Street I suddenly thought, 'What the hell am I doing with this bunch?' I felt a distinct sense of phoniness within myself since I must confess that in my heart I didn't really believe these people cared whether you lived or died – they were merely making the correct political gesture. Everybody who worked at the Court developed this sanctimonious pomposity about them-selves as if they were *the* light of the new theatre. In many ways in the earlier days they were and when I worked there they still had a great reputation. But when I saw Genet's *The Blacks*, which I found utterly confusing and muddled, I asked the lovely casting director Miriam Brickman if she too didn't find it rather confusing. She replied from the full height of her RC status, 'Life is confusing, dear!' I was chastened; of course life is confusing.

I felt the total opposite when I went to Joan Littlewood's theatre in Stratford East and would come away with only a good experience in my pocket. That was *not* confusing. Of course one sees these events as a struggling 'artiste' and while they may seem important at the time from your worm's-eye view and because of the lack of attention you command, to them you were merely another of many actors and 'they' were also struggling to maintain a thriving institution.

John Dexter, who directed *The Kitchen*, was always good-natured to me and fun to work with, since he also liked to deflate the swollen ego of the theatre and could bitch away at the actors, but basically we knew he was having fun. It was barrack-room stuff and most took it well. John reserved most of his acid for Jeremy Brett, calling him every name under the sun and impugning his origins and man-hood with references to Eton, etc. Jeremy, to his credit, never once got upset, nor did he cringe, but took it with the kind of good humour he must have had to learn at public school. John never got him down . . .

Dexter slagged away quite a bit, but I now realize he must have been bored out of his tree. He had mounted *The Kitchen* twice before, once in the full-scale production I had seen. As I write I can see the awesome performance of Robert Stephens before me. I remember his flawless German/Bavarian accent and his manic power. Stephens was one hell of a giant in those days. Jeremy, to his credit, gave a very good performance in the light of Stephens's *tour de force*. He was also full of the nervous, crazy energy that Dexter managed to extract from his actors and he became very good indeed – the whole cast were most impressed. Stephens was a hard act to follow, but Jeremy did it.

John did in fact talk to me about another play and though we never became close he was respectful and friendly. One day during rehearsals of *The Kitchen* we happened to lunch together and we chatted showbiz; he asked me which writers I liked or wished to see performed. Knowing John to be such a luminary and wishing to make a good impression, I said, 'Ernst Toller', who I was reading at the time and who I did find very powerful. He said, 'Never heard of him!' . . . From then on he thought I was a rather serious young person.

The show was most successful again and on the first night we bowled into the pub. I happened to be out first and there was Sir Michael Redgrave with congratulations for each member as they came in. He greeted me warmly as I had dashed out fast and there was no one else there for him to welcome. Ken Tynan was also there and I was most impressed by the way he held his cigarette, between his third and fourth finger. *Très élégant*.

In the formidable line-up of talent in the cast Glenda Jackson breathed her fire over everyone even then and a particularly fierce blast over me in the one sentence I exchanged with her in three months. Perhaps this is what fuelled her, but as I think back there seemed to be a sourness that emanated from this company. Whether it was due to the theatre itself, since waves spread through from the top to the bottom and must have an effect, I do not know, but I had never met such a bunch of whining, bitchy actors before. Insult was the order of the day, and unmitigated bitchiness. It seemed a kind of fashion to greet a fellow actor in the pub with your most abrasive salutation. I never really got used to this as a term of endearment.

Edward Fox played a young German kitchen hand, and very well too. He seems a quite different actor today. Rita Tushingham was cute, buxom and waitressy and had a fling at fame. I played out my fishing egg shells out of the bowl for three months. Wesker used to watch rehearsals, but never spoke to me or to the other newcomers during the whole period. He sat there relaxed like a hirsute young poet relishing his fame. Years later we did in fact meet up when he took over the Round House and he was to be very helpful and positive. It's difficult always to give to everyone and to be aware in the corner of your eye of an actor taking over a role when he is one of many.

This slipstream of memory really came out of my association with the demon booze and I followed its path, and the memories that came with it led me to Sloane Square. During *The Kitchen* I think I was going through a change of life. This happens every seven years or so when the body has its regular upheaval/spring-clean/change of skin or any of the various things that bodies do. Anyway, it was a period of nervousness and I again tried the barley wine method of drama. Because the role was small it helped me syphon off that nervousness and I rolled along with my thrice barley wine. That was to be the last time I used that particular method. I usually only did it when the play or performance was against the grain and I suppose the play, which I deeply admired, the part, the people and the theatre contributed each in their little way to a feeling of depression which my barley wine would help me combat. I mean I was mightily outnumbered.

Emergence of 'The Writer'

At least I was working. That was good. Just six years earlier I had returned from Wiesbaden and now I was a West End actor of sorts. At that time six years ago I had got home and found the landscape barren. I wandered around the town on my first night home, trying to pick up the desultory contacts I had round the spots, the jazz clubs, hoping to see a face, a friend, someone, since I had pulled away the skin that was attaching me to so many of my youthful mates with whom for whatever reason I had lost contact. What was it that I resisted? Why not call Wally, who introduced me to the idea of Europe, or Barry? Why did I feel I had to be such a recluse? I started to drift round like a leaf blown by any wind and go here and there without purpose or will. I had no work to anchor me, only the same monotonous and meaningless wage-earning in these charnel houses of depravity and deadness. Retail! Drifting in with a heart that weighed like lead and pretending I wanted to die a little more in their wretched mausoleum. I've already pushed out this beast from my psyche in *East* and in a short story I once wrote called 'Say a Prayer for Me' . . . I think it one of the most tender things I ever wrote. Somehow I put more of my spirit into my short stories, which appeared under the title *Gross Intrusion* and which John Calder bravely published when no other publisher would go near me.

In plays I was able to start a dialogue with the audience the way you start a fire with two sticks. One actor answers the other and each answer builds the story and raises the ante. Sometimes there are far too many words. If Hamlet had fewer words he would not go mad. He suffers with the responsibility of the weight of words. Words, words, words, he has to chew his way through words, commenting on everything like a human tape-recorder. After a while he must raise the temperature since we will get bored otherwise. He must question life and death and love and hate. While in a novel we can rest our poor tongues and dwell on the description of a street, its houses and characters, or a frown; a white blouse hanging from the window which Joseph K. notices as he is being arrested.

In stage adaptations most writers seize the dialogue as if they were doing a liver transplant, giving the play the most visceral bloody part but leaving out the narrative, the abstract thoughts. It's weighed down with dialogue. With endless spoken dialogue. How can you act *narrative*? Ah, let's put a narrator on the stage, preferably with a book in his hand like the compère. In my version of *The Trial* it was necessary to put the narrative into the action, since the narrative is the landscape without necessarily the human involvement. It is a grey day. Who speaks these things, if not Joseph K.? It is the voice of the book itself. *It* speaks to you, it is the slow pan of the camera across the horizon, but the words are far more powerful. 'It was a grey day in autumn' is of course far more evocative than swirling misty cloud which makes us wait for something. The words curl themselves around your memories and demand that you interpret them with your best thoughts or, as Shakespeare says, 'piece out our imperfections with your thoughts'. In the short story there is a lack of that same tension, since the story doesn't have to become visible through the friction of two actors rubbing up against each other and producing *dialogue*. It can appear slowly and softly, as if speaking silent thoughts. Getting up in the morning from a night of uneasy dreams . . . It tells us so much already about Gregor Samsa's mind. His night of dreams.

Gross Intrusion is a book of fourteen short tales, simple sad tales about the loveless lonely. I wrote them in the seventies during a period when I was extremely happy, working well, sharing a life with a lady I loved. At weekends we would scamper down to Brighton on the train from Victoria Station and try all the hotels until we found the hotel of our dreams, the Royal Crescent. Now it has unfortunately been run into the ground by people who don't seem to know too much about catering, but then it was like staying in the Carlton in Cannes. Even the doorman, Mr Carmichael, was an elegant, charming and delightful man with his insignia of crossed keys over his lapel, the universal sign of the head porter. He always advised us as to what was on in town and which actors were staying, since the Royal Crescent used to attract the *crème de la crème*. The building was dove grey and stood out like an elegant birthday cake. The welcome when you arrived was soft and calming – real class, not the fawning unctuousness following suspicion and dirty looks. From the very beginning I was treated with dignity, very important to an insecure actor who's going for a weekend with his lady in Brighton. It was delight. The sky was always blue then and of course it was always summer and from our room we would stare out at the coast reaching down to the school at Roedean and the Downs sailed away into the distance; we ordered breakfast in bed and were supremely content.

Unbeknown to me at the time, but adding to the general delights of the area, was Olivier's presence in the adjoining crescent. And lo and behold, just as I was parking my motorbike in the Royal Crescent garage amidst the Jags, out comes Sir Larry parking his. Shall I approach and offer my warm greetings and solicitations to someone who has even invaded my dreams? No, let him be in peace.

Annie and I had our rituals in Brighton and one of these was a long, slow walk across the Downs to Rottingdean and a stop-off for refuelling in a little sandwich bar next to the putting green. It was a charming little café with windows on to the sea and then, as in many places, run by a very friendly couple who made delicious cheese and salad sandies. So in this blissful condition with my delightful pre-Raphaelite Annie, her long, silken, chestnut hair reflecting glints of sunlight, and a cheese and salad sandie in my mitt, I wrote the most horrific stories I could think up.

I would sit and write each tale in one go lasting about an hour. I wrote in one huge explosion, without stopping for breath. It just poured out. Everything. It started as fun since I love to doodle and make little verbal sketches, but now, as I was beginning to discover writing and inventing, I took my notebook everywhere. It was a kind of journal and as I wrote I became more enthused. The delights of Brighton seemed to loosen out of me all the débris of loneliness I had felt all my life and I was able to make little allegories out of these fragments.

My way of working them out was very simple. I would let the first line pop into my head, no matter how strange and improbable this line might be. Whatever surfaced in my mind, from out of the murky depths, would be my headline. The débris drifted out and away. Wherever I happened to be over the next five years these stories seemed to come out, little allegoric tales about the loneliness I felt until I found Annie or until I found what it was I wanted to do. It was as if I had a sump down there or a block of ice that was now melting in the sun. Horrors unfolded as fun. I could not deny my fascination with *Last Exit to Brooklyn*, which might have influenced my way of seeing things in a more candid and raw fashion. I thought Hubert Selby Junior a very fine writer indeed.

I enjoyed the wretched existence of my characters and their pitiable and desperate loneliness. The point of the stories was how we try to use whatever means we have at our disposal to break down the walls of loneliness and how we will do almost anything to be able to feel and hold someone. So desperate people use desperate measures.

Each story in an unconscious way seemed to extirpate some knot of bitterness and gall. Each one was a secret confession, even if the guilts were only imagined and never acted out. In 'Daddy' a father goes to a Turkish bath and meets his own son in a scene of horrific confrontation as their mutual sexual tendencies are revealed. The idea of sex is so horrific to your parents or to you vis-à-vis them that you invent the worst possible scenario, the alternative Oedipus. Sexuality in every different form, mostly lonely men looking for lonely women and then failing at that moment. In 'Say a Prayer for Me', a menswear salesman goes back to his lodging each night and tries to cope without love and with a need to make some event happen in his life, to screw the young charlady. He loses the emblem of his manhood when he sees the cuffs of his shirt hanging dirtily over the chair. What is this? Humiliation in this work? Humbleness and feelings of inferiority. In 'She, Or A Day in Brighton' I talk about the present and am sublimely happy in this little eulogistic portrait of Annie. 'Master of Café Society' is about an unemployed person who charts his way through the world of the morning and finds he does everything like a working man from waking, washing, walking to the café, reading his paper and eating his breakfast, but then instead of going the step further, which is on to work, he goes home and eats his heart out. The inspiration for the story was Alfredo's in Islington with its formica-topped white tables and plenty of steam. It's my most autobiographical of them all and so familiar; when I recently saw the young and talented George Dillon adapt this for a one-man show I felt the awfulness and pain of it all over again. His performance was a masterpiece of timing and observation, but most of all he let himself go. I was most proud of my written work when I saw him.

I managed to crawl inside a woman's mind in 'From My Point of View', I found it was not so different from a man's, although as Napoleon said, 'I am glad I was never born a woman, since then I could never love them.' So I drew on my observations of the female world and also on that passive or feminine part of me, since the duality in our nature gives us that sense of balance without which we have a very singular view of life. When someone said that I seem to write good roles for women I was truly proud, not just because of any suggestion of the skill that statement might imply but because of the idea that we flow between our male and female states; when I write I don't consciously think how would a 'she' do this, I simply put myself there and it all 'flows'.

I thought I would tempt everything and write about masturbation in 'Pictures'. This came out well, in my opinion, since it deals even more with the solitary human being throttling his loneliness, in this case accompanied by a gallery of mental pictures that he keeps for reference. 'False God' was a suitable apotheosis for the poor Harry who, having used his introduction card for years, is getting tired as well as lonely and ends up with a plastic replica of a woman. It is a horrible story of loneliness taken to its bitter end. The plastic smiling facsimile. 'North' is, in a sense, a panegyric to the wondrous delights of space, air and freedom, and has nothing to do with sex, loneliness or any other desperate need. It is about the sadness of sudden death and a loving tribute to my wife Shelley, who used to wait for me at home and would tell me she listened for the bike outside when I drove up and parked it outside the railings, in Devonia Road. I imagined what would happen if I had died and she had been waiting for me, and so this time it was about loss.

The title story is a weird fantasy, 'Gross Intrusion'. The title itself means death caused by one car penetrating another. So it's a euphemism in the American auto industry and seemed most appropriate for this collection, since everybody suffers a kind of soul death from being brutally invaded by other desperate people. This time a black man, with his legendary equipment, invades a white man and destroys him. It's simple and brutal. The white man is a mouse of sexual fantasy while the black is the fully grown tiger, and tears him to pieces. Hey, what is this? Some of it was directly influenced by a Tennessee Williams story called 'Desire and the Black Masseur', in which a black man, a masseur, having beaten some poor white to death, proceeds on instruction from the dying white man to be 'eaten', thus giving a literal interpretation to the term usually meant to imply fellatio or a blow job. It made sensational reading and was a big influence on me as a demonstration of daring and being bold, of using all the forces at your disposal. The worse your imagination is the more fertile it is and you should *not* censor yourself for fear of castigation. Was it fear or was it my imaginative flights that took an idea to its ultimate end, to go as far as one could reach? To marry your mother and kill your father is as far as Aeschylus's imagination can reach – was being impaled by death by the black merely an influence from Tennessee Williams or was it the awful fear that I might be harbouring such thoughts and wished to kill them in words, since at the end of the story Harry thinks only of the soft, tender, warm and gentle bodies of women?

These and other stories were written during the years of 1972–77. When they were published they received the most terrible reviews. Some critics loathed the contents of my Pandora's box, while others pretended it was only the style that was so awful. One particular lady made mincemeat of my stories, which I wrote with a total belief in the underlying message: that it was a great tragedy to be denied love and tenderness, and people crave this affection as much as food and become so desperate that they will commit crimes upon their own person to get some of it, even if, like the beggar raiding the dustbin, they find only garbage and filth! That much I thought was clear and that much I thought would be seen to be the motive of the stories.

Over the years *Gross Intrusion* has received a certain notoriety and been praised in those quarters I admire. Parts of it have even been adapted for the stage. One theatre group had a big success with 'From My Point of View' and George Dillon is still performing my short stories.

Exile – Iceland, 1956

The mind swings backwards and forwards in time, pulling this way and that like a water diviner. I cannot really write out my life in chronological order, since one thought is attracted to another, swirling like atomic particles until one particle is attracted by another and led along a different route, in the way that conversation works or dreams associate freely within your mind, clearing the air and making their own logic. It is not the order of things that affects you so much as certain impulses and pains, and these can come from many different times and places. So I try to work this weave with many differing threads, but hope that at the end of it, or even before, there will emerge a pattern that may be perceived. There was not much hope in the past except to work and by working hope that divine light would suddenly hit you and that you would be shown the place and the Holy Grail. Going to the Youth Employment Bureau in Oxford Street. Doing odd jobs. Surely all these things must be leading to some destination and there is a reason for all this. There must be, since when I was a youngster living in a two-roomed East End slum I wrote myself a letter about all the things that I hoped I might be, so I did feel that there was a destiny somewhere over the horizon. It can't be all like this, I thought.

After much gallivanting about for a couple of years of desultory work and then my great escapade in Europe, when I met and fell in love with Fay, I decided that I had to get back to my beloved in Wiesbaden and now was setting myself goals at last. Another firm was competing with Burberry's but with much less class, making suits in the PX stores in Germany. As soon as I knew this I fled to their shop in Oxford St. I was put on the usual trial period to test me for the obvious things like decency, honesty and efficiency and so once again I had to prove that I could do this godforsaken work. The branch was next door to the tube; it was a particularly obnoxious shop full of crappy clothes for the ready-to-wear brigade and my mood was intense as I waited daily for the call that would take me back to Fay.

After a few months of this torture I was summoned and told that I would be leaving next week. For *Iceland. Oh no, how much more can I take?* Why were they doing this to me? Probably because they could see that I really hated the work and the nasty little manager who talked about sex all day gave me a bad report. They said there were no places in Germany at the moment (lies) but if I did this for a couple of months to help them out, there would be a place for me in Deutschland. I knew that if I refused I wouldn't get anywhere.

I left for Iceland from Glasgow on my first-ever flight and wore a smart Donegal tweed suit my dad had made – badly, but it still looked OK. As we journeyed towards the far north it got weirdly lighter and lighter and when I landed I saw no one who wished to meet me. I wasn't going to stand around until some jerk arrived to claim me, so I sat in the nice airport café and waited. Eventually a little goon came up and said he wasn't sure that it was me (since I looked too smartly dressed and cool with my short hairstyle and three-button Donegal tweed suit with slanting flap pocket). He seemed put out, as he was obviously expecting the kind of tatty, shiny-elbowed, dandruffed scab who normally worked in menswear. So he gruffly took me to my Nissen-hut digs where I had to share a room with this chap who looked as if he lived for menswear. It was a kind of eerie early morning light when I went to bed.

The following day, after getting all my permits in Reykjavik and being told all about the town heated by underwater springs, we went to this nasty little concrete box on the base. The first shock I had was when a customer came in and I went to serve him. The little runt pushed me aside, told me just to sweep up and brush the evil suits. He was scared of having any rejects back and wanted to make sure I could measure up correctly before entrusting me with messing up a hundred-dollar suit. It was obvious from him and my other colleagues that all they got to go to Iceland were the dregs . . . and I was one of them.

The days crawled. The nights never came, just this perpetual twilight zone and the shop of the mad in the middle with its group of maniac menswear salesmen caught in a time warp sludging backwards and forwards, not very different from Mother Courage's following the armies and feeding off them in the grim PX stores. Feeding off them like some evil parasites that caught the young men when they were off work and bored and thought they were getting the famous English suit that our great tailoring traditions had developed over the years, our sartorial taste and splendour. You look in the fashion plates and the well-drawn men looking svelte and casual and Joe Palooka from the Bronx says, 'Hey, yeah, something like dat.'

'Certainly sir, zip or buttons on the fly?'

Here in this land of the Icelandic sagas where the Norsemen came out of the hills and bathed in hot springs, where the ethereal lights bounced off the poles and shattered the night sky, it was 'Dust the suits, will you, Steve?' and 'Give the floor a tickle.' Mind you, the food was good and I ate like a king in the soldiers' canteens and as usual made friends with the USA.

I got into a study group of chaps who met and discussed literature and the arts once a week and we got on really fine. One day there was a visitor to the 'school' and I was having a marvellous chat about 'life and art', since I was a bit of a chatterer in those days and so relieved to be able to talk to someone that my lunch hour was passing by and I was due back. The teacher said, 'What's your phone number, we'll call and say you're in a meeting.' They must have thought I had a respectable position in the suit graveyard. 'In a meeting'!! Those turds would have a fit. But they made the call to the shop and I chatted amiably for ten more minutes since there was absolutely nothing to do in the morgue except 'sleeve the jackets'.

When I got back the little gnome had turned into a beetroot and exercised his tiny tongue to try and tell me off. By this time I had had enough and replied that much as I loved this way of life he could shove it up his ample arsehole. Of course I was put on two weeks' notice.

This was heaven and this time I saved and did not squander my money, so I had enough to take a trip to Germany even without a job. I lounged around for a couple more days and saw my gradually expanding group of American friends and our little soldiers' 'class'. I played pingpong and went to the servicemen's nightclub and one night a taxi driver begged me to buy some whisky for him from the PX store; the economy in Iceland was so bizarre since everything had to be imported that a bottle of whisky would cost me three dollars and our friends in Reykjavik thirty dollars. He said, 'I make you a deal.' Would I bring him some whisky and he'd pay me thirteen dollars, giving me an extra ten? I thought this seemed a reasonable if illegal but not criminal way of supplementing my meagre income and agreed with alacrity to let him have my weekly allowance, since I didn't drink and the base was already on to this scam and rationed you to two bottles per week.

Now unbeknown to me, while this was going on, my notice had not been accepted by Head Office – they presumably weren't fond of flying people back and forwards for such short periods and wanted me to stay longer because they had trouble finding staff who were not in the last throes of dementia and who were willing to go to this mad outfitters, which grew more like Alice in Wonderland every day. So the nutter had his little assistants spy on me in order to get some dirt. They knew I kept a notebook, my little tome of secrets, and one day when I was out working, or rather developing halitosis and spine warp, one of the little ferrets went in and read my diary, reporting back my gleeful expressions of joy: 'Sold two bottles today, twenty more dollars, goodee!' or such stuff, which is what I used to write. So now the gnome had a ruse. He confronted me with the nefarious deed.

At the time America was leasing the base from Iceland and did not wish to tamper with its inflated economy. There was a strong communist party who wanted the Americans out, saying they made the nation a military target, confused the economy, brought pox and other undesirable elements; so the US were very careful about black-market trading and the penalties were severe. I was accused by the boss of helping to undermine the Icelandic economy and endangering the base and my crime was blown up to such proportions that I was glad not to have been sentenced to ninety-nine years. Instead they had an excuse to rush me off the base, but before they could do this they needed to write to Leeds Head Office explaining their actions. Since I would get there before the letter, they actually entrusted me with it and said I must hand it in if I wanted to receive my two weeks' notice money, thus ensuring that I wouldn't just throw the letter away.

I was delighted to be going home and getting out of the mad no-man's land. I settled back in my seat on the plane and eventually arrived happily in Leeds, where I stayed the night at a hotel, prepared to meet with HQ in the morning. Well, realizing that it was risky to give me the letter, they had sealed it with tape at the top end where you lick it down but the bottom end, which is already sealed, they ignored. You see how intelligent they were. In my room there was fortunately one of those tea-makers and lo and behold steam was soon furiously rising and the secrets were pouring out. I sat down and read the purulent words of the pygmy manager who accused me of undermining the Icelandic economy, leading to a possible removal of the American forces from Iceland, and in the same sentence of coming in late for work and other macabre habits like keeping secret diaries and laughing a lot in the shop. All these crimes were lumped together to make me appear like some lunatic whom they had no choice but to remove as soon as possible so as to safeguard the grotty stores scattered like so many blackheads around the world.

My masters in Leeds were in fact quite friendly. I said I knew that I had been spied on and thought the worse of the staff for doing this. Since they tended to agree that spying and searching people's drawers for info was hardly British they gave me my salary, put me on the train for London and wished me well. Thank God that little escapade was over. Eventually, these same stores died out since customers have a way of knowing when something smells off.

I could wait no longer to see my beloved Fay. There was also some other fantasy that had to be fulfilled. It was a desire to leave England, to be free, to learn another language, to study in Paris, to be a bohemian, to live without grinding work, to fulfil all those childhood dreams. I knew now that I had to be an actor. This life was no good. But in my naïveté I imagined that to be an actor you had to have the looks of a matinée idol and I most certainly did not ... yet. But I would.

Return to Germany, or 'The Nose' – 1956

I decided to have plastic surgery in Wiesbaden on my nose, which had been knocked out of joint in the detention centre. To speak true it was not a bad knock, but I thought a little straightening would be in order. I took the boat back to Wiesbaden and went to a German surgeon whom I had met on my previous visit. He looked cold and steely with his blue eyes and his long cigarette holder, but we talked and he guaranteed that he would straighten it. He was dressed in starched white and was a dead ringer for one of those German doctors in films who made 'experiments' . . . I was fearful and didn't sleep at all well in the youth hostel the night before. In fact I was terrified but I wanted to go through with it. I even asked an innocent young German boy who was on a walking tour through the area whether I should have it done or not. He said that I must do what was in my dreams. He was so calm and reassuring that I went to the clinic and marched boldly in.

To my horror and consternation, rather than have me change and wait or test my pulse, blood or anything, he made me lie down and started injecting me. My God, I had only taken my sweater off and already I was on the table! *Jesus Christ I still had my Star of David round my neck*! *What if he was a Nazi? Oh shit*! He pulled the sheet up to my chin. The needle went in my nose and face. Feel anything? No, all dead, nothing. Then as I lay there looking and sometimes not looking, I sensed him take an instrument like a hammer, bring it down on my nose and break it. I swear to God I did not believe this was going to happen. It crunched as he broke it, like when you break an ice cube. Cruu-unnnch! Then all quiet. He's working away. Perhaps he won't mind my Star of David or will choose to ignore it. Let's hope so. I feel him scrape, but feel nothing, just hear him and feel the vibration of the scrape. A bit of resetting and more scraping and then suddenly the pain returns. There was not enough anaesthetic and I am coming round in the middle of the op! I start to signal as a burning pain sends shoots of agony through the area. He works on, faster, I moan and he finishes, puts plaster over and I go to bed in the clinic.

The next day my black eyes were the signature of everyone who has made this trip and I set about finding somewhere to live from the To Let ads. I found a little room with Fraulein Schmidt in Grill-parzerstrasse. She was very nice and very accommodating, spoke English, was cultured and I agreed a price and was now living in Deutsch-land – with no job, but living. My own apartment, learning German, a plaster on my new nose and a future.

I lay low for a week until the plaster came off and when it did it looked perfect. The doctor took the plaster off and I shut my eyes and opened them slowly. It was *straight as a die*. I was now a movie actor. Perfect, eureka! But he made me sit with a mini vice over my nose, which was painful since the nose tends to expand slightly when the plaster comes off. I sat for half an hour and then went out into the sweet open air. The German sunshine had never seemed so sweet. I went into one of a thousand bars and ordered my favourite drink. A Johanesbeesaft. A marvellous grape juice drink which I was potty on. I slid down to the Friedrichstrasse and sat and waited for Fay.

The next few days were idyllic. The weather was glorious but the nose had other plans and started to make a slight detour to the opposite side from whence it had been ironed out. So now it was sloping to the right. I was furious and sat for more endless hours with the mini vice stuck to my nose, with a tiny key at the side to make it tighter. It was no good. It would straighten for a while and then begin a slight lean. Horror! However, I didn't care since there was still a slight improvement and I felt psychologically liberated for having had it done and even being able to confess it. It eventually settled and was OK and more than OK. Slightly raffish: the slope gave it a real look.

I went about looking for work and got myself a job first in the bar on the US base. All the soldiers would get plastered there on pay-day and you'd make a fortune in tips, since bars are not like pubs, where you claw the bar like pigs at a trough; instead you get served by an eager young beaver like myself, hoping to make good tips to pay the rent. That was OK for a few weeks. I enjoyed the life and meeting people and hearing stories from all over America. One day as I was entering the American Forces 'Eagle' Club, which was a club for officers to which I had sneaked myself in on a regular basis to take some beginners' piano lessons, I met in the foyer a man demonstrating Rosenthal china. He seemed familiar and we spoke. He was most amusing and an Anglophile and told very funny jokes. I then remembered where I had seen him. He was the receptionist at the *Spielhaus* who used to give me my entrance card eighteen months earlier. He asked me what I was doing and I said I was working in bars, which I didn't like much, either no business or you're too busy. He offered me a job as his assistant with Rosenthal china, going round the US bases selling to the housewives who were bored and wanted to spend their money. We would knock on the door and 'demonstrate' the beautifully clean, pure lines of Rosenthal. And so I did.

His name was Fritz Peilsticker, but he preferred to be called Fritz Peil. I called at his house the following morning and had breakfast in the little courtyard. He introduced me to his old mother and we drank coffee and planned our day. It was great fun and I felt a little like Felix Krull, the hero of Thomas Mann's great novel, *The Confessions of Felix Krull, Confidence Man* ... We would travel to Frankfurt to the great housing units of the US bases and knock at the doors and I would watch as Fritz began a tireless rodomontade on the virtues of Rosenthal china. Thus he and I became yet another pair of passengers on Mother Courage's bandwagon through Europe.

The cultured ladies were always fascinated by Fritz's demonstration. He would preface his spiel by saying he was sent by Rosenthal merely to demonstrate; he was not selling. Only a few minutes to look at the wonderful set. Well, the ladies were bored and didn't mind some free entertainment, especially as the demonstrator had a young man in tow with a reasonably smart new hooter and confidence. The *pièce de résistance* at the end of the demonstration was the sight of Fritz, a fairly big fellow, proving the delicate china's strength by standing with his full weight on a cup. This impressed them and usually they would wish to order a set and he would do reasonably well. He paid me a small fee and the sorcerer's apprentice would carry the bags, put the crockery away and watch.

Later Fritz gave me my own set of china and I would knock on a few doors and try to repeat his lessons. I could never do it so well, but I succeeded in arousing the initial interest; then would promise to call back with the 'demonstrator' and he would knock a couple of days later. After work we would go into Frankfurt and explore a few bars, eat something and fool around. Fritz always had a joke and was something of a clown.

My relationship with Fay had cooled in the eighteen months since we had parted at the station and it didn't seem possible to repair it. Sadly we drifted apart. She still went to the café at Friedrichstrasse, presumably looking for newer meat.

I enjoyed my life with Fritz. He was a really good friend and something of a father figure. It was a sad day when we parted. The police became rather too interested in me since I had no working status and no cards and paid no tax. One day there was a knock at the door and a request to go the next day to the police station, so I decided in a bit of a panic to avail myself of the next train to Avignon. I had a girlfriend there whom I had met a few months earlier at the Astoria dance hall, Charing Cross Road. We went out a few times and she had asked me to join her in the South of France – she was working in a holiday hotel in Ax-les-Thermes, in the beautiful Pyrenees. Now was the time. Fritz and I had a farewell dinner. Sadly I was never to see him again, but would remember him for the rest of my life.

After my sojourn in Ax-les-Thermes I returned to London and Manor House, which I was getting thoroughly sick of. Barry Wise, my old friend, who had also been doing the PX stores of Europe, told me about his new life in the Merchant Navy: you would make long trips, have a good time, spend a few nights in Hong Kong or New York and be off again, and not much to do in terms of work. This sounded a very good proposition and so I asked Beryl, my sister, to type out some phoney references saying that I had been a waiter, knew silver service (big mistake) and was looking for a career in the Merchant Navy. The lads from Stamford Hill talked of big tips, even a touch of romance from young widows, exotic foreign places, so off I marched to Dock Street in the East End and presented myself for work. A few days later I had a call to go down there and was offered a post as waiter aboard the *Chusan*, a P & O liner not going to any exotic places but merely chugging round the Mediterranean. Summer holiday cruises. Fair enough, I thought, a couple of months of the Med and then maybe China and the Far East. So I went to Southampton to buy my uniform and was soon fitted up in a smart white suit and peaked hat. And off I went. Hell!

Life on the Ocean Wave

It was not the fun I had supposed, since this was no ordinary ship. This big white vessel was a holiday cruise ship and the customers expected to be not only served their grub but entertained and fussed, wined and dined at all times. Each service was multiplied by two, as there were two sittings for each meal and no sooner had they announced that breakfast or dinner was served than an avalanche of faces which had been pressing against the glass door all piled in like lava erupting from a volcano. As it was a cruise ship everyone turned up for every meal and for some bizarre reason you weren't allowed to write down the order. There were only two or three choices and you had to remember what everyone wanted. I looked after only two tables with four people on each, so why did I find it so irksome? Some would want soup, but some would want whatever the alternative was or they'd want to start with the main course and some wanted this veg and some wanted that, and then I'd get to the kitchen and have to wait my turn and take two or three dishes out on a tray and I cannot think why eight defeated me unless my memory was failing me.

The soups took for ever, but after a while I worked out that several people would want soup and so without waiting to take the order I kept three or four in my dumb waiter so that I could be quick off the mark. As soon as they sat down I would shout out, 'Who's for soup?' They soon got used to my unorthodox ways and the fact that though the head waiter placed 'speedy Gonzales' right next to the doors of the kitchen my poor customers would still be the last out.

As soon as they left the second sitting would come piling in and again I was spinning in and out of the kitchens getting the various orders and trying to remember the damned things. In the kitchen all hell would break loose with the shouting and screaming orders. These kids had been doing it for years and this was the first time I had waited in my life. I had served drinks but never waited table with the added complications of serving vegs with one hand holding spoon and fork. You dared not scoop them out with a soup spoon but had to grip the flaming fork *and* spoon between your fingers to be elegant, after all the customers were on a ship and you had to preserve the fantasy of a luxury liner for them.

Breakfast at seven and eight, and then lunch at twelve and one-thirty and then afternoon tea at four, one sitting thank God, and the two sittings for dinner meant that I was serving forty-eight meals per day plus teas. It doesn't sound a lot, but it was murder because each tripper had saved for this and was fussy about everything and I would forget something and rush back and while I was rushing back their food was getting cold and by the time I went back for the cauliflower and waited at the line the other guys were on to the sweets and I'd be sweating like a pig. The head waiter was a sport and would help out for a bit, since he was an old hand. I started to admire these men who were cool and had sharp greased-back hair and never seemed to sweat.

Then at the end of the evening when you were shagged out of your mind there were party games and drinks and streamers to give out and they *must have fun*. I had come to hell on water. I'd collapse at night in my bunk, my stomach now taking its vengeance, and fall into a sleep in a cabin with six other blokes. My folly. I wished I had been a deck hand. It would have been peaceful just swabbing the decks. The morning came with shouts to get up and get your breakfast, but not before you had cleaned round your station. Then it would start again, the mad frenzy, and it would go on until 9 p.m.

When we docked at Barcelona I went on deck after breakfast and saw the shimmering, beautiful yellow sun-misted haze over the city. It was a sight I would never forget and then it all seemed worthwhile. After lunch we were given some hours off, if it was our break, and it was such bliss to walk around Barcelona and see the sights. I remember walking up and down the Ramblas admiring all the whores who used to parade there and then getting back to the ship for dinner. That was our one afternoon off. Most people would get off the boat when we docked and we wouldn't see them till dinner; lunch and tea on that day would be served by a skeleton staff. So every few days there was one day of comparative bliss.

The next port of call was Cannes and again we had the afternoon off and swam on the little strip of sand. At night we went round the town like poor sailors admiring all the glittering lights and cabarets in the large hotel gardens; we found a cheap steak and chips place and had a good meal for once. Walking back along the promenade we saw the *Chusan* lit up and glittering on the waters, looking like a demi-paradise, and we all agreed that hell had never looked so pretty.

Naples followed after a couple of days of frenzy and at night I strolled alone around this fascinating town until I was followed by some street urchins whom I allowed to con me into buying them a pizza, which they all dived into. I was glad to have the kids for a bit of company and they were giggling so much because they had conned me for a pizza. When we got outside into the street there was a street vendor selling slices of melon and the smallest of the group, who was still too young to be a rogue and felt some guilt for his mates' action (although it had not cost me a great deal for their pizza), bought me a piece of melon. He wanted to show me that he was aware of what was going on and wanted to treat me. It was such a sweet gesture it stayed in my memory.

After that on the way back we didn't stop and it was work and more work. I slept one night on deck under the stars and it was blissful to see the vast panorama of stars as you lay on a warm deck out at sea. We docked at Southampton and received our tips and wages less deductions. I had had enough and wanted out. That was my first and last taste of the Merchant Navy; from Southampton to Tilbury I stayed on deck, pretending to be a tourist. No more cleaning for me. No more. I had had enough.

I got to Manor House and didn't feel too good. A few weeks later I checked into hospital, since my stomach was torturing me daily. A tube was inserted into my nose and fed into my stomach and I was treated with a milk drip that allows a continuous drip of milk to go into your stomach and on to your ulcer. It's meant to heal you. I was nineteen and a bit of a wreck. I stayed in hospital for four weeks.

Theatre in 1990

It's dark outside. I'm sitting in Brighton. I like getting up before the light and then I seem ahead of it for the rest of the day. It's Christmas again and the beginning of the last decade of the century.

1990 is really the end of the eighties, although last year all the pundits were giving their tips for the future and doffing their hats to their faves of the past. One rag which had championed me for years decided to ignore in print any contribution I had made during the whole of the eighties. It was miffed because I had reacted to some little slur from one of its whingey writers with something less than grace. It's the era of the little people and, as Anthony Burgess so rightly says, sub-art now rules. Or words to that effect. Last year I was the subject of a few attacks and one rag saw fit to make comments of a personal nature, about my face and my age. Now while I don't mind an argy-bargy there are, I think, limits to what these angst-ridden bitches – unfortunately and sorry to say, most of them have been of the gentler sex – have to say. It seems that merely being female and having inherited the agonies of history and the natural rage that women have to amend the crimes made against them gives every little sourpuss a licence to exercise a taste for sadism. *Look what they did to us!* Of course there are a few whacky females around who can mask their innate fascism with a political face. It has become a fashion for some and a new ugly canker has grown into the pages of yellow journalism.

When I read about the 1890s and how the great Henry Irving, who sent his message to me across the century and got me to the Lyceum, ran his theatre like a warrior with an output that was as remarkable as it was seemingly impossible and how he threw all his energy into directing and running a theatre with that rare brand of courage, then I want to salute him across the chasm of years. When nearly dying and playing in Belfast he received a request to appear before the King and his guests at Sandringham. He had to travel day and night, including a rough sea crossing, perform and get back to Ireland, missing only one show. I am amazed at the fortitude of this man and wonder how he could have survived as long as he did. He does the performance and has a nice chat with the King, and then, no sleep, oh no, he has to get the train at midnight and return to Liverpool and then face a *150 mile voyage to Belfast*! When he gets there he is ready to step on the stage to play Mephistopheles. A truly great artist.

Of course we can always hold up beacons of energy and they will always cast long shadows over the wimps, but you never heard Irving whining and begging for money! He may have needed it, but he knew that the only way to make the dosh was – and is – to make yourself and your theatre into a star. The only way is to take those risks the public adore. Hence the actor will do just that. Olivier did just that. Ellen Terry. Sarah Bernhardt. It has something to do with knowing that the money is invested in you. Not in a theatre; not in an institution, unless it has some mystical reputation like the Moscow Arts; certainly not in a director and his cabal unless it is one of the great innovators like Joan Littlewood or Elia Kazan, who really won the people to their work. The living and breathing actor is what the audience come to see. This in some way can help an actor gird his loins to the occasion: his knowledge of his responsibility may make him strike that much harder and plumb deeper into his psyche; not for the money and not for the fame but for the energy and faith that money represents.

Nowadays an actor is cushioned from that 'make or break' feeling and can prepare his role in peace and safety. Even if the play is not a big hit, he will not starve and the theatre will always be 80 per cent full because it's the place to go. The directors will get on their hind legs like dogs begging for money for themselves and chums to keep the club running and keep their careers alive. They will speak to Arts Councils at every opportunity and show figures to demonstrate their good housekeeping, and we will watch and listen as percentages are being brayed and the cost of living index and in 'real terms' and the grant must be higher, must be, always must be so they can run these great institutions and who would envy this task? They are enormous machines that need not the headiness of actors and their self-obsessed temperament but the concept of an overseer, a lord of creation.

Irving would rehearse all his actors and their grouping and action with great care and only then would return home to practise on his own. In those days the actor was a bit of a soloist. Olivier's films show an obsessive interest in the small role, to the extent of sometimes making them too interesting. He was an actor who enjoyed giving to his colleagues and, just as there may be some actors who would ignore their mates, so there are just as many who, because of their leading status, are able to make sure that the actors know they are not being ignored. George C. Scott's direction and performance of *Present Laughter* in New York was a hit for both and the liveliest direction of Coward I have ever seen. Orson Welles, José Ferrer, Olivier, Jean-Louis Barrault, Jacques Charon of the Comédie Française have all directed and starred with very good results, so what I am thinking is that while the director is most useful and vital, he is not the source of creation.

Mind you, I have to take my hat off to them for championing the arts and making sure they are funded. An actor would be too proud to beg. He wouldn't close a theatre, blaming others for not shoving more money down its throat. An actor would blame himself for not bringing the audiences in! Would Irving have closed a theatre? Never, since as an actor he knew his public *wanted him and would miss him*, because he had a one-on-one relationship with them. He could not close the theatre; when it did have to close because of fire regulations he was mortified and had to find a fortune to render it safe for the LCC. He didn't have the money. He sold the lease and the company was declared bankrupt after he had spent years killing himself on stage. He was conned. Of course progress needs good arts administrators and these should be the people who crow for the funds, not the artistic directors, who probably have enough to do. We tend to think that the actor/manager, overburdened and self-involved, could not oversee the whole, but I have seen directors obsessed with their leading player, all but ignoring everybody else, hoping the 'star' will pull an otherwise mediocre production out of the doldrums.

We no longer look at or listen to great theatre actors like Irving unless they are the trash sub-art in LA getting millions for a film and discussing Shakespeare. It makes you want to puke if you have any puke left. Henry Irving brought literature and art to the stage; he brought dignity, power, daring and raised the status of the actor to the greatest heights the century had seen. And he was knighted for it, as was Olivier. Now the actor has drifted back to the flotsam and jetsam. The vehicle for rubbish, the imbiber of trash, the messenger of crap, the spokesman of the people. Millions for dickheads. Can you believe it? Well, Hollywood is an industry that has succeeded in lowering critical and literary standards throughout the entire civilized world. It didn't exist in Irving's time.

Today we revere directors, but the actor brings with him the Promethean fire, and we are also allowed to possess him, to share him and bring our tribute to him since the sacrifice is a vulnerable being. We must be able to eat our gods. It's an ancient tradition.

I know a few directors who create a whole new world and bring to life ideas that were merely hints. But I am thinking of some others who do not. The ones whose faces are splattered like so many potatoes in every paper, weary faces always with the same boring tune in their ever-moving mouths. Olivier's reign at the National was one of the most exciting I have seen since he brought in some of the best directors.

Some directors get credit for productions that bring in choreographers who work marvels and yet are hardly mentioned; or they are credited at the bottom of the programme as 'Movement by . . .' Claude Chagrin is one of the greatest of mime teachers and choreographers. She staged some epics, such as the movement for *The Royal Hunt of the Sun* and *Equus,* and now can't find an outlet for her rare skills in the places that would benefit from it. Perhaps this art is no longer valid, but as a director I have found that years of working with 'straight' companies have rendered actors stiff, unbending, remote, obsessed with 'personality of the character'. Moving with great awkwardness, untrained in any wider sense. Brittle. Parochial in taste and judgement. Claude's skills could take an actor away from his self-obsession and into the idea of performing in a comic, critical and satiric sense. Her lessons saved me from a very dreary year. Her classes were warm and filled with light. And we learned.

Ghosts – 23 December 1990

Sometimes I see the river just easing itself past the windows in the East End and I think of the ghosts that must wonder at the new mega-city being built in what was once Ratcliff Wharf and Highway. A place of filth and iniquity, of cheap and dangerous brothels, poor streets eaten away with disease and poverty. Of course this was a century ago. I read about baby farms where the poor who couldn't feed any more children would give a small fee to an advertiser who wished to take care of babies and after taking the fee from the poor distraught woman would let the child die of neglect. Of streets teeming with the unemployed and poor. Yes, we are lucky today. The tourists are still living through 'Ripperology' and walks can be had that take you around the 'sights' where the Ripper struck his victims down in an orgy of bloodlust.

It was 1888, which is an odd date. Henry Irving is getting made up to play Macbeth in 1888, although his stage murders follow Jack's and may be inspired by them. The public are in a mood for blood. Oscar Wilde, also inspired by the lugubrious atmosphere of Whitechapel and the river, starts writing *The Picture of Dorian Grey*. Oscar invites W. B. Yeats for Christmas dinner in 1888 and in the same year publishes his wonderfully tender fairy tales. Van Gogh is trying to paint in the South of France. The East End is a filthy, unlit conglomeration of alleys and streets and the Jews are pouring in from the four corners of the earth, particularly from Russia where the pogroms have taken a turn for the worse. My mother's family settle in Batty Street, just off Commercial Road. They have brought siblings with them and give birth regularly until eleven have passed through the portals, my mother being one of them. She was born in 1903, when the blood had not yet been washed away from the back of the house in Hanbury Street where Jack had performed his more ambitious deeds. Why do tourists love to tread the path of Jack so many years later, when the 1914–18 war killed millions of young men?

But still the East End fascinates in its awfulness and seething energy. Everything is possible because there is no bar to your imagination. You can be what you want to be, you were told, from the kitchen tables to the slums. You had to do something to escape and so the very conditions may have inspired a greater response to life, forcing you to come to grips with it. In the East End you could be the champion of the world. I have a photo in my possession showing Jimmy Wilde falling to the floor after receiving a knock-out blow, but my uncle Alf, as usual the gentleman, is holding his arms out to stop him crashing to the floor! Jimmy Wilde recovered and Alf went home with his one sighted eye and one blind and eventually lost his sight. When he visited us at Manor House he would say, 'Hey, Les, you're getting bigger every day.' They called me by that name, though in my teens I had changed to using my middle name, which they had fortunately given me. Thank God I had a spare . . .

> MIKE: Mike's OK, after the holy saint . . . Mike with a hard 'k' like a kick-swift . . . not mad about Les.
> LES: It's soft, it's gooey, but choose it I did not, in my mother's hot womb did she curse this name on me . . . it's my handle . . . under the soft – it's spiky, under the pillow it's sharp.
>
> [*East*]

Also I could purge the spots and blemishes out of me in the plays. Alf never lost his humour and always sent up his blindness. He was a unique character; he never whinged and never would have done in a thousand years. He was a fighter till the end of his life. He had anger – and ladles of it – for what he saw around him. For the villains he identified in his mind, the politicians and warmongers, as he called them. The people who lived off and profited by war.

I came back from my short stint in the Merchant Navy and wondered what to do next. At the back of my mind there was still this idea of acting, but then again of writing. Would I be a famous writer, I asked myself, or a great actor? I never considered the idea of directing, since that is an in-between job that has been invented in recent years. There have been actors and writers since the Greeks and so I naturally gravitated towards those archetypes. I had no idea that I would end up spending so much time pushing traffic around the stage, but now I think of directing as more in the realm of painting.

After another ghastly round of dreary jobs I could take no more. In the meantime the YMCA not only kept me off the streets but made me fit again and gave me a sense of purpose. The old premises in Tottenham Court Road were a sanctuary where you could sit and read or play hand-ball, which I did for years and became a dab hand at it.

I had a job in King's Road, Chelsea, at a shop called John Michael. I wandered down there for my interview and got on well with the manager, who was a tiny Jewish guy. I seemed to make him laugh and we were soon on good terms. I was totally unfamiliar with the road, but I liked the little shops which sold old prints and antiques. I took lunch at the Sa Tortuga, which was owned by the family of an actress I was to work with in later years, Linda Marlowe. I would sit in the little coffee shop amidst all the Chelsea bohemians and then return to the shop. It was 1956 or 1957 and we were in the middle of a cultural revolution. The shop in its way had sensed this and was limply trying to capture the new mood. A quaint little shop just down the road was owned by Mary Quant, whose husband would come in to John Michael. Once when I was wearing the last suit I ever had made by Diamond Bros the famous designer passed his compliments – I was rather chuffed, since Mary Quant's shop and fashion pioneering were already the talk of the street.

I had a long way to travel this time but I was intrigued by the street, even if the work was rather dull and sometimes painful in its midweek boredom. I got out of the tube at Sloane Square and would see the billboard on the front of the Royal Court for *Look Back in Anger*, which had not the slightest effect on me, as I remember. I even saw an extract on TV with an actress ironing and I wondered then what was going on in the theatre and what was causing this huge rumpus. This *Look Back in Anger* seemed to me to be terribly conventional. Theatre in my mind was something to do with magic, music hall, Harry Houdini and tightrope walkers. Ideas belonged in books.

John Michael was a very pleasant, civilized chap who wore stiff collars and tailored suits. His mother had a dress shop next door and I have an idea that the shop was a kind of 'gift' for the bright young man. It was on two floors and when it was quiet I would escape for a long read. I had just discovered Henry Miller and that kept me occupied. Before Miller I was getting through Huxley and further developed my penchant for the strange and macabre with *Brave New World* – I wished all his books were like that. I spent a longer time in this place than anywhere else, partly because I had discovered the City Literary Institute. Twice a week I would go from work and attend adult education classes. Those who have missed out in their youthful studies can now go back! It's a wonderful idea. Who thought of it? I made a telephone call one day and asked somebody – I have no idea who – how the hell I got started in acting, since there seemed to be a wall between me and the other side. How did *they* get to these film sets, how did *they* get in the film? What did you do? Who did you have to know? What was this mystery? Ah, I was going to find out.

Drury Lane

That's when a voice told me to try the City Lit. I queued in the corridor for an interview and was duly received. For the first time in my life I became a student of dramatic art.

The first class was a way for us to get up without being embarrassed. The teacher had us sail across the room in a movement he called 'peripheral', which was meant to be open and liberating, and then to repeat the rush across the classroom in a 'centripetal' movement. I was ecstatic. This was indeed Art. At the break we sat in the canteen being awfully impressed by the second-termers, who were already in costume for a rehearsal of *As You Like It* . . . God, the heady feeling of drama. I scoffed down cheese and chutney sandies and flew back into my studies awaiting the second half of the evening.

Now we were confronted with a chap with a reddish beard and authoritarian manner who desired that we learn some text and bring it next week. Ah, the acid test of our skills was to be applied. We would be *performing in public*!! I had never read a play and had little interest in the ones that I now read, so I picked up a short story and set about dramatizing it. It was a little tale called 'The Bucket Rider' by Kafka and is about a man who is freezing in his simple abode; his coal bucket is empty, so that he decides to ride on it to the coal dealer in order to demonstrate by the very lightness of his bucket that he needs some credit for coal lest he perish. It was a story that had heart, soul, pathos, magic, eeriness, lyricism, all the qualities missing in the plays I scoured through, Shakespeare excepted. I spent hours learning the flaming thing, but as yet hardly had the idea for staging and shaping my tale – I would just tell it.

I got up when my time came, having heard lots of Margarets, Beatrices and Juliets. I began, but after a few moments Red Beard got up . . . 'No, no, no!' That won't do, you must find a play, a play with some continuous dialogue that you excerpt. My story had the dialogue plus narration and it was a perfect one-to-one telling of a story. Kafka hardly ever used the third person in the story . . . No, no, no! I sat down chastened.

But I continued learning the story and knew that one day I would perform it. I have performed it several times in a one-man show, acting all the characters. It is a wonderful piece for a student to learn, since it gives you a chance to dissolve from one character to another, far better than tearing a piece out of a play and dangling the creature in front of us like a fish out of water, when you act to an empty chair! A story has a beginning and an end.

However, Red Beard was doing his job and wanted me to read plays and get off this tack. So I sat and read the most dreary bunch of plays and could find little that made any impact on me, since plays are indeed hard to read and must be seen. I ventured into Shakespeare and tossed off a *Richard III*, a piece of *Hamlet*. Then I was asked to do Launcelot Gobbo and I was pleased the suggestion came from the outside. I delighted in all Gobbo's changes of mind and conscience, which were really like a form of guilt.

As the young fledglings performed (and many were there just because they were a bit lonely and wanted to have a go at acting; only one or two were recaptured souls who found themselves in the nick of time) Red Beard asked for comments and then gave his own. These were, as I remember, fairly sound advice. The classroom smelled of polishing and char sweat, chalk, canteen smells, masses and masses of paper, clerical utensils, carbon paper, cheap perfume, sweat from the gym and first-year ballet for beginners, canteen soup, the tinned variety, pipe tobacco. I sat amidst the roll-neck sweaters and the girls with woolly stockings; some of the chaps had come from offices and still had shirts and ties on, but had changed from their trousers into jeans as a concession to non-conformity and the possibility of some active 'peripheral movement'. The City Lit is in a narrow alleyway called Stukeley Street off Drury Lane. I have always had a strange association with this street, and an almost uncanny returning to it as if it were a river and I a salmon that returns to spawn. It was the same fanciful obsession as I had had with the Lyceum, which was just around the corner, since now I seemed to befriend the spirit of Kean, the great actor of the nineteenth century.

Kean had fascinated me since, as with Artaud, someone had thrust into my hand a book whose contents set me aflame. I would carry the book as a symbol of man's awesome achievement over natural handicap. Kean was a small man, perhaps no more than five feet five inches, and really had to fight to overcome opposition to him. In those days, of course, the actor not only had to supply his own costumes, but very often had to walk to his gigs. Kean would generally have his family with him and spent two or three days hiking around the country, perhaps eking out the money with some recitals in the village market for a few pennies. Of course actors were not protected by unions or Social Security – nor were the general population, but once you were a carpenter or tailor or cook you were at least secure in your employment as long as your master was solvent. If you were an actor you were only as popular as you could make yourself and would work only as long as it pleased the guv'nor, who would test you to see if your product was successful, and ditch you if it wasn't. It was a monstrous life, but had its compensations.

I read Nigel Playfair's biography of Kean like wildfire. Kean. I liked the name; Edmund was good, too. A perfect name for a firebrand. An outsider who felt distinct discomfort with the acting profession and with those who went to genuflect at his feet. He was happier in the little club called the 'Wolf Club' he formed in the Strand. There he could relax after the performance at Drury Lane in his limited but powerful repertoire of characters, Richard III, Sir Giles Overreach, Shylock. It was as Shylock that he made his début; he was called on to perform at more or less the last minute and nobody took him very seriously until they began to see his strange and phenomenal power. He was a danger on stage, a wild beast that years of penury, rejection and struggle had formed into a dangerously formidable acting force. Do hardship and pain do this? In some instances I believe they do and I would have been fascinated to see Kean act. I am sure it would have taken your breath away by its sheer audacity, whether lit by candles or by one kilowatt lamps. You cannot take away the power even if the style is antique. Too many people have praised his work for him to be dismissed as the ham of his age.

So Kean was another of those symbols I carried in my mind to help me through the long days. I would call on him, feast on him, dwell on his life and see myself reflected in his prism, hoping that in studying him some of it would rub off on me. Just as you study painters in order to become a better painter, so you study not only the living, breathing form but the essence and the core of the man, his life and his methods, his great successes and the way he lived; you try to avoid the booze, but in those days that might have been difficult. It was a ghastly time anyway in London and poverty was rife, so if Kean saw the other side he would haul himself out of any self-questioning state and soldier on.

I cannot imagine Kean taking direction from a man who told him how to speak verse. He would have butchered the metre and set fire to the remains . . . we read that to see him act was 'like reading Shakespeare by flashes of lightning'. He was a wild animal within a civilized art and he gave that art a new form. Even then it was competitive, but he made it into a boxing ring. You went to see blood and he gave it metaphysically.

I knew Kean must have trodden these very streets and at one time may have lived in rooms nearby. And so every time I pass the Theatre Royal Drury Lane, where the anodyne *Miss Saigon* sits like a great, soggy pudding, I make a special thought for Kean. Each time I go to the little theatre cafés around the Lyceum, I think of Henry going in the stage door in Burleigh Street. What is Kean to me or I to him? I don't know why I fasten on to ghosts of the past, but I get a tremendous amount of pleasure in studying and listening to the thoughts that come from it.

So the City Lit was the beginning of my Drury Lane: we sat and took it all in and dreamed of the future. My association with the Lane continued over the years. In 1967 Jim Haynes' Arts Lab was already open right next door and facing on to Drury Lane. It was there that I had my very first performance as actor–manager in *In the Penal Colony*, adapted from Kafka, less than fifty feet from the classroom where I had done my first performance of 'The Bucket

Rider'! Night after night I was tightening up my technique in a sensational play which gave me tremendous opportunities for performance. Just next door.

In 1963 or '64 I had met a mime artist called Lindsay Kemp and we were both fascinated with the potential of mime. He called me one day to tell me excitedly that he had found the ideal flat. Where was it? Of course it had to be in Drury Lane, on the other side of the alleyway that led to the City Lit. We had a fitful few months, but neither of us was working and we were both too intense for each other's good. I did get him a job, though, in the TV Shakespeare *Hamlet at Elsinore*, with Christopher Plummer as Hamlet and Lindsay and I playing the Player Queen and Lucianus, the murderer King. It was only shown once on the BBC and it was Plummer's finest performance. It cost so much money through overtime and a strange union law that everyone walked away with absolute fortunes and Chris bought a house in Mayfair on the proceeds, I believe. Very different from poor Edmund. No TV then. No actors worrying about their trailers and their 'card' on the film with their petty little billing.

Then in the same year I heard that the Comédie Française needed extras for a Feydeau farce and in those days they would swell the crowd scene with actors who were out of work. I actually performed with the Comédie Française!! Of course, at the Aldwych, Drury Lane.

Jacques Charon, the director of *Un Fil à la Patte*, wanted some extra bodies for a party scene and I was one of those picked. I was able to watch at close quarters the French acting team and be part of it. I was totally astounded by Robert Hirsch, who was and is an actor after my own heart. He took an idea and squeezed every possible nuance out of it and created an armoury of gestures and a vocabulary that was as astonishing as it was erudite and precise. It was taking the art of acting to absurd heights and making the most grotesque art out of it and at the same time moving the audience to gasps of wonder. As soon as Monsieur Hirsch entered the stage he began acting. As he descended the staircase in the most extraordinary convoluted way you knew you were in the presence of a master. Spellbinding was the order of the day. When he took off his make-up he was a fairly attractive Frenchman in his forties.

During the season I became friends with Alain Feydeau, the

nephew of the famous comedy writer Georges Feydeau, whose work we had been performing. Alain wanted to go to a very English restaurant, so I was invited with the French actors to Rules in Maiden Lane and felt very grand indeed. Alain came from a line of theatricals; he was a minor player in the Comédie Française and seemed glad to know an English actor. When in the future I did my summer course at the French mime school Alain offered me a room in his apartment in the Rue de Richelieu, near the Comédie Française. I was invited to look around the Comédie Française and went backstage and saw the dressing room of the 'Societaires', which they had done up themselves since they were there for life. I went to Robert Hirsch's room and it was like an elegant apartment. Alain was a charming and very amusing host who spoke a kind of Agatha Christie English. He was overwhelmingly fascinated with Hammer horror films and liked the part of London that was ghoulish and weird.

When he visited London I always felt rather ashamed. London seemed so drab and lifeless in comparison to Paris. But he would visit the little house I shared in Islington with my future wife Alison, and always seemed quite happy to potter about here. I hadn't seen him for many years when I was in Paris directing Roman Polanski in the French version of *Metamorphosis*. I thought I would look him up. He had moved to the Opéra, where he had a small apartment. He made dinner and predictably talked of Agatha. He was still a charming and generous host, but he seemed much older and sadder and somehow a little remote from the world. Perhaps he never found anyone he could live with. Perhaps having a name like Feydeau was a burden of expectancy that he didn't need.

In the sixties we had the chance of seeing the great theatre companies of the world and observing and watching the strange styles of theatre so different from our own. In the World Theatre season of which *Un Fil à la Patte* was part, I was able to advance my ideas of theatre and develop new cultures in my acting. Where would I have had a chance to do this without that international season which brought together so many different forms? We have nothing of that diversity here. Many of the great European directors who might not only shed new light but give us a taste of something different have not been seen in Britain. If I was a punter I would demand diversity, I would demand that the theatre administrator, whoever it may be, should scour the world looking for the best creative talent and bring it here. I would like variety in my restaurant, not the same old stodge over and over again. Joe Papp invited me to New York to direct *Coriolanus* and it was an exciting event for me and it seemed to work for the others. Susan Loewenberg made it possible for me to direct *Agamemnon* with black actors in LA. These experiences were vital for me; they served the community and refreshed us and stimulated us and rewarded us and reinvigorated us and showed us new routes and delighted us and sent us scampering to the theatre. They made us see ourselves the way others see us and helped to cast a new light on familiar things and bring countries together and cultures and people closer; they helped to break down constipated and antique notions like confetti and taped music and half-digested movement ... No, I know you don't like foreigners too much. They're so foreign, aren't they? I want to see your ugly mush year after year.

One season I saw Ansky's *The Dybbuk*, Schiller's *The Robbers* and Goethe's *Clavigo*. I remember the magic of *The Dybbuk* and the opening scene with the men in the synagogue, each in strange, convoluted positions, one resting with his hand up the wall, each finding a pose which expressed him and his longing. I remember the dance when everyone came on in painted face masks. How all the beggars danced with the beautiful bride, Leah. How all the shrivelled-up wanted to be near a fruit that was so full and ripe and vulnerable. Certain men of a certain age like the intercourse of other men of equal standing in other nations and embrace them as fellow artists; they are cosmopolitan and wish to open our stages and nations to them. I believe that when I saw the Berliner Ensemble at the Old Vic during the reign of Olivier and Ken Tynan it was because Olivier and Tynan were both men of the world and wanted the world to come to them. They did, and it was a rich day for me. Then I saw Ekkehard Schall's *Arturo Ui* and his *Coriolanus*.

Who do the poor mugs here in Britain have as guides or mentors as they slide out into the world full of self-confidence in their little squibs of acting? They have seen nothing and know less and they go out puffed up to traverse the little pond which they think is the sea of their experience. Is that why everybody looks so young? Theatre directors in their fifties look like young men, a bit shrivelled, perhaps, but there is little of the aged look of experience.

But getting back to Drury Lane, there used to be a theatre there called the Winter Garden. It was there that I rehearsed for Murray Macdonald, who was directing *The Amorous Prawn*, starring the wondrous and ageless Evelyn Laye, or 'Boo' to her friends. I was understudying a couple of parts, including that of Harry Landis, but he eventually went out of his mind with the material that he had to shout each night, and he fled the country. We were rehearsing in this big barn which was falling into disrepair. I sat there with sharpened pencil, since I was ASM as well as understudy.

I liked Evelyn Laye very much and she was particularly friendly to me. On the first day she came by our little desk, mine and Chris's the stage manager, who was understudy to Stanley Baxter. Chris was a simple bloke, happy to be doing this the rest of his life, but he was kind and gentle and I liked him. Boo came up and asked for a cigarette. When Chris proffered his she said, 'One with spats?' 'Pardon?' responded Chris, but I immediately whisked out my du Maurier and offered her the tipped cigarette she wanted. I was immensely proud. To my ever greater pride, she asked me to have dinner with her when the show hit Brighton and to the startled looks of the rest of the cast she swanned out of the stage door with me! Actually she must have been well bored with the cast after an eight-week tour of Britain, which is what you did in the old days. You wouldn't dream of opening cold after five or six previews as they do now. Then you had to master your laughs and timing and the author might change something on the tour and you had to have time to see if it worked.

The Winter Garden was demolished in 1965 and the New London opened in its place in 1973. For a while it was a bit of a white elephant, but after *East* closed at that terrible dump of a theatre, the Regent Poly, it went to the New London and did well. The Regent Poly was like a long tunnel; I remember it as a cinema where in my teens I saw a most remarkable French film called *Life Begins Tomorrow* (*La Vie Commence Demain*). Anyway, at the Regent we weren't doing too well and we were given our notice by Brian Rix. I begged him to let us stay at a slightly reduced rent because I knew that *East* would pick up, but he was having none of it. So a few weeks later we heard that the New London was available and we found a new manager to take over the admin and went into Drury Lane with three shows: *East*, *The Fall of the House of Usher* and *Metamorphosis*. A great time to see the canopy of the building with my name plastered over it. Another proud time. So Drury Lane seems to have figured much in my life.

However, while I was still at the City Lit I was befriended by Murray Gilmore, a professional actor who was sitting in on the class as a student teacher. Murray was one of those signposts you come across in life which point in a very definite way.

He was a Scot who seemed to have had some kind of nervous breakdown in his middle years and was seeking work as a teacher. The City Lit was a place various people gravitated to for whatever reason, mostly because it provided a kind of sanctuary for those who had lost their way. Murray would stand up when asked to comment on our little moments of self-exposure and he would get quite carried away, his eyes bulging and the sheer joy and passion for the art pouring out of him. I became quite close to him and for a couple of years he would train me, advising me on how to place my voice and what to look for in a speech and revealing things that I never suspected in the text. He would analyse a speech in *Richard III* word by word so that I would know exactly what I was saying and not give a cod rendering of Olivier. When he broke up the text and hinted at the subtext his fervour illuminated the speech as much as his analysis. 'But I – that am not shaped for sportive tricks, Nor made to court an amorous looking-glass, I that am rudely stamp'd, and want love's majesty, To strut before a wanton ambling nymph . . .' He interpreted this to mean that Richard could be impotent; 'love's majesty' was the flowering of an erection and not just a fair and pretty form. This method of looking at Shakespeare was a revelation and I started to look at his text and the use of metaphor which masked the real and often sexual intent of the speech.

This way of writing is totally unknown and unused today. Writers say exactly what they mean, but do not use language inventively in drama. As Oscar Wilde said, 'The function of the artist is to invent, not to chronicle.' Perhaps my problem with drama as we perceive it in our century is this terrible obsession with the real, the slavish devotion to putting things down as they are without recourse to the mystery of allusion and allegory, which allow the artist to step back from the subject and view it as a symptom of human behaviour in a wider social context. My fascination with Kafka came from the fact that you could not read him simply as describing a real event, one that we must be concerned with by pressing all those emotional buttons. He led us to view the suffering of humankind with a keen invention that lifted the plight of his creatures to a level of great poetic art.

So when I read the plays that I was supposed to absorb I could see no merit in any, but found them pedestrian and dull. They recked of ordinariness and my mind was never engaged by their activities. Of course, after a while I had to engage myself and found some speeches that, through the task of learning and acting, led me to drop some of my high-falutin ideals. I realized that I would be doing very little Shakespeare, which I was getting a taste for, but plays more like *Not in the Book* and *Write me a Murder*.

I had more time for the American dream and feasted on Tennessee Williams, who fascinated me. I identified with his wounded heroines and was distraught at the plight of Blanche DuBois in the movie of *A Streetcar Named Desire*; while I naturally studied Stanley Kowalski, a part I might have liked to play one day and nearly did, I still found the character of Blanche far more interesting and multi-dimensional, as she was intended to be until Brando stole the limelight. All Tennessee Williams plays intrigued me and cast some kind of spell over me. From the first lines, from the descriptions of the locale, the set, 'an adobe house', always adobe . . . what the hell was that? It didn't matter. Arthur Miller I liked too, since he was real in the sense of vital, not merely accurate. His language had heart and passion and I could identify again with poor Willy Loman and his son in *Death of a Salesman* . . . I understood Biff in *Death of a Salesman* in that when he stood in the office of his father's friend, when he had waited for hours to see him, all he could do was to steal a pen. I understood this only too well. The waiting and the knowledge that with all your passion and energy you will be given the bum's rush. To steal a pen, a little rebellion, a little act of pain that is so ancient, you take a token from your enemy to curse him with, or you wish to show that he is vulnerable – instead of him giving you the world or the possibility of it you are left with a 'gesture' . . . a pathetic one. But I found even the successful English plays vapid. However, there was nothing I could do but go along with them.

I was fascinated by playwrights like Max Frisch, Dürrenmatt and Ionesco. I could enjoy Anouilh, Sartre, Rostand, Brecht, Toller, but found no equivalent here. So I was all the more intrigued to discover that Artaud adored Jacobean tragedy. I set to reading the work he much admired, *'Tis Pity She's a Whore*, and immediately loved it. I wrote to Bernard Miles a few years later when I heard that he was staging 'Tis Pity. He *did* grant me an interview and I *did* see the shambles of a production, but I remember it probably because of the steely murderous performance of John Woodvine. The rest is silence. But that was much later. For now I was sitting in the City Lit. Murray Gilmore coached me to win the grant that paid to take me to Webber-Douglas, and I applied there largely because it was the only school that would accept me in the second year. I finally abandoned menswear; Webber-Douglas absorbed me and I soon got into the swing of things. So instead of getting out at Sloane Square I would now alight at South Kensington. John Michael, mind you, had been kind to me and I had had a chance to meet a different kind of client coming in and made friends with lots of the Chelsea 'crowd' of the time. We would sit in the coffee bar and talk; nowadays there are not really the same easy places to congregate and sit without going for a big-deal dinner. Michael White, the producer, was a curly-haired and charming young man then and Peter Wyngarde was a regular whom I got to know when he was so brilliant acting with Vivien Leigh in *Duel of Angels*. I first met him when I was working as a waiter in Au Père de Nico, also in Chelsea. This was my part-time job then, clearing the tables and washing the glasses which helped eke out the pennies. A lot of 'successful' actors came to Au Père de Nico and tipped the poor out-of-work actors who used to work there, but the out-of-work actors would get so self-conscious when a star they knew very slightly came in that they would rush downstairs and clean glasses for half an hour.

John Gielgud came in to John Michael's one day and of course I rushed to serve him. He was extremely courteous and I asked him how the play was going. Now so many years later I might be in a shop and some young assistant might ask me the same question. In fact it is mostly taxi drivers who say, 'What you up to at the moment?' since I am the villain in so many films and taxi drivers see them all. East End hero makes good. All those nasty brutish thugs and funny East Enders.

All that started in the most extraordinary way. My archaeological excavations of my childhood were merely an exploration for writing *East* as an affectionate satire on childhood. Before this event I had never seen myself in this way.

First Exposure to Film – 1958

After an eventful but rather demoralizing year at Webber-Douglas I looked for work. During the terms' breaks I earned some money as a film extra – in those days you could reasonably expect to work once or twice a week and on a film you could work for two weeks continuously. It was the greatest fun and a fascinating introduction to film. I was astounded at how easy it was to get into the extras' union, the FAA, which was in Poland Street. I was actually on a film set for many months before I began to play parts on film and I think this helped in my future work in front of camera. I was able to watch all the 'greats' at work, and no better opportunity could befall anyone. I was an extra in *The Captain's Table*, *I Was Monty's Double* and *The Sheriff of Fractured Jaw* with Jayne Mansfield. There I was watching her go through her paces with Kenneth More; she was fascinating to watch as she was choreographed by her dance coach and singing her song. I was amazed as I heard the rich sound rumble through the set and saw her miming to the soundtrack.

In *The Devil's Disciple* I was vaguely in some crowd, but watched the astounding Burt Lancaster cycle home after work. In a TV series I worked a line or two with Richard Conte, saw Vittorio de Sica, chatted up John Schlesinger, and rode a donkey for the Boulting Brothers. We generally had a good time and I was thinking that this was all good practice; I would bring my books and study since there was a lot of hanging around. At the end of the day I was very pleased indeed to earn a fiver or an extra quid for being in a shot with the star or for some 'special action' . . .

Oliver Reed was an extra then; I met him and he seemed a charming young man. He told me he wanted to be an actor and I told him I was at drama school. It was the generation of improvisation – all the schools were doing it and I suggested he try it while we were hanging about, but I don't believe he was very interested. I was also doing photography to eke out a living; I had made my own dark room and was a dab hand at shooting actors. I took some very good shots of Reed, but seldom saw him after that. There were always some characters on the film set who drifted in as extras and there was a fair amount of interesting chat.

My last day at Webber D. we did our auditions. I had a go at Hamlet and did my William Saroyan, but the Hamlet was well criticized by a rather incisive visiting director and I valued his comments, as I do those of any intelligent being. A few agents were there, one of whom was John Penrose, who had a history of his own and had once been a performer himself. I went to see him in his office in Cambridge Circus and he took me on, so now I had an agent.

Samantha Eggar, the beauty with the freckles, had left, I don't know why, but she had been doing very well, had a wonderful voice and should have been one of those glamorous stage actresses we are so reluctant to have. We do like our old Queen Victoria dowagers, don't we? We simply adore those mother figures who remind us of stern matrons at boarding school and loathe beautiful, sensual, sexy ladies, relegating them to films or not really trusting them too much, but waiting until they get old, floppy, puffy, and then giving them all the juveniles.

John Penrose found a job for me straight off. Did I want to play a small part in *A View From The Bridge*? He was looking for a Rodolpho and mentioned it, but when he asked would I be confident enough to do it, I hesitated and he could see I wasn't sure. My training at Webber D. had not exactly prepared me, with rehearsals held by students since they only booked the directors once or twice a week and then you would 'run' it without the director there. Some system I was paying through the nose for! Of course, it's far better now since I have taught there and maybe this was the system in all drama schools then.

Anyway I played the part of a longshoreman and was ASM, which is the best possible training if you are going to direct. It also means you have an understanding of what goes on and do not become a primping, spoilt arsehole wanting everything to be done for you. I turned up at the rehearsal room in Windmill Street and began. It was a thrilling moment of my life – I was getting about nine pounds a week. I watched the actors go through their paces: they were damned good and all very experienced and they convinced me. Marina Martin, now a successful agent, played the female lead and was full of tender sympathy and utterly believable. I can't recall the others, but remember being sent out to get props like fruit for the table scenes and the company manager asked me always to get receipts. I thought, what, for a pound of apples I have to ask some right tough barrow boy for a receipt! I found that part difficult.

We put the show together and went to our first gig in Bradford. I moved into my first digs. It was great. Three meals a day and bed for four quid a week. Smashing. An old building, the Alhambra, a gigantic barn of a place, and I explored all the little corridors and dressing rooms. For the first week I was as nervous as hell, coming on in those huge theatres after the tiny theatre at Webber D., but after that it was OK. I prepared the record of 'The Love of Three Oranges', the opening music of the play; the director had marked with a special pencil the point where I had to drop the needle. Afterwards we would go home and have supper, me and the company manager. We never drank with the cast. The CM was a funny Ozzy. We had shrieking giggles every night – I can't remember why, but we both thought it was hysterical. When the police came to arrest the Italians at the end of the play we both had to change into our cop gear and if I caught his eye we would both go up.

We also visited Kettering and then the Finsbury Park Empire which was down the road from my home. So I played one of the greatest theatres in London, whose demise must be one of the biggest disgraces any council could possibly have on its copybook – it was one of those great old empires that the dance world want so much today. I had been there many times with Mum to see Variety and so it was rather special to be playing there.

The Amorous Prawn

A period out of work followed, but to keep up the training I would take singing classes three times a week and go to Siegfried Leder's Laban School of Dance in Morley College. I changed agents and read for understudy and ASM for *The Amorous Prawn*. Eureka. I read for the charming and utterly civilized impresario Murray Macdonald and was soon ensconced at the Winter Garden in Drury Lane watching the real pros. In addition to Evelyn Laye and Harry Landis there were Walter Fitzgerald, Hugh McDermott and Stanley Baxter, the great Glaswegian comedian. Peter Barkworth was assistant to

Murray. Fifteen pounds a week. Several weeks' rehearsal and a tour of the *whole of Great Britain*.

Derek Nimmo was playing a wet and made a huge success of doing this all his life, and Ernest Clark tried to fob me off with Irish pennies when paying for his tea. You notice things like that when you're an assistant stage manager. You watch everything because people pay no attention to you except when they want something so you are able to observe at close quarters and see how they behave among themselves. *The Amorous Prawn* was my first real experience with West End actors. They were generally very well dressed and wore suits for work; Murray used to be immaculately attired in a well-tailored suit and had a constant cigarette which looked rather elegant in those days. The company manager was a bit of a bullying turd, but apart from that it was OK and eventually we reached Brighton and all was well. The weekend before we opened there I remember the relief in coming back to Manor House for a good breakfast. Brighton was a charming and easy week and in those days the Theatre Royal had a bar backstage where you could have a tipple immediately after the show. The trip was crowned with my dinner with Evelyn Laye. Later, when we were plonked at the Saville Theatre for our West End run I offered to bring Evelyn Laye my mother's soups, which I seem to remember she rather liked and of course mum was double chuffed to be making bortsch for the great star. It was also a proud moment when Stanley Baxter came back to the flat I had in Knightsbridge at the time and I made a great stew, which he praised highly.

The Amorous Prawn was a fairly silly play about a government minister who has an affair with his secretary and decides to go to Scotland salmon fishing. He stays at a house being illicitly let out to tourists by the wife of a general, who of course knows the Minister of Defence and doesn't know that his wife is keeping lodgers. Stanley Baxter played her aide-de-camp. It's funny for the audience and there's a huge scream of laughter when the general returns. I have seldom heard such a reaction on the stage before or since – the whole audience whooped like one giant being.

We toured to the 'number one' dates, as they are called, and I tried to find things to do in each city we visited. I found Britain totally fascinating. In the beautiful white city of Aberdeen I took up horse-riding. In Glasgow I explored the Gorbals and the whole city, while in Edinburgh there was no end to what one could discover. In Leeds I stayed with my Uncle Sol, which wasn't a bundle of laughs, but I found someone to fall in love with for the week, a girl who worked in a chemist's. Some dates I forget, but I do remember Oxford and I spent a great deal of time in the reference libraries reading a variorum Shakespeare, which had a line-by-line commentary by expert critics and scholars. I enjoyed this since I felt that this was going to be an area of investigation in the future.

The tour wore on. I remember the digs we had in Glasgow where the landlord put a nutmeg in the sugar bowl to keep the sugar loose. The cold was setting in and I adored the backstage atmosphere of the King's Theatre. The smell of those old theatres was a tonic, but the true miracle for me came each Saturday night when the stage carpenter would 'strike' the set – it never ceased to amaze me that the whole thing would be dismantled in minutes, and this living room and walls, furniture, laughter and actors would become just a memory. I'd walk around the empty stage as they were taking down the flats, sensing where everybody had been playing to the huge audience, and I'd look at the empty seats where all those bums had been contentedly sitting, clapping 'Boo' as she came on stage. I was in charge of the props and carefully wrapped each piece in newspaper.

When we arrived at each new venue I felt the same thrill, watching them put down the stage cloth with all the markings for the flats, watching these being cleated together and then the stage wire supporting the bars that held them up. Watching the light bars come down for the lighting rig and checking the sound level on my tape for the car drawing up. Mixing the colours for the coffee with caramel and having to remember to change it two or three times a week so they didn't get a green mould on it, even though they were only 'dressing' and nobody drank them. Getting in twice weekly in the morning to go through our understudy rehearsal which after three months was utter and diabolical torture, and soon reached a climax which I will come to in a moment.

Apart from Stanley the best actor was the great, puffing and irascible Walter Fitzgerald, who gave all and never spared himself. Hugh McDermott was very good as the Yank. Once near the end of the tour, by which time I was bored out of my tree, as I was going round giving the half-hour call, which I did personally in those days, I greeted Hugh with a flippant perfunctory 'Hi!' and carried on. Hugh turned on his heel and said very sharply, 'You say "Good evening" when you come in this theatre! You say "Good evening, Mr McDermott"!' He was furious. Maybe he too was bored and missing home and sick of going to the digs each night and fed up after nearly two months on the road. He was of course right. These people were veterans of maybe thirty years' experience and had won their laurels and gave polished performances. They knew every theatre in the country and when they toured the stage doormen would welcome them like old friends and the landladies would keep a good room for them and their pictures would be up in the local pub. And who was I, a greenhorn, a naïve poseur with high-falutin' poetic ideas of theatre? These people *were* the theatre. They weren't some upstart, wet-behind-the-ears, one-off chancer; they were the backbone of the British theatre and all theatre everywhere and so sorry, Hugh, and please forgive me in thespian heaven!

As I said, the theatre began to tire me with its routine and the loneliness, since there was no real fraternization, no change of personalities as there is in rep and no demanding work for me to do. I was rotting away with a good salary. I bought a black raincoat at Aquascutum and a brolly and went to work feeling rather grand but bored. During the understudy rehearsals, which were now making me feel rather ill, I had a bit of a conflict with Chris, the company manager. What happened was that a package came on stage which I knew to be a prop we had ordered, but it was addressed to the management. I said that this was what we were waiting for, since the size and weight exactly corresponded to whatever it was, and there was no need to be so forelock-touching and wait for management to arrive to open it. Well, poor chap, Chris was a company man to his knickers and there was a row and I hurled the stage management book at him with all my force. This is not a weapon exactly, but it has two hard covers and can be a trifle heavy, especially with that play inside it. I was thrown out and banned from coming back. I was sacked! The stage doorman, who was my mate, suddenly turned company man and refused to allow me in even to collect my cards and Christmas presents from my dressing room. I collected them from the stage door later.

This was the best thing that could have happened and I was released from bondage. I tramped round the agencies and waited for work. In one way I was really glad, though I had been grateful for

229

the wages for a few months, a trip round the four corners of Britain and the occasional party when we were invited to the three-year anniversary of *Roar Like a Dove* at Quaglino's. This time even I was invited by Murray Macdonald. It was a suitably luxurious affair and I got my first smell of showbiz razzamatazz. Anthony Bushell was there – he had given me my first TV part, in *The Four Just Men*, during the run at the Saville. He had been Olivier's assistant on some of his films and was a terribly pleasant and warm-natured man. He seemed like an old soldier and told me why Larry couldn't get the money for *Macbeth* – it had something to do with having enough to cover weather exigencies. I was most disappointed not to have had the pleasure of seeing what would have been a remarkable film. While we were chatting affably and I was feeling most important, who should walk in but the radiant and exotic Vivien Leigh!!! This was altogether too much. Tony actually introduced us but I could only greet her with my best smile and shyly stare at her for the rest of the evening. She danced with all the young men, since they all wanted to be able to say to their grandchildren that they had danced with Vivien Leigh, but I couldn't get up the courage, even if she kept giving me sidelong glances all evening. Damn my cowardice!

Repertory: An Actor Prepares

After a while I went to an agent called Vincent Shaw who specialized in rep. A large, genial bloke who talked down to you, quite rightly, but nevertheless took me on after comparing good and bad acting with Michael Redgrave and Sam Wanamaker. 'Yes,' I humphed, 'of course,' although I was a big fan of Sam's and had adopted his vitality in *The Rose Tattoo* in which he gave an electrifying performance. I am so sorry that we were denied his great animal energy when it was diverted to archaeological explorations on the South Bank; too bad.

Summer season was coming up and the little reps which couldn't function all year surfaced like those desert flowers that lie dormant most of the year, then suddenly emerge in the sunshine. People come out of hibernation, those little producers, who usually live in Bournemouth and whose names the public will never ever know since no accolades will adorn their mantelpiece but who are the very soul of British theatre.

I was lucky one summer to begin my career in weekly rep in Buxton, a charming old town nestled in the hills of Derbyshire, in the Peak District. I met this gentle but vital old couple at Vincent Shaw's office. They must have decided that I was the one on whom to pin their hopes for a long summer season of weekly rep. Buxton is an old spa town and decades ago the wealthy would come for the magical local cures. The architecture was Victorian and Georgian and well-preserved. The theatre was less a theatre than a converted cinema next to the cinema, which used to be a theatre and which now has been saved by the cinema's demise and reconverted to become the Buxton Opera House! Mrs Twigg ruled the box office and had photos of previous incumbents on the wall in her little box. One of them was Frances Cuka, who was already famous for *A Taste of Honey*, in which she had appeared at Stratford East. The producers were Pilton Wilson and Kathleen Willis; I have the feeling that these venerable people had been keeping the repertory system alive for decades. These non-complaining, decent, hard-working old troupers were the foundation of many an actor's craft, providing the launching pads and the gym for us to fail and grope. They were given a round of applause on the first night by the local community whom they had served for so many years.

Their faithful character actor, Walter Wingham, would be the kind of example to me that my boxer uncle Alf was. A dour, tough little man who could utterly transform himself week after week and was the most protean being I have witnessed on a stage. He would be what they call in rep DLP, dead letter perfect, on the first day.

Of course in rep it goes without question that you learn the whole play in daily chunks by the act. So you open a play on Monday night. On Tuesday you block the whole of next week's play, which hopefully is two acts but often in those days three. Wednesday comes the test when you should have learned the first act; Thursday you cope with the second act and Friday the third! Saturday gives you the opportunity to run the beast and make mistakes, but not too many. The play finishes its run on Saturday night and with regret or relief you grease your make-up off and make for the local pub, which is always pleasant. On Monday you explore the new set which has miraculously grown over the weekend. You try out your wig, costumes, new make-up. I once played the young black boy in *Hot Summer Night* and must have looked a sight with blue eyes and blacked-up face, but I had an impeccable West Indian accent and luckily had seen the original with Lloyd Reckord, the Jamaican actor who was so good in the part. It was a moving play about a young black boy's love for a white girl, which was quite controversial in its time. In one scene I left a big black blob on the face of my leading lady and of course she didn't know that she was playing the rest of the act showing some genetic confusion on her face. These events were typical in weekly rep, when there was little time to test out probable hazards and you only found them out on the night.

When I got the list of seventeen plays they were doing for the Buxton season I found I was in fifteen of them and I sped to the British Drama League, of which I was a member. A more valuable institution you could not find. This library would be my weekly outing, coupled with the odd visit to the British Museum Reference Library. I was a keen lad in those days! I had a few weeks before starting, so I found and got cracking with the first play, which was *How Say You?* by Harold Brooke and Kay Bannerman. I played a young solicitor. It wasn't a huge part, but enough for me to worry about and yearn to get right for the first week of rehearsal in Buxton.

As I was not in an evening play I had time to learn my part and was astounded to come in on the first Monday with pumping heart and find a well-made set! Even in weekly rep! From the tour of *A View from the Bridge* I had expected worthy but tatty and here was a well-made, authentic-looking courtroom. Possibly it was because it was the first play. I practised incessantly going in and out of doors and looking smooth and striking all those sudden frozen poses so beloved of rep actors. I wanted my entrances to be slick and look somehow frisky and neat, and while the other poor actors were rehearsing their bits and pieces after the run I would keep going in and out of the doors. I did have a lot of entrances and exits, as I remember.

It took them a while to get my name right and my old programmes that now look like parchment reveal my name as Burcoff for the first play. The Steven was Stephen for one or two, but what matter these things? The play was a triumph. I had a little dressing room which was my cave under the stage and the two producers were never anything but charming to me.

I had learned the first couple of plays that I borrowed from the British Drama League, but now the third and fourth plays were coming up and I had no advantage any more, since I had used up my preparation time and had to learn them by the week like everyone else. I remember it always rained in Buxton. Once it rained for forty days and the warm drizzle washed the hills and the streets and I sat with the gas fire on, swilling down the lines.

Once I was in the middle of a scene and although the lines had not gone I felt 'What am I doing here?' I went into a horrible panic and wondered why on earth I was doing this, since it was sheer torture. The feeling passed and the next night I continued with a certain fear, but less panic. This is the learning stage when the body is adapting itself to situations for which it has no answer. Fear releases the panic button and adrenalin pours forth and instructs flight or possible death. Your muscles, breath, energy are geared for escape, but you stay. You stand there during the most awful, embarrassing, naked and unarmed moments of your life, moments when you should be stunning and winning and entertaining the audience. Your bottle has gone and your belief mysteriously vanishes. You are left stranded with only your weakened personality in the glare of the audience. Even now I can feel similar sensations, but I have the muscle to accept and control, to let it pass so that I can bite into the text and the play once more and a new surge will arrive which says fight, not flight. So each attack of fear, though terrifying at the time, was an instruction to the softer, vulnerable, shyer, weaker part of my mind. That first season at Buxton was truly a baptism of fire.

I started to enjoy the challenge and even to 'wing' certain scenes. I would come on Friday with the third act unlearnt and know I could paraphrase it until Monday. On Mondays I was raring to go and have a good time. I started to experiment but still be safe and keep to the show. I had some favourite plays. I think I had an advantage from having played *A View From the Bridge* on tour and so I jumped into the lead role very easily.

Jan Fogarty was our director for all the productions and an occasional actor. He and Walter Wingham were lifelong friends, and since Walter was so small and Jan so large we used to think of them as Laurel and Hardy. I was rehearsing one of the scenes one day after the run and Jan said rather sadly to me, 'You never ask me to rehearse with you.' It had never occurred to me, since he seemed to represent the theatre and was the director . . . I never imagined these people had nerves and anxiety like us beginners. That sentence hooked into my mind for thirty years and I wish I had said, 'Of course, Jan, I would love to.' I don't remember what I said, but I thought he must be teasing and left it at that.

The plays I remember are *A View from the Bridge*, *Tea and Sympathy*, *Hot Summer Night*, *The Unexpected Guest*, *The Seventh Veil*, *Gilt and Gingerbread*, *Murder at Midnight*, *The French Mistress*, *The Stepmother*, *Not in the Book*, *How Say You?* and *Murder on Arrival*. There must have been a few others. I left just before the season was due to be extended for three more weeks. I had had enough. But it was a sterling experience and I learned a lot. I had a wonderful life in rep. A very pleasant local lass for the nights and weekends off and the occasional respite of visiting juvenile character actresses.

The psychoanalyst Jung defined human behaviour in terms of archetypes and rep theatre is also defined by its archetypes. You have the leading man, who plays sexually desirable and 'good' chaps. Then you have juv leads, who play young sexually desirable fellows who tend to get the leading ladies. These guys are often bores and think too much of themselves. Then you get the character leading ladies who are like old battleships and play wonderfully understanding mums. Then your leading lady, who is meant to be a bit glam and is perfect for all those West End comedies whose authors are desperately concerned with the gin-and-tonic belt. The juvenile character actor like me plays juvenile leads and those troublesome young delinquents bursting painfully into puberty, like my characters in *French Mistress*, *Tea and Sympathy*, and the young Rodolpho in *A View from the Bridge*.

I missed Buxton and always carry it in my heart as a place of growth and study, where the pains of growing and failing were most acute. My favourite time was Saturday night, a Chinese meal up the road and then the long walk home in the dark. Walking up the hills and exploring the moors with Jan, my girlfriend. The wild winds at the top and that 'Heathcliffe-y' feeling. I was sad to return to the trek around the agents once more, but by luck they were looking for a juvenile character for Chesterfield rep, run by Anthony Cornish, who was a little more 'tart' than bucolic old Mr Fogarty. So in 1960 I found myself visiting Chesterfield with its twisted steeple, symbolizing perhaps the spirit of that town. I was there for three plays.

I was pleased to have found work so swiftly and near enough to Buxton that Jan could visit me on Sunday – I wouldn't have to wait eighteen months as I had for Fay in Wiesbaden. I didn't much care for the theatre in Chesterfield but I recognized that it was a real, all-year-round theatre, not a summer season that just might not turn up one summer. This was the biz. It was an active theatre with good actors and actresses, and me and the other new chap admired all the gestures flying about. I was terribly impressed by gestures in those days.

On 24 October 1960 I opened in *The Great Sebastians* by Howard Lindsay and Russell Crouse, a bizarre melodrama with much conjuring and special effects. This was followed by *The Cathedral*, based on Hugh Walpole, in which I felt distinctly uncomfortable. I remember Tony Cornish's pert, sharp voice emanating from his sweet, cat-like face and saying that this would get a laugh if I played it right and if it didn't he would want to know why. Such a command, of course, engendered the opposite response; whenever I came to the line I would hope for the laugh he had so eagerly prophesied. Alas, I was not to get it.

Laughs are the Holy Grail that all actors search for in their text, as if they were mining a goldfield; the terrain is dug up mercilessly in the quest. 'We didn't get many laughs tonight' is a familiar refrain – no matter that the audience enjoyed it and, having bathed, travelled to the theatre and braved the elements, sat and concentrated and tried to make their lives a little more worthwhile by paying lip service to culture in order that they may acquit themselves of charges of spiritual neglect.

There was a little café opposite the theatre where we would go in the morning break and have bacon rolls. It still all felt strange and I remember on the day I arrived, which was the day before rehearsal started, I took a walk to the fields that I could see from the theatre. I walked and walked until I found myself in the countryside. I always feel safe in the countryside.

After my stint in Chesterfield I was out of work again, but not for too long. I don't know why the crooked steeple should come to mean so much to me, but I remember as I write that a friend, Dera Cooper, an actress I met at the Unity Theatre, King's Cross, mentioned it to me. Now, thirty years later, why should I recall a sentence out of thousands? My response is that it gave the place I was going to a special signature and made it an event symbolized by that twisted finger in the sky. It made even what I was doing seem important.

Dera and I used to listen to radio plays together and one night heard *The Infernal Machine*, Cocteau's brilliant adaptation of *Oedipus*. King's Cross Unity Theatre preceded even my City Lit days. I would go along and sit in the cold auditorium just to be part of the atmosphere. A man called McCullum was rehearsing *The Crucible* . . . I recall him as being very gentle to actors, full of wisdom and compassion. When I failed to read well for a part that was not suited to me he said, 'You should play those young romantic parts' rather than 'You read that badly.' I never forgot him for that . . . 'I have always relied on the kindness of strangers.'

Sensory Deprivation

I think many people go to the theatre out of some desire to fulfil a duty. They don't really like it that much, since film has so stretched their aural and visual capacities that the diminished figures on a stage need more concentrating on than ever. They have to strain to hear what is said and sift through the overwhelming amount of verbiage without the necessary visual stimulus that activates all parts of the mind. Writers continue to write the same plodding acres of text without considering that in the twentieth century we may need not only to evolve but to improve and compete with other media. They write as if other media did not exist and make little or no attempt to write beyond the old Victorian and Edwardian conventions; even if the themes are modern, the style is old.

In writing much of *East* in verse I was trying to arrest the ear. To reclaim the battlefield lost to movies and TV and to create a language or form that would prick up your ears. To attack the audience with an avalanche of language. To seize, attack, reclaim, hunt down, and generally say to them *listen to this . . . watch this*, this is my territory. I will not unfold the plot stage by boring stage as if they were watching TV. I will not compete with what that medium does so much better. It has close-ups. What is your close-up equivalent in the theatre? How do you create this in language? Or in form? You don't. You rely on a kind of cultural anachronism and a time warp by saying this is theatre, darling, and the very act of endurance on the part of the live actor is enough.

It is a pleasure to witness great skills on the stage and one is drawn into the actor's craft if he is good and exciting, but what about the time when your star is not on stage and we wait for the big moments and suffer incurable dross in the meantime? Bad, dull staging and having to pretend not to see sets being wheeled on and off . . . Pretend it's not happening, darling. A little amateurish, is it not? And while I must be above and beyond the scrawl of the reviewers and good luck to all who work, I cannot be so quite superhuman as to ignore the evenings I have had of total brain rot when the critics have praised so and so to the skies and crowned some dreary piece of convention with laurels. How can I ignore this when my bread and butter is to some extent validated by a good review? How can I not suffer when I see dross praised as gold and not only praised but regurgitated and like old cud rechewed whenever some critic wishes to make a point? No matter, say I and others, since we are outside the convention that seeks to keep the theatre in the Victorian age. The pioneer always has to suffer to pave the way. If I am a pioneer in anything, it is that I have worked from a kind of desperation and struggle to survive. I think that is valid enough.

So what I am saying is that when we go to the theatre we must suspend all our twentieth-century beliefs and enter a time warp which is called culture. For the sake of culture, which is another word for spiritual deprivation, we will sit and be bored and enjoy a star or two and be gassed by dry ice pouring over the stalls and pretend that this is not happening and watch confetti pour down from the ceiling and see the set being changed by stage hands. So by the end we have in some way *suffered*. Ah, there's the rub. If you suffer it must be good. If you suffer and in that suffering you lower your responses and your sensory needs to a minimum, you will enjoy certain qualities – audiences like to suffer to pay for their spiritual moribundity. But young people will not do this. They do not share this guilt and stay away.

But we do not need the young in our theatres. We need the guilty and the guilty will be fed a kind of stodge. In the big soggy Christmas cake of that stodge there will be sixpences, and these will be chewed and spat on and presented as gleaming treasures. So, you may ask, even if I am so smart and can do it better, why should I bother? I bother since no matter how far out on a limb we may go or how different a route we may take, we still need to put a bum on the seat. I do not wish to wear hair cloth and suffer for my art. There is a spate of youthful theatre about now which dabbles in a kind of physicality and I applaud the intentions of someone actually using some of the great discoveries of the twentieth century and seeing that we are more alert and can use a kind of shorthand language on stage. Symbolic gesture and staging. The more vital body that is the body of the twentieth-century man can be used more inventively. But I still find that these 'gestures' are often no more than that. They may show a desire to do without set, to make the actor the focus and keep the direction spare, but they still lack the gut truth. They are still in a sense peripheral.

Perhaps the theatre is an anachronism like opera. Perhaps attempts to modernize or revitalize it are mistaken and the theatre really is there to charm and to revive Chekhov and bland Shakespeare. Perhaps in the electronic age it seeks to cosset itself in the serenity of the pre-industrial age. An occasional scurry of activity may emerge with a surrogate Peter Brook and a bit of atmospherics, but it will soon gather up its skirts and return to the well-made play in which we must concentrate, lower our expectancy and suffer. Suffering is good for you. But it's not good for me.

January 1991

Popped into Ian McKellen's down the road. He is my friendly neighbour and yesterday was proclaimed a knight. It is now Sir Ian. How these titles become the theatrical profession and endow a certain majesty. I am very pleased for him, since it is a fitting laurel for the tireless work he does and the devotion he gives to his craft. He is a ceaseless prowler around the body of the English theatre and sometimes reminds me of a stalking wolf, ready to seize his prey and tear it to pieces. Even his roles lately have all been villainous and he is developing a nice rogues gallery. There is a quest in his face, a hunger which, like the wolf, will never be satisfied; his eyes reveal nothing to tell you what he will be. Yet last night he had taken off the wolf clothing and was the perfect host, clearing away dirty plates and making sure our glasses were full.

Nottingham Playhouse – 1964

So I saw Ian McKellen, which started this whole train of thought, and he has worn like one of those lions round Trafalgar Square. I remember him in May 1964. I had been doing the rounds for some time and now had a chance to go to Nottingham Playhouse, which was then big-deal time for me. As usual my agent must have put me on the 'B' List and Frank Dunlop cast me for some minute role as a player, in a strange piece about Sir Thomas More, attributed to Shakespeare. I did something with the part, but it was the most hated season of my theatrical career up to then.

We had just sat down to begin our first reading when in walked this very young man with bushy hair, wearing blue jeans and a jeans top. He was playing Sir Thomas More. You gotta be kidding. He looks far too young. But when Ian started to read he had an authority which belied his years. This authority grew and grew and was confirmed when I saw him being brilliant in the stage version of *Saturday Night and Sunday Morning*, which was playing at the time. Here was a big talent already, hardly older than me, and I was tripping around like a damp squib, trying to make something out of my constant entrances and exits and a few lines as a player at the end.

The company were a most unfriendly lot and I spent a miserable time in my digs, alone. I wandered around the godforsaken town endlessly and grew more and more unhappy. Whenever I heard the actors who had parts bigger than mine and saw how weak and ineffective they were, I grew more and more angry with Dunlop. Frank had a whey-faced assistant, one of those 'thrilled' to take rehearsals when the boss is busy. I was making a bit of a scene with my player and one day this assistant made a remark to the effect that he *liked* the way I was playing the player like an awkward *amateur*, in character of course. Naturally I had thought that I was making something more of it than that, since a couple of colleagues had remarked on the fact that I had managed to salvage something from the dross. However, I saw his pale pudding face in front of me and thought that God sends many people to try us in this world and this creature is one of them. I held on to my cool and persevered.

The play was a ghastly mishmash of nothing. When I had a weekend off I rushed to Liz, my current lady, at her home in Bletchley and when I got into her garden and sat in her old garden chair and felt her warmth near me again and the summer trees all in bloom I burst into tears for the wretchedness and loneliness I felt in that awful dump with such pompous small-part actors. It was so grim that even twenty-seven years later I cannot see or think about any of those actors without a shudder, with the exception of Ian, of course, who was the star and had nothing to do with me directly.

One day I was demonstrating some mime to some actors and Ian, who was waiting and standing in his cloak, expressed an interest and said jokingly, 'Where do you go to get that?' as if you could buy it in the supermarket. The fact that I can even remember that incident shows how desperate I was for the slightest degree of attention.

The only really good thing that came out of that production was meeting Maggie Jordan, whom I employed years later when mounting my first revival of *Metamorphosis*. A more dynamic actress I have seldom come across. Also I chanced to meet a pleasant lady who was an ex of Mr Neville who, with Peter Ustinov, was co-director of the Nottingham Playhouse. Whether Mr Neville was otherwise engaged I do not know, but after Thomas More I was swiftly kicked out. Ah, such bliss . . . I have never been back. Kenneth McReddie was an extra in the show and now he is an important agent. Good for him. The rest faded away, and frankly I'm not surprised.

Just as I carry away in my heart only the sweetest joys of some adventures in the play trade which will always give me a resonant and vital skein of memory, so others will give me sourness, bitterness and even hatred. I hated Nottingham, but if I'd played a better role could it have improved? Marginally, perhaps, but I don't think that much. Of course, unlike Buxton, it was a highly professional company, but whereas Buxton had some soul, this had none. Frank Dunlop did his best, I am sure, and a more scruffy and talented director I had not yet had the pleasure of working for. But it looked good on my CV.

Looking for Work – the Sixties

Oh Dad, Poor Dad, Mama's Hung You in the Closet and I'm Feeling So Sad. It was the longest title of all time. By the 20th or so of May I was cast in a small role. The great method actress and teacher Stella Adler had come to England to première it in London; it might have been hot stuff in New York and this was the way of ironing out the kinks. Stella was part of the great Adler family of actors who reach back into the European theatre and with her brother, Luther Adler, she dominated the New York stage at a certain period in the forties. They also were famous in the Second Avenue Yiddish Theatre.

Stella taught until she was in her late eighties and died in 1993. In 1961 she was a young chick in her mid-fifties and being directed by Frank Corsaro. A young lady called Lee Becker, who once played in *West Side Story*, did the choreography and auditioned us, and all our movements were choreographed to an accompanying pianist, who also composed the music. His name was Bernardo Segal. Strangely enough, the producer at the time, as I look at the old programme, was Roger Stevens, who was my producer when I revived *Metamorphosis* on Broadway with Baryshnikov in 1989. Andrew Ray played the juvenile lead and his wife, Susan Burnet, was the female juvenile lead but the grand diva of the drama was the amazing, stupendous, awesome and unbelievable *Stella Adler*. And in the blue corner stood the wonderfully stylish light-heavyweight contender for the crown of European flash, Ferdy Mayne.

The market in Soho was alive with fruit of all colours as I made my way to the Queen's Theatre for the first reading. We all sat around and Stella attacked the text with a ferocity that gave me a new idea of drama. She was spellbinding and magnificent and we all quaked at the force of this driving tigress.

I played a bell-boy and we all had the most immaculate green suits tailored and the play duly opened at Cambridge in the beautiful Arts Theatre on 26 June 1961. It was a fiasco, since poor Stella could not remember her lines. Susan Burnet fell ill and Sarah Miles came up to replace her. She was amazing – Susan was quite pale in comparison. Sarah rolled around the bed and behaved quite madly and was wonderful with her syrupy cat-like voice. She is another talent the Brits have seldom used properly, she was terribly pretty and clever and exceedingly temperamental. But they couldn't keep the little gem, because Andrew Ray threatened to walk unless they reinstated his missus. Sadly I never worked with Sarah again.

We duly opened at the old Lyric Theatre, Hammersmith. By this time Stella had a hold on about half the lines, but after much screaming and shouting from the leading contestants the whole boat sank without trace. It was a bit too sub-Tennessee Williams, which had been apparent to me from the start, but without an ounce of his humour and compassion. It was a young man's first play and had a stream of poetic or sub-poetic particles that didn't really link up; however, I was working for a period and the time passed.

Before we opened we held a party in Chelsea for the cast and I saw my hero Ken Tynan and spoke to him for the first time. Not really knowing what to say, I asked if he thought the critics would object to the colourful language and, for the time, rather risqué things going on in our play. He replied that *Beyond The Fringe*, which was the latest fad from Oxbridge, had done well and been 'controversial'. We dawdled on talking bullshit and I saw Liz from the corner of my eye and signalled her wildly to come on over while I was actually bathing in the same light as *Tynan*!

The play dissolved and emerged later in New York in an altogether better production, with Hermione Gingold, very suitably I thought, playing the Stella Adler part. If anything, it was this experience that persuaded the great lady to retire. She was a handsome woman with large blue eyes, silver hair and a voice that could hit the wine glasses at the back of the bar.

Well, we had no sooner buried this than I was called to the Royal Court to read for Arnold Wesker's/John Dexter's *The Kitchen*, an experience I have already described. It always seems strange to me to have just been to see a play and then to find that I will be appearing in it in the near future. In those days you didn't often miss what went on at the Court. I haven't been there now for a decade, at least not since I was asked to review a piece called *Kafka's Dick*, whose title was enough to make me totally antipathetic to any wit that might be lurking within it. Having read so much about Kafka and been so involved with his life and work, I was hostile to such a gross cheapening of his name. Of course, if you were not involved with Kafka or his stories, his life and his personal agony, or if you were an illiterate yob, or a literate yob, you might find the title amusing and satiric. I found it typical of a current trend in hatefulness and indifference to human feeling. So jolly funny. So British.

I protested to Alan Bennett, sending him a telegram registering my disgust; he kindly and responsibly answered, setting out his reasons for choosing the title. I thought the production well staged and there were some funny lines in it; I might actually have found it interesting had I not already been outraged. While the Brits cannot and have not had a writer like Kafka and our mainstream theatre cannot and does not present his works on stage as Barrault, Welles, Jan Grossman in Czechoslovkia, Andrzej Wajda and I have done, since the Brits seldom have the kind of imagination to enter the interior of man's soul, I feel they tend to mock unusual works. I had a strange, quirky feeling in my gut that the play was slurred with an unconscious anti-semitism. Not conscious, but people like Mr Bennett and other critics and journalists who profess liberal and radical views still vilify people for their differences. Of course, Kafka is different and obsessed and Jewish and neurotic and introverted and palpably edging towards insanity and this is an inheritance of ghettoizing, even if it doesn't touch everyone, or every Jew. His life has been the subject of countless thousands of books and pamphlets and even if the size of his dick was relevant and the play was a satire on all the trash that has been written about him, a kind of persiflage, still I could not get past the title. It was too infantile for my taste.

Newcastle, Rotherham and More Rep

After playing in Arnold Wesker's *The Kitchen* at the Royal Court, I think I drifted again, worked out at the YMCA and was thoroughly miserably unemployed for some time. I was experiencing the detrimental effects and spiralling increase of insecurity as each week turned into a horrible month. I seem to recall Christmas looming up and then a panto at the Flora Robson Playhouse in Newcastle, when I played some insignificant piece of twaddle in *Treasure Island* with Griffith Jones as Long John Silver. I recall little of that event except my little bed-sitter and the endless long days with nothing to look forward to except performing junk at night. It was one of the ghastly experiences, but not the most ghastly. Nothing would beat Nottingham for ghastliness except one that was to come.

Newcastle had its gentler side and though the Flora Robson Theatre now lies in a heap of rubble it did perform some service to the community and introduced me to the addictive qualities of Newcastle Brown Ale. Also I learned what it was like to sit in a dressing room all night and then come racing on to sing 'Yo ho ho and a bottle of rum'. The evils of sitting out and playing Scrabble. One night I rushed out to one of the many calls on stage with my old sword in my hand and ran right into the sweet stage manager, impaling her in the thigh! It was a horrid moment and brought me to my senses. I had to be more responsible. I have never used a weapon since – in my 1980 *Hamlet* we mimed the weapons to great effect.

I was getting to be so lonely again that I started to write poetry in my digs and found that a very good way to deal with isolation. Fortunately my loneliness was abated and somewhat like Joseph K. I was momentarily assuaged by the comforting presence of a very intelligent woman called Paula. We became good friends and I continued our friendship after the show ended.

Back in London Vincent Shaw said there was a one-off job if I liked. It was with the worst and tattiest producer I have ever had the misfortune to work for; I devoutly hope I never sink to such depths that I have to work for him again. The man was a complete liar and actually claimed once in conversation that he had worked with Jean-Louis Barrault! He was putting on, for one week only, a ghastly play called *Not in the Book*, but rather than be out of work I said I would do it. I played a minor role even though by this time I had played the main juvenile at Buxton.

We arrived in Rotherham and had to find digs. This seemed to take an eternity, since for some unknown reason everywhere was booked. So another poor actor and I trudged around this godforsaken sludge-hole from five until ten in the evening to find digs to enable us to do a show we didn't want to do for the tattiest company in England. The local critic tended to agree with me in his review, which said, and I remember it to this day: 'I waited all evening in anticipation of the set falling down.' It certainly looked as if it might.

My friend and I found some awful workmen's digs and when my colleague requested no meat, since he was a vegetarian, the landlady retorted that 'we don't want no fussy customers here' in her best northern twang. The other workers were shreds and shards of humanity. I had stumbled into a Dickensian boarding house of unspeakable squalor. In the morning we all gathered around the collective table and ate our stodge. The landlady thrust greasy bacon, sausage and well-fried eggs under my delicate vegetarian colleague's eyes. Of course we fled. After the show that night I think we might have had a Chinese together and then we all went our different ways. This is the life of cheapo theatre.

There was no place to go in the town and so after walking around hell for a few hours we went to the theatre at about 3 p.m., just to wait for eight o'clock. The manager of the theatre threw us out, would you believe it? At the lousy Civic Theatre, Rotherham, we were told we could not wait in the theatre nor would we be allowed in until the half-hour before curtain-up. We walked around the streets or sat in cafés. The week went past and mercifully I have never worked for or seen this wretched, tatty disgrace to the theatre again. Nor do I want to see it or be near it. It was the worst.

June that year saw me playing Henry VIII in *A Man for All Seasons* and things were looking up again. It was in the Devonshire Park Theatre in Eastbourne, not a classy rep, but a decent bloke running it, some well-crafted acting and I had a peach of a role. The way we rehearsed was to run it three times. I wore the mandatory blond wig and played the scene, which is a cracker since you come on once, as I remember, and steal the act.

Eastbourne is a funny little town, full of the slow and living aged who enjoy a night at the theatre. Elizabeth Spriggs, who was a leading actress with the RSC, came down to see me and told me to work on my voice. It was good advice. I thought I was good in the role but she sternly criticized and praised. I had always admired Liz Spriggs – her huge, enthusiastic smile and grandeur reminded me of an Ellen Terry or a Sarah Siddons and I wondered how on earth such an actress was not made into the luminary that she was so obviously cut out to be. She was brilliant in *The Physicists* by Dürrenmatt when she took over the role at the Aldwych, and in many other parts; she was uniquely gifted with a splendid sonorous voice. I saw her being pushed around by David Warner's childish *Hamlet* and hated the productions that seem to be praised for some reason of topical currency, or adherence to some theories formulated by various experts. I found it rather unappetizing, but then there was seldom anything I did like in those days. I do remember being ravished and sorely jealous of the wonderful acting in *The Revenger's Tragedy*, seeing for the first time the brilliant Clive Revill in *The Jew of Malta* and enjoying a clever and superbly acted *Comedy of Errors* directed by Clifford Williams. And of course I would and did make a journey to see Alec McCowen in *anything*. I captured almost everything he did over several years and have a fond memory of a great afternoon at the Golders Green Empire watching him play in Françoise Sagan's *Castle in Sweden*. I first saw this remarkable actor at the Old Vic as the Dauphin in *St Joan* and then as Mercutio, which was acting after my own heart. Full, strident and technical. Passionate and virtuoso. He had the unfortunate ability to make others around him look rather modest, so he was a dangerous actor to be on stage with. When I saw him in Brook's *Lear* I was fearful for Scofield, whom I also much admired, but Paul calmly kept the magic imp firmly in his place with the great sonorities of that splendid voice, which starts like a river in a place deep down and far away. When it reaches us it is a torrent. I liked that production a great deal for its cleanness, sparseness and timelessness.

To watch these actors was the best training for an actor, to sit and admire but not to copy; some imitation was frankly unavoidable, but once you borrowed a gesture or two you soon made it your own. Or tried. Ian Richardson I also admired inordinately as the most precious carrier of language with his silver tongue.

Meanwhile I continued my peregrinations round the country in one crummy rep after another. Never mind. I was in the third division, that was true, but I was hoping that one day I would hit the first. Birmingham, Liverpool, Manchester – these words were like the top division in acting as in football and you knew that if only you could get there your problems would be over. You would be 'discovered'. But first the weary weekly reps and one-offs. Some better quality, like the odd sortie to Cheltenham or Cardiff, but mostly not. Still, I had to keep going, for the alternative was bleak.

There was the endless round of the agents, since third division actors might have many agents. I was just another figure on the agents' books, so they could use me without having to worry about keeping me in work. The gaps between jobs were growing larger since I obviously could not stage manage any more. I had had a beginner's rush of luck, but now months might yawn between one awful job and another. In between I was sneaking into television and doing odd spots. Listening out for news, meeting actors in the Salisbury in St Martins Lane, then a pleasant and friendly pub. For some reason the Arts Club also became a hang-out for down-and-out actors who would gather in the café basement and exchange dreary gossip and anecdotes. It would usually be the same grim group. After that you might wile away more precious hours of your life in the Joe Lyons tea shop, no longer there, which we called 'Pro Lyons'. And if you were further inclined, opposite the Arts there was, and still is, I believe, one of those 'within the law' afternoon drinking clubs where you could really put an end to your existence and forget everything. Francis Bacon would usually be in there buying champagne for his sub-criminal acting associates. If you wanted to eat, there was always 'Jimmy the Greek's' in Soho, the actors' lunchtime haunt where you'd get cheap delicious moussaka and doorstep chunks of bread. Actors were a noisy lot then and, often fuelled by booze, they'd regale you with what happened when so and so fell off the stage.

I tried to avoid these places at first, but they seemed to be a necessity if I was to meet anyone of my fraternity. Such a shame that the only way was through booze and the pub. The other way was the YMCA, Tottenham Court Road. There were a lot of actors there: my old chum Robert Flemyng worked out well into his seventies. I'd bang out my frustration on the hand-ball court. I think it was the YMCA that saved my life and kept me sane through all those bleak times.

One day I heard they needed actors for a rep production at Leatherhead. The play was *Ross* by Terence Rattigan and I played some Welsh idiot, probably called Taffy. The only time I respected a director at first reading was when David McDonald, now resident at Glasgow, took the script by the corner as if he were holding up something rather smelly, and said we would try and do something with this. He didn't come out like most to say, 'Oh, what a wonderful play' ... His expression was 'Let's see what we can do with it.' From that we all felt at least that we were on the same side and worked at it with a will rather than pretending it's marvellous, darling, and resenting it the whole time.

The week sped past with a few vague memories of a Welshman saying a few things with an accent as if I had beamed dead thoughts from distant galaxies. Most plays left me like that, with no aftertaste, just a gradually fading impression of something a little bit lifeless posing as some nourishment. You put it into your system and it goes through it like polystyrene. You stuff your mouth with it and it fills a void, but then at the end you are left with nothing. All the plays pouring through with no meaning to you, much like the plays today, for is it any different? But at least now there is more choice. The big hits are still the same commercial dross, but at least today you have the National Theatre, which was only a dream then.

I am not sure there are many roles in the contemporary drama that anyone would really want to play. Like you might say I want to play Sir Giles Overreach, I'd die to play Macbeth, or Giovanni or Bosola, or Cyrano, or Danton or Woyzeck or even John Tanner. Are there modern roles that spring to mind? I don't think so. Nowadays there seems to be less of a passionate interest in human beings and more a distancing from them and from human needs and contact in favour of an alleged devotion to the political health of the state. There seems to be an adherence to the principles of objectivity and a sense of Euroworld. Individuals and their unique idiosyncrasies are of little interest. In fact, one senses a positive dislike of people in the contemporary shelf. One actually believes that humans are hated first and then won over. Like being guilty first and then proved innocent. There is a cold remoteness that seeks to address groups and themes since love is so rare and undemanded. So awkward that it is easier to love groups. When I read O'Neill I do feel that he loves human beings with a passion and that he has to write about them, just as Modigliani had to paint them, and even Noël Coward, I felt, had an affection for his creations, a real sense of tenderness; certainly it is there in Brecht. When there is an overwhelming sense of the author's love for his creation we tend to avoid it in England as being a bit too much. Unless it is wrapped in a classical package.

This must have been one of those rare occasions when I struck lucky, since while playing in *Ross* at night I see from my old programmes that on 20 August 1962 I was doing a chunky six-play season at the Cambridge Arts Theatre where the year before I had opened in the *Oh Dad, Poor Dad* fiasco. Now I was becoming a pro. I was actually returning to places I had been to before. Getting the familiar nod from the stage doorman. Knowing where the good cafés were. Punting down the Cam like a Cambridge student. Sniffing out the tea rooms and walking past the great colleges and soaking in the atmosphere of the past. Imagining life at Trinity and hardly being able to conceive it. Liking to walk in the grounds of the college and admiring the great chapel with its flying buttresses and the grand network of arches in its vaulted ceiling. Staring up at it day after day, with a pull, a tug of some desire for I know not what. Thinking of the famous students of the past, walking the River Cam. Being fascinated by the thousands of spindly bikes of the students and in the evening taking my place on the stage with *The Irregular Verb to Love* . . . Of course no student would dream of setting his foot in here.

I have always wondered why the theatres in university towns are unable to respond to the huge student population and can only put on middle-of-the-road junk. They have a built-in audience of the most intelligent young people in the nation and do not cater for them. Of course they hardly ever did. They had nothing much to say to an intelligent mind.

I enjoyed my season in Cambridge. It was a pleasant, drifting summer of small-town adventures. I was in all six plays and actually had the chance to play the lead this time in *The Amorous Prawn*. I probably got the job because I lied and said I had understudied Stanley Baxter, when in fact I had understudied the two other moronic characters in the play, a daft Cockney soldier played superbly by Harry Landis, and an inane gook played equally gormlessly and funnily by Derek Nimmo. However, I had watched Stan and knew the gags. They had obviously needed my insights on this popular piece now being released for the reps. I felt a bit awkward since I had never played it or studied it and now I had to look supremely confident on the first day of rehearsal, but I managed to swing it and it was a big success.

I can't remember much more about Cambridge except my ma came down to see me one night. It was the first time in our lives that she had travelled any distance to see me work and where would I put her up in my digs? I showed her round the colleges and antique sights. She enjoyed it very much, but sometimes I might have felt an edge of resentment in being a substitute hubby, for he never took her anywhere.

Marlowe Theatre, Canterbury – 1962

This was a one-off, *Write Me a Murder* by Frederick Knott. 21 to 24 November 1962. Why does it seem like yesterday? I remember so clearly this beautiful town and the charming theatre and the sheer wonderful and extraordinary luck to have digs inside the cathedral precincts. One of the houses belonging to the cathedral was used for some of the actors. In the morning I looked out over the cathedral. I had never seen a more beautiful sight in all my life. The colours changed every day and during the day on the ancient yellow stone. It was sheer delight to wander in the great, gaunt cathedral. At night I had a key to get in the gate, since there was a small door cut into the huge gate itself. Then I was a lone figure in the grounds and there was nothing so breathtakingly beautiful. I felt I had been given a secret key that revealed Paradise!

Mark Powell, who had played Thomas More in Eastbourne, was to join me in this piece of cod. I got out my best suit and put in a workmanlike performance. There was a bar right next door to the theatre and it seemed as if you could enter it from the theatre itself. Rolf Kruger, the agent, directed the show well and I half-liked doing it as I was getting a taste for trashy plays. You could fool around with the dialogue and play with your interpretation. It was an easy-peasy job and when Rolf came back on the Friday, since he had to go to London after the first night, he singled me out as the only one with any style. Given the company, this was not the great compliment it might appear, but I was over the moon. I cherished the words and feed on them even now.

I needed that praise then. I needed some affirmation that my skills were becoming a little more honed and crafted. It went straight to my head, like alcohol on an empty stomach. I don't need praise so much now, but a small acknowledgement keeps one healthy. It is like food, soul food. Not undiluted praise, far from it, but not vilifying. Nobody needs that and it, too, goes straight to your stomach. I, being a decent sort of bloke, resist writing something or saying something that is too wounding, unless I am responding to a slur against me. I have to hold myself back when I am occasionally asked to review something for TV or radio: I know I must try to say what I have to say without rubbing anybody's nose in the dirt. But I have sometimes felt like doing it and have held back, so I realize what some critics go through. The sheer joy of the taste of blood and the ability to whip with words. Rolf did make me feel a kinder person and I am still proud of that comment.

I will never forget Canterbury. I could have lived there for years. Just calmly writing or painting had I had any skills in either at the time . . .

Lincoln: First Shakespeare – 1963

The days turned into weeks and then into months and I don't remember what happened to them or whether I worked or suffered the ignominy of unemployment. I can't recall anything until February of the following year, when I started to rehearse for my first Shakespeare, *As You Like It*, in Lincoln. This was terrific and was the result of one of the few letters to which I had had a reply when I was seeking work. Kay Gardner, the director, was looking for an Orlando . . . Well, this was to be a bizarre experience to say the least.

Miss Gardner wrote inviting me to come for an audition and paying my return fare, which I thought was just super. When the train arrived in Lincoln I could see this huge cathedral in the distance with its towers soaring above the town. It looked mighty and impressive and I was getting a taste for cathedral towns. There was something solid about them and strong, yet cosy, with this great awesome weight in the centre somehow pulling the whole town to it. I knew when I saw this majestic eruption of stone that I would be passing time here and playing Orlando . . . such a colourful name.

The time came to begin rehearsals and we all assembled in the small hut opposite the theatre and started to read, when lo and behold the good lady began to cut all reference to just about anything that vaguely symbolized 'horniness'. No naughty imagery in this pastoral piece of countryside bawdy. All references out. We went through the morning with our blue pencils and I suspected it was simply that she was reluctant to have to explain any of the obscure double entendres. Cut cut cut. Like circumcision, or infibulation of words. I had never experienced anything like it and made a mild protest, saying that they were so obscure anyway they wouldn't offend, but this added merely fuel to her ardour to emasculate the text.

I was given a little pastoral dress to wear, the sort you might have seen in local amateur reps in the thirties, and I was a real sight for sore eyes. Of course I protested with vehemence this time, and I managed to hoick it up so that I looked a bit more butch. The show was a ghastly mess and must have looked really dotty and soft, but we soldiered on. I got some good reviews and the wrestling scene went very well, trained as we were by a pro; I looked as if I was losing for a long time and then made a big comeback. I was soaking by the time I got off from the match and I think it knocked me out for the rest of the play, but it went OK. I enjoyed speaking the verse: got into the rhythms and wanted to do more of it.

It was a school's programme and each matinée we had scores of nubile and younger screeching kiddies who sent me dozens of letters couched in the sweetest terms and begging for a photo. At last I had fans I could respond to and immediately ordered dozens of postcard-size photos. The letters were nearly all from twelve-year-old school-girls and were so delightful and in many cases so very intelligent that it made me realize just how much of an event it was for them to see something live. The very knowledge and appreciation of its 'liveness' made so much difference to them, compared to the films and dead tubes their mums and dads watched each night. This was real human life and they responded so warmly that I could readily see that theatre as a communion and live event was very important for them.

The theatre was a benign and charming old building on the corner of the street. At lunchtime I'd go home and cook a steak with pota-toes and onion. By God, it tasted something great, since meat was what you lived on then. Lincoln had a touring system which meant that after you had done a week or two there you would go on to Rotherham and then to Kettering, travelling every day. It was a good work-out and once we were back in the coach Kay would give me notes not to change anything, which of course I did. She presided over everyone like a great bullying schoolma'am, even reducing the poor chap on stage management to tears, and by the end we were not on speaking terms.

I found a very junoesque lady in Lincoln with the unusual surname of Smallhorn. Apparently it was of French origin. She was an utterly charming creature and invited me home to Sunday lunch where her father was presiding over the guests. He was obviously a very successful doctor and they had a lovely house. While making some point about the labours of love certain members of society give with little hope of reward, like young doctors and teachers, he then said, pointing at me, 'Look at Steve here, working for a pittance and giving his all . . .' My face went slowly pink, puce then purple. For some reason the idea that I was earning a pittance hadn't occurred to me, since I was still too excited merely to be working to concern myself with such things. Now I had the table sympathizing with my pittance *in front of my girlfriend*. In Lincoln I thought I was a star! Now I was collapsing. This was horrendous. My colour continued to deepen and they began to worry about my health. I made my excuses and left.

You can't help but let old Stamford Hill values and codes of behaviour come back. You must never be put down or humiliated in front of your lady. In front of her you must be seen to be king of your domain, no matter how small that domain is. Why should I remember it to this day if it had not had a wounding effect?

I was always very sensitive to the fact that I was an actor and not in the real world. I saw my old comrades earning their wages and even fortunes by simple hard graft and the weekly grind, while I with my part-time work was forced to sign on at the Labour Exchange and in bad times go to Social Security for assistance since they would pay your rent. I was utterly astounded by this since Murray Gilmore, my friend from the City Lit days, who was such a fund of goodwill and advice, had remained my ally over the years and told me that the State would give you money even if you had a little money in the bank. It was not the government's desire to see you use every penny until you were broke before you came for help and even a couple of hundred quid in the bank would not disqualify you. What a nation, I remember thinking, what an amazing society that could protect its members in this way and wished to do so. First they give me a grant to study and to live on, and now they keep me from starving when there is no work. Pretty astonishing. Perhaps I was being naïve, but I could not compare this to any other country I had been in. Now the State gets it back. By allowing me to thrive and to live when times were bleak, it gave me the courage not to give up and now I have paid back in taxes tenfold what I was given.

Barrow-in-Furness – June 1963

Not too long after Lincoln Derek Golby, who knew me from *The Kitchen*, since he was one of the many who used to hang around the Royal Court, asked me to go to Barrow-in-Furness, which was a strange, gloomy old ship-building town on the north-west coast of England. I remembered Golby clearly as a very articulate young man given to debate and having constant arguments with Harry Landis, who was a staunch communist.

What I admired about Harry, and others with strong left-wing views, was that they knew their history and absorbed facts; they were in no doubt about their beliefs since these were honed out of constant reading and study. Events in politics weren't as they are for most of us, simply the chance collision of opposing interests or conflict of personalities. For Harry and Derek these were eruptions the seeds of which had been sown years, decades before. They quoted chapter and verse to delineate the origins rather than the present event. Their arguments after rehearsal for *The Kitchen* were very stimulating and made me feel that I was totally stupid with my obsessive self-interest in being an actor. These people were conscious of world events. So when Derek asked me to go to this Godforsaken town in the north of England it was no surprise to find that he was doing a double bill by Bertolt Brecht. Ah, my first taste of the German master.

I arrived and saw this grotty little theatre, which was my first shock, and then I got to my digs. A couple of actors who were married were sitting in the kitchen. They welcomed me and made me tea. We talked a bit; she had her feet up, which was a bit revealing, but they were very relaxed. I had a bedroom in the house and we shared a kitchen.

The rehearsals were quite interesting and for the first time I was encouraged to use my imagination. Music was played live and it was very inventive and catchy, so much so that I remember it and can sing it to this day, a kind of quasi Kurt Weill. One of the stories involved a master shooting and killing a coolie. He was acquitted of murder on the grounds that he had killed him in error. He had assumed, since he had so exploited the servant, that the servant was going to kill him, whereas in fact the servant was making a gesture intended to help his master. The court ruled that a master who had always treated his slave brutally could not expect the slaves to be anything but aggressive. It was a good piece to play and I enjoyed it. The town was like a study in hell, with its tiny streets and look-alike houses, but I applauded Derek for even attempting Brecht there. Obviously this show was a bit different from their usual fare, but I remembered it when I lost all the other debris that floated out off my brain as it rejected the hostile material.

There was a very good actor called Bernard Gallagher there who later joined the National Theatre. Donald Sartain, the producer, later went to the Young Vic where he put up a big battle to keep it going but returned negatives to every plea for employment from me, even when I had my own company.

A lot of directors or producer/directors were determined that I should never set foot in their buildings with my productions. Even when they seemed to be gaining a semblance of respectability in the press and were attracting an audience. Even when they were also gaining credence abroad and winning laurels from all sorts of people in all sorts of cities, I found the door firmly barred in every theatre, except those like the Round House that were run by an Arts Administrator. Then of course I had the chance to thrive, and I did on the few occasions I played there. Whenever a theatre, unlike the continental model, was run by a director, there was little chance and the door was locked with a 'We are thinking of you' . . . 'Our season is fully committed.' It doesn't take an Einstein to work that one out. Either your stuff is shit and rightly they don't want it, or their stuff is shit and they don't want you. Sometimes, when I applied for directing work, it was implied that I would be bad for the 'traditions' of the company. One RSC director said that, when all the traditions I could see at the time were a terrific penchant for dry ice, buckets of blood and blokes hanging about the stage. Of course, others would find some reason to hold me at bay while they pursued their own grim policy. I always thought that if you were on a grant it was your duty to liven things up sometimes with a bit of fresh blood. I can understand only too well the scenario that must go on in their minds . . . Why let the bastard in? He might even be popular, and popularity can be a dangerous thing. So it needs a little largesse to put me in their cosy little nest. I do sympathize and I am not sure how I would feel if I had my own nest.

How different from the German model. I have just been to Munich for the weekend to discuss *Coriolanus* in German. Günter Beelitz is at rehearsal for all his companies at least once a week, watching their progress, flying to South America, Russia, East Germany to scour around for interesting directors. He is not 'tied up', 'in rehearsal', since he has to run a company and the intendant has to be there at all times.

However it is and was to my benefit, for water will find an exit no matter how circuitous the route and being rejected so many times may have led me along a more interesting path. With my own team I felt freer and less committed to any rules or policies. I toured when I wanted and hustled for my own work. When I got it I triumphed through my own abilities to find graft, rather than having it all done for me like some of the fortunate but pale creatures who were taken in without flexing much muscle elsewhere and had, so to speak, little combat experience. They came in like pale facsimiles sitting at the toes of the master and cooing to his every word, never seeing the light of the outside world. And when the time came, sitting in his master's old chair and wearing his old slippers. I had no master to follow and if this is arrogant then let it be. It is meant only to show that you do not need a master in whose image you create yourself with minor variations. You hew your way out with the bloody axe. Those who have never used their muscles and reflexes to fight in alien territory never demonstrate to me more than a modest showing in spite of all the heralding they might receive elsewhere. It is these well-meaning disciples who spread the word and who, sucking the nipple of arts subsidy, shriek the loudest for more. Art is as much a need as clean water. It refreshes and cleanses our souls. These people are in some ways right to take it for granted. For me, the first bestowal of Arts Council money was a kind of magic, unbelievable to one who had worked in the mire of wage-earning, unskilled workers. Actually to be given money, when I first applied, by a council which had no axe to grind with me as long as I toured, was a marvel beyond belief. I still see a certain amount of privilege in the idea that someone helps to support my lifestyle when others have to work a coal face or drive a bus or sit in a sweaty workshop.

I am not sure that all those who demand subsidies with such vehemence really appeal to the taxpayers who support their habit. I am not always sure that from their monk-like, cloistered habit they have seen much of the world either. Is art for the masses? At least let us suppose that it must reach a large minority of the masses. Opera, for example, most certainly does not and why pay these vastly over-weight foghorns such sums as £5,000 to £10,000 per performance when they only eat it all up? Why should Paul Scofield be paid only £1,000 per week at a subsidized theatre, if he is so fortunate, since his performance is as demanding, requiring terrific vocal techniques and responses, clear-mindedness, emotional draining and very often a far more exacting detail of staging and memory, since nowadays the actor doesn't just come in a couple of days before like the opera star and fit in. I like operatic singing and I like Olivier's acting. The fact that he rehearsed his Othello with the company for many weeks made the work and the company naturally homogeneous. The idea of his going from theatre to theatre in the English-speaking world fitting his Othello into the resident company is as ludicrous as

Pavarotti flitting from country to country banging out his 'numbers'. Am I to understand that they are like supreme heavyweights? Recent memory has me recalling that Placido Domingo was to play Wembley Stadium but cancelled when it was only half or less full. We actors play to a lot less. So I am not really too sympathetic to these giants and the money poured all over them like precious and holy oil. If the arts are subsidized to the hilt the subsidized companies should have an eye on demotic taste. Not by lowering standards but by reaching for the new.

On the last night at Barrow-in-Furness I got 'well and truly' on barley wines and since I can remember it I don't want you to think that it was a regular occurrence – it was just a celebration after the last night. Hazel, one of the actresses of the next show, and I carroomed around the grim city and ended up in the fish and chip shop. I remember leaving my beer on the ledge outside, getting my fish and chips and, like Buster Keaton, walking past the ledge munching a chip and shooting an arm out to retrieve my precious bounty. Hazel was hoping I might leave it. I think I was very happy because it was the last night. I got back to London feeling a little less happy and tried to settle into my new flat in Drury Lane.

I mentioned during my Drury Lane sagas how the street seemed continually to claim me. Now I was flat-sharing with the exuberant, ebullient Lindsay Kemp. It wasn't going to be smooth sailing but we enjoyed the locale. During this period I seem to have been out of work and we both took to being bartenders in a pub. What cruel fate. But still I was struggling to gain some degree of recognition in London, being turned down with fearsome regularity, getting quite a taste for it and on each rejection growing that little bit stronger, since after the first disappointment leaves you breathless you either build up more muscle or you collapse and go into antiques or catering. In one you can play with props and in the other you can still entertain an audience.

We joined a kind of agency which gave you temp work in different pubs and I could see what a dreary life it was, just opening bottles and pulling beer. Nothing remotely creative, no cocktails to learn as in a bar in New York, where if you were out of work for a couple of months you might at least pick up some interesting facts and crafts. Here, nothing but the dead weight of your body going from one beer to another. You could not even, as in a Munich beer house, prepare sausages and sauerkraut, cheeses and smoked meats. No, just beer, spirits and crisps. Your good old English way.

I was working in some poxy little slum in the West End, one of those karzies that think because they've got a bit of beer-stained velvet on the seats that it's smart. It was in Mayfair, but a very dreary slow trade. One endless Saturday night Lindsay came in with a friend and in his indomitable way started to take over the place with his impressions. Being so full of life he could not help but remind the living dead of their death-like pallor, but while he was gesturing and laughing and doing no one any harm the rotted manager asked him to leave. Lindsay was what you might call a little 'camp' or 'theatrical', so he walked out in a huff. I stayed because I needed the job, but for years afterwards I regretted my cowardice and compromise. I should have walked out with Lindsay there and then.

Twenty years later Lindsay has conquered the world with his shows, his extravagant style, his famous workshops and his bizarre humour which fails to come across in print since you miss all the gestures and inflections, the whole panoply of body language which tells you so much more than the mere words. It's his body and voice which are expressive of his joy and feelings, and so in print it looks all wrong and pompous. He has been practically everywhere and is continuing the tradition of the great silent music theatre. Sometimes his actors do speak but his forte is in the power of his images and imagination. He still recalls that incident in the pub, but he changes the story: the way he tells it, when he is asked to leave I get angry and sock the manager. He wishes to remember that I came gallantly to his defence and I wish it were so as well. But I like him so much for the tenderness of the thought that he wished me to have been a trifle more gallant.

A TV Hamlet – Watching Christopher Plummer, 1963

A few weeks later, in one of my many nagging calls to the Beeb, I managed to get through to Philip Saville's office. They were looking for mime artists for the player scene in *Hamlet*.[1]* 'That's me,' I

*See *I Am Hamlet*.

screamed down the phone and they said, 'Come on in.' The Beeb is a friendly building in White City and the scene of so many visits that it starts to feel like an old ally. The receptionist is always friendly and there are a few newspapers to browse through until you get your call. Will you go to the fourth or second floor? In the lift there will be an actor or director from the past who will greet you like a long-lost pal. You get out at your floor and go down endless corridors, past doors with the names of directors on, and you imagine that behind these doors there are pots of gold that are yours for daring to go in. That each is in the process of trying to find the actor that is you. That there are magically wondrous roles that will shoot you into a million homes and reveal the full spectrum of your talent. Once when I was auditioning for a slight role in one episode of something quite forgettable, I must have made such an impression of pitiful sorrow and naked hunger that when I left the assistant caught up with me in the lift and said the part was mine if I wanted it. I was overjoyed and thanked him profusely. It was the part of a barman with four lines.

Being the Beeb and not committed to making money, it attracted and developed the kind of producer who was looking for and interested in drama and the human condition, rather than in soaps and mild, time-wasting trash, so there was an army of young assistant directors and writers who were naturally of a left-wing bent. Thus the Beeb also had a clubby feel, like a post-graduate course. You might take tea in the canteen afterwards, or go to the bar. The Beeb saved my bacon from time to time, like a benevolent aunt, and just at the right moment seemed to give me a little morsel to get on with, some scrap or leftover once the main role had been swallowed up.

So it was in 1963 that I went along the corridors to meet Philip Saville, who was in the process of putting together *Hamlet*. To be shot in Elsinore as part of the marvellous BBC 'Wednesday Play' series. What a task, and what a delightful piece of creative nourishment for him! I met this very charming man with a svelte voice and playful expression, who was very aware of his maleness and his attractiveness to women, I suspect. He smoked long cigars and wore those kind of tapered beige twill pants you'd buy in Aquascutum. His hair was worn like a crown or mane over his head and he asked if I could play the Player Queen. I said that would be fine. I was a trifle modest and felt simply overwhelmed to get the job, though my elation was at once vitiated by the idea of wearing a skirt. I had not yet got to the stage of acting when I could quite separate myself from the role. Now it wouldn't bother me in the least; in fact I can't wait to have an opportunity to get the high heels on. Then I felt rather embarrassed, since I was still trying to view the drama as ways of extending and amplifying me, rather than seeing it as a skill in which you successfully hide yourself in the pursuit of a creation.

I went back to Drury Lane and told Lindsay of my huge coup. I knew they needed mimes, so I suggested that I would try and get him an interview. When I rang they were quite relieved to know I had another mime in the family and booked him unseen. I suggested that as Lindsay was a very clever professional mime he could be the Player Queen and I would do the Player King, or really the murderer who becomes the King. Lindsay and I would work it out in our front room in Drury Lane. Philip was happy with this turn of events and Lindsay and I worked together for the first time. He did the choreography, which was so extraordinary that we had a sprinkling of clapping when we first did it in rehearsal. He choreographed it in Kabuki style for my role and somehow used elements from different cultures, but it made sense in a kind of Grand Guignol way with strong emphatic gestures. Philip Saville was pleased.

The line-up was Christopher Plummer as Hamlet, Michael Caine as Horatio, Robert Shaw as Claudius and Alec Clunes as Polonius. It was one of the most exciting things I ever saw rehearsed. Plummer's energy and voice were astounding to watch and hear; he seemed to leap over everyone in huge bounds of vitality. At times he reminded me of Henry Irving with his aquiline features, his thin top lip and the immense tone from his resonators and palates. It was sometimes like a trumpet blast. I realized now that I was watching an actor in the full prime of his power and it is an awesome spectacle. I felt sometimes that in his tireless quest to be astounding and mercurial Chris would stretch an idea almost to its snapping point but it worked and never became boring. Years later, on an old, blurred tape, he still conveys majesty and madness in equal doses. The rehearsal went well and on the last day the producers came for the run-through.

Lindsay and I were now a little strained in our partnership since the involvement in *Hamlet* seemed to have got him a trifle overwrought and with his profundity of abilities he was now pushing to design and organize, do make-ups and generally being 'busy' . . .

It was getting on my nerves since he was only in the show thanks to me, but we still worked well together and the scene was very popular.

On the run-through what the producers do is to follow the action around as it goes from scene to scene designated by poles which mark the boundaries of the set. These usually tell us the terrain. Philip Saville requested that we did not even go to the loo during the next two hours. Complete and utter silence when we were not on and no distractions or reading newspapers when you had half an hour off. Just *concentration*.

I like that direction from Philip. It must have impressed me for me to remember it to this day while forgetting so much else. So what is it precisely that struck me? Perhaps it was the idea that something is worth sacrificing ourselves and our comfort for. He asked for our patience and that we treat this very seriously indeed.

The play started and I was like a coiled spring. That morning Plummer gave one of his most searing performances ever. During the rehearsal I kept comparing him to Olivier and even decided to check out Larry's performance when a rerun of *Hamlet* was on. When I did that, I found Plummer wanting in the sheer beautiful lyricism of Olivier, but during this run-through I was totally stunned and so were the rest of the cast. A long silence reigned and Sydney Newman, the producer, was utterly impressed. It was what you might call a *tour de force*. Only Robert Shaw was disgruntled – he felt that we should have just shuffled through it and not made a big deal for the run-through, but I sensed that he was very aware, possibly even jealous, of Plummer's power. We flew out to Elsinore for the filming, but by then Lindsay and I had fallen out. The scene went as well as could be, but since there were hazards all through filming, everybody was on monstrous 'overtime' and it was never shown twice: the royalty payments would have been too expensive!!

The Search for Sanctuary

After *Hamlet* I moved out of Drury Lane and may have wandered back to Mum, which I tended to do between rooms and flats. I seemed to be making a route around London parallel to the one I was taking around the country in rep. My first and very lucky strike was in Ovington Square, Knightsbridge, where I shared a flat with an actor and writer called Randall Kinkead for a couple of years and benefited from the fact that the person who had lived there before me was an interior decorator and had made something of a designer apartment out of it. Of course, heating was by paraffin in those days and you lit it carefully when you came in and then turned it out when you went out. Even if Randall was finishing his breakfast and hanging around the flat I would turn the heating off when I went to work. I didn't want my precious shillings being used up. Now I think how terrible to be so awfully fearful of being poor that I was reduced to such mean, tight-arsed gestures.

I didn't much like the area – it seemed precious and 'Sloaney' – but there used to be a good workers' café nearby and there was a wonderful bakery where you could buy soft, squeezy milk loaves. Randall was interested in many things other than acting and writing, and he introduced me to his Soho set. I met other writers like Dan Farson in the French pub, to which Randall also introduced me and we often went to Jimmy the Greek's for cheapo dinners. I met the film critic David Robinson, and assorted types who would float over to the flat. It was a very social flat and although we fought about who did the dishes, basically we got on well; Randall was a very patient and kindly chap who eventually gave up the theatre and went back to university. During my dishwashing days at Au Père de Nico the restaurant was managed by the prior occupier of my flat, Harry Mann, a very sophisticated South African Jew who was an inventive and creative decorator but for some reason was managing a restaurant which was the flavour of the month in those days.

During my evening stints I came across, as was my wont, a sweet but older lady who was the mother of two young children. My instincts seemed to veer towards protectors. I was still raw in the discovery of my own abilities and a relative beginner, so I can only surmise that I wanted some form of support or encouragement or home. Being the cuckoo I was then, I soon found myself ensconced with this lady in Warwick Avenue, in an enormous white room with a green ceiling and sharing a black bathroom downstairs. This lasted a short time until we decided that we would be better friends apart and I moved to the house next to the Bull and Bush, Hampstead. I was very happy there for a few months except that the walk to the tube was murder and it was an exhausting trek back down the hill and up the hill. So although I had painted my room in fashionable terracotta, I decided it was once again time to pack the bags. Well, why not return to mother earth once more until the going got better? It was at this time, when once again taking classes at the City Lit which were given by some Royal Court directors, including Bill Gaskill, that I met a charming young Canadian with short red hair who was very adept at mime. We went out together for a while and one day she actually got a job, so I sublet her flat and got to know Pimlico. I found it a thoroughly depressing place, but while there I got a job which kept me going and made the first real difference to my career.

In November 1963 I auditioned for Warren Jenkins at the New Theatre, Cardiff, to do *War and Peace*. I travelled up with the Canadian actor Paul Massey, who had apparently had a bad time trying to act Brick in *Cat on a Hot Tin Roof* opposite Kim Stanley, a typically vital New York actress. Like so many of our Brit-trained actors, Paul couldn't deal with the strong male American roles. Now he was consolidating his career with some rep and playing the lead in *War and Peace*. It was going to be one of those Meyerholdian productions with screen projections, music, fire, the full works. It was fun to do and I decided to flex my wings a bit and make something of my relatively small but vital role. Warren Jenkins was a champ to work with, a Welsh terrier, full of good humour and resilience and very witty, even if he did have an occasional tendency to fall asleep in the stalls. I liked the New Theatre and it was an epic show to do there; we put our all into it. I was happy with my digs; there was a very Welsh spinster who lived in the front room and played the harp. She had a divine temperament and I enjoyed talking to her.

The technical dress rehearsal kept us half the night and the next day I heard the news that Kennedy had been killed. The world was shocked and I thought it was horrible in the sense of one of those things that happens at such a remove that one can barely begin to understand it. So much of our understanding of the world is drawn from the accumulated build-up we acquire through the media that it seems to remain two-dimensional; those kind of things never quite penetrated my deeper side. For all I knew Kennedy could have been a figure from fiction, although I did know that he was a good president and a brave and just man, and that did him a great deal of credit as far as I was concerned. But I could not get as weepy about his death as when I heard that Albert Camus had crashed his car and we had been robbed prematurely of one of the greatest writers of our time. I knew Camus in a way I could never know Kennedy.

Of course there was a terrible joke going round at the time which referred originally to the Lincoln assassination; it was a showbiz joke, given showbiz's obsession with itself. 'Apart from that, Mrs Lincoln, how did you enjoy the play?' I was foolish enough to breach all rules of etiquette and repeat the joke in our dressing room, much to the outrage of one of the actresses. I received a blasting for it. She was a pain in the arse to me and seemed to see red each time she laid her ferocious little eyes on me.

In *War and Peace* I was killed in a duel and, determined to make it as sensational as possible, I practised a backward fall, the kind where you fall dead straight without breaking your drop with your bum or hands. You trust to nature and to the belief that your head will not snap back and crack your skull. It doesn't – if you are dead straight, your back, shoulders and bum hit the floor together and it will be painless. The fear is terrible, but you have to trust yourself. I remember seeing Finney doing it in *Luther*, wearing a thick monk's cowl. I practised on my bed in the digs, but the bounce of the springs shook me up too much and misled me into thinking the real thing would be worse than the bed. Then I practised on the stage on several blankets, beginning from a small crouch and gradually building up courage. Eventually I psyched myself up to take the plunge, imagined I heard the shot and fell. Then I asked the actor playing my adversary to do the shot and again I went down in one long plonk. I was most excited, but when I asked Warren Jenkins to witness my act of bravery he was not impressed and said, 'Cut it.' I was horribly disappointed but kept practising and when Warren was not in the theatre, since like most directors he only stayed for a couple of nights, I went back to my backward fall. The audience were impressed and I was satisfied, although I never tried it again.

The season didn't last very long and the next play I did was *Semi-Detached* by David Turner. Lee Montague was the 'star', recruited for the leading part of Fred Midway, so ably played by Olivier in the West End, where I saw it at the Saville Theatre. Jeremy Conway, the agent, was an actor then before he wisely changed course; he played the soppy Tom Midway, and Peter Penry Jones, who had killed me in *War and Peace*, played Arnold Makepiece. The play was successful;

Lee Montague made a big impression on everyone and was very funny. I had developed a peculiar habit of clearing my nose with a kind of snort, a nervous condition brought about by my worrying about being audible on stage, and on the first night when we all traipsed round to the café for our pre-show tea, Lee suddenly said, 'Can't you stop that!' I was so shocked by his blunt and naked assault on my foible that I did immediately stop and it went away. It recurred years later, but in less measure than before. I think the wear and tear of acting takes a toll on a nervous disposition until the constitution strengthens and toughens.

Anyway I was satisfied. I had worked in a large theatre in an epic play with good actors and had for the first time heard of a pop group called the Beatles, which stuck in my mind as a naff name. I had done my famous backward free fall without injury; I had notched up two more plays and it was still only 1963. I had been acting for all of three years.

There seems to be a gap in my mind after this. I can't find any theatre programmes after this date and these fading mementoes are the maps that provide the clue to my past. Each contains in essence the total experience, who was the assistant stage manager, where to eat after the show, and what is coming next. As I look through them everything streams back and the names bring back the faces, even when the faces change so radically.

I was sitting in a restaurant recently and was greeted by Jeremy Conway, who has expanded beyond the small, slim elf he was in Cardiff. I saw him twice that day after a period of twenty-eight years. There is something so precious about the past: the events cannot be changed or improved, but are like ghosts forever trapped in the same repetitive movements and sad journeys. It is dangerous to dwell on it since it can suck you back into reverie and you lose the impact of the moment if you are not careful. The months of unemployment were broken up with bouts of television: I found myself playing small costume parts in *Crime and Punishment* and *Murder in the Cathedral*, eking out a living, reporting to the Labour Exchange with the gang. Then I auditioned for a summer season with Perth rep and was chosen for a leading juv.

I liked Scotland and was happy to go up there, although Perth was a kind of genteel Scotland. The first play was *The Importance of Being*

Earnest in which I was improbably cast as Jack. Rehearsals were a trifle stiff and the director was a woman who seemed to take an aversion to me. I found the part difficult at first, although I knew exactly what I wanted. I had not yet quite polished the rougher edges to my voice sufficiently to be able to let those plummy sentences slide out without some effort. They should come dripping out with elegant ease.

I enjoyed my walk along the High Street to rehearsal and positively purred with joy as I sat in a café and ate my breakfast – bacon rolls in that delicious Scottish bread and tea – and then, well-fuelled, I would endure another day of torture. I was developing a kind of neurosis, either through the discomfort of the role and being forced to be so exact, or because of the wear and tear of my life on the road and constant travelling (though I found that exciting), or maybe I was just acclimatizing to the pressure of acting and the first scar tissue hadn't protected the vulnerable spots. I suddenly felt terribly exposed. Unendurably and painfully raw. I even went to a doctor, since I had developed stage fright. I was scared of drying, although I never did. But before I went on I had this terrible fear and had a glass of sherry to steady the nerves, as did a fellow actor, who also seemed a dash unquiet but concealed his feelings better than I did. At the end of the performance we would gather in the little Upper Circle bar and have a wee dram with the old manageress, who had been there for ever. The play was fairly painful, but I gave it a brave stab – in fact, in the end I thought I was rather good. I rushed to the Perth *Evening News* on the day of reviews. I would wait for the result of my self-flagellation. It seemed the most important thing on earth then to see just some commendation of my efforts. I was a sorrowful creature. I read the review and it was quite good for me: while recognizing that I was not quite the epicene English dandy or chinless wonder, it still commended me for my comedy and so it wasn't quite the wash-out I thought it might have been.

Next I was scheduled to play the lead as an Italian in a Forster adaptation and then to do *A Streetcar Named Desire*. Now this is a play I could die for. I was settling in to do a good, greasy, demonstrative Italian; I had already seen Keith Baxter perform the Forster play in London and knew it was well within my reach when I heard that they had given the part to my fellow actor in *Earnest*, merely be-

266

cause they thought he was better in the Wilde. I was shattered – I knew that he was utterly wrong for the Italian and that I was tailor-made for it. I sat in my depressing digs among the flotsam and jetsam of the gang who make up the cast and crew of provincial rep; every night I came home to noise in the kitchen and drinking and laughing and went to my room alone and mightily depressed. The noise was too much, so I changed digs, but found I was sitting down for dinner with a group of glum working men. I became more and more depressed and one day said to a kindly chap in my digs that I thought I was losing my marbles.

I gave in my notice to the theatre even with *Streetcar* on the way with my name on it. I was so disgusted with the idea of playing a tiny role in the next play and not being given a chance to redeem myself in the part that had been earmarked for me. The old manageress was shocked, but I was adamant. Had the other man been a terrific actor I'm sure I wouldn't have minded quite so much, but he wasn't. Fine as he was in *Earnest*, I could see him way out of his depth in the Forster. I refused to stay on to do the next play and then they started threatening legal action. I even threatened to leave the present production of *Earnest* ... oh I was very adamant on my rights, and headstrong. I knew in my guts that the next play was mine and I had been cheated.

The next two weeks seemed a lifetime and then I left, with no regrets and no work to look forward to. You might think this was the most stupid thing in the world to do, since what is one play with a small part? I could have started learning *Streetcar* and using the free time to get the words and the accent down, and lived a little in this beautiful, if slightly gloomy, town. I had the greatest role to look forward to and yet, like a petulant little git thinking only of now, I fled.

It was to be the turning point of my career. Though painful at the time, it was a decision which was to pave the way towards a new life and a new way of treating myself. I was then so very raw, vulnerable, insecure and prone to too many of the thousand shocks that flesh is heir to. I think that constantly exposing oneself on stage is a shock to the system and can be the most unbearable thing to do. Hence its terrible attraction. You are out there to entertain people and when the chink of vulnerability lets the doubts in, every second becomes a baptism of fire. You wish to escape. You feel foolish, and unworthy.

Worst of all, you feel childish, since 'playing' and 'dressing up' are childhood escapades.

I escaped into the Highlands. I always took off into the icy region when working in Scotland and was fascinated by the great wastelands of moors and lochs. I would travel alone for days, staying in sweet little bed and breakfast houses, and hitchhike to Ullapool or cross to the weirdly atmospheric Rannoch Moor which I love to this day. There is something awesome in waking by Loch Torridan and seeing the clouds gently nestling on the skin of the lake. I was to go to Scotland many times in the future: it would be the scene of many of my premières. I felt safe there. It was so un-English. The accent reassured me, felt earthy and true and had a music in it absent from the English drone. I even like the smell of the cities of Scotland.

Mime Artist

I came back to London and went back to the City Lit, to classes now being held regularly by the marvellous Claude Chagrin. It was my twice-weekly mind saver and allowed me to be creative on Tuesday and Thursday mornings. I was relieved to be back. I felt calmer and tried to regain my equilibrium. Claude's husband, Julian, had devised a show based on some of the techniques he had learned with Jacques Lecoq, and he and another skilled mime, George Ogilvie, plus some cabaret interest, put together a show cutely called *Chaganog*, linking their two names. They had some amusing and clever sketches and I was *understudying two of the best mimes in the country*! Well, it would have been disaster if I had had to go on since I hadn't a clue about any of the sketches – I couldn't possibly have learned them unless Jacques and George taught me, and they were both too busy and too exhausted even to contemplate it. We did a tour of Britain first, doing all the major theatres, and back I was in the Kings Theatre, Edinburgh. So I beetled straight up to the little Traverse Theatre in the Royal Mile to sniff around the place. Jim Haynes had opened it as one of the first fringe theatres in the country: you could eat, drink, sit around or watch a show. It had a pocket-sized stage, but you saw the best theatre you could hope to see anywhere. The plays were usually European in origin and therefore seemed to possess a more universal theme than the current Brit offerings, although

I did see an amusing John Antrobus play outrageously titled *How You'll Come to Love Your Sperm Test*. Antrobus was then the master of anarchy and when I saw him I was surprised to find he was an attractive young man, as if I expected writers to be fat and decrepit.

Chaganog worked well in Edinburgh, but for me it was an uneasy mix of showbiz and mime and this was its downfall. If they had stuck to mime it might have had a chance but they decided (foolishly, I think) that mime wasn't commercial enough and that they should give the show a cabaret feel by surrounding the mime with a singer and a couple of dancers.

It wasn't a huge tour, but we did go to a very unusual theatre in Westhaven on the north-west coast. It was run by a millionaire silk manufacturer-cum-arts philanthropist who invited the company to a huge party at his majestic house. He seemed to be very famous and knew everybody of substance in the country.

We eventually got to London, to the Vaudeville Theatre. I had a dressing room to myself; all I had to do was to get in and wait until the second act and then go. You can't imagine how painful that was. I can't explain why, except that my day was geared to my job, which was doing nothing but sitting in a dressing room. It could be very depressing. During the various acts the other understudy and I would, like ghosts, mimic the actions on stage to try and recall the acts we were supposed to know if ever we had to go on. During the interval the musicians and I would slip into the pub in the alleyway next door and then go back for the second act. Then leave.

The show had lukewarm reviews and business was bad. We all had wages cuts and tried to hang on over Christmas. I was living in my Victoria digs at the time and desperately seeking real work. After five years this wasn't my idea of heaven, being an understudy jokingly paid to perform in something I hadn't the slightest idea of doing. It was a farce. However, the train of events that led me to this after giving in my notice in Perth was beginning to take shape. Indirectly, my benefactor was Orson Welles!

Zoo Story, 1965 – It Begins

I had been keeping up with current trends in the theatre and its overlords, and I was quite impressed with *Who's Afraid of Virginia*

Woolf?, particularly by the acting and directing of the American company I saw in London. Uta Hagen and Arthur Hill were utterly brilliant. So I started to read Albee's other works, including *Zoo Story*, which struck me at the time as an exciting but slightly overheated piece with huge and fascinating arias for the actor playing Jerry. I was still desperately trying to find real acting work and had made most of my contacts through the grapevine. Sitting in the dressing room each night at the Vaudeville was beginning to demoralize me and I felt I would never work again. This is every actor's nightmare at the end of a job. You wonder if by some chance your number will ever come up again or if you will always be at the bottom of the pack when the cards are shuffled each time casting gets under way.

I continued to audition, always arousing a smidgeon of interest which never grew beyond that. I even had a callback from the RSC, but was spared what might have been more frustration and interminable spear-carrying. One day I just happened to hear that David Thompson at Stratford East was casting Molière's *George Dandin* and Albee's *Zoo Story* as a double bill. Stratford had fallen away from the great Joan and now was in the hands of a couple of 'worthy' producers who knew they had inherited a very well-known theatre and were trying to keep its reputation going. They chose good plays with good casts and printed large programmes. I phoned and left a message regarding *Zoo Story*. I was told as usual that it was cast, but we would let you know, etc. Several days later I had a call! Would I come to Stratford to read?

This was big news. The actor cast for Jerry, who had been chosen some time ago, was locked into a schedule in Spain with the much-delayed *Chimes at Midnight*, directed by Orson Welles. The actor was well-known in the lower ranks and had the kind of smouldering good looks and outsider stance that probably looked good on paper for Jerry. But I had the *desperation*. Plus a tinge of the waywardness and eccentricity. Thompson was lucky and so was I.

I took the tube to Stratford, walked down the narrow street to the charming little Theatre Royal and read Jerry for David Thompson. I had borrowed the play from the library and studied a few of the speeches, and was confirmed in my feelings that it was a trifle protesting-too-much but still a marvellous story. What it offered was a *tour de force* for any actor who could cope with it. Jerry's central speech goes on for *fifteen minutes*! It is five pages long and must be the longest speech in theatrical history, rivalling in intensity and bizarreness Lucky's big monologue in *Waiting for Godot*.

I started to read. My accent was pretty good, since I like the freedom of the American pitch and inflection and find anyway that accents take me away from the conditioning of my own personality which is chained to certain responses. In a way an accent liberates you from bondage and enables you to take on a 'new' personality. I hit the text and could see Thompson was impressed. He then asked me for some 'dazzle' or words to that effect, saying that Jerry had to hold the stage and must be 'sparkling' or have other luminous and incandescent qualities. So I moved about a bit; rather silly, I thought, with a book in my hand – he should have asked me to go home and learn a section and come back next week – but I tried to show 'sparkle'. He seemed to like what I was doing and said he would let me know, but I had a feeling that I would be chosen, since there are not many English actors who can swallow American roles and be authentic.

A few days later I heard that the part was mine and I was to be paid thirty pounds per week, which was utterly marvellous, and would I be in the other play as well? Well, I was not so well suited to *George Dandin* as the actor who was moored in Spain might have been, and so they recruited my friend Peter Brett, and I was satisfied to play a tiny part in that piece. I was still going in for *Chaganog*, now on its last gasp but 'gallantly' staying open. I gave my notice and started to learn the part at night in my dressing room.

The lines came easily and flowed, but David Thompson was directing both plays and I had to share his time with Ewan Hooper, who was playing Dandin – this was before Ewan had bravely put together the Greenwich Theatre. But I was *acting* full out and with no holds barred! I swept into it. Played, feinted, jabbed, posed, dived into the text, cried, howled and generally gave one of those performances so beloved of the New York Actors' Studio, although I was not a member of that fraternity. I felt the text drew that out of me. The man's obsession with the dog that he tried to relate to but couldn't. Terrible and bitter loneliness leading to absurd gestures. The outsider who lives or exists in tenements. Albee's fascination with the alienated rooming-house dweller.

It was all going well, but I was suddenly struck down with fear as I thought of that five-page speech looming up on the first night with no try-out in the provinces for a few weeks to get it under your belt. This fear grew and grew as I paced the dressing room in the Vaudeville Theatre, enjoying the sensation of new and exciting lines entering my system, fuelling me and carrying along my dormant emotions. I was getting into Jerry and his dog and the idea of the man who anticipated his own death. But at the same time the fear paralysed me. I foresaw this first-night audience at Stratford East and myself 'drying' in front of the whole world. There were other sizeable chunks as well as the five-page speech.

I spoke to ex-Ophelia Jo Maxwell-Muller about it and she told me about the wonder drug Librium. I got a prescription from my local doctor and lo and behold I felt relaxed and able to rehearse without the slightest fear, only a reasonable amount of good nervousness.

On the day of the dress rehearsal, the Molière play had huge problems with sets and costumes and took up all the time available. I sat and waited. My nerves were now almost snapping, in spite of 'mother's little helpers'. Of course our play was much simpler, the set being a park bench in front of a backdrop, but for me it was the entire world. My nerves finally went when the gentle David Thompson said there wasn't time to rehearse *Zoo Story* and I could go home. I did one of my 'fit' numbers, yelling and being carried along in the released torrent of my emotions. I purged myself and went up to my dressing room, where a distraught David tried to calm me down and said we could do it tomorrow. I went home with Peter Brett and I think that David knew I was plain terrified. This was one of the largest and most demanding roles I had ever played and I was going out there cold in front of the critics of London for the first time in my life. I was near breakdown.

The first night loomed up. I popped enough Librium to tranquillize a horse and duly did my dress rehearsal in front of a few actors who were no longer too sympathetic to me after my demonstration of the collywobbles, which they interpreted as hysteria. I got through the afternoon and sat around in my dressing room. Each hour I fortified my level of Librium until I was pleasantly drowsy but felt sure that it wouldn't interfere with my memory centre as I had been popping a couple a day to help me cope with rehearsals. Two or three were enough, but today I might have risked four or even five. One is normally very effective. An hour to go, what the hell, let's have one more. I felt drowsy but OK. Nervous in a nice way, without too much anxiety. The half-hour was called and I fell asleep. I drowsed in a semi-slumberland where the noises of the outside world mixed with my dream and eventually I heard the 'beginners' call. I had to shrug myself awake. I strolled somnambulantly to the stage and waited to go on. The lights went down and I walked to my place. I stood there half asleep but OK. The lights poured on and I heard and almost saw in a distant, hazy way a sea of faces. But I wasn't fazed, since I was concentrating like mad on my first lines. After a few lines I heard a ripple of laughter. I was encouraged and felt that moment when the nerves give way and power and confidence start feeding on the same fuel supply. I was riding my horse and taking it for a canter. The big speech went on for fifteen minutes or longer without a hitch and without a flaw. I got laughs and even became inspired. I leaped, pounced, played with the dog, borrowed a few cadences from Christopher Plummer. Did bizarre things with my hands and performed weird gestures and finished the play in forty minutes or so to a good applause. I went well chuffed to my dressing room. I was over the moon.

I had not invited anyone to the first night since I wasn't sure I would get through it, but my current girlfriend had come and had been so scared for me when she saw the packed audience and all the press that she went to the ladies to be sick. At the end of the play she came backstage and because I didn't know she was in I was all the more elated that she should have seen me in my hour of struggle and not in my hours of triumph which the actor feels after playing a play for more than a few weeks or months. This was my trial and it was this fear that could have caused me to flee from the theatre. The trial had been almost more than I could bear and I think I came through with flying colours. That must have been one of the happiest nights of my life!

We went to Luba's Russian bistro in Knightsbridge for a celebratory meal and the next morning I read the reviews. It had been a triumph. I was hailed by practically all the national press! I was amazed, excited, elated, but knew I had to do it again the next night and the night after. Word got around. The Sunday papers were no less enthusiastic, discussing Albee as if he was a seminal writer and ploughing through the play searching for meaningful symbols. The radio critics were even more complimentary – words like 'perfection' were used and I thought that the play must have meant more to me than I realized and said more to me and about me than I knew. I attacked it with resourcefulness and bravery; Plummer's attack on Hamlet never far from my mind. To be daring. To go far. To try. Go to the edge.

This was in 1965. I had left Webber-Douglas just five years earlier and Perth six months ago, thoroughly depressed and demoted to playing small parts. One month earlier I had been sitting in a dressing room hearing other people's work, grateful for the chance of being an understudy who would never be able to go on and now I was in the biggest hit play Stratford East had had for a long time and which was meant only as a curtain-raiser to the main bill. Yet everyone really came to see this new actor in *Zoo Story*. It was a bit of luck and my desperation and loneliness over the years really found their articulate counterpart in Jerry.

Anthony Armstrong-Jones was commissioned to photograph me for *The Sunday Times* along with five other up-and-coming actors. Ken Tynan's wife Kathleen interviewed me at the Connaught Hotel, where for some reason I felt out of my depth and didn't know what to say to her. I felt I had to say something important and spewed a lot of rubbish. I was embarrassed being photographed by Princess Margaret's husband in *The Sunday Times* building and wondered what this was all about: it felt very silly. All I was doing was a play. Several weeks later the article featuring Terence Stamp, Nicol Williamson, Ian McKellen, James Fox, Peter McEnery and me came out. I was called 'winsome'!

In later years Kathleen admitted that she had had little knowledge of the theatre then but had been egged on by Ken. So at least he might have gone to see me and recommended me. That would have been a feather in my cap. There are some critics whose respect bestows on you the hallmark of fame or pride. This rare breed can give you the sense that all has been worthwhile and, no matter what agony you suffered in the process, the final tick of approval from one of them is justification for everything. Tynan was one of these. Without him or his equivalent we are left with a gang without a leader. Tynan led, and his brilliance was coupled with a healthy disregard for convention, tradition or cosy bourgeois values. A good review from him was worth years of bad reviews from others, for he sensed the climate of the time. He saw which way theatre was moving and what was becoming defunct. I hoped one day to be reviewed by him.

17 One of the first of Berkoff's companies, on a tour of Holland
with *The Trial*, *c.* 1971

18 Another Berkoff company outside The Round House, London,
where they were performing *Metamorphosis*, 1969

19   *The Trial* at the Round House, London, 1973

20   Linda Marlowe in *The Trial*

21   The horses in *Agamemnon*, Round House, London, 1973

22   *Agamemnon*, Greenwich Theatre, 1976

23 Berkoff and Shelley Lee in *The Fall of the House of Usher*,
Hampstead Theatre Club, 1975

25 Shelley Lee (soon to become Berkoff's
second wife) as Madeleine Usher

24 Berkoff as Usher becomes a chair for
Terry McGinity as Usher's Friend

26 Berkoff as Mike, *East*, Greenwich Theatre, 1976

27 Matthew Scurfield as Dad, *East*

28 With the deadly sexy Anna Nygh

29 Matthew Scurfield as Dad, Barry Philips as Les,
Anna Nygh as Sylv and Berkoff as Mike, *East*

30   Les and Mike, *East*

31 Berkoff in his Houdini period: *Metamorphosis* with Petra Markham (*left*) as Greta and Jeannie James as Mrs Samsa at the Round House, London, 1969

Hoped that he would see and write about one of my productions, but alas it was not to be and after *Zoo Story* I had to suffer some pretty banal reviewers for the first years. When Tynan questioned the time and content of our theatre I wanted him to see *my* theatre. When he said it was full of insulated, non-physical, walking heads, I yearned for him to come to *my* productions.

So I was chosen via him to be in the colour magazine and suddenly I was news. I became famous for a weekend. I remember being too self-conscious to go out for a week. I felt slightly embarrassed by it all. I was not a London swinger and party-goer or giver. Basically I was a quiet soul given to few friends and my idea of paradise was an evening at a restaurant with the girlfriend. Now I had to get *social*. I felt that I should capitalize on my present fame and get some work offers.

Nothing came in. Even after those sensational reviews I could barely get an audition for the RSC or other major theatres. My agent was flabbergasted that no one had the wit to pick me up or encourage my first bold fling lest my newfound bravura wilt from neglect. But nobody was that interested. I was to find this more and more as I got older: all the goodwill and hard work, the audition pieces I studied, the letters I wrote to the major companies were to have no effect. Only 'Sorry, we're not able to catch your show.' I was too odd, or too out of the mainstream, or too something, but the dreams I had of playing Shakespeare were to be constantly dashed against the rocks of indifference. What was it? Was it pure indifference or was there something that had manifested itself in my performance in *Zoo Story* that proclaimed itself outside the British style? Neither for good nor bad, but different.

The director David Scase came down from Liverpool and had no difficulty in giving me a job at the Liverpool Playhouse for a season. He did it with such warm-blooded enthusiasm that I immediately felt at home with him. I was not to start until later that year, so I had a few months to kick my heels. I briefly did some TV, including a play called *The Pistol*, in which I again played a small, worthless role and was so fed up with all the climbing up and down hills and digging ditches that I felt sure was more the work of extras that I complained, along with everyone else. I was promptly put in the BBC's 'black book' and didn't work for them for years afterwards. The only redeeming feature of the play was the presence of Lionel Stander, the American actor with a voice like a cement mixer, who graced every show he did with a massive presence and scene-chewing vigour as well as being a hugely likeable and amusing man. James Ferman directed it and soon afterwards gave up directing to become our film censor.

Zoo Story was coming to an end and I wanted desperately to capitalize on my new-found secrets, to keep the magic lamp burning. I all but begged the next director at Stratford, David Thompson's partner, to let me play Oswald in *Ghosts*. Why not nurture the actor you discovered? Give sustenance and create a core or team of players that people would come to see again and again? But no. This was the shopping casting that was to be the keynote of most British directors. Let's try a different flavour next week. *Ghosts* went on and died a death and the theatre eventually went bust through a mixture of overspending on sets and bad management. It had started well, but died of over-confidence and no real ideology.

Zoo Story was the one and only time I was to work in Stratford East, but I always retained a distinct impression of going there. The tube to Stratford and then the walk down the quaint street of neat terraced houses until you came to the theatre stuck in the middle of them. Only Joan Littlewood could have made it work the way she did, expressing the needs of the people and relating to them in a way they could understand. Because the theatre had life force and energy, the West End flocked to it. Now on the rare occasion when I go back, I can hardly find it. The area has been devastated and resembles a madman's dream of urban planning. The theatre is like an island in the middle of a roundabout.

Mum, of course, was dead chuffed to see my mug with a cap on looking 'winsome' and distinctly unrelaxed in a soppy colour print – she straightaway bought about twenty copies. Her pride must have reached new heights as her son was becoming the artist she could have been, or at worst a mere actor. She duly came down to Stratford, as did Auntie Betty, and my former English teacher, Joe Brearley from Hackney Downs Grammar School, mentor to Harold Pinter.

I spent some time out of work after this and cursed the industry for being so short-sighted and insulated. Now, years later, I do not revise that opinion. The reviews and success of *Zoo Story* were more than ordinary and I would have thought that invitations would be forthcoming at least to meet or audition, if not to be invited to join a major company, but there was a big zilch. Perhaps they thought I was a Russian.

By this time I had met my future wife Alison and had moved into her maisonette in Islington. To protect myself from the guilt of being another out-of-work actor I took to trying to construct shelves. I even rejoined the British Museum library and researched a theme that was inspired by my time with Lincoln rep, when I saw in the cathedral a plaque to 'Hugh of Lincoln'. The plaque went on to say that the deeds committed by the Christian community did not redound to the benefit of Christianity. Apparently the Jews of Lincoln were charged with the 'ritual' killing of a Christian child who was found dead from causes unknown. This myth was repeated throughout Europe and the supposed killing became one of the many pieces of infamy for which Jews were to be blamed. This was a very convenient charge, since according to the law of the time the State also confiscated all possessions of anyone found guilty of a major crime. The Jews, being the bankers and money lenders, had in their debt many people who would be nicely let off considerable sums if some charge could be trumped up. And so it was, and it became a terrible scandal and set off waves of bloody persecution.

I sat in the library ordering the books from the giant catalogues. What a fascinating time it was to be, and how much I learned. The trolleys with my requirements would be left at my table and the pit-a-pat of the books would echo around the circular room. I spent a couple of weeks there writing out my notes, but after a while would get bored dealing with all the dates, facts and historical cross-references and sneak out for a fag on the steps of the museum. But in the end I felt I had enough material to go on. I went home and wrote my first play.

It was an emotional, albeit sentimental, reconstruction of the events and featured a trial which owed a lot to contemporary religious analysis and research into the laws and customs of the time. Of course nobody was interested; a few agents expressed admiration for it, but no companies either for stage or for television would touch it and it has been in my drawer ever since. I think I spent about a month typing it out and then another few weeks refining it and in the end I had a pretty good reconstruction of the events leading up to the persecution and trial of the Jews of Lincoln in the year 1290. What strange times, that such atrocities should take place in the sleepy hamlet of Lincoln.

The most illuminating aspect of the many hours in the museum was the sheer amount of material I found on anti-semitism. I was amazed at how many famous schoolboy history heroes were contaminated by that virus, including quite a few popes whose utterances have been preserved and handed down in books of prayer while their other manias have been allowed to fade away.

I finished my play, which I called *Blood Accusation*, although at an earlier stage I decided on the odd name *Hep, Hep, Hep*. This strange cry was purported to have been uttered by the crusading knights as they swept down on the unbelievers. The letters are an acronym for 'Hierosolym est perdita'. Jerusalem is lost. Funny what you can pick up at the British Museum. As a treat for me when I completed the first draft I sat down and immediately wrote another play, a little two-hander which I called *Lunch* and which dealt with the famous old situation where man meets and picks up woman, goes through the seasons of fascination, familiarity, contempt and then the first shoots of love.

Lunch has been performed many times but *Hep* never saw the light of day. 'Jewy' themes are difficult to set down without falling into the trap of making all the Jews holy, good, decent and all the gentiles villains and cold-blooded tyrants. I fell right into it and I had to find another way.

Still, I had assuaged a great deal of guilt and had a purpose. I enjoyed my little room in Islington where I had a typewriter. Alison and I shared a two-floor flat and were happy for a time. When it was hot we found the only thing to do was to get the train from Victoria and beetle down to Brighton. It was paradise to leave the hot, dusty streets of pre-trendy Islington, step out of the train at Brighton and walk down the long street leading to the perfect blue sea which you could see as you came out of the station. I remember that first time so distinctly – it was so easy to go from unemployed and desperate depression to unalloyed and ecstatic pleasure that I wondered why I had not thought of it before. It was so blissful that when we went on a hot summer morning the following week I was amazed that it was just as marvellous as before. Each time never ceased to amaze me. We'd take a few sandies and walk down to Black Rock and sit on the stones. We'd eat and read and I'd jump into the sea, since that was mandatory for my seaside experience, and then we'd get the train back in the evening, feeling a great deal better than when we'd started out. I thought then, as I looked at the white, bulbous-fronted Regency houses fronting the beach, how wonderful it would be to live there.

Islington, like most London suburbs in the sixties, was a font of utter depression enlivened by a couple of street markets which I always enjoyed. I made it my Sunday pilgrimage to go down Chapel Street market and sit on a stool by the window in the greasy spoon café and read the 'Sundays'. The café was run by Italian twins, who specialized in ice-cream. As I looked out of the window I saw a man with blond hair and very Saxon features selling vegs and doing a brisk trade since his prices were fair. I think he was there most days, but I tended to see him only on Sunday. Over the years that I sat on my stool with my sausage and salad roll I always saw him in the same position, always moving and doing a good trade. He never smoked and always seemed to be very fit.

Many years passed and one female partner turned into another; I would take each one for Sunday breakfast and the man with the glasses and blond hair was always there. He became a fixture in my mind as a man who never changed. His hair looked the same and his expression was always one of cheerful buoyancy. I even came to be a little in awe of him. He might have been a character from a Greek myth. Like the trusted ferryman who would guide you across the River Styx. Dealing in simple and unexotic vegetables meant that he always had a queue of housewives who needed and trusted him and he seemed to understand this bond. He would throw me a smile or a chuckle as I passed, but not much more. Over the years he appeared in my mind to have that quality of honesty and purpose given to men who devote their lives to one end, be it the priesthood or selling vegs, and no matter how far from each other the two occupations are they are both attested to by the devotion of their protagonists. I even became a little shy of going to him and buying his vegs and would send someone else. I left Islington after eighteen years, but when I go back to Chapel Street he is still there and hasn't changed. In fact I call him 'The Man Who Never Changed'. He works in all weathers and now we exchange a little banter.

I was glad when I came to rehearse in Liverpool. We started with *Seidman and Son*, a bland comedy which was a vehicle for David Kossoff. It passed away quietly and was soon forgotten about. Its one distinguishing feature was the appearance of Duncan Weldon, who was Kossoff's assistant at the time. Duncan has now gone on to better things and recently we joined up again when he took *Salomé* to the West End.

The next play was slightly better, Willis Hall's *The Long and the Short and the Tall*. It's a classic war story for a mixed bunch of actors, a good tense war drama with all the right ingredients and stereotypes. I was cast as the lead, Bamforth. I saw Peter O'Toole perform it in Lindsay Anderson's stunning production. The play certainly packs a punch and is the same kind of well-crafted piece as *The Bofors Gun*. This gave another soldier/hero a great acting opportunity, in the shape of Nicol Williamson's dynamic portrayal, even on TV.

We got into rehearsals and I started to feel a release from bondage and an ability to 'play' again that I hadn't found since *Zoo Story*. It is the writer's craft to be able to give you words and thoughts that inspire you and set off trains of thought that get you going in all directions and most of all engage your vitality and sense of self. David Scase had done the play before, twice I think, and so knew all its pitfalls. He gave it a swift, powerful and moving production.

We had been booked to take the play to Florence for the anti-war Festival of Theatre. We duly flew in to Florence, rehearsed on a set that was an exact duplicate of the one we had in Liverpool and opened the following night. With simultaneous translation we were getting delayed laughs as if they had to bounce off the moon. Despite that the night went well, although I was astonished by the forty-minute interval we were forced to take. At the end there was an ovation the like of which I have never heard. Again and yet again, and even I was in full operatic mood since we were playing the Teatro della Pergola, a beautiful opera house. I blew kisses to the audience. The next day the papers were as enthusiastic as the audience had been and singled me out as a natural clown and performer – they seemed to think that I had communicated beyond the language barrier. We were all well and truly over the moon and sat in Italian restaurants with our guv, David Scase, whom we all loved without restraint!

Most of the others flew back, but I wanted to see the Italian countryside and opted to be a companion to the driver, Duncan Weldon. Duncan drove as if he wanted to get home and had no real interest in the scenery, so in the end I had to get out of the car and run behind it just to experience the wonderfully exhilarating atmosphere and deep-running valleys, gorges, forests. Then I could get back in the car and suffer more endless driving until we came to another great view, when I would ask Duncan to stop and I would do my ten-minute run in the fresh open air. I don't think Duncan cared too much for fresh air.

Eventually we got to Paris and I checked into the Hôtel de Louvre, which was the height of luxury for me. I got back to Liverpool three days later in time to carry on with the last two weeks of playing Bamforth, without the attendant strain or pleasure of rehearsing another play during the day.

For some reason I was then cast in a ridiculous Australian play called *The Piccadilly Bushman*, which I can only surmise was given to David to try out in exchange for paying all the expenses, since a greater load of abominable twaddle can never have reached our shores. Even if it was written by the estimable Australian playwright Ray Lawler. I played it as if I were Peter O'Toole for the first weeks and was accused by one of the actors, Bill Ellis, of 'insensitivity'. I then found a curious way of playing which I have seldom captured again, a kind of hyper-sincerity. Of listening intently and answering quietly and civilly. I was so enraptured by this new discovery that I pleaded with David Scase to witness my awesome inspiration. He had to be dragged in, since he hated the play more than all of us, and he thought what I did was 'interesting' . . .

What I tried to do was to release that part which is the 'me' crying out for attention at all times and in a way dissolve into the background or be very still. This way you have a strange feeling of giving up all those quirks and bumps, all those 'character' signatures and letting something flow which is newer and more interesting; then when you have a 'moment' you let rip all the banked-up energy you have saved. It's a curious way of playing, but I was gaining so much experience now that I could afford to experiment. It was still 1965 and I had only been in the biz for six years.

I left Liverpool, since I felt there was little else for me to stay there for, which could have been a rather large mistake – there was much I could have played had I had the knowledge to understand it. They were rehearsing *Twelfth Night* with Bill Ellis playing Feste. He is an agent now, but I remember him being very good. There was a character called Malvolio I could have played, but I didn't understand Shakespeare well enough to see what opportunities I was letting fly from my grasp. I went back to our basement flat in London and more unemployment. It was a grim Christmas and I couldn't wait to get started again.

A Midsummer Night's Dream, City Lit Institute

During a bleak period of unemployment in 1965 I went to my old workhouse sanctuary, the City Lit, and asked if I could be an assistant to a director. I wanted to learn about production. I was fascinated by the idea of directing and the City Lit gave me the chance of working with a venerable director who was pleased to have an energetic assistant who couldn't really keep an idea to himself. I watched with awed and deep fascination how my director would conduct the twice-weekly rehearsals of *A Midsummer Night's Dream* (it would take a whole term of three months). He was highly professional and showed them the set that they would be using. I was astounded by the detail that had already gone into it. The stage manager would gather music of his choice and tape the sections to be ready to give the appropriate colour. I was again dazzled by the difference some music made, how it merged so well with a scene and produced something that wasn't there before. I liked the old chap immensely. He was obviously in cahoots with the drama director, since they would meet afterwards; I now realize they were a gay couple who were devoted to each other and were highly sensitive to the needs of the school. Perhaps they even had an awareness and dedication that a family man might not have had the time and space for.

After a while the director asked me if I would like to comment, and remembering David Giles' production at Cheltenham so well, I was tempted to use some of his ideas, since I had no others. The director was most impressed and left me to do a lot of the staging. He was not in the least resentful and in fact encouraged me. One day he did not turn up and I, for the first time in my life, took a rehearsal. I felt at home and enjoyed it. I was *creating* the play anew and adding so much of my own business that in the end I scrapped my boss's biz. I hope and trust he didn't mind, since he was able to come less and less. He worked during the day and was kept busy, and confessed that he was relieved to step out of the production. ATV, a television station that he worked for, needed him rather more than the City Lit, and I was put in sole charge. I felt he trusted me because he sensed that the students responded strongly to me and to my ideas. Of course I was also able to fuse the beginnings of my mime training that I was still doing at the Institute with Claude Chagrin, whose other pupils included Edward Petherbridge. I am sure that much of Edward's expressiveness and superb control of body was unlocked by Claude.

The play doddled along as it must when you meet only twice a week for three hours, but we achieved much and I added every luscious, exotic sound I could think of, particularly Fauré, the nineteenth-century composer, whom I had just discovered. A great deal of fun was had with lovers and fairies and the production was a resounding success. Lindsay Kemp was inveigled into designing a poster, which he did – it was suitably shocking and ablaze with fertile life and looked a little rude in the reception hall of the City Lit along with the canteen smells of tinned soup and polished floors. I watched the show each night and felt a strong sense of responsibility or even bonding with the actors, as if in some way they had become my family. This paternalistic spirit has never quite left me and may have in some way compensated for the family I never had, since the actors needed and responded to care and affection and were people in a vulnerable position. If you are able to give to people in this situation then you must, since the more confidence you give them the more they can bear. That's why I find it so strange when I hear of directors who bully or intimidate. It is easy to do that – possibly this is one of the reasons that they do it, precisely because it is so easy. The power a director has can so easily intoxicate those for whom power was never an ingredient in their early lives; sadism thrives on vulnerable and accessible people. The danger can also work in reverse, in that you become too attached and too fussy, like a mother hen; I recall being so enamoured of my new family that I would go and get them baked potatoes in their jackets during the interval. I was clucking far too much. A sense of balance is preferable. The show worked well and the audiences were charmed and laughed a lot. I had made my first ever production and the City Lit once again provided a safe and gentle harbour for my journey.

More Rep – 1966

In 1966 Anthony Richardson, not to be confused with Tony Richardson, invited me to the Belgrade Theatre, Coventry, which was then in the top division of repertory theatres. So at least my *Zoo Story* platform gave me access to the best reps. I went up to appear first of all in Shaw's *Misalliance*, directed by a young and talkative Bill Bryden. It was an odd play, full of those pithy Shavian polemics, and I had some fun with it, but at the end of each rehearsal Bill would talk for hours. I never met anyone who could talk so much. Some directors feel this is necessary to inform and enlighten the cast. Bill's chats were full of fervour and always interesting, even if this approach sometimes prevented a more spontaneous eruption taking place.

Once *Misalliance* had opened I started rehearsing *Who's Afraid of Virginia Woolf?*, my second Albee. I played the visitor, while the splendidly passionate Maggie Tyzack played Martha. She was a fascinating and convincing actress to work with. Brian Phelan played George and had a good go, but his Irishness might have edged the role away from its crusty professorial origins. I found again that I could respond very easily to Albee and scored a minor success in the small part. It was a happy company, but I only really remember Maggie and was glad to have had the chance of working with such a talented actress. I seemed to be in a much happier mood in these sojourns from London, knowing what I would be doing each day and each night – it's so much easier than planning a day with no real focus to it. Coventry itself was fairly horrific. I remember a ghastly shopping precinct which seemed to go dead at night. I imagined that it was populated by creatures who lived under the pavement and came out in the morning and walked around like zombies. In the centre of this deadly testament to man's philistinism was an army recruiting post.

In due course I returned to London and more months of aching unemployment and odd jobs. Then Michael Blakemore auditioned me to do three plays at the Glasgow Citizens' Theatre for the autumn season. I was well pleased to have a go at doing *Zoo Story* for the second time, plus *The Creditors* in a double bill. The third piece was a play by Doris Lessing called *Play With a Tiger*, which Michael thought a lot of. He was cross with me when during rehearsals I said I found it '*Woman's Own*-ish' . . .

I loved Glasgow. I liked the rawness of it and the rough seediness of the Gorbals, most of which was still standing, about to be pulled down and yet still nestling the theatre within it. The butcher's shop next door was where I would buy my 'Pope's eye steak' and cook up a good meal in my digs. As usual on the first days there was a mad scramble for all available actresses – it reminds me of some mating ritual on a faraway Galapagos Island. I had my eye on a sweet young thing called Nicola Pagett, but she was swept off by some gamin young man. So they found comfort in each other while I had to forage among the leftovers and boilers, which suited me very well since by then I was less prone to romance and just needed company, friendship and a bit of real contact.

John Warner directed me in *Zoo Story* and this time Edgar Wreford, a wonderful character actor, played the man on the bench. Edgar was quite as effective as Ewen Hooper had been two years earlier, but Warner was a stickler for getting the lines exactly right and wouldn't let me off the hook. *The Creditors* was an odd play in which I played the tortured hero, a sculptor being deceived by his wife, who drives him insane. This was directed by an ex-actor called Michael Meacham. I looked, in the terrible outfit they put me in, like a hairdresser and having Blakemore's current lady playing the lead didn't help matters. Edgar came into his own in this play and was quite satanic.

I again won very good reviews for *Zoo Story* and crowds turned out to see it at the small studio theatre which was attached to the main house. I loved the studio. It was the first time I had worked so close to an audience and I found it very exciting. After the show the bar was open and you could eat and drink until late, so it was a social time too. I hate theatres where you go in and go out with nothing in between. I like an environment in which the actor might come out and have a drink in the bar, chat to a member of the audience, get some feedback and praise for his efforts, and meet for a drink with a friend too shy to go backstage, since you never know who else will be hogging the actor's attention and often a visitor can be standing backstage like a lemon. And the poor actor might just have given his all on stage and must try to remember the names of his guests and introduce them and even supply drinks; he must be careful not to enthuse too much to one guest and ignore, or worse still, forget completely not only the name but the face – which can happen, since after a show you are often bushwhacked. And so in the Close Theatre you drifted out and caught the eye of a chum.

The same thing used to happen when I started at the Round House in the early seventies. The bar was the place to go after the show or even to wander into before the show. Later, on my return to the Round House, all that 'fraternizing' had been stopped. The Mermaid Theatre also had that feel to it with its long bar and restaurant. Theatres would gain more if they could be more generous in their services, but alas, the Victorian theatre had no such need or concern. It's sad to watch actors leaving the stage door having busted their guts to a delighted house and having to go home without so much as a drink or a thankyou or any informal response. It's a shame to have to plan to have a friend come in order to have someone to eat with after the show. In Paris you would just slide into the café next door and wind down, with none of that insane panic around you as the curtains are about to descend on your drinking.

Play With a Tiger was in fact the first play we did in Glasgow. Doris Lessing came up to see it and liked my portrayal of Alex very much, so I was well chuffed by that. I think the play was a bit of an autobio for her.

On Sunday I would go to the markets, which I love in any city and particularly Barrow Land. The shouts and cries were all the more poignant in the broad Glasgow accent, with the acres of old clothes and secondhand utensils testifying to the awful poverty that still existed up there. My fave was to sit in the steamy, greasy womb of a workman's café and munch a greasy sausage sandwich and drink tea.

Michael Blakemore was a firm but caring director, never less than supportive. If I did a bit of biz I would say, 'Michael, is that too much?' and he would say, 'No, that's good, keep it in.'

Next door in the large theatre they were doing *Stephen D*, based on Joyce's novel *A Portrait of the Artist as a Young Man*; it was a good piece of staging and an Australian actor called Lewis Fiander played Stephen very well. I saw him in Melbourne in 1994, having not heard about him for some years, but, at the time he was one of the actors one had to look out for.

There were so many brave young actors and actresses who one felt were brilliantly talented, but their genius crashed against the morbid rocks of indifference and stupidity represented by casting directors, directors and even writers, who seemed to view theatre as an aspect of themselves and a mirror for their own limited world, whereas the actors' world was a different mentality. Directors seemed to distrust idiosyncratic actors or beautiful actresses. If you were either handsome or beautiful there was some doubt about whether you could act well, since you were obviously too blessed by nature to be really gifted. If you were on the plainish side and a little dumpy you were reliable and you could also play the great sexual beauties with a little extra make-up on. I think this unconscious weeding-out has enabled a kind of type to develop, a genus of player who has been purged of any exotic contamination.

Glasgow took me into the winter and when I left I photographed much of the Gorbals; these remain some of the best pictures I have taken.

I was sorry to leave my little flat in Pollokshaws, but it was time and there were no more invites to do more plays. I headed back to London and rented a flat in Islington which was the lower two floors of a house. In the upper floor were controlled-rent tenants and an old lady who kept saying to herself 'I don't care cause I can't care' over and over again. It was to be my theme tune in later years. I was glad to move out of my girlfriend's place and have for the first time in my life my own unfurnished flat. I decorated it myself. Alison's friends were all architects, since she used to go out with one, and one of the chaps showed me how to do inventive carpentry in making shelves. I set to work and was intensely proud of having made a whole wall of staggered-level shelving. I went up the road to Sanderson's wood yard like a real 'worker' . . . Then I would put all the clean shaved timber on one shoulder, cross Essex Road, beetle down St Peter's Street with my purchases and get to sawing. The sweet smell of freshly cut wood permeated the room. I liked the purity of it, the clean lines and the strength of 'two by two' or 'two by four' pine. It seemed simple and basic and that was my paradigm, simple, pure and clean. That's if I could achieve it. Unfettered, uncluttered, open and simple. Once a woman who visited me said, 'This room is so male.' I rather liked that, since I had thought of rooms as being neutral. A bit of this and that, but the idea of a *male* room suddenly made me feel very male. Perhaps she meant that it was not soft and curved or full of feminine touches. It was male and had a large, long wooden desk built by my friend Alistair, who had been an architect and then decided to be an artist when the freedom of the sixties seemed to cut him off from his moorings. He had the style of building great wooden pieces made to appear thicker by the addition of architraves and mouldings. I was so proud of his wonderful desk and I wrote many plays at it. It sat up against the window in the basement and I stared up into the grim Islington street.

Next door an Irish family with a yearly dropping would assemble and chat with the neighbour who would gabble incessantly while I was trying to work. The woman would never invite the neighbour into the house but would gas on and on outside the door for ever and meanwhile her rotten little son Michael would be running up and down the street. So at intervals during the long gossip I would hear the shriek, 'Mayyyychel!' This went on for years and became unbearable, especially in the hot weather when I was unemployed and was sitting in the basement trying to work.

As time went by I gained control over the house as the old tenants grew dangerous and decrepit and were moved out. The last ones to go were an old man and his wife who lived on the top floor. The room stank beyond belief and the windows were never opened. The man had a metal plate in his head from a First World War wound. He would get pissed regularly and come slumping in, aided by his long-suffering wife who had warts all over her face. They were the most decayed couple I had ever seen, but they were independent and defended their territory fiercely. Many a fight we had on the stairs. When he lunged at me drunkenly and I made to defend myself, his wife would scream, "E's got a plate in 'is head, 'E's got a plate in 'is head!' They had the two rooms on the top floor and even so sublet one of them to an Italian widow who got fed up and left.

The old lady on the first floor, the one who used to moan 'I don't care' all the time, had meals on wheels each day. They would knock loudly and keep on knocking since she was half-deaf. Then she would thunder down the stairs and they would all thunder up the stairs and down again. Sometimes when I entered the house I would smell gas and discover that the old lady's little kitchen on the first landing was saturated with it, because she would turn it on, put a saucepan lid over the unlit gas and then look for matches in her lounge. While she was looking she would forget what she was looking for and just settle down to whatever it was she was doing or not doing. I complained to her welfare worker that she was in danger not only of doing herself in, but of taking all of us with her, but they always thought that people who had bought their houses were trying to get rid of the tenants.

I bought the house for £3,500 in 1970, because nobody else would buy it with controlled-rent tenants festering in it. I got a mortgage from the Chelsea Building Society and borrowed the deposit from the bank and felt truly, what a remarkable system we have, that with a bit of effort a poor actor can buy a cheap house. I was helped by going into partnership with another architect friend, Martin Beaton. It looked better having an employed architect's name on the mortgage application.

The garden at the back was my breathing space. The cats would loll about in it and shit all over the place. In the back area under the stairs I built a dark room and went about developing pictures and eking out a living taking actors' mug shots. Very good many of them were, too. It may be surprising, since I had really tried to attack the business and gain work, that I was in fact working less and less. The more 'well-known' I became, the less work I got. So the more I would hunker down and dream of plans to make my own show and retain a bit of independence and work when I wanted and not be reliant on the bloody phone and somebody's roulette wheel calling out my number. I liked printing my photos and watching them slowly come to life, and many a peaceful hour I had in my dark room, often to wake to the morning light and see that I had underdeveloped them.

Lodgers came and went and the main thing was for the house to be self-sufficient. I kept lodgers for years. One of them, a Polish man, ran away with my girlfriend of four years, Anne, to whom I was deeply attached. She had long, straight, silken hair and was like a pre-Raphaelite painting. I loved taking her picture since she always looked so serene and happy.

The house had four floors and from the garden when I looked up it looked really huge and I was proud of it. I had a cat called Pottle who lasted eighteen years and was a gift from the actress Eliza Ward, who asked me to look after her when she was doing a stint in Glasgow rep. Pottle was a tortoiseshell cat with the most beautiful nature. She was incredibly affectionate. Of course after a few weeks of looking after her I found myself growing quite fond of the thing and felt like a character in a Tennessee Williams story who had a strong attachment to his cat.

I believe I have already mentioned the café called Alfredo's up the road, where I would read my *Guardian* and order a toasted liver and tomato sandwich and blissfully ingest the first delicious corner, but going back home in the morning after breakfast I always found incredibly depressing and the out-of-work syndrome was getting worse. The other café I would visit would be Itala's Green Angel café on the corner of Colebrooke Row, before it turns into the Essex Road. Itala was like a mum and wanted to know how was Annie when I was with Annie, and then how was Shelley, and then how was Helen and so on as the years and the women in my life flowed past and stopped off at Itala's on the way. The Green Angel was a little sanctuary and is still there at the time of writing. Itala's son Tony has grown up from the tiny tot he was when I first visited to the strapping man he is. Any favours needed, Tony will be there with his long-affianced girlfriend. Tony's dad died and Tony had to replace him – in Italian households you can't leave a widow to fend for herself.

On Wednesday the Camden Passage was alive with the antique market and that was always good for a bit of browsing and time wasting. It was also about this time that a pub in the passage called the Camden Head became the first base of operations for my theatre work.

It was at Glasgow that I met Bruce Myles, an Ozzy who shared my belief that the actor should have more control over his product. We were resolved to try and find our own path and devise a method of workshops where we would keep our precious techniques honed each week in front of other actors and be spared the humiliating exercise of waiting by the phone, driving agents crazy and making the constant barrage upon poor casting directors. I had already had a taste of teaching and holding workshops at Webber-Douglas and now we were to embark on our first ever meeting at the Camden Head, which was conveniently around the corner from me. As I mounted the stairs I remember to this day, beyond the stale smell of beer from downstairs, the incredible excitement that everything was going to change. Bruce, being a little formal, had brought along an accountant, which I thought was a bit silly, but he had him there to keep the books, to make the small charge we levied and to keep minutes. To begin with we had agreed that I would conduct some movement classes and then anyone in the group would volunteer their skills or we would perform audition speeches and work on scenes. We were all a bit reticent, but eventually someone broke the ice and did a piece and we all commented on how good it was and bathed in the same euphoric excitement that we were holding the reins. We had never experienced this sense of power before and it gave us hope and dignity.

I had a dream of playing the extraordinary and unplayed part of Yank in Eugene O'Neill's *The Hairy Ape*. I got up and went through it and all were most impressed, since the sinewy bite of O'Neill and the bigheartedness of the character could not fail to make themselves felt. I always like characters much larger than life and believe these are the people the audience craves, that they may gain hope and energy from their example. Audiences don't want creatures who are the mirrors of their own ghastliness and pettiness. As I write, the film of *Cyrano* has just come out and everyone is astonished at its extra-ordinary popularity and emotional force and vigour. Cyrano is of course so much larger than life, yet he epitomizes and embodies the essence of life itself. The play is about external beauty versus internal beauty and the real value of the qualities of the soul and very much more. It gave hope to all who felt ugly and as such performed a marvellous service, especially for those of us in the East End or Golders Green!

The Six Day War – Israel v. the Rest

In 1967 we had the Six Day War when the united Arab armies decided that it would be a unifying factor to get rid of Israel. Instead of killing each other they would turn all their murderous energy in on the Jewish state. This did help to give an overlying motive to all the Arab nations who had been slaughtering each other at frequent intervals – why should Nasser be killing off his own people when he could save his poison gases for the Jew?

Unfortunately, people who fight for their very lives tend to defeat those whose lives are not so much on the line and the collected armies of Egypt, Syria, Jordan, Lebanon were routed and left in a dishevelled mess. But at the time I remember the Israeli Foreign Minister circling the world looking for allies and asking the leading nations to intervene since it looked for a moment as if a massacre might take place. Now that maybe a million Kurds may die at the hands of the insane Sod Hussein, where are the Arab voices spewing up their rancid bile? Where are the voices clamouring for Jihad and death to the Jew for daring to exist in Israel and killing Arabs – which is bad enough and which I protest against as loudly as possible, since it contaminates what might have been an oasis for the Jewish race and one doesn't want it poisoned. However, if the Jew committed 1 per cent of the atrocities that this slug is committing you would not hear yourself for the uproar. Where is the voice of V. Redgrave now? Where Arafat?

In the Penal Colony – 1967

In 1967 we were all in trepidation, fearing the possible end of Israel, and there were many marches in that long summer, but the war was quickly over and nobody had to volunteer after all to man the domestic front while the soldiers fought. In the meantime I was looking for work and yet not daring to make that leap into the unknown. It is a leap I have always feared, but eventually undertaken out of a desperate need to work. I have plunged in with trepidation, riddled with the angst of not knowing if what I would eventually do would work out. Now I don't have to leap so much since I can work, but it is the leap into the unknown which takes you on the journey and when, out of some misgiving or fear, I lose the opportunity that I am offered, then I am lost. When I take the leap I am in a glorious world where everything adheres to me. Ideas, love, peace, adventure all in the full turmoil of creation. It doesn't matter if you don't have a single idea at first, it will grow, as it did when I was asked to direct *Coriolanus* in New York. I had ne'er a clue and started to filter out and regurgitate some of the ideas we used in *Hamlet*, but eventually it started to live on its own as a kind of monster. I am now asked to direct *Othello*, but turn it down, pleading performances of Titorelli. It's true I have four shows which would collide, but my understudy could go on: it would be a buzz for him and a release for me, and yet I use this excuse to legitimize my cowardice. Am I a coward? Who calls me a villain? I am always testing myself out and when I do not then chaos comes. I sit by the window in Brighton in sedentary calm, staring out at the jade green sea.

I think that work is my only salvation and the place where my chaos is sent on urgent errands to achieve and clarify, to investigate and form, to inspire and set down. What is chaos but unorganized energy? So I have never directed in Central Park, New York, and I turn down this golden opportunity like some mad creature who only wants to throw away the choicest fruit. I sometimes believe it is a fantasy and that it all never happened, so precious was the time and so fruitful and sustaining.

So during the Six Day War we did our little workshops and walked up the stairs of the Camden Head in Islington feeling very proud of ourselves, but I had to start the very first production. This was the biggest stumbling block, since I had no idea of administration or organization. I had no idea how people got those sets around the country by train and who made them and how on earth you toured them and the million and one questions that seemed to need to be answered before you could even attempt to start. Then there was the choice, the decision, which play, how many people, how, when, where, with what, where's the money coming from, and who would even dream of giving it, and how do you ask for it and so on and so forth. It seemed hopeless. Perhaps we would stick to our workshops with our simple and useful exposure of our audition pieces and the bit of mime I taught.

Having been fascinated with Kafka for years I did see the enormous potential for theatrical presentation in his work. I tried to make a version of *Metamorphosis* and did in fact have the play for some time before performing it. I knew at the time that it was a one-act play, although it has grown lovingly since then. I needed to start with a smaller play which would accompany *Metamorphosis* and I chose *In the Penal Colony* with its fiendish plot of the cruel officer rigidly obsessed with tradition. What a curious piece for Kafka to write. How bizarrely sadistic in its descriptions of the refined and awful form of torture with its savage *double entendre* of the man receiving his sentence both physically and literally as the actual sentence is scrawled on to his back with a machine that inscribes it deeper and deeper until at last the man 'reads' his sentence! Horrific, and very strange indeed. Is that the sentence that poor Kafka feels is etching itself into his own body? The life sentence that he has been condemned to?

Of course, such a machine was beyond one's wildest imaginings and how on earth on our budget of nothing could we even begin to consider building a monstrosity that contained wheels and pulleys, writing needles – as described by Kafka it could be something out of the drawings of Heath Robinson. A machine made into a nightmare. Someone suggested that it should be a plain block and one should merely describe it and mime its function. I daresay this could work and enable the actor being tortured to express the pain and movement of the 'bed', which actually turns the prisoner over to allow the needles to write on some fresh space! In the end my inventive architect friend Alistair Merry conjured up this machine made out of wood with each section beautifully carpentered. It looked like a coffin and had struts across the base. To this we kept adding an assortment of wires, tubes, pulleys and anything weird that was ripped out of a radio, flashing lights and pulsing ones, until at last we had assembled this monstrous concoction. In this instance the thing looked menacing before anyone had even opened their mouths and realism was seen to work. When I described the function of the machine the audience would look at the various non-working bits of wire glued in and they would endow them with awesome qualities.

I was very proud indeed of my first ever production. It came out of the blue when I submitted the play version to Jim Haynes at the Arts Lab and he put up the poster advertising it coming. Somehow the poster did it. If someone had sat down and painted an elaborate poster by hand, then the least I could do was put the show together. It was a memorable summer and I recall that I seldom suffered any nerves; I was always on a high when I finished the show and my performance felt strong and inventive. We did three shows a week, at the weekends, and it was usually full.

The play lasted only forty minutes. That was how Jim would run the 'lab' . . . Rather than have to go in for a whole evening you could just sample half an hour or an hour's worth, and you had time to do something else; so it was in effect like a living gallery.

As I pass the building now in Drury Lane I feel it never really happened. There is no sign that it was ever there, no plaque, no mention that here was one of the greatest seeding houses of renegade arts in Britain. Now it has reverted to its old, familiar use. Shops and offices. One day everything will be shops and offices. All familiar and dead. Lifeless streets where once life trod. The City Lit is still round the corner, but now in need of funding and threatened with closure by the Tory government. A greater crime I, for one, cannot conceive of.

A very strange assortment of creatures wandered in and out of the Arts Lab. Sometimes a visiting celebrity would stroll in. Even the great Jean-Louis Barrault stuck his head in when appearing with the Comédie-Française in the World Theatre season at the Aldwych, where we used to be able to see how theatre should really be done.

I have seen Shakespeare in Germany far more exciting than anything in England, particularly Heiner Müller's *Macbeth*, which was directed by a disciple of Brecht's company who was visiting in Düsseldorf. I could in fact say without too much contradiction that the art of directing Shakespeare has been lost and that the idea of Shakespeare is totally misunderstood. Shakespeare requires and stipulates that there are no sets in his production and that the words do the action. He stripped his stages down to the minimum and his actors were given high-definition text with which to accomplish their task. The idea of confusing theatricality with realism, of pretending so and so is bleeding with his buckets of paint, of expensive sets and revolves, is a total misrepresentation of Shakespeare's intentions.

So I walk down Drury Lane trying to recall the entrance to the Arts Lab and the strange world within of exhibitions, mime shows, performance artists, movies and me. Even the sandwiches Tony Crerar made were good, and what a brilliant mime he was! I saw him recently in Wales tramping around looking skint, with his wife and a little cold-looking kid in tow. At least at the Arts Lab he had a good home. Now what is there? Cold-blooded theatre with a get in and get out policy. The Donmar became a squirty little theatre with high-priced glasses of cheap wine. The Round House was ruined before it closed. What a pity that the snot-nosed yuppie generation who discovered theatre in the eighties are now the guardians of the theatre. Ignorance and bile are their only credits.

Macbeth – 1970

Because I had directed *Macbeth* at Webber-Douglas I felt it necessary to put some Shakespeare under my belt. I decided to stage *Macbeth* and went about my usual way of recruiting actors, putting ads in *Time Out*. Then Chris Muncke and I met the applicants.

To do it yourself seemed to be the obvious way of doing anything, rather than waiting and waiting, hoping against hope; when you actually got the cherished job you found that the play was directed in such a perverse, indifferent way that you could not be satisfied with your part in it. One famous director, I was told by an actor who had the less than satisfying experience of working for him, never took his eyes off the script to see what you were doing, but only heard what you were saying. He had no interest in the actor's mind and its relationship to his body, face, expression. No interest at all. The actor kept looking to the director for confirmation or acknowledgement, but he only saw the top of his head!

Do it yourself and in the doing you may create more than is required. You may find that necessity provokes an awakening of the imaginative juices that might be locked up while you wait for the director to be 'inspired'. It is often the case that the director will object to too much invention or spirit, since he or she is sitting out and not a participant in the furore going on within. It will seem on first ignition to be excessive and you may find a great deal of curbing of the spirit going on. Self-creation unlocks many of those doors kept shut by the 'outside' eye, which is not really an eye at all but a kind of censor that appears to put the stage in a kind of order. Without question, a skilled director can help unlock many insights in the actor, but these directors are few and far between. I have watched actors being hopelessly trapped by bad direction, unable to release the powerful part of their psyches which could in turn make the actor the 'sacrifice' we all need. In a recent 'praised' production of *Othello* I saw an actor hopelessly and helplessly trapped behind a desk when making one of the greatest speeches of anguish Shakespeare ever wrote. Perhaps the director spent a great deal of time behind desks and related to that artefact. The actor was unable to see 'what happened if' . . . it was fixed and staged like this and so the poor man had nowhere to go. So one may make mistakes and commit sins of excess, but one also may just, because of that responsibility, try harder and be uninhibited by the eye which is often thinking of something else when you believe it is watching you.

While it was easy for Chris and me to audition actors at the Drama League, the first day of rehearsal was difficult. We recruited Pip Donaghue, who was then a wiry actor with a mass of curly black hair and a lithe and flexible body, made to be a leading player. He is now highly respected, but this actor is dynamite. Within our system such rare creatures seem to have too much energy or originality for the directors. Pip was as inventive about the production as he was creative as an actor, and he would continually feed ideas into the group. He brought along some mates from the Drama Centre, including Glyn Grain, who also seemed gifted with that special physical dexterity and grace, and I began to suspect that the Drama Centre had something over the other schools; under Yat Malgram the students were looser, less egomaniacal and more disciplined through the use and reverence for the body and not the ego, as text-orientated actors seem to be, always talking about 'characters' they wished to play.

The first day of rehearsal was a Sunday and I had Alison make some sandwiches since there were no cafés open on a Sunday in those days in the bleak deadlands of Islington. We had the church hall in Devonia Road and a strange bunch of people made their way across the road and started. I was incredibly nervous because I not only had to get the sandies organized but had to play Macbeth and had that fear all those of us who direct and play the principal part have, that we have to earn respect on two levels simultaneously.

We began with the arrival of the spirits. I was at the time mightily impressed by a brilliant, animalistic production of *Futz* that La Mama brought over to this country, directed by Tom O'Horgan at the Mercury Theatre, Notting Hill, and I wanted some of that earthiness in our opening. In *Futz* the characters entered crouched, shooting out one leg at a time and so from the beginning you saw legs shoot out as if they were frog-like creatures inhabiting some hot, swampy, steamy, sexy southland. This opening stuck in my mind and worked equally well for a *Macbeth* I directed first at Webber-Douglas.

The La Mama actors played instruments made from wine jugs and the whole feel was eerie and queer. We took the idea of their opening and played drums and flutes, which also created a strange atmosphere until it felt like a witch's cauldron outside the pot. Murky, sinister shapes emerged and the sounds seemed to glue it all together. Then gradually the shape became soldiers performing a series of battle moves as if this was created out of the morass or was a part of it, evil somehow co-existing with slaughter on the battlefield. You imagined the invisible succubi licking up the lives and the pain. As the soldiers changed their physical positions from the crawling, earth-hugging creatures and became fighters, the whole team turned into a line of warriors like a vast centipede of arms and legs moving in rhythm. During this, our three witches rose from the line of thrashing, moving bodies and started their text as if in the thick of battle. 'Where hast thou been sister?' This worked very well and 'A drum, a drum! Macbeth doth come' merely heralded Macbeth's arrival. The witches were in this early Shakespeare of mine united almost as one being, a multiple image I have used over and over again. We see it in Indian dance and in painting, the image of three people somehow in unison, sometimes behind each other moving in and out of the rhythm like a delayed-action photo. They spoke in and out of the rhythm of the drum, which gave it an almost Brechtian bite. Again, use of imagery like this was developed by the American groups like La Mama and Living Theatre and was further reinforced by Nancy Meckler's Freehold Theatre, who also made some stunning images and were blessed with one of the most powerful actresses I had seen at the time, Dinah Stabb, who is characteristically seldom heard of now.

A well-known director beat a drum for Peggy Ashcroft at some wretched award ceremony the other night and while I salute the venerable lady's talent, most of the world has no idea who she is or what she has done in recent years and yet we keep trotting out our fave old character bags. No disrespect to the great Peggy, but surely after the longest speech in award ceremony history we might also salute the unknown actress. The poor bird who has trundled from place to place around the reps for years, dropping babies where convenient, living in Fulham in a house that has to be sublet and relying on payments from lazy ex-husbands who contribute a pittance, and never ever getting just a morsel of the curious adulation that these old faves get year after year. And yet the unknown actress knocks spots off all of them. The unknown actress often saves the show. Her guts, grittiness and day-to-day experience make her like a highly strung instrument ready to give out the right tune.

Anyway, with *Macbeth*, I was the unknown actor, but not quite unknown since *Metamorphosis* which I had done at the Round House the previous year had placed me smack in the forefront of theatrical attention. I found keeping the workshop together a real strain. Actors would come and go, but Pip and Glyn and Chris were my stalwarts who kept on. I am grateful to them for ever, for without their help I might have chucked it in. Sometimes we would do classes and workshops if there were not enough of us for a real rehearsal. One of our tricks was diving over chairs onto a mat. We'd lay a chair down on its side and then place more and more until there were at least five. Each time it got more and more nerve-wracking, but Pip would put another chair out until we all gave up and then he would sail over six or eight of them. It gave us some 'guts' perhaps, for the rehearsal.

We decided that the witches should be the servants in the castle of the Macbeths and the servants would somehow metamorphose into the witches. Pip devised a movement which was as brilliant as it was simple. By bending low and pulling one's arms over one's back one could, with some deft movement, impersonate a bird, a kind of black, vulture-like thing. It was necessary, in order to retain the bird-like movement, not to bend at the knee but to hop from leg to leg. Those who were not too stiff or muscle-bound could impersonate those half-human, half-witch/bird-like creatures beautifully. When changing from human to witch/bird one would merely slowly up-end oneself.

It was one of the myriad things we did in those days, since it seemed so very important to liberate ourselves physically before we could deal adequately with the text. Text you could read loud or silent; it existed, but we did not exist and had to make ourselves exist theatrically. We had to make a signature and language that would express what the words had stimulated inside us and not be just a mouthpiece with resonant tones.

During this halcyon period of rehearsal and the exchange of many, many actors who got work, since no one was being paid with us, we ploughed on and got through the play. If an actor got a job I would take a deep breath and telephone around and find another actor to start within a couple of days and begin the process all over again. Pip was getting a bit pipped, but still he stuck it out.

One day when we were actually thinking of putting the show on at

The Place theatre I had made an appointment to meet the administrator, Alwyne Scrase-Dickins. In the morning I went to the YMCA for a work-out and lo and behold, as I was practising my best somersaults off a springboard on to a gym mat, my foot caught behind me and I broke my ankle. The pain was terrible. It was the first time in my life I had broken a limb. Off to the hospital off Tottenham Court Road. My foot was plastered up and Alison came to fetch me. In the evening I distinctly remember my agent coming around to console me. She was a sweet young woman who worked for the Eric Glass Agency and I never knew what happened to her in future years. Then the actors came. We were sunk and had lost our date at The Place theatre, though they did promise us another one.

The next day or two I took it easy and then the actors suggested I go to the rehearsal hall and conduct the rehearsal from a wheelchair! What a team! I thought by then that they would have blown the whole thing out, but I was to reckon without the kind of stalwart characters who wanted to work and to learn and to keep practising their art. I found this most moving and stimulating, that actors never tire of learning and improving themselves, even if there is no money. So Pip and Chris got me up the stairs and across the road and for the next six weeks I wheelchaired the rehearsals. After six or eight weeks the plaster came off, but the pain was still severe if I put too much weight on it. Still actors came and went. Even Pip, with the greatest will in the world, had to take a job that was offered. I was deeply sorry to see him go, since he was the backbone of the company, but he had given so much and I was indebted to him.

Some of the things we did were not just physically inventive, but made more sense of the script. We threw a lot of bodies on the floor as representing all the people I would murder and I sat on the top of the heap. But from beneath Banquo peeps out and says, 'Thou hast it now, king, Cawdor, Glamis, all, As the weird women promis'd . . .' During the time when Macbeth goes to visit the witches for the second prophecy I had the idea that they were like sirens, luring men to their beds in order to destroy them more easily. So I devised an orgy, choreographed of course. It was a little embarrassing to say, 'Well, boys and girls, let's get into different positions,' but to my astonishment everybody did and it was also very funny. Then I had an inkling that I was already getting older, since I could barely have allowed myself to do this at their age. We had some attractive witches, so the chaps didn't find it hard to comply, and I don't think the girls minded too much either. We were a happy group and each night I went to the church hall I felt blessed that I was no longer out of work. As I watched the working-class kids in my street just hanging around all night I felt sorry for them not having anything to do but let their brains waste away.

After a further four weeks, we had now been rehearsing for the best part of six months, allowing for breaks, and felt it was time to put the bloody thing on the stage. We rented the LAMDA Theatre where we had tried out *Metamorphosis*. I felt distinctly odd at first, since I hadn't joined in the opening crawl across the stage and the battle scene, so after we got into the theatre I walked through the beginning. I was exhausted before I even opened my mouth! However, I soon got used to it and tried not to limp too much.

Eliza Ward (what happened to her?) played Lady Macbeth. She was a vivacious woman with great blue eyes and a perfectly shaped mouth. She was a strong lady and a very good singer.

We put much that was 'current' into the play in terms of my popular group images, but I was beginning to get the acting bug back again and enjoyed the scenes of pure unadulterated acting. I love the scene with the two murderers when I invite them to kill Banquo. It's a great piece of muscular writing when Macbeth compares the different grades of men to qualities in dogs. Also the scene after Macbeth has slain the King's protectors and begins his speech with his defence of 'Who can be wise, amazed, temperate and furious, loyal and neutral, in a moment?' All wonderful stuff to enact and put yourself through, Shakespeare. It activates those parts of yourself other texts fail to reach. It animates a superior being, perhaps, or allows you to drift away from the moribundity of life and enter worlds where greatness lies. You taste power or the privilege of kings.

We did our week at LAMDA and had a modicum of success. The play was a bit of a black tights and string vest production, but the action flowed from scene to scene and we had some stunning effects and innovations. It was certainly popular and the audience laughed a lot and were generally fascinated by it. We then, thus emboldened, decided to take our production forward. We had one snotty review from Mike Byrave, who was scribbling for the early *Time Out* (and has since disappeared); it was so vicious and intemperate that he left a mark on us, if not a nasty stain. However, we soldiered through it and prepared to take on the London press with a real opening at The Place for a three-week run.

There were by now many factions threatening to tear the company apart and threats of not going on if some conditions weren't met. I cannot now remember the details, but it had to do with a sourness and a boredom with the play that we had been working on for several months. I was shocked at the time, since I had always felt we were a great team of friends and allies, but I also think there were some sexual liaisons that may have muddied the waters. I was distraught and determined never to work with any one of them ever again. And I haven't. We might have grown into a real ensemble and gone on to bigger and better things, but there is always a fly in the ointment, an actor who, after a few days or weeks, forgets how horrible and soul-destroying being unemployed is.

The reviews came out and were mixed, predictably, but many had some good words about the inventiveness of the group. The dullest was by J. W. Lambert, in *The Sunday Times*, which said, 'We must have a moratorium for experimental groups that get into a circle and hum' . . . the blind critic *par excellence*. There was so much invention in our play with our battle scenes, mimed horses, thrilling death scene of Duncan, that the circle did occur once and once only – we created a table at the beginning of the play and sat round and quite effectively created the sound of bagpipes. I thought it was a superb piece of business and deserved a maturer consideration and some degree of respect, rather than the slimy kind of cynicism Mr Lambert gave it.

Curiously enough, years later the main Shakespeare companies tried to imbue their productions with some small degree of ensemble and even resorted to leaving the actors on stage during the proceedings to 'demonstrate' that this was 'theatre', but the poor creatures often just sat there trying to look significant but with nothing to do since the director had not the foggiest idea of how to use movement to supplement the text. The exception was Peter Brook, who did make the actors part of the chorus or orchestra.

I remember going out at midnight to get the reviews and being so disappointed and angry, as if there was such great theatre going that they could be so cavalier. However, we did miraculously get audiences and most people seemed to be very excited by what they saw. More importantly, the students at the recently emerging school of

Martha Graham's London branch under Robert Cohan loved the work and could relate to our attempts to merge the text with physical structure and not sets. Of course, we might have gone too far the other way in our reaction against the RSC syndrome of hang-about actors; so determined were we to avoid this clump of thespians standing around while the star did his turn that we made sure the ensemble was paramount.

Nicholas and Alexandra – 1970

We finished our season and I went to Spain to play a monkey or small role in the epic movie *Nicholas and Alexandra*. That was one of the worst experiences of my life, since having been with a bunch of reasonably dedicated stage actors for six months or more I was now thrust into the midst of a bunch of drunken slobs who, although good-natured, revealed all the more distinctly to me what happens to actors who are ill-used or used in the conventional way of the natural-istic theatre: wait in the dressing room for your call. These creatures were the result. Shouting, raving, boorish. I knew they could not help themselves, since no one had ever demanded that they be part of a group or responsible to their fellow men. It was each one for himself. We had the unfortunate fate of sharing a trailer between shots and I felt even then I was speaking a different language. We were emerg-ing from a hippy-influenced era and I liked my actors, who wore their hair like long manes and did warm-ups and yoga and smoked pot. They were to a man physically and vocally strong. This bunch were the relics of a bygone age where an infusion of the pub became the loudspeaker through which they spewed. I loved Spain, hated the work.

I think part of the over-enthusiastic drinking, shouting, eating binges came from the contrast between living in a restricted, law-bound Britain and the late night-life of Madrid. I must say that Madrid was astounding in its sheer variety of things to do and see. Even something as simple as going into a bar with its clean, cold, zinc counter and its perfect little glasses of wine and triangles of Spanish omelettes was a treat of the highest order. There was a café in the old area where they had guitars on the wall for the patrons to play and in every room people were singing that gutsy, rasping, crying sound. I sat in wonderment at the profane abandonment of the players and our twerpy British uptightness and mealy-mouthed text in this bunch of twaddle, *Nicholas and Alexandra*. Franklin Schaffner directed it. He was the old American-school director who worked with a jacket and tie on and yet with a ten-inch cigar, very elegant stuff.

I walked around a lot on my own and took loads of black and white photos of the city. I took a beautiful day trip to Toledo, where El Greco lived and painted and where there is a museum housing his work. I wandered around the old streets for hours and relished being away from the ghastly set and its people. I even managed to find a ladyfriend to spend time with. She was a complete beauty in the full Spanish style, but I was too enamoured of 'Chittle', the lady who was at the time my steady sweetheart.

I had met Anne Cheatle at LAMDA when I applied for teaching work there and then later on when I was looking for actors for *Macbeth*. I remember a lady behind a desk on one side and another lady behind a desk on the other side. When I started to communicate mainly by phone I was never sure whom I was addressing. Anne sat there with her long silken hair down to her waist and beyond and two of the roundest and most penetrating eyes I have ever seen. She just looked at you with full, open gaze and of course such a scrutiny is irresistible. She was out of Peter Pan crossed with Rossetti. A pure pre-Raphaelite beauty and yet very sensible and down-to-earth. We enjoyed the most idyllic four years together. I was heartbroken when she ran off with my Polish lodger.

Eventually we finished filming and had to return to the grimlands. The film did not do well and I made my brief appearance as a Russian revolutionary, somewhere behind a lot of faces. I had very little to do, which helped my sense of utter frustration.

Peter O'Toole had been meant to play the crazy Rasputin, but in those days if you were doing as well as he was you could afford to be picky in the most absurd way. He turned down this marvellous role and it went to an actor who went on to achieve his greatest fame in *Doctor Who*. Apparently he had once studied for holy orders and was one of those eccentric actors with storms of curly hair running down his neck. He was a very free spirit and seemed to come out with whatever was in his head. I recalled him from a dinner many years before when a young Welsh director brought him to the house of an older director who was his mentor. The older man's wife was a doctor. It was the early sixties and the great planet of 'liberation' was swinging over us, impelling everyone to shed their inhibitions immediately. The dinner was most pleasant and the director, trying to inspire us with confidence in directing, talked about taking a trunkful of props and making them fit your situation. When lo and behold, this actor started talking about *fucking*. The couple's two young children were there and he was saying he hadn't had a fuck for ages. I was not so much horrified as repelled, since this was an area that you discussed only with those involved in your carnal life or close intimates. My eyes shot across the table to the children and to the mother. They seemed at ease and laughing, but I thought I could detect the strain of not admitting to themselves that this was an outrageous assault on their dignity and family, but this was also the sixties and acid and Beatles and they mustn't look uptight! Or maybe he was trying to shock us and the family knew him, since he seemed to be part of the family table. I was never to forget that evening.

I came back to London and immediately saw Chittle. She looked very glamorous and wore a strange brown lipstick. I was keen to show her the suede Spanish trousers I had bought in Madrid. I felt I had to get back to doing my own productions, but the wear and tear of casting, directing, producing and finding the few bob with which to do it was as enervating as it was exhilarating. I found again that, just in order to act, I had to do everything but build the theatre. However, this was preferable to the free-for-all market where everyone was competing with everyone else and the actor of the day tended to be a strange new working-class bloke with chips a mile high for whom O'Toole and Richard Harris were the role models! Everyone seemed to want to fight you over nothing.

I needed to get rid of surplus energy, but I went to the gym, not the pub. I loved the feeling of the cool air on my skin when I left the YMCA. A lot of actors went there. I didn't much appreciate this new 'working class' actor so beloved of the Royal Court mandarins, as I have already made more than clear. Actors became overnight successes on the strength of one role that reflected the times, rather than for a series of great roles played. Gerry's Bar in Shaftesbury Avenue was the watering-hole for the piss-artists and actors. It was a friendly basement where you could see the actors deep in their cups.

I started to feel I was from a different planet with my group of actors in the church hall off Devonia Road. What another world we inhabited with our concerns for creating ideas and movements. How idealistic we all were. The other world seemed hostile to us and very alien. I could see no real reason for this attitude. Dustin Hoffman was astonished, so he says, when he found that British actors boozed so much. Here they spend their time in the pub while in the USA, he said, they spend their time in the gym. And yet paradoxically these same actors would be employed over and over again by the major companies and the companies would have to put up with them as if they were at least the enemy you know. You can always deal with an aggressive boozer, but not with an actor with ideas or, more dangerous, ideals. So we remained under-employed and unemployed.

The Glass Menagerie – 1971

Macbeth was a great experience, though I never had the time to concentrate my ideas on the acting. But I thought at the end I was getting close and now I felt like another bash. There was a period of floating and Bruce Myles, my Ozzy friend, and myself still entertained the idea of working together, although by now I was well ahead in terms of going my own way. Bruce told me one day they were looking for an actor to play the gentleman caller in *The Glass Menagerie* at Greenwich. I flew to the post office with letter and CV.

The director was a pleasant bloke whom I had known from my Lincoln days and had cast Helen Cherry, wife of Trevor Howard, as Amanda. A nicer lady you couldn't hope to meet in a lifetime. But I run before my horse to market. I received no reply for a few days and then I called and was told that they were still searching for Jim the gentleman caller! I was in a state of utter fury, since I *was* the gentleman caller and nobody could do it as I could. I knew the play very well and had played the long speech of comfort to Laura as an audition; it was the most moving and eloquent statement of a simple man I had ever read ... 'You know what I judge to be the trouble with you? Inferiority complex! Know what that is? That's what they call it when someone low-rates himself ...' Kirk Douglas played it in the film and it was really a study of solid American values that had heart, mind and soul. I loved the part, the play and the man, and knew that if the director didn't take me it would *not* be because I couldn't play it. He had known me from Lincoln and may have thought I was trouble.

I wrote again accusing him of being the incarnation of every reason I had for starting my own group, and insulting him for his moral cowardice in not giving me even a crack at the reading – I wouldn't have minded him turning me down after he had auditioned me. He actually phoned me, as I remember, and was miffed and angry in a slightly put-on way. He demanded an apology, then insisted I come in to *read*. I did, and he offered me the part. I admired him for ever after that, for having the decency to see through my anger and the pain of my rejection.

So Bruce and I were working together. We took the train to Greenwich and played around with the scenes we were in together. I knew that Bruce would make sure I didn't steal the limelight from him and I didn't. Bruce gave it an honesty and heart that was terribly moving. I loved doing the play and I did get very good reviews for my portrayal. We did it for about four weeks and Helen was charming in the role. The great Trevor Howard came. I was duly introduced to the legendary man and was amazed to see him looking so powerful with a mane of red hair. Annie would come down and sometimes help the usherette she had made a friend of to count the stubs. One night Annie's mum and dad came with Roy Strong, who had just become the director of the V & A. I was amazed that someone so intelligent should come and see us and me. He seemed incredibly young, but I thought well, this *is* my territory and he couldn't play the gentleman caller. But I always had to give myself these little directives to enable me to deal with people of obvious education. I was very happy at the Greenwich Theatre and was to use it again a few years later.

During this period Keith Hack, the young up-and-coming prodigy from Oxford who had done a stunning *Seven Deadly Sins* at the Edinburgh Festival, asked me to play a slip of a part in *Titus Andronicus*. It was one of those big mistakes, since the part wasn't worth the getting up in the morning, but I was seduced by the idea of it being a special production. However, it was not to be, and I left after a few days. Saw the thing in performance and congratulated myself on getting out. I went home and worked on my version of *The Trial*. Bill Stuart, who was the husband of the usherette at Greenwich, asked me one day straight out for the role of Joseph K. and with such insistence that I gave it to him. Not only was he brilliant, he became an ally for years to come.

Forming a Company – 1971

I worked slowly through the book of *The Trial*, basing my work on what I did in my improvisations at Webber-Douglas. I looked at the version Barrault created with André Gide and thought, I am doing this alone. I completed the first draft, which of course ran an inordinately long time since there was so much one didn't want to lose, but I eventually got it down to two hours and forty minutes. Gradually I recruited the actors and of course started with Pip Donaghue, who as usual knew interesting actors and would introduce a carefully chosen new member into our midst. I brought back Steve Williams, with whom I had worked at Webber-Douglas. He had played Titorelli there and was a born comedian, but has since become a leading member of the EST Institute. Thus we lose a talented performer. I liked Steve very much, since like a lot of natural comedians he didn't view life through the miasma of a career. He was all joy and life and he would not pursue a career, a career must pursue him.

Paola Dionisotti lent her considerable talent to the event and was a find from the ghastly experience I had rehearsing *Titus Andronicus* – she played Lavinia and expressed an interest in working with me. Pip continually wanted to work out with me and be taught everything I knew about mime. On the days we couldn't rehearse he would suggest we did workshops together. Paola, overhearing, asked if she could come and watch. She was keen and another member of that marvellous school Drama Centre.

Pip brought along Boyd Mackenzie, a tall, handsome, rogue actor who had the most marvellous enthusiasm and was working in a small capacity for the RSC. He used to enthuse about how great it was to be working like this and we all repaired to the pub after listening to his endless recommendations of our 'school'.

Other actors came and went. Peter Brett, with whom I had worked at Cheltenham rep years earlier, joined us. He was a director himself and watched with a slightly jaundiced eye; he was inclined to be critical, but in the end gave his all to the proceedings and, being an ex-dancer, had good movement and looked good. The women tended not to last long, but Paola stayed to the bitter end. The rehearsal period was about three months. Tony Meyer joined us near the end and came into the studio exclaiming gleefully about our architectural screens. He had read architecture at Oxford and I was proud to have such a smart chap in our team, which was now becoming a formidable ensemble.

Since Steve Williams was working in a West End show he could only perform the play late night, so we booked to open at the Oval House on a Saturday night. We wanted to do two nights as a try-out, or maybe three. We opened at midnight! The Oval House was packed and the audience cheered us at the end. We used every technique at our disposal to bring the play to life. The methods of Jacques Lecoq were so well suited to the play and my theory that it would work came to fruition; not only did my set design work, but it suited Kafka's thought process whereby his book dissolved from scene to scene through a series of dream images. Years earlier, George Ogilvie, whom I had understudied in *Chaganog*, had mentioned to me his desire to do a work based on *The Trial* and then I knew that I had to get on with it.

In the end I had the beginnings of a production I was intensely proud of, one that would tour the world and end up in Vienna for the International Festival, where it would sweep the honours above all other entrants. Bill Stuart was nothing less than memorable and invaded the stage for every second he was on. A panicked weasel searching for ways and means to extricate himself from his guilt, but knowing, as many of us do, that we feel guilty as soon as we pass a policeman and keep our eyes averted. There are some of us who feel guilty just for being alive and Bill Stuart played K. like one of these.

At this time, in the early seventies, there was a chap from the famous Mickery-theater in Amsterdam who had a fascination with anything British that came from the fringe. Group after group made their way over to Holland and we became one of them. We opened in Amsterdam at the Nooderkerk, a huge church in the centre of the city, but found that if we played on one level the audience in the pews would not have a good view two or three rows back. We begged and pleaded for rostra to lift us higher. The poor director of the Mickery scoured Holland and the following day, at great expense, we had our rostra. Alas, the screens we had devised for the play were free-standing and wobbled on the uneven rostra. So we had to say the rostra didn't work and we got rid of them, which started our relationship on a very poor footing.

The play went on with all the problems that could exist in a church. In those days I was obsessed with lighting and would fret for hours about the look of the thing, since light has such an ability to change mood and affect atmosphere. Eventually, after much wobble and sweat, we crawled through a first night which had none of the élan the play had had at our midnight specials at the Oval House. Those midnight runs were electrifying and the dynamic of the company was perfectly co-ordinated. For Amsterdam and the tour through Holland we lost our mainstay, Pip. Steve Williams took over the part, as I remember, but was not the same and we lost a lot of the focus. The actor playing Huld was so glad to be away from his home life that he fell in love with a Dutch drink called Genever and our best actresses were not with us either – we missed Paola Dionisotti's perfectly played characters. It was a rum crowd we had in the end, but after a while they jelled and the show became good again. There were some awful factions and, as usual in touring groups, certain people tended to stick together like shit to a blanket. I of course felt this wasn't the democratic thing to do. Bill Stuart stayed with us and Steve Williams was an ally, but everyone else seemed to go potty, as if it was merely a paid holiday.

The actor playing Huld had to leave before the end to go back to the RSC, where he was a spear carrier, and I took over his part of the lawyer as well as playing Titorelli on the last night. It was one of those sensational evenings when everybody chipped in and pulled through. In the end it was one of the most successful shows, with necessity truly the mother of invention.

I recall the next day with utter sublimity as we crossed the Channel on the ferry. I was in heaven, with a kind of glow of satisfaction mixed with the feeling that I had purged myself of all terror, sickness and evil. That I was pure and angelic because of the baptism of fire the night before. I remember going for lunch and everything being white: the tablecloths, the fish, the napkins, the white foam of the sea. The brilliant sunlight, the white, clear, translucent wine. I felt so at ease inside my own body and never forgot how wonderful work can make you feel after the event. We got back to England and we were satisfied.

The Trial had begun life at the Oval House on 6 November 1971. I just looked in my diary and it's got D. DAY WAS GREAT, MAG-NIFICENT, and under that: 'to prove that one must go on and do it in spite of incredible odds!'

Touring with My Own Show – The Actor-Manager, 1972

On 24 January 1972, David Aukin and I had an appointment with George Hoskins, who was the Round House's financial administrator. David and I met in the lobby and he instructed me in a quick accounting course while we waited for George. He wrote down what we would need to do to break even if we came to the theatre and worked out the losses going from 10 per cent, 20 per cent, 30 per cent, etc., so that we would know what to respond to in the meeting. George was a very charismatic character and sat in his great office with windows over the vast wasteland of Camden's railways, which seemed to stretch out for ever. His little Cupid-bow mouth looked incongruous in his large face beneath tumbles of steely grey hair. Like a cross between Oscar Wilde and Arthur Scargill. But he was enthusiastic and passionately wanted us to perform *The Trial* at the Round House. David and I both felt good about it, but we never did become partners and in the end I produced *The Trial* in December 1973 by myself. However, David was to be very helpful in getting the production launched. He arranged a tour for us to take *Metamorphosis* around the country. It was the first of our British tours and made us feel as if we were a real company.

On 6 March came the traumatic news that the Arts Council had given us a grant and the first panic after the elation was that we had to create on demand. Up till then I had worked from need and desire. Now we would need administration and accounts, an administrator. Many groups who were now funded by the Arts Council had hitherto worked like roving players and split the money at the end of the evening. The necessary administrative and organizational skills were quite beyond them and everybody was foraging around for these mythical administrators who could work wonders and were models of planning and accounting. With the grant we now had to organize ourselves into some kind of company with plans and policy and so, with our ambitions greater than our capabilities, we planned to do a three-play season starting with *'Tis Pity She's a Whore*. We began what we laughingly called workshops, but which were really tentative bites at it to see if it tasted right. Steve Williams, Terry McGinity, Tony Meyer and I would gather in a hall near Richmond which Steve had found. We would read and play around with the text and wonder why it was so bloody hard. We would fool around, break it up, accompany it with guitar, which did give it a good Mediterranean feel; we even had puppets made to play the smaller roles. But it didn't go anywhere, although at times some sparks were struck. We'd sit in the coffee shop after and wonder what on earth to do. Shall we cancel? Forget the grant and be free, because the grant was driving us all insane?

We had also planned to revive *Metamorphosis* and do one other play which I forget. Terry was slotted to play my role of Gregor Samsa, which I was willing to relinquish so as to be able to entice a good actor to the company and not appear to be grabbing the best roles. Terry was also rehearsing Giovanni in *'Tis Pity* so he was doing very nicely. The exciting thing about Terry was his voice. A deep, mellifluous and sonorous sound which was extremely classic and suggested great dignity. As was the style, he had long, flaring reddish hair and was extremely good looking in a classic-profiled way. He reminded me of a nineteenth-century actor.

Terry was willing to try anything and when he started playing the beetle I found him extremely moving: he had nuances and registers of emotion I had not even thought about. We ditched the idea of doing *'Tis Pity* and convinced the Arts Council of our intention to do it later. For now we would tour *Metamorphosis*. They were quite satisfied with this. It was only I who felt this overwhelming guilt about having to kill myself for the grant.

Once we were back on familiar territory everything slipped into place. Of course no one in the provinces had seen the Kafka piece and so naturally it was the most acceptable and sensible thing to do. By chance I met Maggie Jordan in Camden Passage one weekend and so I found someone to play the mother. Steven Williams played Dad and I did the lodger. Tony Meyer helped and started playing with the back of a piano, and so I discovered 'music' ... I noticed that when Tony pulled or struck a string it would give such an emphasis to a line or movement that the absence of it would strike me forcibly. I began to wonder how I had managed without music before. It changed the play from what it had been at the Round House three years earlier and gave it rhythm and mood, so much more colour and intensity than before. Maggie Jordan was splendid and also had a curiously musical voice with an Edinburgh lilt. She was pound for pound one of the best actresses I have ever seen. She looked simply magnificent with her Titian hair wound like a turban round her head and put me in mind of Sarah Bernhardt. That she was difficult to work with is an understatement and she drove everybody insane, but to watch her perform was to be electrified and her vocal swoops were bird-like and thrilling. What happened to Maggie Jordan?

Eventually, in order to justify our grant, we rehearsed a series of Kafka sketches called *Knock at the Manor Gate*, a collection of simple, beautiful and haunting stories, and we prefaced *Metamorphosis* with these 'skits'. They were fun to work on and are such skilful and pithy tales that the audience can relate to them quickly and easily. They worked as *hors d'oeuvres*. Now was my chance to do *The Bucket Rider* all these years after I first attempted my little recital at the City Lit in 1957! Our sketches were well received and had an atmosphere all their own. From the strange *Knock at the Manor Gate* story to *The Eagle that Pecked at the Man's Feet*, the tales seemed somehow possessed and that was what drew me to them. We were going to try them out in Brighton and were now joined by Denis Lawson. Maggie Jordan, of course, didn't wish to be part of this nonsense. At first she watched from a distance, then for whatever reason she walked out. We rushed around to Jeanie James's house begging her to come back, although she had not played the role for four years since our Round House début. Jeanie seemed very old-fashioned compared to Maggie and resisted the innovations and the music, but she kept at it and relearned it for Brighton, where we were a huge and resounding success after our première of *Knock at the Manor Gate*.

We had successfully created another show. Oscar Lewenstein came down to see it and thought that while it was very inventive theatre the acting wasn't good enough for the West End. He was of course right. Since the strict period of 1969 when I cast steadfastly to age and type I had 'hippified' myself to the extent that I thought Terry's long hair was OK for Gregor the bank clerk, that our improvised bashing on the piano guts was real musical effects, and that Steve Williams, who was younger than I, could play Mr Samsa. I had become slack and too 'liberal' in my thinking, but would return to my old form and discipline eventually.

We enjoyed Brighton and the tour of England that David Aukin had worked out for us, going to Newcastle, Cardiff and Brighton. We finished up in Hampstead Theatre Club in the boiling hot summer. Since this is the worst time to play, Michael Rudman

313

offered it to us with a tiny fee, but we took it gladly and played to packed houses for four weeks in the height of summer. Since we fooled the critics by calling the piece *Knock at the Manor Gate* and not *Metamorphosis* (which was a bit silly really since the main bill was the beetle play), they all came again and re-reviewed it and gave us generally good notices for our short 'expressionistic' pieces.

The summer slid by and I waited impatiently to go to Greece for the first time with Annie. We took a train all the way there and it was the trip of a lifetime. I had a surplus air ticket from my trip to Israel with the ghastly film *Bloomfield*. I kept renewing it each year and now converted it to a first-class train ticket and so we watched the countries slipping past the window and slept through Europe, stopping off at Venice and then Lugano and on to Athens. From there we went to Skyros, which then was the island of my dreams, quiet, solemn, stately, full of wondrous walks, small villages, drenched in pine, heavy with figs, shadowed with vines, and the water teeming with fish.

It was one of the happiest times of my life and I realized for the first time in years just how much of a life there is out there away from the theatre and the desperate need you think you have to express yourself!! I used to swim each day and afterwards, when Annie was sunbathing on the beach, I would drink a small bottle of retsina, eat a salad and write. A great deal of what I wrote there became passages in *Agamemnon* and they fitted in very well ... 'Sea is the colour of paradise.'

We returned to London and again decisions had to be made. I tried to give mime classes at the Dance Centre or the Mayfair Gymnasium in Marylebone, where I would find eager souls – one of the best ways to find actors is to give a class to them if you can. By October I was so frustrated that I wrote in my diary, 'Oct.11.72. I must get off my arse, I am draining myself of my manhood, I sit around playing at nothing with my life dribbling away.' I would get very frustrated if I could not manage to put a project together, but for some reason it always took me a long time to do it since my organizational ability is much weaker and more untutored than my creative ability. When I have someone to do the organizing for me I just go in and get on with the play, but when I don't one pulls the other back. In the end I jumped from *Salomé* to *Usher* to *Miss Julie* and plumped for a double bill of *Miss Julie* and *Zoo Story* so that I would at least have something familiar. But how to do *Julie*? There's a point and of course it couldn't be realistic . . . no, I would have to find a *difficult* way of doing it.

Miss Julie versus Expressionism

I had to work out a new piece of theatre. Why I decided on *Julie* I don't quite know, except that I thought it would be a good double act for Maggie Jordan and myself. Having made up our differences, we sat down and read it together. Then we went to the Old Red Lion in Islington to block it and work on it, but we were getting nowhere fast since I was congenitally incapable of doing it for real, with a real table and chairs and pots and pans. I knew then that this would be a dull method and that we just could not in the latter part of the twentieth century resort to the same tired old methods of realism. That that was lazy, unimaginative and in the end destructive to theatre. Young people brought up on movies, videos, and TV are staled by the simple processes of theatre and theatre must either match, keep up with or improve.

I wasn't conscious of this at the time in that militant way of expression, but I felt it nevertheless. I wanted to explore the core of *Julie* and Strindberg and just acting it out, though momentarily satisfying, often felt a little fakey. It would have been fine in the end since you would have become more and more immersed in the character, but from the beginning I wanted an explosion of the theme of the play. I was going crazy and wished I could just plot it and rely on good acting, but I for some reason couldn't do it. Eventually Maggie went berserk with all my indecision and arguing and walked out. That night I sat down and looked at the play in my basement kitchen. I stared at the beginning and saw where the energy seemed to peter out and conventional narrative take over . . . I stared and stared and suddenly I started to reshape the play . . . Eureka, I felt within me that surge of discovery!

I changed the order of events, much like a collage, and pieced together themes of the play so that one scene collided into another, much as if you were watching a series of trailers for a film. What this did was to release certain forces from their structure and let them flow wildly, without the constraints of building up exposition. This may have mutilated the original intention – though it was never my desire to do disservice to Strindberg – but at that time in my life I was always experimenting with ways to free drama from its plodding build-up and conventional narrative.

I sat in my kitchen night after night reworking. I recall to this day as I started at midnight a trembling feeling in my body as if I had really discovered a method that would be a viable theatrical experience. It was a strong feeling and one that I get when writing a play – suddenly a force unlocks a surge of ideas that have been fermenting deep inside you. I had that feeling most strongly and I went to rehearsal saying to the new Miss Julie, my ex-Lady Macbeth, Eliza Ward, that this was the new Strindberg play. She liked it and was able to cope with it. The servant Kristin was played by Carol Cleveland, who was in the *Monty Python* series and was a dancer/actress. She too was very responsive to the new order of events, and also this new version kept Kristin on the stage throughout as a kind of helper and chorus, a figure who was never far from our minds and therefore always there and visible. We rid ourselves of all furniture and had just three white cubes as seating positions and a large pair of boots standing huge and threatening on stage. The impression was surreal and stark.

I then, and with trepidation, called in Colin Wood, a cellist whom I had met in Edinburgh and who improvised with dance companies. I was so in awe of real, skilled performers like singers and musicians that I felt my efforts would seem awkward and unformed. I warned him that I had only just started the play and he replied that he too had to start from scratch and expected nothing; that put me completely at ease. Colin came in on a Saturday morning with his huge cello in its case and I watched with fascination as he took it out and rested its point in a little cup. I ran a few moments from the beginning when Julie comes in with Jean and Kristin which we had reshaped to include everybody in a kind of abandoned dance with midsummer flowers. I asked him to play something and he pulled his bow across the strings and made the most beautiful sound I had ever heard, the more so since I was connecting this sound with actions and *it worked*. It took off and we were all thrilled to death with the effect.

We did it again and again and it got better each time. Now gradually Colin would shape his improvisations to our actions and to the text. As the play grew I started to adjust my words to the cello's theme and even half sang or used *sprechgesang*, a kind of speak chant. The music was the key to this method and then he added piano and some percussion. Each day was more exciting than the last and I felt I had discovered not only a new world but a genuine way of exploring this play in an Artaudian fashion. It satisfied my conscience in that I made a new form of drama, yet still expressed Strindberg, and the result demanded a very skilled and physical form of acting.

After only three weeks we had the piece intact and each event in the play that might have become a realistic problem – killing the bird, for example – we solved poetically rather than realistically. Julie came on with a long feather boa which she played with and this, stretched out over her arms, became the bird. As she pleaded with me not to kill her bird her hands fluttered and then her arms like a frightened bird until she became the creature whose head I cut off. Julie's head! It had moments of such raw power that I felt could never have been extracted from a naturalistic rendering.

The scene when Julie and Jean go off together while the servants are dancing (usually played by a lot of bored extras in a large company) was done in the following way. Julie and Jean stand against the wall as if in two doorways. What they do is represented by a series of extraordinary pornographic stills projected on to the wall. These stills came from a magazine on Victorian pornography I purchased in Amsterdam. As they are shown, Kristin comes up to both of us, one at a time, and makes us dishevelled; she rubs lipstick all over Julie's face and smears some on mine. When the pictures are over we dash out as if we have been in a furious erotic tangle.

The scene was powerful and to the point. It was graphic, crude, but creative and startling. It showed the audience what we had been doing and what was in our minds. When we came out the play's headlong assault downwards required no further changing and so we followed the text closely from then on. Of course, as a dissection of the play, Kristin was allowed to step out of her slice-of-life realism and be an imp throughout, taking pleasure in our downfall and ringing the infernal bell of the master which had me furiously shining boots as if in some Pavlovian reflex action. When I did cut off the bird's head Julie delivered her great aria of hatred to my masked face. A mask of the devil. It was very thrilling stuff, not to everybody's taste, but it certainly made some waves. We toured the play to Brighton, Glasgow, Edinburgh and Newcastle. When we opened at Brighton the rather prim lighting man said, 'All right, let's see these slides of yours.' I gave him the slides and slid under my seat, half expecting him to say, 'Aye, aye, we can't show this kind of stuff here,' but he only said, 'How large do you want the projections?'

With ne'er a preview we opened in Brighton. I performed *Zoo Story* with John Joyce as part of a double bill and was quite glad to get back to Albee again. Irving Wardle came on the first night. He was working for *The Times* and in a way I was flattered that such an eminent critic would come all the way to see my piece of theatre and review it for such an eminent paper. I don't know why I felt this, since I had been working for a decade and directing for four years. I imagine the feeling of being on the outer limits or sometimes having had to struggle inordinately tends to have the undesirable effect of making one feel like a beggar, and beggars aren't usually reviewed in *The Times*. However, Mr Wardle was and is a civilized critic and when I asked where he was after the show I was told he was in a room writing his review. I like that idea of a solitary scribe in his monk-like retreat writing words that will be in my box of reviews for the next eighteen years, until I take them out for dusting. I thought his review was precise, analytic, concise and to the point; without praising me he made me sound like an adventurous spirit and most of all gave me sufficient hope and confidence in myself and my work to enable me to carry on.

We all read the review and were pleased as punch, except Eliza, who was a little pallid; the very fault Wardle found I could re-echo and had tried to warn her of. Nevertheless, Eliza was a good ally and we completed our week in Brighton and arranged to meet in Glasgow.

We arrived in Glasgow shattered and it was suggested we open a day late since there weren't many bookings. For some reason, on the first night I gave my worst performance in *Zoo Story*, at the very place I had scored such a hit in the same play seven years earlier. I was shocked at myself for having developed a habit when things weren't going too well of throwing the rest of it away sulkily. Still, it was a first night and that's like a dress rehearsal in a strange theatre, getting used to working in the three-sided Close Theatre, now unfortunately no more. Having performed it within the proscenium arch I had to adjust the bench that Jerry fights over to be able to play three sides, so John Joyce and I used to battle with the damned thing.

Glasgow was fun in the end and then we toured to Edinburgh, where it went down well and I was getting used to the turbulence of playing two 'heavy' roles in one night. At the end of the evening I felt high and purged when I joined John Joyce in the bar for a couple of Special Brews. J. J., as we called him, was an ace company member and enjoyed playing Peter to my Jerry in *Zoo Story*. J. J. was very good indeed as Peter; he always got favourable mentions and he was an easy person to be with.

From Edinburgh we went home again and since the little tour had been a morsel of a strain we all parted company. . . . In Edinburgh on 28 February 1973 I wrote in my diary, '*Julie* best performance yet, tore thru it like volcano. *Zoo Story*, by developing and holding on to "type" stronger laughs returned naturally.' After the week I recuperated on Rannoch Moor.

A New *Miss Julie*

On 28 April 1973, I re-rehearsed Julie with yet another pair of girls, Teresa D'Abreu and her friend Judith Alderson, the night before I saw the great French actor Robert Hirsch in *Richard III* – he was brilliant but needed calming down. I was thinking at this time also of creating Stage Two of *Agamemnon*, having rewritten the tired, stale translation I directed at RADA, and so the two things were fighting for ascendancy. I had another date I had to fulfil for my Arts Council grant and that was at Newcastle's Gulbenkian Centre.

Teresa was a perfect Miss Julie; although her natural upper-class horsiness made her awkward at times, she had that real thorough-bred quality of the character and didn't have to 'act' it. She was a cousin of the Queen, so she let out to the world, but to me she was a truly sweet ally, a charming, devoted actress and never less than fun to be with. Judith came in late but was excellent in the part of Kristin and did marvellous acrobatics. I enjoyed these ladies and found the younger ones of the hippy era much freer, more inventive and care-free than the pre-hippy rep actresses.

We opened in Newcastle on 17 May. I got rid of my uniform for Jean and played it in dungarees and no shoes like a ranch-hand or hillbilly, but I may have been again corrupting the sheer discipline of my work for the sake of a loose hippydom. However, the notices the next day were brilliant:

Imagination – and power

The London Theatre have brought the most imaginative and powerful production so far to Newcastle's Gulbenkian Studio.

Their adaptation of Strindberg's *Miss Julie* is one of those rare creations that leaves the onlooker totally drained at the finale.

Basically a story of a humble-born lad torn between his love for a kitchen maid and the temptations of a countess, *Miss Julie* is, even when played straight, a taut, complex study of a self-destructive trio.

The group bring to it an oppressive, almost horrific, atmosphere. To the haunting and desperate strains of cellist Colin Wood, the three play out their tragic roles, each in turn conjuring up their internal devils.

Their brilliant use of body movements and facial expressions coupled with a lighting programme that picks them out in a complex kaleidoscope of colours, adds to an atmosphere that totters between tragedy and insanity as the play progresses.

Teresa D'Abreu as Julie is outstanding. At one minute she is a satanic woman, and the next a desperate, cast-off lover. The bizarre Jean is portrayed by Steven Berkoff with uncanny power and Judith Alderson, as the maid Kristin, completes a professional trio.

The play is a coiled spring, stretching relationships tighter and tighter until the inevitable break.

The white painted faces, the almost surrealist tang of the set and the brooding, underlying sexuality make it a steamroller of a production.

The London Theatre, certainly one of the most adventurous of the experimental groups, continue tonight and tomorrow.

Peter Mortimer, *Newcastle Journal*

We worked hard and well in Newcastle and we all had a good time up there in the Arts Festival of touring groups. I recall one yobbo from some group with one of those names so beloved of fringe-y groups like 'The Perfectly Absurd Theatre Group' or some such title, saying to me ' "The London Theatre Group"? A bit dull, who does your PR?' Well, we scooped the honour despite our dull title.

Agamemnon – 1973

From Newcastle I went back to London and started in earnest on *Agamemnon* with a cast I had workshopped from the wanted columns in *Time Out*.

We had a really enthusiastic group. Teresa D'Abreu was my first Clytemnestra, I played Agamemnon and the rehearsals were full of the joy of invention. I've always liked the idea of rehearsing without a fixed date or venue hanging over me so that my work is not determined by schedules, deadlines, programmes, publicity, tickets, subscribers and all the other useless impediments to one's creativity.

I don't know how big organizations cope with the production-line values they have embodied within their system, but see why so much of their work stinks. How they have so many flops when the rehearsal period is so rigid and actors have to walk from one rehearsal room to another and they have to wait days to get the actor back again since the poor brute is rehearsing two or even three plays at once. How can you take the risk of attempting to create in a spontaneous fashion by trial and error? So instead you inherit all the stale conventions of having a set built as a little model that the actors all stare at dutifully on the first day as if this will be their home for the next weeks or months. No matter what they might invent, it will all be circumscribed by the ponderous set, which has to be decided on before you start because the workshops need four weeks to build the bloody thing and it's a ten-to-one shot that it won't be ready and if it is it will get stuck on the first night.

That such conjectures become fact is astonishing when you hear of the same thing happening season after season – you might be inclined to think that another system would be in order. In business a management would be sacked if the work methods produced such disasters on a regular basis and a new system would have to be installed to respond to the public taste and demands. However, boorish attitudes ensure that defunct and antique machinery is used. Like the ostrich attitudes of British industry after the war, when traditionalism impeded the need for change and lost Britain its markets, the theatre pursues the same hopeless and stale methodology. Why? Because it is largely a closed shop. It does not have to compete with foreign companies since the language barrier protects it in its insularity. If it, like film, had to compete in its own and foreign markets, it would have shrunk, much like the poor film industry which can only just protect itself by clinging to the skirts of commercial TV or importing Yankee talent to push its goods into America. Here theatre is the most closed shop on earth. Its talent has no yardstick by which to measure its formlessness, though that may be in the nature of theatre itself and not just on our shores. The alternative method would be to reduce the number of shows and make each one something special. To keep to a schedule for some productions but to have others on an open-ended rehearsal to see what might materialize creatively, like any large industry that puts aside money for research.

So, we did not have to conform to any standards or timescale when working and therefore we were not committed to following the pattern of convention. We were, after several weeks, able to see that, as usual, we did not need the set. As we worked we saw that music was to be a considerable and vital part of our equipage. We found that if we wanted to change we could and if we couldn't think about how to do a section it didn't matter, we would do it another time and go on to something else. I never believed that I would ever finish any play, since this way of working does not guarantee success or even completion. *You take a risk*. So as each day passed and we were moving from scene to scene I decided that we should run what we had and time it, and lo and behold it was one and a half hours and playable. The Arts Council wished us to do a date in Manchester which was a kind of festival of groups, so we hired a van and went up and did it. It was one of the most exciting nights of my life. I watched something that had come together calmly and in good spirits with actors coming and going and with no rush; it was performed and it worked.

We performed for just three nights for our 'work in progress' and even on the first performance we all remarked how calm we were, as if it came out of us quite naturally, with none of the panic or first-night nerves that one is normally heir to. Afterwards we all piled into the usual Greek restaurant and celebrated our success. There is a feeling of family that is so very strong in a group of actors touring, brought together by a mutual need not only to work but to feel part of something that expresses the energy of each member and is not a factory processing actors to fit seasons and directors' tastes. This was a one-off and we all lived and survived by this play.

On the last night Linda Marlowe came up to see it. I had not worked with her for a long time. She came from the traditional rep system and was sufficiently excited by the unity and idea of 'company' that she was willing to become part of it.

I felt very proud of the show that last night in Manchester when Agamemnon came storming in after a mimed entrance of horses charging down the plains of Argos. So after I had kissed this good soil of Argos and made my speech, I examined the troops and, for some reason unbeknown to me but in the spirit of freedom that our company engendered, I plonked a strong kiss on the mouth of Barry Philips, who was playing the Herald. Not in a sexual way, but as a Greek welcoming his men. It seemed good at the time and it was an act of crazy masculine bravado! I remember uncles doing this to me in the past and it was like that. A pure act of affection.

Barry was rather taken aback but quite liked it. I was perhaps feeling the warmth of camaraderie that I had missed for all those years in my youth and lonely school days. Now I had my eight male mates around me, plus of course Teresa D'Abreu as Clytemnestra and Judith Alderson as Cassandra. It was tremendously satisfying to sense that I had found friends. I wonder if many of us go into the theatre for precisely that warmth and that sense of danger in action on the stage; I suppose that's what soldiers miss after their life in the army. We all got on well and Hilton McRea, who many years later took the lead in *Miss Saigon*, gave his all as a glamorous Paris. We were a unique team and even then I was starting to feel a pang of sorrow for those straight actors for whom release was not on the stage but getting pissed in Gerry's Bar after an unsatisfying show.

To keep the impetus going we also did a performance at the Oval on a particularly hot night, but my confidence and euphoria in having created a new work were beginning to reap strange blooms – I started getting 'clever dick' and adding bits I had seen from this and that!

I had always started with a pure idea of what I wanted and tried my best to achieve the fantasy through a series of exercises, impros, choreographic input and images; and lo and behold it would suddenly snap into place. Some things took for ever and never did work. I had the idea of trying to create the city of Argos by using doors and arches created from the limbs of the actors, an exercise in mime we had used before and which works for certain needs such as entrances, since a door is both a barrier and an entrance, much as an arm might be. We worked for hours dissolving the images and then creating them and showing the inhabitants in their city of Argos when we spoke the first lines ... 'This is Argos, Argos is a clean city, this is Agamemnon's city.' Sometimes in the old days I would get stuck and continue to work it to death, although it palpably wasn't right. Suddenly it would illuminate for a few seconds and then go dead again and so it didn't work, but on we would go. In such circumstances I would feel a sense of shame and embarrassment and say, 'Try again,' but I couldn't get off the treadmill of my own failure. Eventually we changed it and relied on the text and the simplest movement for the opening.

I even tried to compose the musical changes and stresses myself on a piano. I would not leave the text and choral speaking to chance or bring in an 'expert'. I felt each line deserved a rhythm and musical inflection. Some choral speech I would try to achieve by one person saying the line as individually as possible, then two saying it the same way, and then the others until it sounded extraordinarily real and at the same time ear-catching. We are all too familiar with choral speaking being rather flat and characterless as many must speak and they must go for the timbre and melody as opposed to character. When a chorus speaks with the personality of one man stamped on it I feel it come to life. And so we would experiment with different ways of speaking the choral text, sometimes singly, sometimes in pairs, sometimes one person countered by the whole chorus. There was no end to the variants that could be used. Most of all one had to avoid the speaking clump keeping in synch, the deadly Greek chorus.

All in all I found a mode of expression that would not have been remotely possible in any other form of drama. We could express ourselves with total abandon to whatever stimulus would fit the act. Also we could be ourselves as young men and women, as youths, as athletes, as warriors, dancers, singers.

Where could you do this in some play full of the constipated worries of contemporary author? We had a battle for which we used the words as weapons, hurling them like javelins to impale our foes. Not only did it make sense but it was great fun, so the group not only expressed itself but became homogenized and fused by the mutuality of the 'games' ... It was a stirring and stimulating time and much invention went on, not to the detriment of the text but to its enhancement. We mimed the horses riding into Argos and it was a thrilling and evocative entrance. Our horses breathed heavily as they stopped and pawed the ground while Agamemnon made his speech. Of course the critics gave it dismissive reviews, but for one or two, and poor *Agamemnon* bit the dust.

You don't really analyse the cause until much later. You just think they must be so stunted from years of reviewing that they can no longer separate the good from bad or rather they have been institutionalized to a particular, logical construction of plays. This is as serious a defect as a colour-blind person reviewing painters. It's to do not with intellect but with understanding ideas out of the one-two-three sequence. Logical minds like to see logical progressions and love the play and production that gives this to them. They do not see symbols or are unable to understand why you do anything allegoric or symbolic, or reduce anything to a cypher. They reject playing with language or juxtaposition of text with its opposites. Bathos or exaggeration, imaginative playing with meanings they cannot bear – this will be called simply stylistic. So you are up against it if you wish to 'play' or direct non-realistically.

As I find out more I will reveal it. As I read books on ways of thinking I continually see that most critics think only in a quotidian manner and along logical, predictable lines. One actually reveals more about a subject by approaching it laterally and finding its 'symbolic' counterpoint, which in the end illustrates your point more by expressing its essence. This does not make your work obscure; on the contrary it refreshes by driving it out of the niche of its contemporaneity; it takes it into all time.

East has just opened in New York as I write this and surfaces without its creators at La Mama's theatre in East Third Street, which is a good place for it. It received very good reviews from the *New York Times* and the *Village Voice*. It was performed by a group of Americans from San Francisco, and transferred after a successful run there. For years I've thought of reviving it, but like so many intentions it has crashed against the wall of my procrastination and indecision. And so it waits, but shall be done soon. I see another Tennessee Williams revival is about to surface like a bout of herpes. Not T. Williams's herpes, but the God-awful Brit version which no doubt will be praised for its crimes while being protected by the woman who was mistakenly entrusted with administrating it. Poor

Tenn, with friends like these you don't need enemies. This lady jumped out at me, attacking me like a rottweiler for daring to cast an unfavourable comment on the dull production. The face of a worthy actress stares out of a poster of another Williams revival as if it were a one-woman show and the onus of the production fell on her shoulders. I hope she does well – she has apparently been visiting some Italian restaurants to get the flavour of the accents. Well done!

Back to Reality

Let's get back to *Miss Julie*, which is a long time ago. I decided to do *Miss Julie* and *Zoo Story* in London, and so booked the ICA for four weeks in August/September 1973, which helped to fulfil my Arts Council dates. These grants were a terrific way of getting you off your arse, since you had to do a minimum of dates to qualify – you couldn't sit around moping about what to do. You just *had* to do it!

I started by calling my version *Miss Julie versus Expressionism*, which was my way of informing any purists who were expecting a 'straight' version that this would be a little different. I liked the title and it seemed apt, since the play was seen through its fracturing by expressionistic technique. I continued my affair with *sprechgesang* and Colin Wood was now playing throughout.

People liked it or hated it and I, even when I in my dotage play back the tape we made of the show – sound tape only in those days – I am now horrified at my self-indulgence. But it was a phase I had to step through in order to come out the other side. It was a love affair with the art of performing, being a radical, going through theatrical puberty, contaminated by hippydom while not really being a hippy at all. Pot made me quite dizzy, but I liked the idea that in some way I might be an eligible member. I was not for the hippy parade since I was classically trained by the routines and demands of the repertory theatre with its strict disciplines and conservatism, its love of sharp timing and projection. Years of that could not be washed away.

The 'hippy' theatre scene was composed largely of people who loved performance, but not the utter discipline, training and commitment that went with it. They had a go and had flair and could sing pop songs and form pop groups, but basically were illiterate morons.

What they had was a charming friendliness and generosity. An ease at dealing with life and people and freedom to have a go. They were adventurers and would explore the four corners of the earth and were investigators of the spirit, but technique had too much to do with tradition and conservatism. They might do a voice class if it had to do with inner investigations, like primal screams. So I allowed the wash of hippydom to bathe me and wore wide, bell-bottom jeans and was certainly halfway there.

The reviews for *Julie* either stank or were incredible, Naseem Khan of *Time Out* giving it one of her most positive comments, saying, 'What stops this being one of the most exciting shows in town . . .' etc. A French magazine said that Berkoff was a new Artaud, and of course I was thrilled by this. *The Times* gave it the worst review of all time. A chap called Charles Lewin began his review, 'It's longeth and it stinketh,' which was a bit strong since most people seemed fascinated by it.

I loved doing the two shows with Teresa, Judith and John Joyce in the hot little theatre. We spent our month there with modestly good houses and after the Saturday night show I would speed down to Brighton. There is nothing more exhilarating than getting on a train a minute after a performance with all the adrenalin running through you and a half-bottle of champagne nicely chilled to drink on the way and a hotel at the other end where supper is waiting for you. They would do this at the Royal Crescent, lay out a cold supper for those actors who arrived late.

The season at the ICA ended and once again I took off with Annie Cheatle for the Greek islands, having first booked the Round House for a season of *The Trial* and *Agamemnon* to run in tandem. It was to be a six-week season and the most ambitious one to date. I went happily to Athens and this time we knew exactly where we wanted to go – the idyllic island of Skyros. Travelling with Annie was always a joy since we had such fun together and liked the same things. We enjoyed each other's company, loved walking, exploring, taking photos, eating Greek food and talking. It was unforgettable and, like Hemingway's movable feast, stays with you for ever to warm you when in doubt. We went from Skyros to Skiathos, then on to Milos and other exotic places and there was always a friendly Greek in each port of call. On one island we saw a caged sparrow and released it, but since it had not flown for so long it flew low and slowly. I saw a cat about to pounce on it, but before I could curse myself for my misguided good intentions the bird gained strength and flew out of danger. It flew into the pine-laden hills and became a little dot. I felt like that bird, set free. You struggle for a while with freedom but then it gets to you.

When I returned to Heathrow Airport after my month in the Greek islands I was so laid back that I could not possibly conceive of directing two shows simultaneously for the Round House. I could not wait even to get home but rang from the airport to tell George Hoskins I couldn't do it, couldn't possibly take on so big a task now. Perhaps we could wait until later when I got more organized. He listened and said, 'Steven, you've just returned from a Greek island and don't feel like work, but screw your courage to the sticking place!' He was fond of such pithy quotations and even as he uttered the magic words of Lady M., I felt my resolve stiffen and knew I had to do it. Annie and I fell into a nice café, one of those new hamburger joints with wooden tables and large black and white pics of forties movie stars and potted plants dotted here and there – we couldn't bring ourselves to go home and thus put a full stop on the trip.

Eventually we started work in the Mayfair gymnasium in Marylebone. We began rehearsals at 9 a.m. for various reasons, the chief of which was that we could stop with impunity at 2 p.m. for the day. The rehearsals went really well and what was incipient in our try-outs here became polished and refined. I was building up a pool of reliable actors like Terry McGinity, Bill Stuart and Barry Philips, as well as Wolf Kalher and others from *Agamemnon*. In the end I felt I was working with friends and countrymen. They didn't feel like employees or people I had auditioned. I played Titorelli and decided to eschew the mask. The great and bovine Barry Stanton played Huld the lawyer and did it brilliantly, as well as contributing mightily to the invention. After three weeks we started rehearsing *Agamemnon* and that too was jelling. We opened *The Trial*, as we thought, triumphantly, but gained rather patchy reviews, some sardonic, some mealy-mouthed, but the audience thought it the most exciting theatre. We did well and were of course invited to play in many other countries. One of our many visitors was the director of the Vienna Festival, a Herr Baumgartner, who wished to talk to me in the interval. Obviously he had seen what he wanted to see, but since I was going on in the second half I would see no one and he was forced to wait until the end. He remarked with a wry smile that he didn't usually have to wait for people, since everybody wanted to play the Vienna Festival. He confessed that he had seen *nothing* from London that he wished to take for the Festival and was giving up all hope until he saw *The Trial*. We were of course delighted with his comments and never doubted the veracity of them. *The Trial* was successful but *Agamemnon* much less so. We washed off our silver faces and for the last two weeks did *The Trial* only and it was much better. We lost a little on the season, but felt a great sense of achievement.

We had a party after the Round House and I always felt it was the most momentous event, the celebration of a victory and struggle together in the pursuit of our art. Here we had worked and slaved, been close as thieves, brothers and sisters and the finale was to be our revelling in our triumphs. A party was always anathema to me since I sometimes worried more about that than the performance in the evening and started to fret days before the event. I would be discussing how and when and how many and it would eat into me. It's a silly complex that has its roots in childhood when I was constantly denied the privilege of a birthday party. I watched my sister's yearly events with some fascination and yet was denied one myself. I couldn't decipher the reason, unless I was thought too young for such treats, but I see now how these things sow the seeds of greater discomfort in later life, when the idea of a party becomes a source of trauma. Anyway, Hemingway did say that an unhappy childhood was the best training ground for a creative life and mine was unhappy in trumps. I dreamed of being an adult as if I could unmoor the childish craft of childhood and let it float away. Now I am not so sure. So we had our little party, but some of the cast had another way of celebrating and decided to go to a party at the Hard Rock Café. I was mortified that these people who were so much part of my life and had made such a huge contribution to the show's success should not want to drink with us at the end of our triumph. We went to our stage manager, Fiona's house in Islington. The party was predictably ordinary and simple and I wished I had just jumped on the stage and invited the audience to share the last night's festivities with us.

The Evolution of the Villain – 1978

While I was performing in *East* at the Regent Street Poly, a film on the life of the ex-con John McVicar was being made, with Roger Daltrey playing McVicar. Until then I had been more interested in the classics and adapting Poe, whose *Fall of the House of Usher* I had performed the previous year. This was almost an eccentric discovery, my writing and playing *East*, but it had the effect of stamping me as a certain type usually played by the energetic Bob Hoskins. Roger Daltrey asked me about the play and I gave him some 'verbals', which he seemed so delighted with he actually threatened to film it; but like a lot of these ventures the second stage following the fore-play failed to come. So I was cast in *McVicar* after I spattered out a few high-octane blasts from *East* as an audition.

The part of Les in *East* captures your energy; it has cheek and verve, allows the actor to strut his stuff and gives him a sheen or veneer. In other words it can make you look good, like a song that suits you. It's a good vehicle and makes you feel good too when you speak the words. I say this not because I have an undying belief in my own work, but because many people who play Les tell me how 'high' they feel afterwards. Maybe one can feel good playing Chekhov too, but I haven't heard from anyone in my limited circle who has expressed that opinion. I suppose it must make the actors and actresses feel more worthy than good; when they mention that they are doing *The Seagull* their voices get a little breathless and worthy, as if they are going to church. I have never had a yearning in that direction, which is just as well since everybody else seems to be doing Chekhov anyway. It reminds me a little of *The Archers*, 'An everyday story of country folk'.

So Roger had me cast as McVicar's nemesis, a character based on an ex-London villain called Charlie Richardson, who was in jail with him. I found McVicar to be tough, charming and very lucid for an ex-villain, although I don't see why he should not have these qualities; he has now earned himself a big reputation as a journalist of very sinewy, readable prose. At the time we seemed to get on well and I enjoyed his advice about Charlie, whom I got to know years later. The director, Tom Clegg, did a workman-like job on the film and astonishingly I was nominated for some British Screen Award in 1979. (In the end the award went to Jonathan Pryce, I am glad to say, since it saved me having to make a speech.) Adam Faith played the co-starring part and the escape scene was good. But I felt that the cast weren't nearly tough enough for prison lags, and too much emphasis was laid on trivia like whether they were allowed to wear trainers. I felt utterly daft most of the time since I wasn't really 'in it', but it seemed to go OK. I don't think McVicar was too happy with the end result, but I enjoyed motorcycling down to Pinewood and hanging about.

There was an outrageous scene that was unfortunately cut when my character was being visited by this delicious 'bird' I was involved with. Tom Clegg wanted to show Charlie as quite a lad and suggested that his authority in jail was such that he could do almost anything he wanted in front of the screws, so he asked me to fondle this strange actress's breasts! Well, it's all acting, you know; I asked her if she would mind and she said, 'Well, it's all in the job, I suppose.' So on the takes I held these very pleasant parts and because we were complete strangers I did feel an element of arousal and so did she. This went on all morning and I must say I was glad when lunchtime came, since we could barely refrain from clawing each other's clothes off. That has never happened to me again on a set. It was a rare occasion and it was *cut*.

At the première I saw Roy Scheider, the actor, and I wondered what the hell he as an American would think of our pathetic romps in the underbelly of society. We seem to have little idea of showing the depredations and violence of prison life. It all looks like the TV series *Porridge*. I read McVicar's book later and was very impressed by his style, which was lost in the film.

So I became a 'villain' on the casting books.

More Villains

Having established this imprint upon the British public I was stopped in the street by heavies who claimed to like my interpretation of the notorious Charlie Richardson. The next villain came when I met Barbara Broccoli and John Glen, who were casting *Octopussy* and were looking for a Russian heavy. I had been cultivating a shorn look for some years, since I no longer needed to keep my hair some adaptable length so as to be useful for whatever part might crop up. I was now a writer and creator of my own works and thankfully freed of the torments that other poor players must go through if they are losing their hair, as if their genius lay to some extent in the follicular power of their hair roots. I did what I wanted with my body or hair and this meant that my cropped-lawn style made me look harder and thus villainous. So I was cast as General Orlov. *Octopussy* was entertaining and pleasant to perform, even if John Glen unfortunately curbed some of my excesses; I don't think this helped the film, since its essence was fun. But I found filming a hell of a bore. My first scene might have taken off, we were going great guns, but when I saw it I looked to be in shadow half the time and my lips didn't always match the shot. There were a lot of ladies around and I thought the two leading girls were OK, though they didn't knock me out. My scenes with Mr Moore were a trifle dull, but he was exceedingly pleasant to work with. The day of our 'big' scene the poor man couldn't remember his lines, although up till then he had been very strong on lines. I wondered to myself, as one does, if he felt some discomfort with me. Did I make him feel ill-at-ease. He was such a bold, extroverted individual on the set that I felt he might have found me a bit odd or difficult to believe in. I was not that comfortable myself. It was as if night met day. Eventually we shot it almost a sentence at a time.

I liked going to locations and sitting in hotels. I shall never forget that on the first day one of the regular actors asked us all up for drinks and made everyone feel at ease. He was an old Bond trooper. Filming in Pinewood finds you queuing for lunch in what looks like a palace or the alternative of sitting in a greasy, smelly workmen's café; the class system permeates even the declassé world of the film studios. Louis Jourdan was charming and taught us little word games to play while we were waiting around, like identifying movies through a series of codes in your chat. When we all played these games I knew that I had 'arrived' . . .

I happened to be in New York for the première and saw the ghastly finished product. I wanted to crawl under my seat, but I do tend to feel this on the first look at anything. I thought that all that money and all those locations furnished a very thin tale.

Beverly Hills Cop followed in 1984 when I was playing *Decadence* in a flea-pit in Los Angeles, courtesy of our producer. Even in this shabby little flea-pit on Santa Monica Boulevard, where the male hookers of the town would parade to sell their wares, we couldn't get an audience. We were trying *Decadence* out in America, but I have a theory that when you try out something which has been tested and proved already and you crawl back into a little hole in the wall, you may not necessarily even get the audiences who would normally be willing to enter this flea-pit. But if you have the bottle to put it on properly and put your money where your mouth is you will attract the town and the public who wouldn't dream of entering the stuffy little fringe pits. Theatres that are tame and predictable love subscribers. The producers make little speeches to them on the first nights, apologizing to those who may have lost their regular seats since they had to take one row out for this show. They did this at the Mark Taper Forum, a beautiful theatre in LA, when the curtain was waiting to go up on *Metamorphosis*. Usually the producer will appear as if he were an entertainer at an old people's home, which is not far off the truth. In fact during *Metamorphosis* in LA there was a constant rustle of polyester as brain-dead spectators walked out, the men in their synthetic blazers and the women in their recycled bin-liners. They didn't know what they were watching.

So during this caper in LA, I was called to meet Sly Stallone. The casting agent had seen *Octopussy* on a plane and she called me in. I drove to the studio, got my pass at the gate and thought this was to be an historic occasion – for years I had wanted to be in Hollywood and this was it. I saved the little white slip of paper, 'the pass'. The culmination of dreams, the apotheosis, here I was walking to the low, white-framed houses that had been there for fifty years and more. I floated down the long roads between the great sound stages. It looked like all the films I had ever seen and now I was shaking hands with a little bit of destiny; I didn't need it any more, I was independent, but it would be a 'treat', a bit of fun. So I did not enter with the attitude of an actor for whom life is a pair of strings attached to his shoulders and running through his heart that he hopes someone will pull for him. I went in for a bit of a giggle. Anyway, the name of the film was so puerile. *Beverly Hills Cop*, I mean, what an inane title!

There was a group of frightened people sitting round the table since they were in the presence of the Superman of the cinema, a man who not only acted tough but was indeed very tough and built like a Patton tank. They grinned when he grinned and laughed when he laughed. Or so it seemed to me, but these occasions are always strained when you come face to face with a man you have spent years of your life watching. Stallone was very friendly and charming; and we chatted and made a little small talk. He admitted he loved British actors and their voices, the way they delivered their lines like O'Toole with his marvellous aggressive shout. I replied that they get these voices because in Britain the pubs close at 11 p.m. and the actors usually get into the pub only shortly before closing time and in the crush at the bar have to shout to make themselves heard. They all chortled at my little invention, Sly replied that I had dashed his illusions and we wound up and I got the job. Martin Brest, the director, came to see me in *Decadence* to make sure I wasn't just a one-joke wonder. He was suitably impressed and then the word got around Hollywood and the trade people started to come in just before we closed.

On *Beverly Hills Cop* my unctuous costume designer was billing and cooing when he talked about putting me into 'dove grey', which looked like a sack of potatoes, and some fancy watch whose name he pronounced as if he was going down on it. The first day Martin told me to relax – Eddie Murphy had now replaced Sly, since Sly had wanted some incredible stunt that might have been expensive to stage and there had been a falling out. 'Don't do too much, remember you need only press a button for your gorillas to come steaming in.'

The film was a huge hit. Eddie Murphy was entertaining to work with; we sized each other up and went to it. Martin enthused about the rushes, as did the producer, Jerry Bruckheimer. Martin warned me that Eddie liked to improvise, which suited me perfectly since I like to improvise myself. Many of the shots were improvised to hell and ended up on the cutting room floor but in some cases they were funnier than the stuff that was kept. Brest did an excellent job on only his second movie and was a creative and actor-friendly person to work with, highly intelligent about film acting; he and I became friends after this.

The film had such a wide showing that I became a well-known face in America – and, it sometimes seemed, in every other country in the world. I could barely walk down the street. I started seriously to question whether I wanted to be a face that's splattered all over the place. I like to wander in crowds and be at least a bit anonymous and sit in simple cafés and stroll along the beach in Venice, LA, and not have guys screaming at me – and they do out there – screaming from cars, 'Hey, *aren't you the guy in* Beverly Hills Cop? *Hey, you, what's your name? Hey, hey I saw you in . . . didn't you . . .? Weren't you . . . Hey, see that guy, he's Victor Maitland! Shit! Yes!'* And so it went on and on and I avoided the flickers for a while thinking that I had destiny elsewhere.

So now taxi drivers ask me what I am doing next and why haven't they seen me and now they have caught me again as the villain in a film loosely based on the Kray twins, and I mean 'loosely'. I play a mad tearaway called George Cornell who gets his come-uppance in a pub in Whitechapel, of course, not far from where I once tried to sell biro pens for the Pen King . . .

Top Villain! Adolf, 1986

So much for some of my screen villains. They were topped, of course, by Hitler, my TV villain of villains in the epic *War and Remembrance*. After him you can go no further in villainy. Just a pity one had to wade through so much post-vital Mitchum and the rest of the stuff to get to me. Dan Curtis wrote the whole monumental thing and directed each episode. He was and is one of the most phenomenal people I have ever met. His energy was awesome to behold; Americans can work on a scale that is quite breathtaking and he was staggering even by American standards.

Dan and I got on well. I wanted to make this the truest Hitler of all time and Dan would tirelessly tell me that it was; after each shot he would say, 'That was fucking great' and his large American teeth and big Jewish face were like a powerful animal that concealed nothing and gave you every tremor of his being within. There was no concealment and no affectation. He was the Michelangelo of the TV screen and if that sounds flippant it isn't meant to be. He directed something like a thirty-hour movie costing $120 million. He wrote and directed and researched every second of it and it was a labour of ten years of his life. His workload was colossal and he was able to take such a subject and speak on it like a professor, since this just wasn't another movie for him to direct, not just another job, but the sole purpose of his existence. He ploughed his way through the history of Europe during the Second World War and I believe the scenes in Nazi Germany describing the gradual disintegration of Hitler from 1942 are authentic, chilling, perceptively done and stand as a lesson in Nazi history for future generations.

Dan was the only person ever to have dared to reconstruct the gas chambers and thus show the entire progress from arrest to Armageddon. He took his camera to places where other directors would have said this was impossible and we must cut away to the moon and a cloud pulling itself shamefully over the gaze of the great orb to mask it from the horrors. Dan bravely and fiercely took us into the bowels of death, into the very hell itself. I believe he was right to do it, even if our spineless British TV cut the scene and had John Gielgud looking at the moon as he went in since it would be his last glimpse of the wonder of God and now he must face the inventions of man. Dan filmed the chambers, the pellets dropping into a basket made of wire so that no one could throw themselves on it. Right until the last moments as they screamed and clawed the walls. Since millions actually went to their ends that way, surely the least we can do is to hold our stomachs and watch. Not just be moved by facts and figures and the nasty emotive words that hang on our language for all time like a permanent chancre on the face of mankind. Gas chamber.

When I got to Vienna, where we were filming, I strolled the beautiful boulevards and sat in the great cafés where I could write and write. I went each day to one particularly beautiful café, the Café Delma. The last time I had been in Vienna was in 1974 for the Vienna Festival, when we were performing *The Trial*. There were two *Trials* that year. A Polish company and mine.

The other actors were good soldiers and did well, but I felt Dan had invested in me his cause and *raison d'être*. I *was* Hitler for him and the irony was not lost. In order to play a guv'nor I think you have to have been one. Not just a leader among actors. I felt I could not only play the swine, but I could readily identify with his mania. His armies and ambitions became my plays and their conquests. His enemies could be the critics who had unfailingly shot down my works. We tend to hug the bad reviews to us like the long-lasting effects of a whipping, while the good ones are like an act of love that tends to dissolve the moment it's over. My antagonists became Hitler's enemies and dealing with his staff became dealing with the actors in my company, with the theatres, with the producers. And so running a country wasn't so different from the emotional stresses of trying to put on a play. You want to win votes.

The creation of Hitler's face was an hour-and-a-half job every morning, and it was a time to relax. Chris Tucker, who did the make-up, was a good chatter and I seemed to let the world flow out of me in those cold, bleak mornings as I got ready to play Adolf. I believe Chris was also famous for having created not only the Elephant Man's head but Tony Sher's hump in *Richard III*. Herman Wouk turned up on the set one day and watched me do a quiet scene when Hitler speaks to one of his favourite men, played by Jeremy Kemp. He watched with great interest and I was glad to have him there watching me work, since I was always acutely self-conscious, when playing Hitler, of any movement on the set. I became aware of a head that turned in the distance, since for the most part my antennae were out on stalks. But Herman Wouk was a soothing influence.

Hardy Kruger played the 'good German', Rommel. We had a scene together and before the first take he said to me, 'You know, Steven, everybody has a tendency to play Hitler as if he was a raving maniac, but he couldn't run a country like that, and besides the scenes will start to take on a sameness.' He was, of course, quite right in many respects, not least the repetitive quality. We did the scene and I started quietly and then went into my predictable overdrive. Dan was delighted and said that was exactly what he wanted. We were shooting Hitler not as he was before 1942 but after, when the war was beginning to turn and he was in a state of paranoidal psychosis for much of the time. Books I have read on that period describe him as going into paroxysms of rage until he was nearly foaming at the mouth. This may not quite have been his method in 1936, but it became so in 1942. Dan was showing Hitler *in extremis* and each scene was a pivotal point for the monster as the world was closing in on him.

Hardy Kruger was a very warm and engaging man on the set. When he finished his shoot he had a giant keg of beer brought on to the stage and we all had a little party. I liked that. So this is what stars do when they finish on the set . . . they give a little treat for the 'lads'. I will do this, I thought, when the time comes and as the day drew near this became a little bit of an obsession. We were filming in the bunkers which were some cellars in the slums of Vienna. I would be finished early. Should it be beer, like Hardy, or should it be wine? Oh, let's go for some modest champagne, sod it! I deliberated how many bottles and settled on a couple of dozen.

My shot finished and it was a wrap and everyone got busy taking out tripods and camera. The first assistant made an announcement that Steven was providing a farewell drink. The crew walked right past the offering. They were a German crew to a man and had liked Rommel, but didn't care much for Hitler. They blanked me out. I, who had worried about giving them a little treat and wanted to be like the 'stars', kind to your underlings, to be like Hardy, had fallen on my arse. 'Have a drink,' I called out to the fleeing figures. 'After,' they shouted back and I stood there with all my full bottles. A few small-part players gathered around and Dan grabbed a quick glass and then I gave the bottles away. *Never again*. I was never good at giving parties anyway and this was a party-giver's nightmare, when nobody turns up. However I enjoyed my drink.

I must say I looked staggeringly like Hitler once I had the wig and moustache on. When I had the audition, which I had expected since they were looking for cold blue eyes, Nazi Satans, I had to be tested first and went to Wig Creations in Marylebone where they fixed me up nicely with a wig and moustache. When I put on the wig I felt I was getting somewhere, but still looked too much like me. When I put that little smudge of black under my nose, the transformation was complete. Eureka! Everyone was astonished and said I was his double, when made up of course. I took the wig and moustache off and put them gently in a small, strong cardboard box they used to protect wigs and made my way to meet Dan at the Kensington Palace Hotel. It was a summer's day and I strolled in, looking fairly round-faced and healthy, and said, 'I've come to read for Hitler.' He looked at me and his expression held out little hope. I saw the doubt in his eyes and attempted a little spiritual resuscitation; I predicted that he had now found his Hitler. He looked tired and shaggy-eyed and replied doubtfully 'I hope' . . . I think he had been seeing the cream of Britain's actors and found them a trifle sour in the role.

I went into the bathroom and put on the uniform and the wig, just as before, but it was still too much me with a floppy wig, and then the little hairy pelt applied gently between lip and nose . . . aaaaaaaaaah! I pulled the hair down a bit. I knew *exactly* how he looked! I injected just a whisper of that arrogance and walked into the lounge where Dan was sitting with the beautiful Barbara Steele, who was acting as an associate producer. They both looked up. Astonishment registers in their faces. They think they are looking at

Hitler himself. It's weird and we all feel weird at once. A chill goes through the room. Dan recomposes his face and says, 'You look good, but let's do some dialogue' – after all, looking and acting are far apart. I had had some lines to learn but hadn't bothered to learn them because I knew I could play them better than anyone. This was *my role*. I said the text and tore it to pieces on take after take, whining, screaming, cajoling, whingeing, and performed my little bag of thespian tricks. It felt good. I got the job. I had to. That was my last real villain. But I never thought I would be playing villains when I started out into the theatrical world after leaving Webber-Douglas. The idea would never have occurred to me.

Greek – 1979

I just start writing without too much pre-planning or cogitation. I write for the sensation and pleasure of it and may not go past the first few lines. Like a fisherman I may drop my hook and see what I might catch that is lurking deep down there in the unconscious, and so it was for *Decadence*. I had just staged *Greek* and reneged on casting myself in the role of Eddy. I particularly like that part since it was modelled around me and expressed what I had felt at the time and drew deeply on the experience I was having with a difficult but passionate relationship. *Greek* exuded love, sexual and otherwise, and it was an outpouring, a love letter as well as a play drawing its nourishment from the London I saw in the seventies. I didn't know what I was going to write when I started but the pen moved my hand and what came out was an extraordinary compilation of ideas that were stewing in my pot. I was fascinated with Oedipus and Greek mythology and the play became an allegory of London life, transferring the plague of Thebes to the virulent spiritual plague that I felt was responsible for the physical decay of London. The yobs, cheap and grim pub life, the emergence of the drab media and corrosive TV, ever-present and ubiquitous violence, football yobbery, the murderous activities of the IRA bombers. It was all there and in my plot Eddy became the man to rid London of the sphinx, of the plague, by being better, fitter, more idealistic, a warrior, plus a lover. A modern samurai. Yet simple, honest, an everyman hero. I idealized myself into Eddy. 'Rid the world of half-arsed bastards clinging to their dark domain and keeping talent out by filling the entrances with their swollen carcasses and a sagging mediocrity,' says Eddy in his peroration to his public, but it doesn't take a genius to guess who I was talking about. Of course the play became my credo for the young, the frustrated, the idealists, the romantics, the renegades, and I wanted to be part of it but at the same time knew in some way because it was so close to the bone, that is my bone, I couldn't be. I felt that now I had created a play with plot and purpose but that was still satiric and mythic and was rooted in working-class speech patterns. Most of all it was a romance, a story dedicated to my own 'Helen of Troy', except she was a Helen of New Zealand. Cleverly she gave me a fascinating book called *Seven Arrows* and pointed out to me an incident in it. It was a story that was very simple and profound concerning incest, and I took the story where a son loves his mother and the mother soothes the son's anxieties about incest by contrasting their deep love with the horrors of warfare and slaughter going on all around them. My Oedipus defies the legend and runs back to his ma. Almost immediately I found the key to the production. Finding this, struggling to establish the physical shape that was a counterpart to the language, was to be more and more my method of working. There always is a shape and through observation, elimination and patience one will find it. It is the signature, so to speak, and lifts the play immediately into orbit. There is an actual physical counterpart to the language at the onset of a play and there may even be many alternatives but you have to find your own key.

The key for me was stillness. The family sitting at the table but all facing front while Eddy the protagonist stands behind the table. I watched and enjoyed the stillness making reverberations in me. It became a modern Greek fresco of family life. Thinking further on the Greek model I decided to have the actors play in white face, taking further the impression of Greek masks, an eternality of spirit. The angst of family life reaching across the millennia. Thus we had classicism crossed with urban grunge, poetic flights of language linked by the foulest imprecations of verbal street warfare. Then the stillness. Eddy stands or rather rises to that position. It felt like a painting, one of those Lucian Freud paintings from his West 11 period. Ordinary people somehow become extraordinary by the intensity with which we observe them. They are dead still, as if frozen for ever like the preserved figure from Pompeii. Sitting so still until we realize that they are watching television! It was a way of kicking the play off. Eddy then rises and begins his speech. From the stillness which created a tranquillity each gesture became stronger and more visible. The family reacting to Eddy with a turn of a head became a form of language

By finding what I felt was the 'image' or key to the beginning, the structure almost began to unwind itself like a coiled spring. It flowed so easily without all that terrible imposed 'moving around the stage' so beloved of theatre practitioners. By controlling the physical movement the energy of the players seemed to be compressed, gesture became more archetypal and the characters flowed into the mould. It also intensified the players, and the audience paid far more attention to the event. The liberation of the body. Each of us is capable of such dizzying possibilities of movement and gesture and yet most of the time they are blurred in the non-specific generality of what is loosely called naturalism. While this works well for certain subjects, for others it becomes wearily repetitious. Now all the movement was centred around the table, which itself became a form of mini-stage. We clung to it like space travellers moored to their craft. The actors became more and more adept, creating dozens of 'images' around the table, using their bodies as a kind of sub-chorus, and in this way they relayed, amplified, commented upon and thereby strengthened the position of the figure speaking. Or else they were still and in their stillness was created another emotional state. *Greek* was one of the most satisfying works I have done.

After the success at the Half Moon, that wonderful little ex-synagogue in Halley Street round the corner from Dad's old shop, we decided to transfer the play to the colder regions of the West End, to the Arts Theatre, which had once had a reputation for staging some of the most exciting theatre to be seen in London and where years ago I had been mesmerized by Burgess Meredith's brilliant production of *Ulysses in Nightown* with the late, wonderful Zero Mostel. Now it was a second divison theatre for tatty shows and during the day was requisitioned as a children's theatre. You had to fight with the management for space to put your photos up and hope they were not too adjacent to *Snoopy Goes to Town*.

The late Charles Ross produced the play and was proud, he often said, to be doing so. Unfortunately some damp reviews hit the box office and takings were struggling just to meet the rent, and yet the audience were coming in and since I've always been best when my back's to the wall I was determined to fight it out. 'Look, friends,' I said to the actors, 'we have a chance to stay and even change the profile of the West End a little with this kind of work and so let's keep going for less wages.' I was prepared myself that we should even perform if we were reduced to a cheese roll and a cup of tea! However, without the long-term memory of bleak unemployment that I had, the actors too soon forgot what it was like to be hungry both physically and spiritually and unbelievably turned down even a wage reduction, which would have at least kept the show running. I was astonished at this short-sightedness and the play folded after six weeks. The actors fell into long stretches of unemployment and the actor who was so marvellous as Eddy found difficulty working in Britain and eventually emigrated to California. However the seed had been planted and apart from cretinous comments from the likes of James Fenton, who donated a one-word review, the play started to arouse interest and become more and more performed in universities and by young groups and became their Alma Mater. The young actors trained themselves and toughened their vocal skills on the text, which is by no means an easy one. The word was spreading far and wide! *Greek* was becoming the number-one choice for groups performing at the Edinburgh Festival, and after it was published it started to travel round the world. It has been translated into half a dozen languages and has even been made into an opera! Now would you believe it, my 'Yukky' little play that started life as a germ of an idea and a doodle scrawled into my notebook:

> 'So I was spawned in Tufnell Park that's no more than a stone's throw from the Angel/a monkey's fart from Tottenham or a bolt of phlegm from Stamford Hill/it's a cesspit, right . . . a scum-hole dense with the drabs who prop up corner pubs, the kind of pub where ye old arseholes assemble . . .'

Of course what I am describing is any old suburb in bleak sixties and seventies London, and more particularly the long grim pre-gentrified street called Devonia Road in Islington, but then again everything looks worse when you're out of work. However, *Greek* is not just a wailing symphony of the depredations of London life, it is also a hymn to the joys of sexual love and my favourite speech is

Eddy's: 'I love a woman / I love her / I just love and love and love her.'
Barry did that so well, and I knew initially he was having some
difficulty with it.

The next time *Greek* surfaced was two years later, in 1982, when
news had crossed not only over the Atlantic but also the great width
of America and it was being considered by Susan Loewenberg of the
Los Angeles Theater Works, a company dedicated to finding new and
interesting material for her small theatres. So under the bright blue
skies of LA I found *Greek* reborn, and this play reminds me of the
Israelites scorned, scourged and vilified by the Romans and travelling
from the Orient and reappearing somewhere in China or India and
starting up once again. A play is a bit like a people since after all a
'people' are a group of human beings who are linked by an idea
which seems unpalatable to the host country and are extirpated. So
the 'idea' or 'ideology' if it has a seed within it capable of growth will
be blown across the seeds of time and bloom elsewhere. Susan
Loewenberg, an attractive woman with a good sense of drama, had
put together the cast for me since I had to fit the directing in between
a tour of *The Fall of the House of Usher* in Australia and a European
tour of *Hamlet* which I had previously directed at the Round House.
So I fitted this in and was glad to be back in LA, one of my favourite
cities on earth. A lot of actors complain with their supercilious
British tone of superiority about Lotus Land and Lala Land and how
it is awful, materialistic, plastic, phoney, etc., etc. Well, I find the
opposite. It's a fantastic fantasy world of extraordinary diversity,
energy, playfulness, and to hang out on the beach in Venice where I
was lucky enough to live – I'd never seen anything like it in all
my life. Merely to step out of my door was like going on some kind
of mind trip. Living out in Venice some 15 miles from the actual
downtown area I had the beautiful early-morning sea breeze and the
wildest mixture of characters this side of bedlam. Rollerskaters
zoomed by led by their dogs as if they were charioteers, musicians
played, dancers danced, seers told fortunes and the sheer variety of
human invention was there to witness in Venice, and I was never so
happy in my life. I think I had actually found my Nirvana, and
so why did I go back to London? Well, my livelihood, even against
the odds, is in acting and writing for the theatre, and perhaps the
compost heap of London drudge is what fertilizes my work.

Rehearsals for *Greek* went as well as could be expected with an ad hoc company and the play opened to the most positive reviews it has ever had! At the Matrix Theater on Melrose Avenue under the canopy of stars and playing also to quite a few stars that made their way to the source of all the noise, *Greek* was reborn in America! It made quite a noise in the trade and it became the thing to see both for its abrasive, punkish, in-your-face dialogue plus the mechanistic and choreographed staging which made me proud. It was a style I had evolved over the last ten years, of honing things down to a minimum until the bare essence remained. I was to take this a stage further in my next work, *Decadence*, where movement was reduced to two people on a sofa. *Greek* had a very happy nine months in LA and for a change the actors earned a little, but very little, money, since they were not protected by unions in houses under a hundred seats and the producers could pay what they felt they could afford. Something strange seems to happen to the actors who play Eddy; since it is such a heroic role they seem to identify to an enormous degree and never seem quite to shake off the mantle of hero, wit, lover, revolutionary, and find the other world out there, when they are demoted back to hired player, a little difficult to cope with. A Welsh actor called John Francis who was passing through LA heard about the audition, read for it and was given the role. As a Welshman, no one could have been more miscast for Cockney Eddy, but he had a brave stab at it and endowed it with a great charm and earned some good reviews. The play transferred to Off Broadway but whatever faults I felt it had in LA were multiplied in New York and even the wonderful Georgia Brown's efforts did not save it from being shot down in flames by the most ignorant bunch of thugs posturing as critics that I have ever had the misfortune to read. The main drive of their reviews seemed to be that the language offended their delicate American sensibilities. They couldn't see beyond the language and seemed to prefer the redundant junk plays that discuss money or problems. Their loss.

Eventually, my scatological piece of vituperative spleen, enriched of course with passages of lyricism, inspired Hans Werner Henze to commission an opera using the text of *Greek* as a libretto. I was to see my reviled child set to music and delighting the well-heeled *aficionados* of the opera at the ENO.

Having felt a distinct sense of frustration over not playing Eddy and regretting the decision, yet knowing it was also the right one, I set about writing something that would give me a chance to get back on the stage again and let my pen doodle once more, 'let the moving finger write'. Even as *Greek* was playing in some godforsaken provincial town I found I was doodling the beginnings of *Decadence*. I started writing on little cards and as usual I had no idea what was emerging or what I was going to end up writing. I just let the free association take place. I imagined a dialogue and let the characters play with each other: 'How sweet of you to come on time / Bastard! Sweet darling! My you do look so divine'. I just let it drift along on the river of my subconscious, picking its way here and there, wandering up tiny tributaries until I felt it had to have an answer, a conflict, and the woman must ask the man what is so troubling in order to get some kind of response. This led to the improvisation taking on the familiar form of the triangle, which led to the two couples cheating on each other, which then led to the idea of conflicting emotions plus conflicting classes. That in turn led to the examination of the habits of the two opposing classes and the indulgence of one over the other. This then led to writing episodes in which we examine all their most sacred desires. After that the play seemed to write itself and it became a kind of parable on the seven deadly sins. I just picked them out of a hat: gluttony, sexual greed, public school debauchery, cruelty in the hunt enacted out by the pair of them, fashion slavery, drunkenness, snobbery in the white enclave of the Englishman's club.

I finished the play and Linda Marlowe and I rehearsed on the sofa in her Fulham flat but I couldn't seem to get the thing under my belt. It was a bastard to learn but I persevered and we both played the two roles by merely changing our body language. This was going to be a *tour de force* or nothing. I was making up with a vengeance for losing *Greek*. Linda was gobbling up the text like a cat on cream and I was plodding behind until one day after an awkward session I started to get one of my vocal panics. I couldn't get my voice out in the way I wanted. Let me find someone else, I begged her, I am sure it will be better and I'll just direct. We'll get Peter Wyngarde or Peter Bowles. She wasn't having it and said, 'Steven, no one will do it like you and you are absolutely right in the role and in fact both of them!'

Comforting, making coffee, she made me start again, and I was never to look back, though someone else might have said well, maybe you are right and it would be better to stand outside, as one of my colleagues had suggested when I cast *East*. Linda is direct, forthright and honest. She says what she feels and she feels plenty. When you have someone like Linda for an ally you have a strong woman on your side who doesn't take shit for an answer. We first met when she took on a part in *The Trial* and agreed to work for nothing initially as an apprentice of sorts since this work was totally unfamiliar to her and she was brave enough to say that and wanted to stretch herself. Since then she has worked as Gertrude in *Hamlet*, the mother in *Metamorphosis*, the wife in *Greek*, and co-lead in *Decadence* – which she created.

Eventually we decided to give it a bash and approached a very low-key theatre called the New End in Hampstead, which had once been a morgue. It was run by a very supportive and enterprising young chap who did everything possible to make us feel at home. We tried a run-through which was so utterly exhausting I was left wringing wet and my once pristine stiff collar a limp rag. My confidence was not high although I knew the play could work if we sustained the energy and made the changes work from the two upper-class to the two lower-class characters. They did and the audience laughed, howled, cheered, and we grew stronger and stronger with the experience. We were both on the stage for nearly two hours and by the end we were in ecstasy just to have got through it. We didn't wish for reviews just yet but maybe a little ripple in the press would be OK to give it a bit of a launch. Since we were mainly fixed to the sofa our moves had to be *creative within a confined environment* (a phrase which could symbolize my life). We mimed everything – drinks, cigarettes, horses and even rats! I never felt so liberated in both movement and language, and the play started to take on the feel of a Gillray or a Scarfe cartoon. We invited only a couple of reviewers, including Nick de Jongh and thankfully, luckily and happily, Robert Hewison from *The Sunday Times*, who fired our confidence with one of the most interesting and informative reviews I have ever been blessed with:

> Steven Berkoff's play is a stream of pure hatred for you, me, and I suspect the entire readership of *The Sunday Times* . . . The pressure on actors and audience is unrelenting. We are not so much

in the theatre as in the *Neue Sachlichkeit* world of the painters
Max Beckmann or Christian Schad, or the self-torturing environment of the performance artist Stuart Brisley. Berkoff's nihilism
is in tune with a section of the disaffected young, and for that
reason alone, *Decadence* is worth seeing.

I learned something from this critic and he helped me to understand my relationship to the visual arts. Even if I was not familiar at
that time with the *Neue Sachlichkeit*, I saw from the hard-edged
painting of Otto Dix my own image reflected as 'Steve' in *Decadence*.
The polished made-up face, the rictus grin, the straitjacket dress-
suit, the braying whine, the stylization which for years I had been
aiming for – to rid myself of the grim plodding attempts to be natural,
so beloved of the British theatre since it eschewed all necessity to
study movement and shape or to be more physically alive on stage.
Instead of 'Let them eat cake' here in the nineties one might say, 'Let
them have their revolving stages!'

My advice to an actor who on the first day is facing a director
who discusses his little toy revolve, his merry-go-round, his little
carousel, is to *walk*. Don't go near it since when you have left the
show all you will remember is this spinning, effing top, while the
actors look busy being shunted like so much luggage from station to
station. You might recall the leading players but all they do is trot
counter-clockwise to the next port of call and all the hustle and
bustle covers up a great hole which is the centre of the director's
head. What is lost on the stage is the entire space since the ugly
monster sits like a great turd in the middle and the playing area is
reduced to a quarter. There are no great walks, movements, group-
ings or activities and thank God since the revolve moves the whole
ghastly ménage. The director is let off the hook and the fact that it
fools people is even more monstrous since they confuse activity with
art. Even the actors are fooled by the technology and stand there
proudly as they are carried off like little horses on a fairground
carousel. I love the great spaces of the stage and the actor's body
and movement thereon. What is this Victorian device doing now
upon our stages? If I go to the theatre and see one of those things on
a stage my heart sinks since there can be no art of the player, no
choreography, since the director knows not that form. The only
satisfaction I do achieve from the overuse of such mechanical

replacements for ideas is when the damn thing breaks down, which happens frequently, and some flushy-faced administrator has to go onstage and offer the audience their money back or tickets for another night.

So Robert Hewison restored an element of pride in my work and I studied his review, taking it to pieces and looking up the references to the painters he mentioned and in turn studying them. Following the New End, where the distinguished director Deborah Warner was learning admin and being a very helpful assistant, we performed at the Edinburgh Festival in the converted left-luggage room of the Caledonian Hotel. Even the sofa had to be made up and covered with some plastic leatherette. Still we were happy performing and honing *Decadence* in our style, which was to perform it until we felt it worthy of being seen by the wider London audience. We wanted it to be at an advanced stage in terms of input, business, refining, so that when it was eventually reviewed we would be at our potential best and more. To take something beyond the norm was always the ambition. I remember the great actor Paul Scofield coming to see us and writing me a card of congratulations, and that for me was the best review of all.

So *Decadence* was about excess, taking an idea to its limit so it exists on the edge of dissolution before it destroys itself. In fact where the best theatre should lie, on the edge of our human experience and as far as we dare to go and then there is a point of no return. To the edge – is that the area of theatre?How seldom or how often do we see that? The torrent of language that was still boiling inside me, was able to come seething out in *Decadence*. The characters inspired me to see them raw and juicy in an acid bath of language, to see them turning themselves inside out. Hate, jealousy and vengeance became the rallying cry from the working-class couple as they planned and plotted macabre deaths for their elusive and luxuriating enemy who were seldom aware of them throughout the entire play whereas Les and Sybil, the proles, couldn't be more aware of them. Those of us who are forced to do without, who beg, plead, and whistle to be allowed to dip our spoon into the public soup bowl, can think of nothing less but vengeance. In fact, after the initial mention of them to trigger the plot, Steve and his paramour Helen hardly mention the other pair at all. The two couples are a strange split personality in that the four characters are played by just two people, as if the very nation was one being split into two opposing halves and at war with itself like a schizoid personality.

There are flecks of me in Steve as well as touches of me in the disgruntled Les. You have to start from somewhere. There is the fantasy establishment that Steve flirts with and the distaste, contempt and ridicule for it. Notwithstanding, the loathsome twitty couple in *Decadence* embrace a kind of enviable freedom with their total guilt-less abandonment to the seven deadly sins as they take each on to its nauseating and vicious climax. Steve gets drunk in fine abandon until on the stage I was able to heave myself for a good old mimed barf behind the sofa which was tremendous fun, and after I had barfed I couldn't get up for slipping in the sloshy sludge and the audience screamed at this point which impels me to think that they need to escape from conformity like all of us and be released into high lyricism or disgust (but spare me what's in between). The two continued their assault on their senses discussing homosexual rape, blood sports, and sexual debauchery as Helen describes a 'gorgeous' blowjob she bestows on a handsome waiter who brings the morning breakfast to her suite in a hotel in the South of France – she does this while 'hubby' is asleep beside her and he welcomes her with a waking-up kiss blissfully unaware of the stigmata glistening on her lips. Fashion slavery, racism in that great British institution the gentle-man's club, and the grand bouffè at the end of the play when Steve explodes and detonates himself all over the restaurant like a rapidly deflating balloon became the ingredients of the dish called *Decadence*. When Steve was off then I would 'rest' as Les came on, and indeed merely the break from the intensity of Steve would make the performing of Les feel like a holiday and I know that Linda Marlowe felt the same way towards her characters. The white sofa became a mini stage in and around which everything was enacted, including the fox hunt which was done on the carpet as Helen 'shows' me how she rides her horse thereby giving an unexpected bonus for the fetish-ists and players of charades who use their games to camouflage their repression since they are given a licence now to be 'free' and silly. Since we seldom used props and were able to act them out we could determine the shape, size, weight of anything and effortlessly expand them at will. It was a most satisfying but exhausting experience. Linda Marlowe's characters in the two parts complemented each other and significantly it was the women who had a seemingly stronger grip on their sexual identities and motives while both men were satirized as strutting, rutting, posing exemplifiers of the phallocentric male dancing on the hotplate of his own insecure desires.

So we ran it at the New End, then Edinburgh, then back at the New End and kept the play going for a further few weeks. In the winter of '82 I booked the Arts Theatre for a thousand pounds per week and paid all expenses. I was well aided by a very able administrator, Paula de Burgh from Australia, who ironed out the creases and gave her considerable administrative skills to the project, as well as Charles Ross who acted as an associate producer. Again I was risking my money but felt confident that even if the critics didn't like us they wouldn't be able to close me down, no, not with just the two of us and one of the actors being me. I would never 'go down', as Jake La Motta says using the mouth of Robert De Niro in the remarkable film *Raging Bull*. I was still thinking of *Greek*'s dive two years earlier when the actors preferred to throw in the towel. However they have to live and don't have the same vested interest perhaps as I have, and they had been performing it at the Croydon Warehouse for a try-out and then the Half Moon for a second try-out and then the Arts, so I expect they were glad to have a break. But they should have stayed on to beat the system. This time I *would*. The critics came and the decision was unanimous. I had a mini-hit on my hands and eureka, I was saved again.

Christmas 1990

The sky is washed blue today in this Christmas lull when the world becomes increasingly turgid and dull. Christmas seems to epitomize and symbolize the climate of the country. The TV drones on – each year it gets worse. Obsession with doing things becomes paramount and more idiots throw themselves like lemmings on to jets in the giant panic not only to do something but to be seen to do something. To be in any way a misfit of society, an outcast, poor, divorced, unmarried, single, introverted, alone, foreign, mad, anti-social, odd, a stranger, is to render this time of year something akin to one of Moses's plagues. You pray for it to be over. You suddenly ask, 'What are you doing?' to people with whom you are perfectly at ease the rest of the year; now you are reluctant to bother them or imply you are alone, yet you desperately need some company to protect you from the spotlight being trained on you. Now is the time to count your cards, hang them on a line, display your popularity, have friends and family over, the ones you don't really like that much but are part of some inner clan. Or wait at home and sit it out.

My Christmases were only good when I was able to escape and one year I escaped with my wife of the time, Shelley Lee, to the Canary Islands. When I first heard of the Canaries in 1973 they sounded so exotic and strange that I thought they were some extra-ordinary far-flung isles in the Pacific, but then I learned that tourists were going there for Christmas and New Year. So we set off and on the first night a friendly taxi driver took us to a little village in the hills where no doubt he wished to give some friends business. We had a small room overlooking the street and the family lived downstairs, where they had a grocery shop. I used to go downstairs early in the morning because it was really an enchanted village and the little boy would give me a boiled egg, bread, jam and coffee, and I was so happy I can still feel the happiness in my bones as I write. I sat and wrote my journal while Shelley slept a bit more and then she would come downstairs and write her journal; she never stopped writing her journal, like a silkworm weaving the tapestry of her life and thoughts until she boasted she had about thirty volumes. Not boasted; she was proud of having committed to paper millions of words, each of which carried a wisp of memory so that in rubbing them you produced the genie of the lamp who appeared and con-structed the world of the past, coloured and transformed with the emotions of the present.

We were in Tenerife, an island that has over the subsequent years been worn down by the hordes of Europe, but then it was still a sweet and charming island. On Christmas Eve the whole town went to Midnight Mass and when they returned the family had their dinner downstairs and the men played guitars and sang all through the night. In the bright silver-blue morning I went downstairs for my favourite, looked-forward-to, large cup of steaming coffee and the idea of an unburdened and fruitful day, and I saw the family sleeping against each other's shoulders and the man still plucking his guitar. We went on Christmas Day to the beach and swam and thought of the hordes probably trying to have a good time and screaming. It felt so good to swim, not to eat and gorge ourselves but to delight in the cool waters and in the evening sit outside and drink the special Canary tomato soup and watch the kids playing and chasing each other up the street. We slept like the sinless. Then we found a little village on the sea's edge and would walk through the banana plantations each day. This became our ritual, since we didn't drive cars then and I certainly had no intention of becoming acquainted with parking meters. So we walked through the hot fields of bananas with their great purple leaves and the tiny little fingers of the bananas peeping out; we watched the lizards and sat by the water's edge and walked back and ate our dinner and talked.

The next year we went back and found an old hostel on the water's edge. Still there was a bright breakfast room, so sunny and light; and this time there were others who had discovered the joys of leaving England at Christmas and walking through the fields and gorges and valleys in the sun. But halfway through this second wonderful journey I was struck by a recurring thought about what work I would do when I returned. This grew and grew into an obsession until it was taking over my every waking minute. I was sick with it and that spoilt the holiday, since mental obsession, when you churn things over and over, is like watching the window of a washing machine . . . for ever.

Christmas in the USA – 1947

My first Christmas in the USA was in 1947, a lonely and dreadfully sad time that Mum, Beryl and I spent in the New York attic in the Bronx, utterly alone and ignored by the rest of the family. Marlon Brando had just opened in *A Streetcar Named Desire* at the Barrymore Theatre while we huddled in our attic in 173rd Street East, Bronx. Forty years later at the same theatre I would be directing Baryshnikov in my play *Metamorphosis*.

Harry's Christmas

Christmas reached its nadir in the year of 1982. I had travelled much of the world that year, playing *Hamlet* in Paris, directing Kafka in LA, winning awards for *Greek*, also in LA, making *Octopussy* in

England. So then why not celebrate a great Christmas with all my champions and world-touring colleagues? Instead, I let the glumps get to me and went into the hypnotic state which had conditioned me for years: this is the gloomy season and verily ye shall be ultra miserable. This is the Christmas of your deprived youth, the time when you watched the world enjoy itself, but ye shall not since ye are an outcast.

I took myself off to my sister's home in Bristol, a ghastly hole that looked as if a plague had decimated it; the one place to go was the Wimpy Bar, even on Boxing Day when you needed to escape from the family for a few hours. Britain does invent perfect horrors that seem to suit it so well. I strolled aimlessly round the docks and returned to the house, where my relationship with my sister was becoming more and more strained and the evil telly continued to spew out its numbing waves . . .

I was glad to have someone at least to visit, a table to sit at and someone to talk to, but during that holiday I was inspired to write Christmas out of my being for all time. I wrote *Harry's Christmas*, which details the journey of a lonely man in the days leading up to Christmas. In a way it becomes his 'Passion'. I originally called the play *Death and Transfiguration*, but this was considered too bold a title and so it was reduced to *Harry's Christmas*. It was commissioned to open the new Limehouse TV Studios on the Isle of Dogs. I was very chuffed to see the name of the play on all the canvas 'flats' in the studio. A set was built, largely to try out the facilities of the studio, the staff and the whole set-up from editing and sound to final transmission. I think it was very well directed and reasonably acted by me and it was a very moving piece, although I am sure I could have done a better job with a little more time than the two days allowed for shooting.

The play was never shown, which is a great shame as I believe it is a very powerful antidote to Christmas. The main character, Harry, commits suicide on Christmas Day; he is thus 'crucified' for his lack of involvement in the make-believe world of Christmas in which so many people feel alone and neglected. I don't think the play would have encouraged others to copy the example; rather I believe they would have found comfort in it and may even have been discouraged from joining the ranks of those who do themselves in during the Christmas period. I enjoyed writing it and it flowed out of me as something does when I feel I am on the right track and have hit a main line of inspiration.

Although *Harry's Christmas* never went out on TV, I did approach someone at the little Donmar Warehouse who was 'thrilled' with the idea of my doing it as a one-man show in 1986/7. I performed it along with *The Tell-Tale Heart* for six weeks; the theatre was packed throughout and I had never before received so much mail in response to a play, from people who felt the same as I did and were in agreement with its theme. I found it a tough evening, doing two plays per night. The whole show lasted two hours with an interval, but I enjoyed it. Some nights I felt strange dealing with Harry – it was a semi-naturalistic play but I mimed most of the props. I wanted to show him as he was going to bed, getting up, having a crap (great fun with that; mime does allow you a lot of bonuses), having a bath, going to the kitchen, getting on the phone to the dwindling amount of numbers he dare call on the days leading up to Christmas.

The Tell-Tale Heart of course was a gas after that and I didn't have a lonely or bad Christmas that year, in fact it was a good one with just a few days off to cool down and then back again and dinner in Smith's restaurant after the show. I felt successful, and pleased to be doing something useful that Christmas. Simon Callow, acting in his capacity as occasional critic, gave me such a generous review, the like of which I could only be as proud as Punch about, although he chiefly liked *The Tell-Tale Heart*. Bob Hoskins came to the first night and we had dinner afterwards in Smith's; Simon Callow came over and asked when I was going to finish the play on Oscar Wilde I had been threatening to write for some time. I said I had the title if not the play, but I would work on it since I wanted to write a play about Wilde and homosexuality. The title would be just Wilde's initials, with an exclamation – *OW!* It might need some gesture to go with it. I was in earnest.

Back to 1990

Mind you, Christmas 1990 was a nice one. Total isolation with my present lady, and typing this book. So I have been with old friends. The turkey was cooked to a treat and I ate the lot, didn't watch much TV but had to catch Jackie Mason taking the piss out of his audi-

354

ence. I like his act enormously. A Jewish comedian who tells Jewish jokes all night, breaking down all the taboos we have about racial stereotypes. It is refreshing to hear him, particularly as I often get accused of racial or sexual stereotyping myself.

I once made a joke on late-night telly at festival time about dragging the Irish out of the pub to go to work because they were enslaved to Guinness. The comment arose out of a question about our technique and I answered light-heartedly. The interviewer was curious to know why I chose to stage much of the play in slow motion. Following the circuitous route of satirizing something I care very deeply about and so masking my love with humour, I parodied the slow motion that is used in the play with an image of an inebriated person leaving a pub. Well, what a performance I had after that from every worthy watchdog. The fact is I was trying, even unconsciously, to play on the prejudices of the Brits re the Irish and I was, after all, the man who had written *Decadence*! The BBC took it in good humour, since it wasn't a serious show, and I had a strong affinity with my Irish actors and felt I could afford to make this comment. They were a smartly disciplined team and they knew I loved them and would never in a thousand years do anything to hurt them or anyone else by some vicious or scurrilous remark. But it may be that the famous Irish drink problem is too near the surface and they were more sensitive than I realized, though the most offended was a chap in the company who wasn't even Irish. You can't say anything these days without treading on someone's corns. Well, apologies all round and we forgot about it until some wretch in a fringe rag felt that she had to air her pompous concern and repeat the slur. The Irish actors rallied round me when they saw that this was getting out of hand, but then the shit really hit the fan and the non-Irish of the company wanted to whip up a kind of witch hunt. All very bizarre. However, sometimes people function better when they think they don't owe you anything and can behave in the mean-spirited way they felt too inhibited to do before.

So when I saw Jackie Mason I was relieved to see him pop each stereotype as if he were bursting a purulent boil. It was gentle humour, but to the point. An idiot could not have taken grievous offence. Jews are ashamed of being Jews. They hide their names, their origins, their noses! Too true. Jews don't like being thought of as Jews. Tell a girl she looks Italian or French or Spanish and she loves it, but tell her she looks Jewish and she'll hate you forever, especially if she is Jewish. It was all very funny. The audience laughed and we were in stitches. Why? Because it was daring to say we don't wish to hug our fears. We can hear that word without blushing. Jews are born satirists anyway, or comedians. It's one of the most effective defences against pain that there is. So we have been ashamed of being Jews for years and ashamed to say it and ashamed that we demanded so much pity for the holocaust and ashamed that we died so easily in the war and ashamed of our Arabic genes in our noses that became further accentuated in the restricted inter-breeding space of ghettoes, and ashamed of the funny names we got landed with; who wants to be Finkelstein or Fagenblum, even though the second means a flower. With all our shame we are glad when someone holds up the rags of our humiliation and we can laugh. And so the Irish have their shame about their booze problem and I was exposing this slur by pretending they had to have their fingers pulled off the bar to get them to go to work. But it seems only Jews can take jokes against themselves. It goes with the territory. But then again your 'family' can joke about themselves – while outsiders can't.

Jewish Theatre

Of course one is a product of one's environment. My family came here in 1888 or thereabouts and at first they lived as if they were in Russia. They spoke only Russian or Yiddish and understood nothing of the culture they were in; they had brought their own culture with them. The children grew up in that environment but they went to school and spoke English. They still managed to speak a simple Yiddish – my mother used to tell me that when they went to the silent movies in the East End she would have to translate for her mother; all the mothers took their kids along and every time the subtitles came on there was a great whispering and head-turning and kids' shrill voices, then all was silent again.

They would also go to the Yiddish Theatre and watch the great old Jewish actors play in *The Merchant of Venice*, *King Lear* and of course, when they could, *The Dybbuk*, the great Jewish mystic classic. There is something cabbalistic about this piece and in those days the theatre was closer to the synagogue. If the Hassidic Jew developed music and dance into his prayer rituals and announced that God should be worshipped with joy since He is a manifestation of the abundant miracle of life and one should feel this ecstasy right into one's very bones and sing, then this idea must have dropped some of its sparks into the old Russian theatre. The Habimah, the Jewish Russian theatre, would have embraced this and further developed the idea of theatre as an ecstatic ritual of celebration. I only once saw a relic of the Habimah, *The Dybbuk*, a production that had been carefully preserved over the years, delicately pieced together at the Habimah Theatre in Tel Aviv, where the older actors would carry the information of past actors and remember that so and so used to do it this way. The music, gesture and text went together and so one was satisfied at many levels, most of all sensually.

Theatre has always meant a means of celebration to me; even if the subjects were hard or tough, violent at times or flagrantly to the point, they had at the same time to be celebrations of the art of theatre or they were nothing but a mean polemic. So perhaps trickling down through the years, from Moscow, from the last century, from the early stirrings of *The Dybbuk* with its wild ecstasy and mystery, its poetic grandeur, its dance, its expressions of the deepest wonders, this germ came to me. Perhaps in the next generation after my mother, when we no longer spoke the quaint language of Yiddish nor went to synagogue and had emasculated our more exotic-sounding names (I changed mine back), when we spoke English and tried to sound posh, when we eschewed the legends of the ghetto, the wistfulness of Chagall, the curse of the centuries, the alliance with a distant land and merely wished to be Hamlet and Jimmy Porter, just to be a part of and contributor to the sum total of the culture we lived in ... there was always a tiny shred of longing that wished to play *The Dybbuk*.

Having said that I must add that out of the enormous hothouse of the East End and its thousand strands of life, out of the biggest exodus since Moses took the Jews out of bondage, out of all the thousands and tens of thousands of dramas in every tiny room, tenement, street, school, drama, persecution, Blackshirts, poets, anarchists, dreamers, riots, social upheavals, murders and madnesses, achievements and glories, there is hardly one play, film or other work that expresses any of this. One of the largest transportations of culture from one land to another has so shamed the race, so dulled and quietened the people down that they're relieved merely to be left unmolested. Who can blame them – they even put in prayers for the Queen in the synagogue. Apart from some books, one of which is the great biographical novel *Jew Boy* by Simon Blumenfeld, and another his *Diary of an Immigrant*, both of which are terribly moving and fascinating stories, there is no desire to unleash that particular animal. The only vaguely Jewish culture we see is in those commercials for British Telecom where the famous Jewish mother is seen, a ghastly travesty, a fussy, mouthy, busybodying gossip who we must see as 'cute' and which frankly makes me feel quite sick. This is Uncle Tomism with a vengeance.

Anyway, I believe you express your culture through your work, if you allow it to come through. To me *Death of a Salesman* could only be a Jewish play in a neutral setting. The desires and hopes for the children and the terrible shame of their failure to understand the mysteries of commerce, the salesman's gift, his tongue, since traditionally he had little time to absorb science and culture. His children, who became Aryanized and would rather play sports. The terror of faithlessness in one father, the overwhelming love and pain for the betrayed mother. All these things are felt by all races and so the play was so famously successful because it felt it just that much more. Like Kafka's Uncle in South America, the great adventurers shaming us while we hustle for a living at home. Chagall-like dreams hovering over our heads like a mist.

Salomé – 1988–9

I suppose that, to paraphrase Wilde, naturalism is the theatre's way of showing the middle-class public its own ugly and dreary face. I think it's more than that, since I believe it compounds the limitations of achievement and endeavour. It stops up the bung-hole of free expression, it circumscribes its limited terrain, it makes its little vision seem like vast horizons, it proscribes imaginative or non-conformist behaviour, it loves itself and loves all who worship at its vapid, bourgeois box office. Naturalism is the writer using the theatre to express his world view, but this view is mostly gleaned from sitting at his desk and visits to his local lunchtime pub. Some critics will mourn the loss of vital, gutsy and trenchant theatre, yet they condemn it when it appears. One hears continuously, 'Where is the new theatre, where are the new writers?', while any sign of vitality, life, passion, iconoclasm is ignored and swept away because this same force sweeps away their own views. What they profess to admire or seek, in reality they cannot bear.

Why does this paradox exist? It never ceases to baffle me. Naturalism appeals very much to the modern director, who loves movies and wishes the stage were really a movie set and directs actors to have real feelings, real tears, real spit, real nudity, real sets. Although for a while there was a touch of symbolic setting in Shakespearean production, now we are back to clinging to the real world. We love those nice pieces of furniture. Those hugging Chekhovians. We keep doing it. For whom, may I ask? I really need to know, then perhaps I may see the light. Chekhov was a wonderful storyteller, but the plays suffer from a surfeit of the sweetest things . . . as the saying goes.

Wilde's *Salomé* I am sure of. The ideas leap from the page and the language penetrates and curdles into your senses like a twisted curl of smoke from incense. When you discover this play it lights you up. Everybody who has been introduced to it eventually succumbs to it. Even Al Pacino wants to play it . . . good luck to him.

I had these feelings even at drama school. When I left they were taken over by the need to mark out a prompt script and write down the complexity of moves on a page. I loved to do that. 'The actor xdlc' – the actor crosses the stage to the left and moves down the centre, and you can add a small circle if there's a pause since you mustn't prompt during a pause or you will get an '*I'm pausing!*' in a very irate tone of voice.

A critic from the eminent listings mag *Time Out* seemed to think I had somehow used a company to try out a play and had then absconded with it. Quite a reasonable assumption to make if your mind has that perverted bent, especially about Berkoff. In fact I was invited to try the play out since it had been my desire for a decade to perform Herod. I was obsessed by the role and the play and gave it a life it would never have had in Ireland had I not done it. It would have come and gone like all the other plays that get chewed up in the repertory system. It was my strong love for the play that guided me into its interpretation.

Michael Colgan had intended to stage *Salomé* for the sixtieth anniversary of the Gate Theatre, Dublin, and since this coincided with my desire to do it he invited me to stage it with the view that I would then be able to play Herod without the attendant worry of directing in the future. This is much how dance works – a dancer/choreographer will put another dancer in in order that the choreographer may shape the performance from an eyes-front position, then he or she can step in. This was the agreement written in blood. Mike knew this and everybody knew this and if they didn't then they were misinformed.

I don't believe this is necessarily a good way of working since what happens, as in this case, is that the success tends to turn the heads of those who have a gem on their hands and all words, thoughts and promises go by the way. And so when I came to restage *Salomé* in London, it was somehow let out that the Irish company of very worthy actors were being denied the fruit of their work. Not so. Not even for a split second, since I would be the first to create situations where the companies I direct would seek fulfilment. I have fought for companies all my life, for the betterment of their conditions, wages, exposure, etc., and it is not within my nature to rip people off. The only person I rip off is myself.

To say that I could have performed this work with any group of actors would be true. The company was a good company, but not the Moscow Arts, and the success I must modestly say was due to the production, which I had conceived down to the last note, aided by an excellent Herod and Herodias. But it was the conception, which I had worked out on the streets of Paris, that was the star of the show, that and Wilde's text, for I had married the text to a language of movement and music that was as a casket in which to carry the gems of Wilde's text. Nobody else could have done it in this way. It was not created, as some shows are, by mutual improvisation and discussion plus the natural creative flow of mutual discovery. No, this play was 'dreamed up'. I wanted it to be spectacular and awesome in a way that nobody had ever seen.

For many weeks in Paris I had watched a group of dancers in front of the Centre Pompidou do a street act which impersonated slow-motion movie scenes. The way the action is slowed in a spaghetti Western and we see the villain bite the dust and watch the infinitely slow crumble and the flap of the limbs on the ground and the head bouncing up and down slowly until it finally comes to rest. The skills of these boys and girls were mesmeric – I could watch them for hours. Music accompanied their scenes and they worked to it and we saw every tiny moment amplified by their slow, careful movement.

I thought Eureka! I will do my production like this, only with words, and this slow style will enable the density of Wilde's ornate language to be examined and turned over in people's minds as you would turn over in your hand a rare piece of craftsmanship, a beautiful bracelet or ring, something that you found dazzling and admirable, like the skills of the maker combined with the natural beauty of the gem. So I wanted the skill of the director/jeweller to let us see the beauty of the words in all its aspects.

It was a difficult rehearsal period until the musician came in and then it all jelled together. In the end each person, musician, actor, producer felt *they* had created the show, such an effect did the play have on people, but it was only one conception that mattered and that was mine. It was my baby and I had given birth to it – aided by some wonderful and good-hearted people, but it had been gestating inside me for years.

When I have a success the producer of the company I do it for is always terribly pleased and so is everybody else, including me. In this case there was from the beginning a divided loyalty. I had agreed to do the production on one condition, that I would take it and own it and use it. The benefit all round was considerable. The Gate Theatre would have me and I would give birth to a show. I wasn't inclined to work for just four weeks' wages. This was happily agreed, but when the notices came in and Michael Colgan saw how successful the show was to become it was natural that he should want to push the originator to one side and bat for his actors. However, he kept to one side of the agreement, which was that I would take the major cities and he would take the smaller ones and odd festivals.

Well, he was offered a space at the Lyceum for the 1989 Edinburgh Festival, which is to all intents and purposes the same as playing it in London. I was well and truly pooped. I would have to compete with myself. I had made arrangements to take the show to the National Theatre, which coincidentally made a space for me, since Olivier's death had caused his widow Joan Plowright to drop out of the show she was rehearsing. So in effect it was Sir Larry who got me into the National Theatre to play Herod in *Salomé*. A more suitable début I could not imagine. (In fact I gained more from Larry Olivier dead than I get from most producers alive.) Now with mixed feelings would I welcome the appearance of *Salomé* at the Festival, since it would be compared to my new production at the National. Most directors don't face this problem, since they stick to what they know, which is directing, and most critics are spared the knowledge of the difficulties of playing and directing simultaneously. To the well-meaning little *Time Out* critic it looked as if naughty Berkoff had taken the bread out of the mouth of these sweet wee leprechauns. I felt I had no alternative but to call the legal dept.

So *Time Out*, which had been my ally in the old days of editors like John Ford, since he at least recognized that it was an uphill battle and we needed all the help we could get, is now a platform for puking twerps and is given from time to time to sub-Nazi purges like 'Shit Lists', in which my photo was proudly presented. I, who had almost single-handedly revitalized a large section of the British theatre and a lot of that without a huge grant to back up my flops. I, who had given them articles before going anywhere else with them and who had always created a good story for them, was on a shit list because I had dared to object to their ill-informed and vitriolic abuse. I dislike those who for the sake of puny personal prejudice, deny to my public what is in front of them. It is a form of censorship that I loathe and detest. Now I have written for the *Guardian* and other papers and journals and have grown an even bigger audience. So it all came out in the wash, but what is sad is that in olden days that mag was a bridge between me and my audience, which is a young audience. Still, people change and one day someone a little enlightened will surface at *Time Out*. After all, Robert Cushman didn't stay for ever at the *Observer*, nor James Fenton at *The Sunday Times*. With those two I was even considering the possibility of giving up working in this country.

The National Theatre – 1991

I'm getting ready to perform, or direct rather, but that seems like a performance, a version of Kafka's *The Trial*. It will be my second production at the National Theatre. I am deliberating about whether or not to repeat my performance of Titorelli, a crazy Italian painter whom I based on Salvador Dalí after I had the rare and distinct pleasure of seeing him on television. He was asked whom he liked as painters. He recounted some of the greats, including Velázquez, and was then asked whom he admired among living artists. He replied, 'No one.' It was a special kind of arrogance reserved for the great. When pressed to say well, who did he believe was the best of the bunch, or words to that effect, he replied, '*I am the greatest painterrrr in the entirrrre worrrld.*' Of course it was arrogant, but it was being true to himself, and to his spirit, and to the imp that fired his spirit. The imp is the child that all original artists keep within themselves. And why do they keep this imp, be they Chaplin, Dalí, Picasso or Modigliani, Lenny Bruce, Robin Williams, David Lynch or any others whose works have done more than merely defy convention? All artists feel they defy convention in some way. So what makes these people stand out? It is because the child within has not been conditioned. This child still lives within us and helps to release us from constraints of bourgeois constipation. So the child acts as a warning and sometimes screams within us for *release*. It cries for the things denied and will affect us throughout our lives. Joyful children are easy to see in the adult, and bitter, repressed, tight-arsed little farts also exist. We keep the child alive inside so that we can refer back to pre-adult life like pre-Ice Age. Before an age of curb and petty ambition, the thwarting of which is the source of drama. So Dalí kept the child that never died within him happy by claiming, as a child might, that he was the best. 'The greeeeatest painterrrr in the entire worrrrld.' So if I play Titorelli at the National this Feb. I will try and remember Dalí.

Tony Sher will be playing Joseph K. Tony I recall from my teaching period at the old Webber-Douglas School, when I directed him in a mid-term *Midsummer Night's Dream*. He played Puck and I remember him as a sensitive and creative young man. He is such an inventive actor that I am sure we will get on fine, since inventive people are always struggling and in that struggle they are open and responsive.

I have now started *The Trial* at the National and Tony Sher is in the swing of things. Some ideas of the past seem now to be wooden and I am struggling to redefine them. Some things feel 'choreographed' and 'worked out' . . . I have no confidence in the orchestra that once helped to unify the group and I am not sure I can find this living orchestra, but I will continue to try rather than always rely on electronic music.

The music should thrill. If I change some of the style it certainly feels more alive.

I worked out an arrest scene based on the actors acting the room and walls of the house, but then cut it. I think it now moves better and is less contrived, but Tony liked it and I feel mean taking away his pleasure. The cast seems less strong at the moment than my old team and I can see that the independence of my own actors made me highly selective and less prone to be satisfied.

As background to this the Gulf War rages and the TV tube continues to supply the world with talking heads and experts on the Middle East. Saddam Hussein represents the ultimate black devil who must be extirpated from the face of the earth. Tel Aviv has been struck by missiles but fortunately without the poison gases that add the flavouring. Saddam has obviously lost his nerve, since that would have provoked the most almighty response, but I don't think that was necessarily the reason he resisted the temptation. Also Saddam would be less than loved if a poison-gas missile accidentally fell on Jordan. So he had to test their efficiency first.

I go to the National with a heavy heart since I have to deal with a lot of people and put them into positions as in an army and I want this chorus to be something special and not feel wasted and unused. The war absurdly takes second place. I would like them to feel that they are a star unit. Some voice work with Patsy Rodenburg, the National's voice expert, might help. A composer is needed. I always remember Vladimir Rozienko's stunning classes when I did *The Trial* in Germany – afterwards we felt light in spirit and high for two days. I listened again to the German tape, which I am grateful to have kept, and learned that I have included a scene from the first Round House production which wasn't working in the least. In Germany I had made the rooming house of Joseph K.'s landlady into a gossiping nest of frustration. In London I had made it into a house of sexual depravity. My long-term memory was stronger.

The war continues and the TV shows the same limited shots so often that I am now an expert on Scuds and Sidewinders, chemical weapons and extended Scuds. In the future I can see two blokes in the pub discussing them as they used to discuss the relative value of Messerschmidts and Spitfires during the war with Hitler. In the end did we do anything? We dropped more bombs than on Hiroshima and yet the next day we see the city intact and cars driving along as if nothing had happened and news of this smart missile that was seen going along the street and pausing at the traffic light and then turning right until it found the right house. More jokes about that and then the telly shows you the same missile being shot off our boats – we see this so often that it must claim royalties.

Kafka

Still thinking about whether to do Titorelli. I tried running it by myself. It felt OK and I could find some improved methods of playing what is, after all, a cameo, but last night when I played the tapes from my most recent production in Düsseldorf to Mark Glentworth, the enormity of the whole thing struck me. I had tried to create an improved 'opera' at the same time and formed a chorus within a chorus. So I will have a great deal to do without concerning myself with myself. If I am free from that 'anxiety', I will be better able to relax and concentrate on the others. I won't be obsessed with my own costume and make-up, let alone my role. And will it fit in with Tony, who has to fit in with it? And do I need it? But another part of me says, 'Yes, go ahead, have a bit of fun with a role you created.'

It's as if some demon of perversity was nagging me, a screaming child pulling at my coat sleeve and howling, 'Let me get on that bloody stage,' while the adult says, 'Now, honest Berkoff, cease running after parts with thy heels; there will be a play to do after, when you can create your long-awaited production of *Kvetch*.' But the imp says, 'I don't care, I don't think of the future ifs and buts, I want it now.' It's terrible to have an imp inside you that can seldom be satisfied.

So Mark and I heard the fierce German language in which each word is ripped out of the vocal chords and the vocal music I created. At that time I felt very comfortable with it but now I think, will the cast accept this form of sound effects? Will they think it naff and resist it and will it be awkward to 'show' them? I never had that difficulty in Germany – I even did vocal classes and experimented before each day's rehearsal, something I am reluctant to do now. But I will create this vocal singing chorus so that when the guards mime opening K.'s drawers we will hear the sharp sound as if the drawer has life. When Miss Burstner moves around the room, the 'chorus' will amplify the sound of her underwear rubbing against her silk stockings. We will hear the hiss that K. hears in his head as he focuses his love-starved soul into his ears, which become sexual organs stretched to full alert, or like radar screens picking up each tiny sound from secret regions that K. has never discovered.

Poor Kafka desiring love of a sexual nature and putting it all into letters at the rate of two or three *a day*. And waiting impatiently, panting for the response to his missive, and tearing it open as if this was making love by delayed action. A caress is sent and responded to and he examines the response like a dog sniffing around a newly stained tree. He pulls her letter to shreds, analysing the pieces and imagining himself within it; already his feverish brain is coining new responses. He can't go on like this and so he writes *The Trial* instead. He is charged with the crime of not getting on the train and seeing his girlfriend who can barely keep up this *coitus interruptus* relationship and verbal masturbation and wants the real being in the flesh. Throughout *The Trial* K. is given opportunities which slip through his fingers and yet they seem to offer themselves to him the way women do in dreams. That easy, selfless, beautiful dream where your most ardent fantasies are presented to you but slip away.

K. is attractive because he is an accused man; he is guilty of unnamed crimes, but they give an aura of non-conformism to him. The priest says, 'You rely too much on the help of women.' How could Kafka write this? How could he not write that his sensitivity was so acute and his gentleness so extreme that he needed the constant touch and contact with women to ease his pain in the same way that Marat needed his bath? Somehow with the Germans I felt quite free, although I did not speak much of the language.

Günter Beelitz invited me to direct *The Trial* in his first season as artistic director in Düsseldorf in 1976. In Germany it is usual for the director of a company *not* to direct plays, but to direct the course of events and put together a policy and régime. He achieves this by travelling around the world, seeing interesting shows and meeting directors of various faiths and persuasions. He could not do this if he were in rehearsal and had to catch up with his office duties at lunchtime and never had the time or energy to see anyone else's work. That's why our theatres have a rather insular look. Günter Beelitz from Germany, Joe Papp from New York, Avital Mossinson from

Israel had come thousands of miles to see me and other productions which resulted in major cultural changes and infusion into their respective countries. Here they couldn't even make it to the Round House in Chalk Farm. So I could never get my work seen nor bring it to fruition in Britain and often would repeat my own successes. However, abroad saved me. Thank God 'there is a world elsewhere', as Coriolanus so shrewdly says. Of course once you do your own work you feel you are your own man and won't take direction as an actor; also you tend to think you don't need the work, since you are capable of doing your own thing. In my early days of staging my own plays, some of the notices were so good that I wasn't surprised not to get one offer after them. Nothing puts people off more than adulation.

I started rehearsal in Düsseldorf aided by my good friend Estella Shmidt, who was translator. I was given a pleasant apartment where, like Joseph K., the landlady would bring me my breakfast at 8 a.m. sharp. I will never forget it. A tray of steaming coffee plus bright yellow scrambled egg and a roll. Perfect. I'd walk to the theatre through the park and it was summer still, 26 August 1976. I had just got married to Shelley and was getting used to talking about 'my wife' again, which was a really lovely feeling at first and made me feel grown up. The park faces the Düsseldorf Schauspielhaus and you could have a good tomato soup with cream for lunch.

I'd go into the theatre and get in the lift to one of the many rehearsal rooms; the lift would open right on to the rehearsal floor. The actors would be waiting and behind a desk would be an army of authority. I was used to my own company with a single stage manager, but here we had the stage manager, translator, prompter, assistant stage manager and me. It was all too much, but we plodded on. We would do a little vocal warm-up first – I would try to make it explore some of the sounds that we might use for the play.

The actor playing K., Christian Sell, was excellent, and totally devoted to his role and the style of the play, but the others were not so dedicated and found the physical work a little tiring. They would keep forgetting the moves since, like many actors, they were used to remembering only their own lines and cues. If they forgot the moves they would lazily shout out to the stage manager, who was trying to take down all the moves, 'Where do I go now?' I wanted to shout, 'Why don't you write down your fucking moves?'

This was a feeling I had even more strongly years later in New York, when the textbound actors could hardly remember anything. To be fair, the young members of the cast of *Coriolanus* were champion. But the older ones were vague and when, on the third day's rehearsal of the same scene, the actors didn't remember where they were supposed to be, I felt sick. Then I was accused of being difficult or 'demanding' ... I find this reputation dogs me whenever I am working with incompetent people. And I have words about this as well. I inherited the incompetence of nincompoop directors for whom actors audition and work as if their bodies are something they use for sitting in restaurants. I inherited the whole lousy, lazy, stultified system of bad acting and bad physical discipline and creativity. They were, not to put too fine a point on it, shameful. And most of these actors had worked with major subsidized companies. If I had been fighting a war with them we would have been wiped out. The exceptions were some of the actors who had done some integrated work involving thinking with their bodies, like Barry Stanton, who had worked with Peter Brook, or the inventive Wolf Kahler, a German actor who worked with the Freehold and many others, of course, who had worked with various small groups at that time.

In Germany they were not much better but they made an effort and I think eventually got to like what we were doing. If I gently reprimanded the German girls for not remembering something they would burst into tears and run to the Intendant ... They were a rum lot. One guy would smoke every single time we broke for a few minutes. I said it wasn't doing his breathing any good to smoke so much and he was very offended and instead of the response you might have here of 'Oh well, it's a bad habit and I'll try to cut it out', he said, 'That is my business and you have no right, Herr Berkoff, to make any comment on my personal life.'

The rehearsal groaned on and the sounds got better and the women's chorus was very good indeed – they really threw themselves into it, with the vigour of women who have been under-employed for months. They all seemed to have a need for injections and breaks to visit doctors from time to time as if these German actors were all in various stages of physical and mental breakdown. One girl had to have all her teeth remodelled and then when she came back after a week off found that they didn't quite fit and had to have them done over again. At the first break at 2 p.m. (we would work from ten till two and then from six till nine or ten, a very good system), the actors would rush down to the canteen. They asked to be released on the dot of two, when the bell or announcement came through the loud-speaker. They explained that if they didn't get to the canteen on time the best dishes would be gone. So if it was even five minutes after the bell and you were in the middle of some breakthrough, it was down tools.

In the afternoon I'd walk around Düsseldorf and sit in one of the many coffee houses and drift. Sometimes, and mainly before work, I'd try to play some Mozart I had learned when I had a piano for those few months and had memorized two or three pieces. Well, a very strange thing was happening in my mind and that was that I was so confident about restaging *The Trial* in the German language that I felt a sense of guilt for my under-used brain! Of course it couldn't be true, but I kept feeling this sense of guilt unless I learned something painfully new; so I decided to relearn a piece of Mozart, an Étude in C. I practised every single day and hoped that by the time the production was on I would be able to play it perfectly, at least the first part before it got too complex. I would get into the studio at about 8 a.m. and bang away for a couple of hours, ordering the tiny black notes into my brain as if they were a magic and secret code that would bestow on me some immortal gratification to my longing. It also helped balance my mind and acted as a meditation.

I loved the small music room and was at peace. Afterwards, when I went to rehearsal, I had no sense of guilt any more and could proceed fluently. I have always needed an alternative 'job' when doing something slightly familiar. In Israel, while directing *Metamorphosis* in Hebrew, I wrote *The Murder of Jesus Christ*, which still hasn't seen the light of day. When touring *Hamlet* through Europe I kept a journal and made an analysis of the text each morning, which became my book *I Am Hamlet* ... It was as if I wanted to defuse the angst of responsibility by syphoning some of it off into other areas.

I did relearn the Mozart and thought of it as a kind of brain food. I believed that music was an example of real art and genius, the power to speak other languages, and without those attributes I was some kind of a slob. At times this complex reached acute proportions until I could feel positively uncomfortable with people who were gifted in even one other language. This sense of innate inferiority never left me and reinforced my desire to at least bring the level of the theatre I presented to the high standards required by musical accomplishment and the sheer intellectual drive needed to learn the language of notes. After my Mozartian bath I entered the room ready for work and was clear, having 'concentrated my brain' for the previous hour.

Eventually the play came together and I was braver with sound than I had ever been before, thanks to the lessons with my voice teacher in London, Vladimir Rozienko. I was astounded at what could be done with the voice, how it affected the scene and how the music of the actors united the chorus. They didn't have to sit around while the tape or the live musicians did everything for them. Here they were aware that the voice was capable of other things than merely being the servant of the writer, ennobling and illuminating as this may be. It can also be an instrument of fear, passion, irony, ecstasy, tension and music itself. We could use all these voice-boxes and make them expressive. How, is another matter; I was not a musician and could only work within the limited sphere I had learned, but even so it was sufficient to enable me to create a text and almost a choral work.

I had the actors express what would usually be conveyed by sounds that tell the audience what to feel, the way film music does. I wanted to avoid that use of music, and the need for actors to sit in dressing rooms smoking and playing Scrabble while waiting for their entrances. Or worse still, standing in the canteen drinking schnapps or pints of bitter. When actors are off stage it is not free time, it is a kind of dead time when they can neither relax nor enjoy their peace, unless they are the star playing Hamlet, when it might be sheer joy to have those moments off stage. But when you come back on stage it feels distinctly strange. Years earlier in *The Amorous Prawn*, I used to watch Stanley Baxter from my perch in the stage management corner. He would joke and fool about just before he entered; a split second before his cue he would put his cigarette out and as soon as he came off would light another one up. But he was used to it and was an old trouper even then.

So these players in *The Trial* were on stage for the whole event and felt better for it. While it is not a rule that actors should be on stage I find it generally better. The last time I did a 'group' piece was *Coriolanus* in New York, when I found it was preferable to let them sit it out in the Green Room and eventually disposed of the 'chorus' method. I couldn't see Irene Worth or Chris Walken sitting through the whole play on the stage, although I did see Irene do this very thing in a version of *Oedipus* by Ted Hughes.

The Trial opened and was generally acclaimed by the press throughout Germany. I had a good time and my isolation came to an end when Shelley came over to see the play. When it finished I took a train to Amsterdam for a couple of days' break before returning to London. I think I had a mini-breakdown, because I suddenly became utterly obsessed about music again and as I couldn't drag a piano with me everywhere, nor would there always be one handy, I bought a guitar and ruined my fingers trying to learn to play the monster until I threw it out!! I think at the completion of a project you may not have perceived as being a strain to your reserves, something happens to rush into the gap. It was a syndrome I was going to see more and more of.

National Theatre – First Time – 1977

When I was a guest director at the National Theatre in 1977 with my own team of actors I performed three plays in as many weeks and Sheridan Morley wrote a rather glowing profile of me in *The Sunday Times*. He flatteringly, but not quite accurately, stated that I was the only playwright in history to have three plays running at the National at the same time. Technically it was true, but the plays had been evolved over the past eight years and were hardly commissioned, even by the National. I had merely gone in with my repertoire at the invitation of Peter Hall, who needed to find groups to fill three auditoria. Ken Campbell opened it up and we followed; later we would somehow fit in when there was a gap. Michael Halifax would come around with a big book of dates and say, 'What about Tuesday week for three days?' and you'd be expected to find another show from your repertoire to go in. I found that challenging and exciting. We filled the theatre each time and yet were never asked back when the gaps closed up. Since we did so well and had filled a hole and were a good plug I had difficulty reconciling myself to the fact that year after year passed and when my agent rang them I was just at that moment 'on their lips', as if to say belt up and put a sock in it or you'll get nowhere. It was always 'just thinking about you' or 'on their lips'. I liked that one. We had been good and not even got drunk, as many of their stalwart players were in the habit of doing.

Anyway, there I was in full colour in *The Sunday Times*, being heralded as the phenomenon of the National Theatre with three plays in one season. *East*, *The Fall of the House of Usher* and *Metamorphosis*. *Wow!!* And whether this pissed off the National's administrator I don't know, but it was the last time I was to work there for thirteen years!

Back to the Future

I am still deliberating about whether to act in *The Trial* or not. Seventeen years ago at the Round House I played Titorelli and the Narrator. I sat on the side of the stage and made appropriate comments, headlining certain scenes; sometimes before my scene I would get up quietly, go backstage, put on my little moustache and creep back on. I had a great deal of fun playing it, although it might have gone on a tad too long. I mean, it's the end of the play when I come on and it's time for a change of pace and a little comic interjection. Now seventeen years later I feel like a sentimental revisit, but at the National a successful play is kept in the repertoire, so I would either go on and on playing it or leave to do a full-length part. If I go in it's a bit of an ego trip and a chance to display my wares and even bring the show to a bit of a halt, but then someone else will eventually have to take over, with the attendant hassle of programme changes and expectancy of the public. If I give the role to one of the under-used actors he has a great cameo and I take off to play *Kvetch* at long last. That has to make sense! But a part of me wants to do it and create a strange Italian, half sane, half a fantasy of Kafka. The decision is becoming clearer. Then again, I am not doing it with Bill Stuart, with whom I had such fun before and could more or less improvise the scene; I am doing it, or would be, with Tony Sher and I have no idea how he would respond to my 'performance'. Also by making an entrance at the end I would be making some kind of 'statement' . . . Oh, here comes Berkoff type of thing. No, it seems the clean answer is to *let it go*. (But I didn't.)

Politics in the Theatre – *Sink the Belgrano!*, 1986

As I tread the long corridors of the National Theatre in 1991, where I am grateful to have an opportunity to restage *The Trial*, I feel a dullness in the ranks of actors. There are virtually no exotic women or great beauties such as I saw in the Munich theatre a few weeks ago when I did a workshop. I saw three women on stage who looked like movie starlets and acted like viragos. Is theatre a kind of penance or is it becoming a platform for the serious-minded and monastic, purveying only the most weighty themes, whose gravity must reassure us that we are not giving in to too much sensuality or playfulness? Must we always have plays about pregnant mums dealing with their emerging feminism? Good quality plays with a good porridgy feel to them, since we are all becoming so drearily politicized that I almost feel the Thought Police might be watching in case, God forbid, the word 'art' is used. No, we have to show the moral decline of Thatcherism! Of course this can be done with great wit, verve or danger, but inevitably it will redound with the dull, clanging syllables of worthiness.

I recall two esteemed directors, one from the Royal Court, one from the RSC, bleating about the dearth of plays that expressed the malaise of the Thatcher years. They both felt that writers could not address issues that were contemporary, that they needed time for reflection. They lamented the absence of any plays that really dealt with the theme head-on and wondered why. I could have told them. They wouldn't know it if they were hit on the head with one, since their understanding of theatre is worthy but representational.

I sent both these companies my play which dealt with the Falklands conflict. *Sink the Belgrano!* was written in verse and even by my modest standard was one of the best things I have done. Both companies hardly raised an eyebrow and rejected it. The Court because it was out of date, having been written a mere four years after the event; the RSC just sent it back. Eventually Chris Bond produced it with great enthusiasm at the new Half Moon and it played to packed houses for six weeks. Thank you, Chris! This encouraged us to transfer to the Mermaid where it was butchered by those few members of the press who did not ignore it altogether. That such a play could be ignored struck me as very odd indeed, since it was in every sense an anti-war play, not merely a Thatcher-knocker. I stand by it and will always do so. I carefully researched every single fact and concluded that a conspiracy of some kind could have taken place. I created a *mise en scène* using the chaps in the submarine as a chorus. It was a very moving piece of theatre, as the many letters I have received over the years have testified, but even that is not enough. The important thing is that the form and nature of my piece was unacceptable. If it had been written like a dreary documentary with real politicians it might have had some chance. I took great exception to the torpid lie that there were hardly any plays dealing with the Thatcher years, when all my plays dealt with was those very years. *Greek, Decadence, Sink the Belgrano!*

Anyway, in the end I produce my own plays, since if I waited for approval none of my works would exist in print today. Each play of mine was rejected by all and sundry, which is why I started to produce myself.* This is healthier anyway and allows you freedom. It also forced me to learn my craft. Now for the first time I have written a play for TV and of course every single turkey has rejected it and it's like starting all over again. Yet I think it's the funniest play I have written and a caustic satire on the people who love to bask in the limelight of the world's adoring gaze. They are like little balloons of self-importance, myself included, since there are aspects of me that are self-important and a little craven, but I had no hesitation in lampooning my own miserable ego. The play is perhaps a satire of the nineties and fits TV like a glove. Even if the viewers were not to recognize the individuals it would not matter a jot. But no luck. I could take a play like *East* to Dan Crawford at the King's Head, do it on a shoestring and work it up until some producer woke up enough to put up at least some dough, but how can I do this on TV? So I am in the same position and the climate hasn't changed.

Back to the National – 1991

I'm now into the fourth week of rehearsal for *The Trial*. I went ahead and did Titorelli. For the first time I sweated off buckets of fear, since it's a strange thing to hear yourself acting again, after some years of single-mindedly directing and revealing yourself through the

* *West*, the exception, was produced by Ian Albery at the Donmar.

intermediary of your concept. Now I had to go on and 'perform' . . .
Tony Sher encouraged me to do it during rehearsals rather than top
and tail the scene and go on to the next. I did it one afternoon and it
started to come together: I was very grateful to him for pushing me
in, so to speak. Now the snows are here and we've taken a couple of
days off.

As usual I get there a trifle early and now we are into polishing and
shaping. The show is looking very good and Tony Sher is a typical
Joseph K. He has a firm grip on the character and will, I know, be
excellent in the role. He doesn't waver but goes after his game like a
hunter, relentless. When he loses the scent he'll explore another field,
but he won't hesitate. He goes on trampling through the fields until
he finds the scent again. I know when he's got it.

So far I am getting a small whiff of it again. It's right that it should
be at the National Theatre, even if I doubted so at first, since it
should belong to the British public and not be concerned about box
office or reviews. Here at the National we are above and beyond
reviews. People just come if they want to see the subject since the
very fact that it is there at all implies some worth! The cast have
come together quite well, though the play lacks some of the dangerous eccentricity of the 1974 version at the Round House.

The Gulf War rages on and everyone opines on the state of things –
dependent on the status-fix you can predict the resultant expectora-
tions. The Left clan with a clutch of plays and worthiness bedded
within will naturally see everything as an American imperialist plot.
When you carry that kind of baggage you are forced to lean in certain directions, which gives everything you see the same slant. I think
the war is evil and perpetrated by an evil man and that's as far as my
sophistication takes me. But I do question why we should, and why
anyone should, supply arms to weird, evil and despotic régimes. If we
enjoy the fruits of the murder trade then we must expect to get our
fingers burnt. It is a terrible price to pay in that human beings are
sacrificed like so many pawns by the madman of Iraq and while
he cares not a fig for human life or any life, the West, which has
politically and culturally democratized itself enough to value the
individual, now professes an awesome respect for human life, even if
it's a sentimental one at times. However, America's real attitude to
human life is seen in the wholesale slaughter of its population

each year through unbridled gun buying, which loses far more people than are likely to be killed in the Gulf War, but that seems to them to be acceptable. Twenty thousand people will die by the hand-gun in one year! An extraordinary double standard seems to be at work here. Poor Saddam is waiting for a ground war, getting bored out of his mind, but hoping that when this confrontation takes place he can show his mettle. He sits unwashed and stewing in his bunker, reminiscent of Hitler's last days.

It's a freezing day on 14 February, and we have another week to go with the show in good shape. I can predict the critics. Since Kafka is a reality slightly tilted, the production goes right over the top. What Kafka hints at, Berkoff 'bludgeons you with'. They will believe that the cold grey world of Kafka should be reflected in the cold grey world of the stage. Reality and conformism to reflect the theme of the book. But underneath there is in the man a heightened reality and the turmoil of K.'s inner life is what I show and anyway it is fun. They would probably praise Andrzej Wajda's version I saw all those years ago in Vienna with a cast of seventy.

Sher seems to be creating a real Joseph K., making him pompous, self-important and a touch humourless. I think he brings the right qualities to it and will get even better, but must not treat it all too seriously or he will be too Kafkaesque. The cast are better now and the chorus work, in fact the meat of the show is excellent and more inventive than ever. I think Sher was used to the method of working across the water where the star is given the golden gloves treatment. I suppose this is unavoidable in institutions where the directors are tired out and let the stars dictate the mood of the piece. However, he adapts to my style, is an excellent mime and learns fast.

I will be glad when the rehearsal period is over. We keep finding ways of refining and that is very good. Sometimes you can't just sit there and give, give, give and not get much in return except the re-run. After a while you feel like a caretaker and that is not a feeling I like. I wish to go back to directing and acting leads again, so that I feel the play within me and do not have to watch others take my work.

Last night, 2 March 1991, we did two shows of *The Trial* and each one felt good. For once Titorelli was on top of things. So now, when it works, I feel on top of the world. I only have to be on for twelve minutes, but those twelve minutes leave me in a state of exhaustion as if I had sprinted a mile. The show looks wonderful from the front and each scene is now a perfect miniature and very, very clear. This work gives me great satisfaction in that I am not so responsible for the acting, but have enough to keep me on my toes, and at the same time can shape and watch another actor take the helm without feeling left out.

All the characters seem to work and each has something particular. Alan Perrin is perfect as the guard, along with his compatriot Michael Jenn, and the arrest scene now chills in the right way. It's never been better and the change in each case from the Round House version is towards refinement. I like the fact that the chorus are now K.'s 'room' and are thus involved; the scene has greater brio as a result. Tony welcomes the changes just as much as he fought for the original version in the 'old days' of rehearsal, so at least, like me, he can change his mind and go from one extreme to another. I think this is a sign of talent, since it means that what you found in the beginning was merely a structure until you replaced it with something better.

The bank scene is far stronger: I have put K.'s opening speeches in it rather than at the front, where they were a kind of abstract plea of pain. Now the pain belongs to the bank as he works. Imogen Claire plays Mrs Grubach perfectly, with a sharp malice. She dances well and that scene has a nice cold edge. The lodgers as waxworks is new and I love to see their leering faces frozen as K. walks through the house. Myriam Cyr is a real find. She presents her words with the precision of a dancer. This scene is obviously better than it was before. Tony plays it also with elegant timing, since he seems to sense he is with a clever cookie. It's a good scene played by two deft artists both determined to mine the scene for all it's worth. Joseph K. is like a boxer fighting fifteen rounds, but each round is with someone different so he can't get too bored. He has to deal with madness at every turn and rarely gets back to someone he's met before. This gives the whole cast bar two an intense scene with him, so everyone feels they are the stars for five or ten minutes of the play, including me.

The nice thing about being at the National is having someone to create things like wigs and a tailor called Dave from the East End to measure me up for my costume. The wig for Titorelli is marvellous and has helped me enormously. I nearly cut it the first or second day because its long hair got in my mouth, but I had to learn to use it like a mask and let it grow around me. I glue some wisps around my skull so now it doesn't get in my mouth. I am sinking into the role and feel some pride that my old bones can repeat a part I first did nearly twenty years ago. Now I define it more and make the points clearer. Having Tony Sher makes me think the text out, since I have to convince him – he is a person who needs convincing and smells out when it doesn't work. This caused a bit of tension at the beginning, but now we each seem to have made a bridge from his side to mine and some of the play has been improved by his suggestions. Particularly the length. I tend to think because I love it so will everyone, but everyone isn't so devoted and now we have trimmed and streamlined much of it. Tony is a dedicated worker and takes his work seriously, but he should have fun with it more as the play runs. At the moment he looks like the only sane person in the play and plays this off very well with the other characters.

Paul Benthal is another discovery. He does both a funny bailiff and a very moving priest. His chorus work is very good, too. Tony absorbs our madness without flinching and I think it's rather bizarre that I, who have in my own world nurtured, accidentally or wilfully, my own needs and style, should, near the end of that working life, link up with someone who has for the last twenty years been nurtured on the legitimate side. I rather like this ultimate marriage at the end of twenty years. I carry in my mind the memory of Tony as Puck at the Webber-Douglas in the hot summer of 1970, twenty-one years ago. He hasn't changed so much.

I have the same dressing room as I had for *Salomé* and the same dresser, Ralph. After a while you begin to develop an affection for the National as you might for the Garrick. It's a club and everybody is intensely proud of that fact and wishes it to be the flagship of British theatre, beyond politics, scandal, begging bowls. It manages its finances well, or seems to.

Much of the second half of the first act follows the pre-arranged plot, except that Myriam now speaks the ship's song instead of singing it and it is clearer. Some of the images and ideas come from my original show and some of the vocal structures come from the German production in Düsseldorf. Perrin again delivers a superb cameo as the smart man and the act concludes well with a neat lighting effect as K. disappears into the distance.

The second act starts as usual with Leni and K., but here the great difference is that I have cut the chorus out completely from one of the funniest scenes where they were at their most surreal. So I have sacrificed some of the most ludicrously outrageous slapstick in exchange for a three-handed scene. I knew that Matthew Scurfield could handle the Huld lawyer scene himself and it would allow him to be as grotesque as he wished with no help from the chorus. I was uncertain for a while, but I had tears running down my face every time Matthew did the scene with Tony and Teddy Kempner as Block, and so that was my litmus test. Even up to the first night, until Matthew got into it, I worried lest it be perceived as mere vulgar slapstick and not a Daumier-like satire on the feebleness and rottenness of the legal procedure as defined by Kafka. I wondered whether to bring the chorus back into the scene but waited, since I thought it might demoralize the actor, implying it would work better with more people. However, we waited and it grew and now it is one of the funniest scenes in Christendom. The topping is putting the chair that Huld cannot get into on top of his bum while he lies spread-eagled on the floor. Then he is hoisted up. Tony did this during rehearsal and it is such a piece of silliness it brings the house down.

Matthew Scurfield has replaced Barry Stanton, who did the part in the first full-scale production, and brings to the role all the demonic energy and playfulness that he might otherwise let out on society. Here his energies are given free rein, but I suppose that is true of all of us. He looks and sounds like a King Ubu crossed with Gargantua. It is a *tour de force* for Matthew and I am glad to have been part of its conception.

I watch the first act from the director's box, which lets me observe in secret, and I see the audience coming in in a state of expectancy. The curtain goes up like an eyelid of steel, parting up and down, and of course I had to seize on this 'safety curtain' and project 'THE TRIAL' in huge letters on the front; the title then slides on to the back screen in true epic fashion. I watch with intense pleasure as the 'eye' parts and I see the sitting figures surrounding the standing figure of Joseph K., who looks as if he is already being tried by a heavenly court. It's the most stunning beginning I have ever devised and knocks out the old one, although that was good in its time.

In the interval I go back and slowly make up. I put my Dalí wig on and generally watch a bit from the wings, especially the Huld scene which has me in fits every night. Then I feel my pulse start to race as I get nearer my scene. The first few nights I thought I might have a heart attack on stage but I grow braver and reach the core which is in the speaking of the text. Patsy Rodenburg gives the company voice, but most importantly for me she is a good ear. She suggests to me that Titorelli's voice should be more 'inventive', 'as inventive as the movement', and her advice I have taken to heart.

At the end of my scene I come off the stage sweating buckets but truly relieved and calm, as I have been through my ordeal once more and can put it behind me until the next time. I wait for the end from the wings and watch Tony struggle against the rope and lean right into it. The two guards lift one leg as if in effort and bring the feet crashing down as they execute him. At this point, as at many other moments in the play, there is complete and utter silence, such as I have rarely experienced. Standing in the wings you can hardly believe that there are nearly one thousand people breathing and living out there in the audience.

Lights go out slowly and there is quiet, since the audience are not quite sure; after that terrifying death and that awful cry for help from Tony, which is terribly moving, no one wishes to break the silence. The lights come on and Tony turns upstage to welcome the cast for the curtain. Cheers ring out as he takes his solo call. He welcomes me for my little solo. The audience don't all know that I directed it but clap politely for my performance as Titorelli . . . I am exalted and in a state akin to grace if my little scene has gone well, even though I know that the whole show is more important and is of course my concept. I chose a very good cast and Tony's sanity and clarity, his simple small chap who is lost in this welter of crazy logic, is intense and moving. He has succeeded admirably and I feel joy that the mammoth undertaking is over. He has been on the stage for two and a half hours.

The night before I had again seen, on dreary old BBC Screen Two, four actors in two pairs screwing their hearts out in such a prudish, phoney way that my contempt for actors reached new heights. Perhaps having to see this invaded my dreams in the form of an actor baring himself and then simulating the most sacred and personal act in the human experience. The curse of naturalism. Baudelaire talks of distortion as the means by which you perceive something and not this blatant reproduction. I think of how *Salomé*, which is so magical and enchanting, is spurned by all these lazy-minded gits in TV who have no feeling whatsoever for what is dramatic or vital and nor for what might be rare. When would anyone have the chance to see such a play?

For six shows Titorelli left me exhausted and puffing during the twelve minutes, but on Saturday I was exalted and felt right in it, and also on Thursday when my ladyfriend, Clara, came. So perhaps now I have the measure of it more and should have expected a little torture in the beginning. I must also not be afraid of changing something to make it clearer. It's my little number, like coming on and doing a comedy routine, but I must confess I do it better if I have exercised or skipped on the afternoon of the performance. Skipping seems to pour endorphins into my system; it puts me in a better mood and makes me more able to cope with the stress of going on.

The Gulf War is over but the horror of all those deaths leaves the worst possible taste in one's mouth. On German TV last night was a programme on napalm casualties which should be compulsory viewing throughout the world. Limbs being sawn off. How like a butcher's shop it looked. Young children burned and roasted. Mandatory viewing.

My Trial – 18 March 1991

First of all this is a wonderful typewriter and all that electronic shit can go to hell! *The Trial* has been on since 23 February 1991 and today it's 18 March and so it's been almost a month. We all enjoy it enormously and are getting full houses and ovations and cheers each night. Last week escaped to Madeira since my partner and I both wanted a rest and love to swim in March while the world is freezing in damp old England. We had a lovely time there, but my mind was thrashing about this tiny weeny problem, whether to say one word or another – it's one of my obsessions that I could well do without, since no matter what you say there is always a way of saying it to make the sense you want. Some actors never check the text once the play is on and eventually tiny changes will take place and little words are left out or 'have to be' is said instead of 'must', which is a much stronger word. The cumulative result of this is that in places the impact is softened, but on the other hand it's organic and flowing. If one night you return to your text and see that you have said 'really innocent' instead of 'completely innocent' you will worry all the next day about one word, that's if you are an obsessive like myself. You might just say to yourself, 'Oh well, it works fine as "really" and I put all the emphasis as if I was saying *really* innocent.' But the other word started to be like a sweet I was denied and took on the hues of the forbidden fruit. Suddenly 'completely' seemed a perfect, definitive word and summed up the whole state of Joseph K.: he was not just innocent or really innocent in the way of really and truly innocent but he was *completely* innocent! There is no way to go beyond being complete, that's it, final and utterly.

And so I thought about this in Madeira, where I had gone for a rest. I tested it out. The difference in the performance would be the weight of a hair and yet it seemed to be the linch-pin, as these things always do when you become obsessed. I like 'really' because I can repeat the word and make the Italian painter say 'rrrrrrrrrreally innocent' like an exaggerated Dalí, whereas with 'completely' I wouldn't have the same licence unless I said, 'completellelli', which deforms the meaning more than 'rrrrrrrreally'. So I practised the different variants. My method was to try it out and what suddenly grabbed me or *felt* good or seemed to catch my nerve or send a spark to my spirit would be the one. So as I sat in some fish restaurant in Madeira hearing the roaring of the waves and feeling the burnished sun on my neck, I would smile at the huge fish on my plate and sip the sangría and enthuse on the view and the amazing miracle of life; would marvel that last year the sun had set at exactly the same point on the horizon and how miraculous was the celestial engineering of the universe that the world could traverse the great acres of space and return to its original spot where the sun set at exactly the same point. But at the back of my mind was a little tape going 'completellelli or rrrrrrreally'.

I don't know what guilt drives you to make yourself into a whipping boy for every 'mistake' you think you have made, since we are not computers and a little adaptation of the text, especially if it is modern and not in verse, should not be a crime. In each play, if 1 per cent of the text is slightly paraphrased is that so important and if you reach 99 per cent accuracy isn't that enough? You will never achieve 100 per cent and if you do and methodically check your text each night before you go on you will then find problems with your gestures or 'business' . . . One has to, as my old actor colleague Matthew Scurfield says, 'live in the now' or one truly perishes in a welter of self-doubt. The problem is two-fold: firstly, since I am the director I have no father to turn to and must resort to asking questions of myself, but that myself might be in the nervous quandary of the actor and be unable to make the switch to the guise of director. Or perhaps this is what keeps me on my toes and has me tuned up. A little 'tweaking', as my dresser at the National Theatre says euphemistically before I go on. I have even asked him if I should try something different tonight, as if I need someone to *tell* me. I scour the world for advice and put it all in my pocket. Each phone call will have me debating the merits of the two choices . . . Oh by the way, which do you think sounds better, and I go through this little pantomime of choices. It must seem as if I have really lost my marbles, but I know I haven't. I have just got overtuned in some places.

The second part of the problem is that since the National has gaps of five days when you don't play, which can be completely (aaah! that word) marvellous, any problem that has arisen the night before may have to wait five days or even two weeks to resolve. After several weeks of performing, you have usually ironed the problems out, since I regard the performances as rehearsals and it is not unusual for me to try different things each night – I like the challenge of keeping something loose in the performance. As if to say, 'I don't need to make it cast iron since I am not afraid. I can keep my guard down so that I may improvise and "play"', since this is what I love about acting, the possibility of change, even each night. But in *The Trial*, since I have been working with Tony Sher, I have been keeping to a format which in many ways works better for the sense of the piece and for the comprehension of the audience, since he is very sharp and accurate. On the other hand he is fast to adapt to any changes that I make and I suspect would give me a good run for my money. He is also a quick improviser, as witness the send-up he does of me as Titorelli when I ask him to play me in order to demonstrate Titorelli's 'prestige' in the eyes of the great judge.

So while for a few nights I was actually happy, on the last night before the five-day break I chanced to check some text and, oh fatal, I was thrown into the abyss where self-doubt lay. Even as I took the curtain call on that night and heard the cheers I was saying to myself, 'Comple . . .' So now I don't look at the text, or not so much.

Last Saturday I had another one of those horrors and decided to ignore the bastard. That can work sometimes if I tell myself I have the strength to resist, since in the end it's not really about the word, it's about how weak I am. Of course, if it were a Pinter play I know accuracy is the rule, and naturally for Shakespeare or even one of mine, although there are grounds for minor changes! So I sweated on it and decided not to be a victim any more, but when it came round to the bit where the word was left out I felt like a coward. That is also how it 'gets' you. It attacks you where you are vulnerable and that is my 'are you a coward' syndrome. In the evening I could stand it no longer and put the missing word back in. I even made something of it and used it as a wedge between the two arguments and it seemed to work. I returned to my dressing room satisfied for a change and had a good dinner afterwards. Perhaps these tiny things are what keeps the piece together and perhaps if you didn't have something specific to focus on you might be overcome with a strange fear of the whole thing. So you give yourself a tiny morsel with which to become obsessed so that you can distract yourself from the idea of coming on at 10 p.m. and doing your little twelve-minute scene.

The reviews on the whole were scathing, as if I had trodden on some collective British corn. A howl of pain could be heard and in that howl not a great deal of coherence. I believe that critics are unused to seeing much that challenges the *status quo* and that they are so taken aback by unfamiliar techniques that they believe they have no place on stage. The book of *The Trial* lends itself to figuration mime whereby the actors become all the instruments of K.'s life – it is a technique that I have explored too little in the theatre and would really like to take to its limits. Why should not a human being be a table, a blouse on a window, a sink and running water? I think it works very well. Not only that, but audiences respond to it. When K. watches Miss Bürstner undress, the other actors become the mirrors and her clothes. This could never be done without mime training and skill to invent. Mime isn't just there to be a flight of stairs, but to suggest and give to the audience a magic way of presenting certain facts which are in the book but would be impossible to translate on to a stage in a naturalistic way.

So when the critics complain that it is more Berkoff than Kafka, I throw up my arms in despair, since if it were not, I would have let down the book. I have to recreate through my own form, which is the theatre so that you are watching a *play* and not a boring rendering of a classic where all the 'dialogue' has been filleted out and shoved like cardboard into the actors' mouths. Here at least I have tried to keep the complexity of the book and its swift change of locale, and again it is through devising the technical means that one is able to convey pure, unadulterated quaffs of Kafka. I am sure that his own febrile imagination would have responded well to it. I have kept most of the book's characters and their multitudinous environments and even tried to take us into the nightmares of Joseph K. I feel that had I been duller or milder or less successful or used a big set, I would have been greeted with less calumny.

However, I am one of those who can fly on one good word and we have had more than a few of them to keep us going. I need far less than unanimous support to survive. Give me two out of ten and I am in with a good chance, since word of mouth is, fortunately, very effective. I have been blessed with a good team of actors and people generally believe they are going to get not only value for money but something original. With two or three good critical souls we are packed out. Wonderful, and I hope it continues. The *Sunday Times* critic had the impertinence to question what we were even doing at the National Theatre. The only answer I can give is ask the nearly one thousand people who turned up each night. They might be able to explain to the dullard!

In the end I expect that the theatre is only as good or challenging as it's allowed to be and that eventually critical myopia will reduce the possibility of entering a new world. What is left will be the dross representing safe and well-guarded areas of what we call realism. Those who plough this region year in and year out will be successful and only the odd maverick will creep in. Subsidy is the only hope against the philistine. In the same way as the National Health Service safeguards the well-being of the population and gives all human life dignity, albeit chipped away by Thatcherism, so subsidy gives the artist, writer, director and actor some protection against the crass market minds of dull critical response. We can survive and the world will be a better place for it. Human achievements and discoveries are traditionally condemned by the pleb, who is well pleased with things as they are – a little change here and there, but not much. We are a bone-headed race that fears change and fears also the representation of ideas in different forms. Not that I am necessarily claiming that I am such an original, but the hostility aroused by *The Trial* was beyond criticism; it reached the bounds of idiocy!

In New York we would have died on the first night or two, but at least here we are in civilized Europe, though not for much longer if we emulate our unfortunate American cousins. They must hang their heads in shame as one play after another hits the deck and all must sit and wait for the one review like poor beggars hoping for a hand-out. When I saw the great Roger Stevens, producer of *West Side Story* and my producer for *Metamorphosis* on Broadway with Barysh-nikov (for which experience I must thank Roman Polanski since he persuaded him to do it), wait for the *New York Times* to trash a work that had received only praise in every nation on earth and in which Mischa played so well, then I could only hang *my* head in shame as well and feel contaminated by the loathsome experience. I feel contempt and pity for a city bereft of theatre, where no writers write except in tiny caverns, where they sit and do readings for backers and beg, scrape and whinge, and where *Nunsense* can run in its grimy little theatre for years. I walked into that theatre one day to audition and could barely stay in the atmosphere of that endless run with its set worn-out and frayed, and the grime of the building where no new life emerges as from a fruitful womb, which is what a theatre should be. But this monster, dead and repeating its loathsome message year after year, is the kind of hell that American 'freedom' espouses.

The Trial might have died on the first night in New York, but it did not in London, where a few good allies cheered the production. We played to capacity each night since the British are a bunch of individuals and demand more than one or two daily papers. If we only had *The Times* and two tabloids, imagine what the nation would have come to. We would have died.

So the National made room for us and we were truly thankful but after all it was my money, as a tax-payer, so who am I thanking? I paid for it and as a practitioner in the arts I am given a 'go' . . . Our season was to have been extended, but is now not to be, but at least in our fifty performances we might reach 30,000 people, which ain't too bad.

Sometimes I wait in the canteen after the show has begun and have a coffee and chat to the fine actor Terence Rigby, who has to walk round with a tail sticking out of his arse for his performance as a horse in *The Wind in the Willows*. I'd hate to have a tail sticking out of my arse!

The audience cheers us each night and Tony Sher gets a good ovation, but probably it's time to move on from the protective arm of the National. Still, what a relief not to have to count the money in the box office or even care what the critics say, since our advance was colossal and the reviews have only dented it. But I am glad that we live in a nation that believes what is worth having is also worth protecting.

At the time of writing the Kurds are being slaughtered by superior numbers and arms and nobody wants to interfere because it's not in the charter! When I think of what scum politicians are I am glad I am not sitting in Parliament which, when I hear it on my car radio, sounds like a bunch of pigs. When anybody with whom they disagree speaks they all shout abuse and insults like the lowest form of life; the dregs of an East End school would allow their mates to get their words out. I find it quite unbelievable that they conduct their business in this way and I am grateful to the radio and TV for allowing me to eavesdrop on how the nation's affairs are conducted by this rabble. So it does not surprise me when some peanut-minded Tory Foreign Minister parrots the same old clichés about not interfering with bloody murder – genocide more like – intolerable suffering inflicted by a man whom we have just fought and defeated. Saddam is then allowed to go and slay his minorities while Bush, mouthing one monstrous cliché after another, like the bits of paper you get in Chinese cookies, plays golf and fishes. To us, me, anybody, this is beyond all belief and I shall never again have any reason to have faith in the politics of this age, since it is a morally worthless and gutless one. Gutless most of all. Evil in its self-centredness.

Finale

My mind goes back over the swirling years and the decades. The mists part and reveal a new world in the sixties, when my hair was dark brown and abundant and I was ever seeking the roles that would let me show my bird of paradise, but always thwarted, and always so happy and satisfied to get a job. And what were the jobs? *Not in the Book*, etc. But I was so happy to be employed. If I may say so, a touch immodestly, a young actor today can at least break his teeth on a Berkoff and get his mouth round some gritty text; he can put on my plays at the Edinburgh Festival and revel in them, but what did I have? Agatha Christie and *Write me a Murder*. What idealism can this possibly fire, what feeding of the very heart that gives us our blood flow? Sure, we need to act and we can be brilliant in *The Unexpected Guest*, but you can't spend the rest of your life being an ice skater showing off your marvellous arabesques. Eventually there must be something that *moves you*! There must be something of what made you want to be an actor in the first place.

You start with the desire to perform as the desire to eat, but then you develop taste, judgement, feeling and know what you respond to. You have favourites that you recite around the kitchen and whose words you never tire of. I did. I loved Hamlet for years and eventually played it; I also loved the role of Herod in *Salomé* but loved the play too and its outpourings of absurdly exotic delights. I like the music in the language, its feast, its glorious colours. I loved Cyrano, but never played it. And of course I write my own parts and they're the best feast of all, but for years I had to be happy with crap.

The young actor today wants to identify himself with his culture and environment and seeks inspiration to show his power and his daring. An actor wants to show off, to strut his stuff. To be awesome, stunning and reveal his gift. Who allows him this? I read Irving Wardle's yearly round-up of the year's best writers, leaving me out, of course, they all do and I am not only used to this but really don't mind. The distinguished critic who has more than once honoured me mentioned three writers he tipped or admired as in some way holding the flag. Let them be anonymous, A, B and C. I have no quarrel with his choice. He had a fair opinion of three successful writers. They deserve their dues and there is a place for all of us, even me. I hope. Just sometimes.

Now let me look at this objectively, as if I were someone else. I ask why I am not included? Is it because I'm also an actor and director and we mustn't be seen to be too busy must we, eh? Who cares, I always say to myself, but some part of me weeps inside, even if the outside is scarred and weathered like old leather. I look at Mr Scribblemuch rounding up the decade's writers and not mentioning me once and I think, bollocks. I think even a little squib would do, but nothing! Not for *Decadence*, not for *Greek*, not for *West* and not for

Sink the Belgrano! I feel like those artists in the Third Reich who were cut out of the history books.

But actors want to perform my plays over and over again. And they do. They perform my plays at the Edinburgh Festival. I am performed in every campus, university, college and prison in the country. Hey, that's quite an achievement.

Is it bad taste occasionally to blow your own trumpet? It may be a little, but the time comes when the expulsion of a little bile may be in order. Anyway, who knows what good or bad taste is? To sit and absorb poisons and disappointment is OK for a while and nothing puts people off more than the Berkoff trumpet. There is sometimes a deep need inside oneself for that tiny pat on the back, and perhaps my need goes deeper than the approbation of my colleagues. Perhaps it goes down to the pits of my being in childhood. Perhaps it stems from the sense of outsiderishness. Perhaps it is a groan of yearning from neglected youth and a desire, nay a passion, to have my creations, gifts, efforts, call them what you will, reacted to sometimes. Not too much. But the truth of the matter may be that we are a divided nation and the people who like to put on my plays, who get sustenance from them and would die to play a role are not necessarily the same people who write about the theatre . . . aaah! Now I see . . . I may actually be a little . . . dare I say it? . . . *Persona non grata.* Ah! Now there's a different turn of view. Is it possible that what engages youth, energy, passion and the desire of young actors to express themselves through my words may be the opposite of what engages some journalists . . . i.e. the pillars of the establishment?

Well, it's going to be an uphill battle this last decade, but since it will definitely be my last I suppose I can take it. I don't want to be acting past sixty or fighting for a place or getting angry when I should be calm and serene, nor feel sick when I take too much notice of reviews, so nineties here we go. All the lads are lined up at the starting post a bit wobbly and hoping against hope to have the low-wattage lamp of theatrical critical approval. They feel, and I do too, that the millennium is something a bit special and as we totter towards the year 2000 there is a sensation that some kind of immortality will be splattered over them. I'm afraid they may be due for a shock! I don't want to be too pessimistic, but I sense a change in the wind and it's a good change, a change for the better. I do not wish to define it too much, but I say there will be a change of values as we hurtle towards the figure that puts an end to the 1990s.

2000 is the year of the future, setting us off on the next thousand years, and the dross of this century will be cast aside like bell-bottom pants, with the honourable exception of those for whom observation and truth went beyond the mere recording of now. Those who held the mirror a little too close to their warty, ugly faces will see only that; those whose mirror was held at a distance will bring in some background and those who need no mirror except the workings of their own imaginations will touch audiences in all years and for ever. What did Oedipus tell us except the torments inside the mind of man? Torments of the soul. Show me a tormented man. Show me a writer who gives me the workings of a spirit racked with pain or ecstatic with pleasure. A Van Gogh or a Walt Whitman. Who? You tell me where I can see this on stage and I will run, since I too am a spectator at the feast. That's why I adapted Kafka and Poe. It is more interesting and more nourishing to be next to a man who expressed the human dilemma as Shakespeare did. And Ford, and the other Jacobeans. As O'Neill did and Tennessee Williams and Miller at times, and . . .

A well-known playwright was recently asked which of his plays would be performed in a hundred years and he answered that he would sound arrogant if he said what he really felt and nauseous if he were to be humble. Let me spare him his pain or his guilt. The answer is *none*! Sorry, you won't be performed in one hundred years' time. You'll be in the libraries and you will be honoured and read for the sheer pleasure of reading your plays, like Galsworthy, Priestley and other literate and well-bred writers, but you will not be performed. The twentieth century, like all centuries before and after, takes to itself the past works that it can identify with most deeply. Once the flesh has rotted away it is still left with a bone structure that is recognizable. Will 'literary' allusions have any currency in the future? No. No, unequivocally.

What about you, Berkoff? I suppose, you arrogant bastard, you believe that the world is going to be populated with Berkoff plays. You think you are the answer to the twentieth century's cry for the new. You with your handful of scatological tripe that only punks and students do at a festival bash so they can cock a childish snook at authority and spew out a few four-letter words. Huh!?

Well, to be truthful I would have to answer yes. Yes, I would have to say, if I were to search my heart. Yes. For the very reasons you gave. My plays are performed by the young, and the young have strong hearts and stronger ideals. They are not impressed by cleverness or literary brilliance. They are not impressed by writers of polemics and people telling them what to feel or what to think. They do not like to be taught. They do not like to be bored. They do not like to see plays about the angst of the middle-classes or middle age or be concerned with the tribulations that ageing brings into the workings of the spirit. They are concerned to express their song, their spirit, their sex, their ideals, and if some of them find these in me, then I am proud, since they are the seed that grows into the tree. The young are the adults of the future. So that is what I believe and not only believe but must believe, not with arrogance or anger but because that is what the plays are to me. They are living embodiments of my life.

EPILOGUE

It's a cold winter morning in London as I stare out of the window contemplating the river Thames which flows past me twice a day with mechanical regularity. In 1990 when I began this journal I admitted to pangs of envy when staring at a brochure for a company that was touring the world. It was visiting Japan, I remember, and I wondered about what mysterious strings have to be pulled to release one from this earthbound existence and allow one to soar over the world. Eventually we found them, with a bit of persistence, and we ascended. We visited the four corners of the earth, taking both *Salomé* and *The Trial* to Japan where they were both received well and I was invited back to direct *Metamorphosis* in Japanese, which was one of the most fascinating experiences of my life.

Salomé went on to play 235 performances around the world, ending up last November in New York. At last I actually performed as an actor there for the first time at Brooklyn Academy at one of their beautiful theatres called the Majestic. Harvey Lichtenstein the impresario told me it had been converted at vast cost for Peter Brook's visit with *Mahabharata* and it served us well too. With their usual generosity the audience gave us the greatest reception we have experienced. Since beginning these memoirs I have written and performed in *Decadence, Sink the Belgrano!, Kvetch, Acapulco, Brighton Beach Scumbags,* and a one-man show. I toured the world with *Sturm und Drang*. I directed the movie of *Decadence* with Joan Collins and eventually I played my beloved *Coriolanus* in Leeds.

I continue to write as I plan the next move, which is to complete this autobiog and to fill in the last decade. At least no one can stop me writing and that is one pleasure for me if not always for the reader. It enables me to try and give form to the chaos of life with its immense stimulus. When I write things start to appear to have a predestined shape, like those patterns that you stare at that reveal an image if you concentrate hard enough. It has been an extraordinary decade and now I watch with some pleasure and amazement as my plays are performed by actors all over the world.

In a few weeks I shall go to Paris to see *Decadence* performed in French, directed by the distinguished Argentinian director George Lavelli. It's wonderful to hear one's plays performed in another language, particularly French. It makes one sound so intelligent.

Index

Aberdeen 227
Adler, Luther 241
Adler, Stella 240–41, 242
Aeschylus 51, 152, 194
Agamemnon (Aeschylus) *see under* Berkoff, Steven
Albee, Edward 270, 271, 273, 284, 318
Albery, Ian 65, 70, 374
Alderson, Judith 319, 320, 323, 327
Aldwych Theatre, 217, 245, 295
Alfredo's café, Islington 193, 290
Alhambra Theatre, Bradford 226
Alice (aunt) 85
Altona (Sartre) 185
Alvarez, Al 60
American adventure (1947) 6, 72, 81–94, 352
Amorous Prawn, The (Kimmins) 220, 226–9, 249, 370
Amsterdam 309, 310, 317, 371
Anderson, Lindsay 125, 280
Animal Farm (Orwell) 182
Anouilh, Jean 180, 222
Ansky, S. 219
Anthony Street, east London 6–7
Antigone (Sophocles) 108
Antrobus, John 269
Ape and Essence (Huxley) 30
Arafat, Yasser 292
Archers, The (radio programme) 330
Arden of Faversham 109
Armstrong-Jones, Anthony (later Lord Snowdon) 274
Artaud, Antonin 109, 117, 176, 182, 215, 222, 317, 327
Arts Club, Dover Street, London 246
Arts Council 256, 311, 312, 322, 326

Arts Festival of touring groups 320
Arts Lab, Drury Lane, London 107–8, 109–10, 121, 216, 294–5
Arts Theatre, Cambridge 241, 248
Arts Theatre, Newport Street, London 17, 341–2, 350
Arturo Ui, The Resistible Rise of (Brecht) 125, 219
As You Like It (Shakespeare) 213, 251
Ashcroft, Dame Peggy 298
Aspern Papers, The (James) 181, 182
Astoria Cinema, Finsbury Park 173
Astoria dance hall, Charing Cross Road, London 203
ATV 283
Au Père de Nico restaurant, Chelsea 223, 262
Aukin, David 311, 313
Auschwitz 80
Ax-les-Thermes 203
Ayckbourn, Alan 62

Bacon, Francis 247
Baker, Chet 150
Bannerman, Kay 232
Barcelona 205
Barkworth, Peter 226–7
Barrault, Jean-Louis 95, 110, 117, 208, 243, 244, 295, 308
Barrow-in-Furness 253, 254, 257
Barrymore Theatre, New York 352
Baryshnikov, Mikhail Nikolayevich 102, 241, 352, 386
Basie, Count 150
Basle 95
Baudelaire, Charles 380
Baumgartner (director, Vienna International Festival) 328–9

Baxter, Keith 266
Baxter, Stanley 226, 227, 228, 249, 370
Beatles, the 265, 305
Beaton, Martin 105, 107, 289
Becker, Lee 241
Beckmann, Max 347
Beelitz, Günter 255, 366
Behan, Brendan 113
Belgium 95
Belgrade Theatre, Coventry 284
Belita 91–2
Bells, The (Lewis) 106, 142
Benedictus, David 65
Bennet, Mary (aunt) 70, 71, 94
Bennet, Sidney (cousin) 44, 45, 67, 70, 94
Bennet, Willy (cousin) 44–5
Bennett, Alan 242, 243
Benthal, Paul 378
Beowulf 65, 68
Berg, Jack 'Kid' 6
Berkoff, Abraham (Al) (father) 11, 47, 79, 92, 166, 341; in America 75; as an absent parent 7, 15, 88, 89, 90, 93, 138; bike episode 76, 77, 80; and the detention centre episode 137, 138, 142, 143, 148; family of 70; gambling 5, 71, 90; portrayed in West 65, 67; relationship with SB xiii, 6, 28, 58, 138, 139, 140; as a tailor 5, 6, 25, 67, 81, 174, 196
Berkoff, Alison (née Minto; SB's first wife) 105, 123, 130, 218, 277, 278–9, 287, 297, 300
Berkoff, Barry (cousin) 92
Berkoff, Beryl (sister) 6, 65, 81, 82, 88, 90–91, 93, 99, 100, 203, 329, 352, 353
Berkoff, Betty (aunt) 92, 93, 94, 276
Berkoff, Polly (mother) 7, 8, 9, 15, 31, 47, 48, 73, 76, 130, 133, 136, 139, 140, 165, 166, 226, 261; American adventure (1947) 6, 81–5, 88–92, 352; death 94, 99–102; and detention centre episode 137, 148; and Evelyn Laye 227; family of 70, 210, 356; and gambling 71; illness 148–9; and Israel 132; marries in America 75; piano playing 79;

portrayed in West 65, 67; relationship with SB xii–xiii; and SB's beating at school 11; at school 72; sees SB at Stratford East 276; visits Cambridge Arts Theatre 249
Berkoff, Sam (uncle) 71, 93, 94
Berkoff, Shelley (née Lee; SB's wife) 50, 51, 140, 194, 290, 351, 367
Berkoff, Steven: acquires an agent 225; acts in first rep (1959) 225–6; acts in first Shakespeare (Lincoln, 1963) 251–2; ambition to be an actor 141, 211; American adventure (1947) 6, 72, 81–94; army medical 149–50; BBC commission 63; birth 92; childhood 5–16, 72–93, 223; at the City Literary Institute see City Literary Institute; and death of his mother 99–102; duodenal ulcer 58, 150, 162, 206; evacuated to Luton (1942) 73–80; first exposure to film (1958) 224; first jobs 26, 48, 87, 135–6, 160, 161, 162–74; first television part 230; first tours with own company (1972) 311–15; first visits Israel (1969) 124, 125, 127–32; in Germany (1955) 164–73; guest director at the National Theatre (1977) 371–2; in Iceland (1956) 196–9; on Jewish humour 355–6; on Jewish theatre 98, 99, 356–8; meets Shelley 51; in the Navy 111, 203–6, 211; nominated for a British Screen Award (1979) 330; plastic surgery in Germany 199–201; plays villains 330–39; RADA teaching 51–2, 54; relationship with father xiii, 6, 28, 58, 138, 139, 140; on his Russian family orgins 131; school days 7, 8, 11–12, 25, 73, 85, 86–8, 89, 90, 92, 111, 112, 135, 143; singing lessons 27, 28, 226; as a student of Jacques Lecoq in Paris 53, 96, 103, 121; as student and lecturer at the Webber-Douglas 54, 55, 110–16, 120–22, 223, 224, 225, 226, 274, 290, 296,

297, 308, 339, 363, 378; studies
with Chagrin 53, 54, 115, 210, 268,
283; as a teenager in Stamford
Hill 30–46; in trouble with the law
(aged fifteen) 111, 136–8, 140–49;
turning point in career 267; writes
first play 278

AS DIRECTOR: *Agamemnon* 17, 51,
52, 55–8, 61, 98, 152–7, 159–60,
219, 314, 319, 321, 322–5, 327,
328, 329; *Coriolanus* 1, 2, 64,
219, 255, 292, 368, 370–71, 392;
Hamlet 27, 58, 59, 94–6, 98, 99,
101, 120–21, 132, 153, 244, 292,
343, 346, 352, 369; *Knock at
the Manor Gate* 313, 314;
Macbeth 25, 51, 120, 121,
296–303, 304; *Midsummer Night's
Dream* 282–4, 363; *Miss Julie*
314–20, 326, 327; *Salome* 314,
359–62, 378, 380–81, 392; *The
Tell-Tale Heart* 354; *Zoo Story*
314–15, 318–19, 326

PLAYS AND ADAPTATIONS:
Acapulco 392; *Agamemnon* 17;
Blood Accusation 278; *Brighton
Beach Scumbags* 392;
Decadence 56, 57, 332, 333, 334,
339, 344, 345–50, 355, 374, 388,
392, 393; *East* 16, 18–21, 45–51,
56, 60, 63, 66, 67, 68, 153, 158,
161, 190, 211, 220, 223, 236, 325,
330, 346, 372, 374; *The Fall of the
House of Usher* 60, 220, 314, 330,
343, 372; *Greek* 2–4, 5, 17–18, 49,
56, 62, 70, 153, 154, 159, 339–44,
345, 346, 350, 352, 374, 388;
Harry's Christmas 353–4; *In the
Penal Colony* 107, 119, 122, 124,
128, 216, 293–4; *Kvetch* 56, 365,
372, 392; *Lunch* 164–5, 278;
Metamorphosis 56, 60–61, 98–9,
102–7, 122–4, 129, 130, 218, 220,
240, 241, 293, 299, 301, 311–14,
333, 346, 352, 372, 386, 392; *The
Murder of Jesus Christ* 369; *Sink
the Belgrano!* 4, 373–4, 389, 392;
The Trial 19, 29, 51, 57, 121–2,
190, 307–10, 311, 327, 328–9,
336, 346, 362–4, 365–71, 372, 373,

374–5, 376–86; *West* 3, 16, 35,
36–8, 41, 46, 47, 49, 63–70, 157,
158, 388

WRITINGS: *Gross Intrusion* 34, 190,
191–5; *I Am Hamlet* 94, 258, 369
Berlin 125
Berliner Ensemble 97, 219
Bernard Baron Settlement, Berner
Street, London 10
Bernhardt, Sarah 207, 313
Berwick Street Market, London 175
Bespoke Overcoat, The
(Mankowitz) 127
Betts Street Baths, London 7, 10–11
Beverly Hills Cop (film) 332–5
Beyond the Fringe 242
Birmingham 246
Bitburg 166, 169, 171
Blacks, The (Genet) 187
Blakemore, Michael 125, 284–5, 286
Bloom, Claire 60
Bloomfield (film) 124–30, 131, 314
Blumenfeld, Simon 358
Bofors Gun, The (film) 280
Bogart, Humphrey 151
Bond, Chris 373
Bostic, Earl 30
Boulting Brothers 224
Bowers, Raymond 114
Bowles, Peter 345
Bradford 226
Brando, Marlon 151, 222, 352
Brave New World (Huxley) 30, 213
Brecht, Bertolt 108, 126, 184, 222,
248, 254, 295, 298
Brest, Martin 334
Brett, Jeremy 184, 187, 188
Brett, Peter 182, 271, 272, 308
Brickman, Miriam 187
Brierly, Joe 11–12, 60, 276
Brig, The (Brown) 97–8, 109
Brighton 1, 61, 70, 81, 191, 192, 206,
220, 227, 278–9, 293, 313, 318,
327
Brisley, Stuart 347
Bristol 353
British Broadcasting Corporation
(BBC) 27, 63, 65, 68, 70, 182, 217,
258–9, 275, 355, 380
British Drama League 232, 233

British Museum library 179, 232, 277–8
British Telecom 358
Broccoli, Barbara 331
Brook, Peter 110, 116–19, 238, 246, 302, 368, 392
Brooke, Harold 232
Brooklyn Academy 392
Brown, Georgia 3, 344
Brubeck, Dave 150–51
Bruce, Lenny 363
Bruckheimer, Jerry 334
Bryden, Bill 284
'Bucket Rider, The' (Kafka) 213–14, 216–17, 313
Budd, Mr (supervisor at Sandersons) 165
Bunyan, John 103
Burberry's 165–6, 195
Burgess, Anthony 68, 206
Burnet, Susan 241
Bush, George 387
Bushell, Anthony 230
Buxton, Derbyshire 231, 232–4, 235, 240, 244
Buxton Opera House 231
Byrave, Mike 301

Café Delma, Vienna 336
Cagney, James 16, 151
Caine, Michael 260
Calder, John 190
Callow, Simon 354
Cambridge 248–9
Cambridge Arts Theatre 241, 248
Camden Head pub, Camden Passage 290, 293
Camden Passage, London 290, 312
Cameri Theatre 129
Campbell, Ken 371
Camus, Albert 264
Canary Islands 351–2
Cannes 191, 205
Canterbury 249–50
Captain's Table, The (film) 224
Cardiff 246, 313
Carmen Jones (film) 151
Carteret, Anna 117, 118
Castle in Sweden (Sagan) 245
Cat on a Hot Tin Roof (Williams) 263
Cathedral, The (Box, after Walpole) 235
Cats (Lloyd Webber) 60
Caves de France club, Soho 174
Cecil Gee's Menswear 37
Céline, Louis-Ferdinand 30
Cendrars, Blaise 30
Chagall, Marc 357, 358
Chaganog 268, 269, 271, 309
Chagrin, Claude 53, 54, 115, 209–10, 268, 283
Chagrin, Julian 268
Chaikin, Joe 97
Channel Four Television 66, 107
Chanticleer Theatre 121
Chapel Street market, Islington 26, 279
Chaplin, Charlie 363
Charon, Jacques 208, 217
Chassay, Tchaik 59
Cheatle, Anne 191–2, 193, 289, 290, 304, 305, 307, 314, 327, 328
Chekhov, Anton 103, 238, 330, 359
Cheltenham 179, 181, 246, 282, 308
Cherry, Helen 206, 307
Chesterfield 234–6
Chichester Theatre 23
Chimes at Midnight (film) 270
Chopin, Fryderyk 150
Christian Street School, London 72, 79, 92
Christie, Agatha 218, 388
Chusan (P & O liner) 203, 205
City Literary Institute 53, 111, 213–15, 216, 217, 221, 223, 236, 253, 263, 268, 282, 283, 284, 295, 313
Civic Theatre, Rotherham 245
Claire, Imogen 377
Clark, Ernest 227
Clavigo (Goethe) 219
Clegg, Tom 330, 331
Cleveland, Carol 316
Clockwork Orange, A (Burgess) 68
Close Theatre, Glasgow 286, 318–19
Clunes, Alec 260
Cocteau, Jean 236
Cohan, Robert 303
Coles, Michael 113
Colgan, Michael 359–60, 361

Collins, Joan 392
Collins, Mr (of Burberrys) 166
Comédie Française 208, 217, 218, 295
Comedy of Errors (Shakespeare) 245
Confessions of Felix Krull, The (Mann) 202
Conte, Richard 224
Conway, Jeremy 264, 265
Cooper, Dera 235, 236
Copland, Aaron 150
Coriolanus (Shakespeare) 1, 2, 64, 219, 255, 292, 368, 370–71, 392
Cornish, Anthony 234, 235
Corsaro, Frank 241
Cottesloe Theatre, London 60–61
Coventry 284
Coward, Noël 113, 248
Cox, Brian 176, 177
Crawford, Dan 374
Creditors, The (Strindberg) 285
Crime Passionnel (Sartre) 22
Crime and Punishment (Dostoievsky) 265
Crouse, Russell 235
Croydon Warehouse 2, 350
Crucible, The (Miller) 236
Cruttwell, Hugh 51, 55, 58
Cuka, Frances 231
Curtis, Dan 335–9
Curtis, Tony 151
Cushman, Robert 4, 362
Cyr, Myriam 377, 378
Cyrano de Bergerac (film) 291
Cyrano de Bergerac (Rostand) 154, 388

D'Abreu, Teresa 319, 321, 323, 327
Dagger, Mr (headmaster) 93
Daily Herald xii
Daily Mirror xii
Dali, Salvador 362–3, 379, 382
Daltrey, Roger 330
Dance Centre 314
Davies, Windsor 180
de Bleik, Jan 95
de Burgh, Paula 350
de Jongh, Nick 59, 154, 346
De Niro, Robert 350
De Sica, Vittorio 224

Dean, James 151
Death of a Salesman (Miller) 222, 358
Decroux, Etienne 121
'Desire and the Black Masseur' (Williams) 194
Devil's Disciple, The (film) 224
Devonshire Park Theatre, Eastbourne 245
Dexter, John 184, 187, 188, 242
Diamond, Gillian 21
Diamond Bros 165, 212
Diary of an Immigrant (Blumenfeld) 358
Dillon, George 193, 195
Dino's cafe 113
Dionisotti, Paola 308, 310
Dix, Otto 347
Doctor Who (television programme) 304
Domingo, Placido 257
Donaghue, Pip 297, 299, 300, 308, 310
Donmar Theatre, London 3, 69–70, 116, 295, 354, 374*n*
Doris (aunt) 83
Dostoievsky, Fyodor Mikhailovich 168, 171
Douglas, Kirk 14, 306
Drama Centre 297
Drama League 297
Duel of Angels (Giraudoux) 223
Dundee 175–8
Dunlop, Frank 239, 240
Dürrenmatt, Friedrich 222, 245
Duryea, Dan 151
Dusseldorf 95, 295, 365, 366, 367, 369, 378
Dybbuk, The (Ansky) 98, 219, 356–7

E & A Milk Bar, Stamford Hill 13, 30, 33, 42
Eagle that Pecked at the Man's Feet, The (Kafka) 313
Ealing comedies 169
Eastbourne 245, 250
Eaton, Gillian 3
Edinburgh 228, 318, 319
Edinburgh Festival 94, 95, 125, 307, 342, 348, 350, 361, 362, 388, 389

Edwards, Rory 68–9
Eggar, Samantha 114, 225
Eilat 129
El Greco 304
Ellington, Ray 41
Ellis, Bill 281, 282
Ellis, Janet 73, 86
Ellis, John 73–4, 78
English National Opera (ENO) 344
Equity 160
Equus (Shaffer) 209
Eric Glass Ltd 300
EST Institute 308
Everett, Mr (of Luton) 78
Everyman Cinema, Hampstead,
    London 162

Faith, Adam 331
Falklands War 373
Fall of the House of Usher, The (Poe)
    see under Berkoff, Steven
Farson, Dan 262
Fauré, Gabriel 283
Fay (in Wiesbaden) 169–73, 195,
    196, 199, 201, 202, 235
Fenton, James 4, 342, 362
Ferman, James 276
Ferrer, José 208
Festival of Theatre, Florence 280
Feydeau, Alain 217–18
Feydeau, Georges 218
Fiander, Lewis 286–7
51 Club, Newport Street,
    London 134
Fil à la Patte, Un (Feydeau) 217, 218
Film Artists' Association (FAA) 224
Finney, Albert 176, 184, 264
Finsbury Park xi, 40, 133, 173
Finsbury Park Empire 226
Fire Raisers, The (Frisch) 185
Fisher, Harry 163–4
Fitzgerald, Ella 150
Fitzgerald, Miss (saleslady at W.
    Bill) 163
Fitzgerald, Walter 226, 228
Fleming, Miss (voice teacher) 113
Flemyng, Robert 247
Flora Robson Playhouse,
    Newcastle 243
Florence 280–81

Fogarty, Jan 233–4
Ford, Henry, II 91, 92
Ford, John 390
Ford, John (*Time Out* editor) 362
Forster, E. M. 266–7
Fountainhead, The (Rand) 87
Four Just Men, The (Wallace) 230
Fox, Edward 185, 188
Fox, James 274
Francis, John 344
Frank, Anne 84
Frankel, John 66
Frankenstein (Shelley) 109, 122
Frankfurt 202
Freehold Theatre 108, 368
French Mistress, The (Monro) 177–8,
    234
Freud, Lucian 60, 340
Freud, Sigmund 5, 103
Frisch, Max 185, 222
Furies, The (Aeschylus) 54
Futz (Owens) 97, 297

Gallagher, Bernard 254
Galsworthy, John 390
Gangster, The (film) 91
Gardner, Ava 163
Gardner, Kay 251, 252
Garrick, David 24
Garrick Theatre, Charing Cross Road,
    London 378
Garrigue and Sons, Golden Square,
    London 174
Gaskill, Bill 263
Gate Theatre, Dublin 359, 361
Genet, Jean 69, 116, 187
George Dandin (Molière) 270, 271,
    272
Germany 95, 164–73, 195, 197, 199–
    203, 295, 364, 365–71
Gerry's Bar, Shaftesbury Avenue,
    London 305, 323
Ghosts (Ibsen) 276
Gide, André 308
Gielgud, Sir John 98, 119, 223, 336
Giles, David 179–80, 184, 282
Gillray, James 346
Gilmore, Murray 221, 223, 253
Gilt and Gingerbread (Hale) 234
Ginger Paul 15–16, 32, 33, 43

Gingold, Hermione 242
Glasgow 227, 228, 285–7, 290, 318–19
Glasgow Citizens' Theatre 285
Glass Menagerie, The (Williams) 306–7
Glen, John 331, 332
Glentworth, Mark 70, 365
Goethe, Johann Wolfgang von 219
Gogol, Nikolai Vasilievich 127
Golby, Derek 253, 254
Gold, Jack 125
Golders Green Empire, London 245
Golem, The (Leivik) 98
Goodman, Henry 56
Graham, Martha 4–5, 303
Grain, Glyn 297, 299
Grand Guignol 260
Grant, Steve 3
Grays Dance Hall, Finsbury Park 40, 134
Great Sebastians, The (Lindsay and Crouse) 235
Greater London Council (GLC) 112
Greece 314, 327–8
Green Angel café, Islington 290
Greenwich Theatre 271, 306, 307
Grimm, Jacob and Wilhelm 103
Grossman, Jan 243
Group Theatre 97
Guardian 122, 154, 290, 362
Gulbenkian Centre, Newcastle 319–20
Gulf War 364–5, 375–6, 381

Habimah 98, 99, 129, 357
Habimah Theatre, Tel Aviv 357
Hack, Keith 307
Hackney Downs Grammar School, London 8, 12, 15, 25, 52, 111, 112, 135, 143, 276
Hackney, London 173
Hagen, Uta 270
Haggard, Piers 175, 177
Hague, the 95
Haifa Municipal Theatre 98, 99
Hairy Ape, The (O'Neill) 291
Half Moon Theatre, London 2, 5, 17, 341, 350, 373
Halifax, Michael 371

Hall, Sir Peter 371
Hall, Willis 280
Hamlet (Shakespeare) 17, 27, 58, 59, 94–6, 98, 99, 101, 120–21, 132, 142, 153, 214, 244, 245, 292, 343, 346, 352, 369
Hamlet at Elsinore 217, 258–61
Hammer horror films 218
Hampstead, London 162, 164, 262–3
Hampstead Theatre Club 313–14
Hard Rock Café, Old Park Lane, London 329
Harringay Stadium xi, 173
Harris, Harold 38, 41
Harris, Richard 125, 127, 128, 129, 305
Harry Fisher, Regent Street, London 163–4
Hassidic Jews 98, 356–7
Hayes, Helen 84
Haynes, Jim 107, 110, 216, 268, 294
Heath, Ted 16, 135
Hemingway, Ernest 177, 327, 329
Henriques, Basil 138, 142–3, 146
Henry V (Shakespeare) 65
Henze, Hans Werner 344
Hewison, Robert 346–7, 348
High Noon (film) 65, 66
Hill, Arthur 270
Hirsch, Robert 217, 218, 319
Hitler, Adolf 74, 80, 126, 335–9, 364, 376
Hobson, Harold 106, 107
Hoffman, Dustin 306
Holland 309–10
Hollywood 72, 209, 333, 334
Holt, Thelma 94
Homer 93
Hooper, Ewan 271, 285
Hope, Morris 14–15
Hoskins, Bob 330, 354
Hoskins, George 107, 311, 328
Hot Summer Night (Willis) 232, 234
House by the Lake, The (Mills) 114
How Say You? (Brooke and Bannerman) 232, 234
How You'll Come to Love Your Sperm Test (Antrobus) 269
Howard, Trevor 306, 307
Hugh of Lincoln 277

Hughes, Ted 51, 371
Hussein, Saddam 292, 364, 376
Huxley, Aldous 30, 213

I Was Monty's Double (film) 224
ICA (Institute of Contemporary Arts),
  The Mall, London 326
Iceland 196–9
Imperial Turkish Baths, Russell
  Square, London 139–40
Importance of Being Earnest, The
  (Wilde) 265–6, 267
In the Penal Colony see under Berkoff,
  Steven
Infernal Machine, The (Cocteau) 236
Ionesco, Eugène 23, 113, 222
Irregular Verb to Love, The (Williams
  and Williams) 248
Irving, Sir Henry 22, 24, 106, 112,
  134–5, 176, 207, 208, 209, 210,
  260
Islington, London xii, xiii, 25, 29, 52,
  218, 277, 278, 279, 287–9, 329,
  342
Israel 17, 94–102, 124, 125, 127–32,
  153, 154, 291–2, 314, 369
Itala, Tony 290

Jack the Ripper 97, 210–11
Jackson, Glenda 185, 188
Jackson, Milt 150
Jacobi, Derek 154
Jaffa 128
Jago, Ralph 115, 116, 122
James, Jeanie 313
Japan 392
Jenkins, Warren 263, 264
Jenn, Michael 377
Jerusalem 99, 100, 127, 129, 130,
  131
Jerusalem Festival 94
Jew Boy (Blumenfeld) 358
Jew of Malta, The (Marlowe) 245
Jewish War, The (Josephus) 132–3
Jimmy the Greek's, Soho 247, 262
Joe (uncle) 84, 85, 88, 94
John Michael, King's Road,
  Chelsea 212–13, 223
Jones, Griffith 243
Jones, Peter Penry 264

Jordan, Maggie 240, 312–13, 315
Josephus 132–3
Jourdan, Louis 332
Joyce, James 286
Joyce, John 70, 318, 319, 327
Jung, Carl Gustav 30, 234

Kabuki 260
Kafka, Franz 27–8, 29, 76, 77, 98–9,
  103, 106, 107, 121, 122, 126, 168,
  176, 182, 213, 214, 216, 221–2,
  242, 243, 293, 294, 309, 312, 313,
  352, 358, 362, 372, 376, 379, 384,
  385, 390
Kafka's Dick (Bennett) 242
Kahler, Wolf 328, 368
Kaleidoscope coffee bar, Gerrard
  Street, London 165
Kanner, Alexis 116
Kassit café, Jerusalem 130
Kazan, Elia 5, 97, 207
Kean, Edmund 24, 176, 181, 215–16,
  217
Keaton, Buster 257
Keith, Penelope 114
Kemp, Jeremy 337
Kemp, Lindsay 108, 217, 257, 258,
  260–61, 283
Kempner, Teddy 378
Kennedy, John Fitzgerald 263–4
Kenton, Stan 30, 150, 151
Kettering 226, 252
Khan, Naseem 327
Kidlington, Oxfordshire 143
Killer, The (Ionesco) 23
King, Curly 32–3, 40, 67, 135
King Lear (Shakespeare) 246, 356
King's Head, Islington 374
King's Theatre, Edinburgh 268
King's Theatre, Glasgow 228
Kinkead, Randall 262
Kitchen, The (Wesker) 184–9, 242,
  243, 253, 254
Knightsbridge, London 262
Knock at the Manor Gate
  (Kafka) 313, 314
Knott, Frederick 249
Kossoff, David 280
Kott, Jan 109
Kray twins 40–41, 335

Kruger, Hardy 337, 338
Kruger, Rolf 250
Kuhn, Mr (singing teacher) 28
Kurds 292, 387
Kurosawa, Akira 162
Kyd, Sylvia 67

La Mama 97, 109, 297
La Mama's Theatre, New York 325
Laban School of Dance 226
Ladd, Alan 151
Laine, Frankie 14
Lambert, J.W. 302
LAMDA see London Academy of
    Music and Dramatic Art
Lamda Theatre 117, 122, 301, 304
Lancaster, Burt 224
Landis, Harry 185–6, 220, 226, 249,
    253, 254
Last Exit to Brooklyn (Selby) 192
Lavelli, George 393
Lawler, Ray 281
Lawson, Denis 313
Laye, Evelyn 220, 226, 227, 228
Le Fanu, Joseph Sheridan 30
Leatherhead, Surrey 247
Lecoq, Jacques 53, 96, 103, 121, 268,
    309
Leder, Siegfried 226
Lee, Harry 43, 44, 45, 67
Lee, Peggy 150
Leeds 199, 228, 392
Leeson (at Kidlington detention
    centre) 144, 145
Leigh, Vivien 223, 230
Lesnevitch, Gus 6
Lessing, Doris 285, 286
Levene, Ralph 30
Levin, Bernard 117
Lewenstein, Oscar 313
Lewin, Charles 327
Lewis, Ted 'Kid' 6
Lewis Trust, Hackney 37
Lichtenstein, Harvey 392
Life Begins Tomorrow (film) 220
Limehouse TV Studios 353
Lincoln 251–2, 277–8, 306
Lincoln, Abraham 264
Lincoln Cathedral 251, 277
Lindsay, Howard 235

Lion in Winter, The (Goldman) 98
Little Malcolm and his Struggle
    against the Eunuchs (Halliwell) 123
Littlewood, Joan 113, 186, 187, 207,
    270, 276
Liverpool 246
Liverpool Playhouse 275, 280, 281–2
Living Theatre 97, 109, 122, 298
Livingstone, Douglas 180
Loewenberg, Susan 154, 219, 343
London Academy of Music and
    Dramatic Art (LAMDA) 304; see
    also Lamda Theatre
London County Council (LCC) 8,
    208
London Palladium 151
London Theatre Group 320
Long and the Short and the Tall, The
    (Hall) 280, 281
Longden, Robert 19
Look Back in Anger (Osborne) 123,
    212
Los Angeles 3, 62, 151, 153, 154,
    159, 160, 209, 219, 332–3, 334,
    343, 344, 352
Los Angeles Theater Works 343
Luba's Russian bistro,
    Knightsbridge 273
Luther (Osborne) 184, 264
Luton 73–80, 82, 84, 85, 86, 90, 93,
    138
Lyceum Dance Hall, Wellington Street,
    London 16, 68, 134–5, 141–2, 160,
    207, 215, 216
Lynch, David 363
Lyric Theatre, Hammersmith 241

Macbeth (Shakespeare) 25, 51, 112,
    120, 121, 230, 295, 296–303, 304
McCowen, Alec 21, 245–6
McCullum (of Unity Theatre) 236
McDermott, Hugh 226, 228–9
McDonald, David 247
Macdonald, Murray 220, 226, 227,
    230
McEnery, Peter 274
McGill, Donald 20
McGinity, Terry 311, 312, 313, 328
McGrah, Neville 180–81
Machiavelli, Niccolò 178

McKellen, Sir Ian 238–9, 240, 274
Mackenzie, Boyd 308
MacRea, Hilton 323
McReddie, Kenneth 240
McVicar (film) 330–31
McVicar, John 70, 330, 331
Madeira 381, 382
Madrid 303–4, 305
Mahabharata 392
Maidenhall Elementary School,
   Luton 73
Mailer, Norman 176, 177
Majestic Theater, New York 392
Malcolm, Chris 4
Malgram, Yat 297
Man for All Seasons, A (Bolt) 245
Manchester 246, 322, 323
Mandragola (Machiavelli) 178
Mankowitz, Wolf 124, 125, 127, 128
Mann, Harry 262
Mann, Thomas 202
Manor House, London xii, 5, 8, 11,
   15, 111, 130, 132, 133, 135, 137,
   165, 173, 203, 206, 211, 227
Mansfield, Alf (uncle) 6, 71, 79, 88,
   211, 231
Mansfield, Jayne 224
Mansfield, Paula 88
Marat-Sade (Weiss) 116
Marceau, Marcel 180
Mark Taper Forum, Los Angeles 333
Marlowe, Linda 212, 322–3, 345–6,
   349
Marlowe Theatre, Canterbury 249
Martin, Marina 225
Mason, Jackie 354–5
Massada 131
Massey, Paul 263
Matchmaker, The (Wilder) 180
Matrix Theater, Los Angeles 344
Matthew Hall Ltd (engineering
   firm) 135
Mauretania 81
Maxie's barbers, Stoke
   Newington 141
Maxwell-Muller, Jo 272
Mayfair Gymnasium,
   Marylebone 314, 328
Mayne, Ferdy 241
Meacham, Michael 285

Mecca 34
Meckler, Nancy 108, 298
Medea (Euripides) 152
Meditations on 'Metamorphosis' 102
Merchant of Venice, The
   (Shakespeare) 177, 356
Mercury Theatre, Notting Hill 286,
   297
Meredith, Burgess 341
Mermaid Theatre 97–8, 373
Merry, Alistair 30, 294
Meskin, Amnon 98
Metamorphosis (Kafka) 168; *see also*
   under Berkoff, Steven
Meyer, Tony 308, 311, 312
Meyerhold, Vsevolod Emilievich 98,
   121, 263
Michael, John 212–13, 223
Mickery-theater, Amsterdam 309
Midsummer Night's Dream
   (Shakespeare) 65, 116, 179–80,
   282–4, 363
Miles, Bernard 223
Miles, Sarah 241
Milhaud, Darius 150
Miller, Arthur 113, 222, 390
Miller, Henry 30, 213
Milos 327
Minto, Alison *see* Berkoff, Alison
Miranda (Blackmore) 113
Misalliance (Shaw) 284
Miss Julie (Strindberg) *see under*
   Berkoff, Steven
Miss Saigon (Bonblil and
   Schönberg) 216, 323
Mitchell, Ronnie 42–3, 45
Mitchum, Robert 335
Modern Man in Seach of a Soul
   (Jung) 30
Modigliani, Amedeo 248, 363
Moisher 43, 44
Molière 270, 272
Montague, Lee 264, 265
Moore, Debbie 18
Moore, Roger 332
More, Kenneth 224
Morley, Sheridan 371
Morley College 226
Morris (cousin) 75, 83, 90
Morris, William 186

Mortimer, Peter 320
Morton, Roger 57–8
Moscow Arts Theatre 98, 109, 207, 360
Mosley, Sir Oswald 47
Mossinson, Avital 94, 366–7
Mostel, Zero 341
Moving Picture Mime Show 53
Mozart, Wolfgang Amadeus 369–70
Much Ado About Nothing (Shakespeare) 154
Müller, Heiner 295
Mulligan, Gerry 150
Mummerschantz 53
Muncke, Chris 55, 296, 297, 299, 300
Munich 255, 258, 373
Murder at Midnight 234
Murder in the Cathedral (Eliot) 265
Murder on Arrival 234
Murphy, Eddie 334
Myles, Bruce 290, 291, 306, 307

Naples 205
Nasser, Gamal Abdel 291
National Theatre, London 23, 29, 125, 209, 247, 254, 361–4, 371–2, 373, 375, 377, 378, 383, 385, 386, 387
Nazism 107, 336
Neue Sachlichkeit 347
Neville, John 240
New End Theatre, Hampstead 346, 348, 350
New London Theatre, Drury Lane, London 60, 63, 220
New Theatre, Cardiff 263
New York 1, 71, 72, 82–92, 93–4, 102, 208, 241, 242, 257, 292, 293, 325, 332, 344, 352, 368, 370–71, 386, 392
New York Actors' Studio 271
New York Times 325
Newcastle 243, 313, 318, 319–20, 321
Newcastle Journal 320
Newman, Sydney 261
Nicholas and Alexandra (film) 176, 303, 304
Nietzsche, Friedrich Wilhelm 113

Nimmo, Derek 227, 249
Nooderkirk, Amsterdam 309
Not in the Book (Watkyn) 222, 234, 244, 387
Nottingham Playhouse 239–40, 243
Nyack, Upper New York 83, 84, 90
Nygh, Anna 19, 67

Observer 362
Octopussy (film) 331–2, 333, 352–3
Odets, Clifford 113
Oedipus (Hughes version) 51, 371
Oedipus (Seneca) 110, 116
Ogilvie, George 268, 309
Oh Dad, Poor Dad, Mama's Hung You in the Closet and I'm Feeling So Sad (Kopit) 240–42, 248
O'Horgan, Tom 297
Old Red Lion, Islington 315
Old Vic 24, 116, 142, 219, 245
Oliver 127
Oliver, John 165
Olivier, Sir Laurence (later Lord) 23–4, 25, 98, 119, 120, 125, 185, 191, 207, 208, 209, 219, 221, 230, 256, 261, 264, 361
O'Malley, Ellen 112
O'Neill, Eugene 248, 291, 390
Open Theatre 97
Oresteia, The (Aeschylus) 51, 54
Orwell, George 182
Osborne, John 184
Othello (Shakespeare) 292, 296
O'Toole, Peter 280, 281, 304, 305, 334
Oval House 309, 310, 323
Overview 152
Oxford 102, 181–2, 228

Pacino, Al 359
Pagett, Nicola 285
Palance, Jack 151
Palaseum Cinema, Commercial Road, London 7, 72
Papp, Joe 1, 64, 219, 366
Paris 53, 55, 95, 103, 115, 117, 165, 199, 218, 281, 286, 352, 360, 393
Pavarotti, Luciano 256–7
Payne, Bruce 3, 69
Pearl (cousin) 83

Peilsticker, Fritz 201-3
Penrose, John 225
People Show 108
Perkins, Anthony 84
Perrin, Alan 377, 378
Perth 265-7, 269, 274
Perth *Evening News* 266
Petherbridge, Edward 53, 283
Petticoat Lane, London 9-10
Phelan, Brian 284
Philips, Barry 2, 18, 19, 49, 152, 153, 154, 323, 328, 343
Phoenix Theatre, Charing Cross Road, London 184
Physicists, The (Dürrenmatt) 116, 245
Picasso, Pablo 363
Piccadilly Bushman, The (Lawler) 281
Picture of Dorian Grey, The (Wilde) 210
Pimlico, London 263
Pinewood Studios 331, 332
Pinter, Harold 8, 11, 60, 276, 384
Pistol, The (television play) 275-6
Play of the Week 108
Play With a Tiger (Lessing) 285, 286
Playfair, Nigel 215
Plowright, Joan 361
Plummer, Christopher 217, 260, 261, 273, 274
Poe, Edgar Allan 22, 30, 107, 176-7, 330, 390
Polanski, Roman 218, 386
Pollock, Ellen 113-14
Pooley, Olaf 181
Porridge (television series) 331
Portnoy's Complaint (Roth) 60
Portrait of the Artist as a Young Man, A (Joyce) 286
Powell, Mark 250
Preminger, Otto 151
Present Laughter (Coward) 208
Priestley, J. B. 390
Pryce, Jonathan 55, 56, 59, 153, 330
Psycho (film) 84
Public Theater, New York 1

Quaglino's 230
Quant, Mary 212

Queen Elizabeth 81
Queen Mary 81, 90
Queen's Theatre, Shaftesbury Avenue, London 241
Quinn, Anthony 151

Rabin, Oscar 135
Raging Bull (film) 350
Raine's Foundation School, Arbour Square, London 7, 8, 11, 93
Rand, Ayn 87
Rattigan, Terence 247
Ray, Andrew 241
Ray (aunt) 83, 89-90
Ray, Johnnie 16, 30, 37, 134, 151-2, 160
Rea, Stephen 108
Reckord, Lloyd 232
Redgrave, Lynn 175, 177
Redgrave, Sir Michael 182, 188, 230
Redgrave, Vanessa 292
Reed, Oliver 224
Regent Cinema, Stamford Hill, London 12, 13
Regent Street Polytechnic, London 220, 330
Regent Theatre, London 60
Revenger's Tragedy, The 245
Revill, Clive 245
Reykjavik 196, 198
Rhinoceros (Ionesco) 23, 185
Rich, Mr (teacher) 86, 88
Richard III (Shakespeare) 112, 214, 221, 319, 337
Richardson, Anthony 284
Richardson, Charlie 330, 331
Richardson, Ian 21, 246
Rigby, Terence 386-7
Rix, Brian 220
Roar Like a Dove (Storm) 230
Robbers, The (Schiller) 219
Robinson, David 262
Rockwell, Norman 83
Rodenburg, Patsy 364, 380
Rommel, Erwin 337, 338
Rose Tattoo 230
Rosenthal 201-2
Ross, Charles 341, 350
Ross (Rattigan) 247
Rossiter, Leonard 125, 126-7

Rostand, Edmond 222
Roth, Philip 60
Rotherham 244–5, 252
Round House Theatre, Chalk Farm, London 19, 57, 59, 94, 102, 105, 106, 107, 109, 122, 123, 126, 189, 255, 286, 295, 299, 311, 312, 313, 327, 328, 329, 343, 364, 367, 372, 375, 377
Rowton House, Whitechapel, London 31
Royal Academy of Dramatic Art (RADA) 51–2, 54, 57, 58, 59, 61, 319
Royal Court Theatre 108, 109, 184, 185, 186, 187, 212, 242, 243, 263, 305, 373
Royal Crescent Hotel, Brighton 191, 327
Royal Hunt of the Sun, The (Shaffer) 209
Royal Shakespeare Company (RSC) 21, 28, 56, 57, 123, 245, 255, 270, 275, 303, 308, 310, 373
Rozienko, Vladimir 364, 370
Rudman, Michael 313–14
Rules restaurant, Maiden Lane, London 218

Sa Tortuga coffee shop, Chelsea 212
Sagan, Françoise 245
St Joan (Shaw) 246
Salisbury pub, St Martin's Lane, London 108, 174, 246
Salomé (Wilde) 280, 314, 359–62, 380–81, 388, 392
San Francisco 48
Sanderson Wallpapers and Fabrics 165
Saroyan, William 22, 225
Sartain, Donald 254
Sartre, Jean-Paul 22, 113, 185, 222
Saturday Night and Sunday Morning (Sillitoe) 239
Saville, Philip 258, 259, 260, 261
Saville Theatre, London 125, 126, 227, 230, 264
Scarfe, Gerald 3–4, 47, 346
Scase, David 275, 280, 281
Schad, Christian 347

Schaffner, Franklin 304
Schall, Ekkehard 219
Scheider, Roy 331
Schell, Maximilian 185
Schiller, Johann Christoph Friedrich von 219
Schlesinger, John 224
Schneider, Romy 125, 128
Scofield, Paul 116, 182, 246, 256, 348
Scotland 265–8
Scott, George C. 208
Scrase-Dickins, Alwyne 300
Screens, The (Genet) 116
Scurfield, Matthew 19, 379, 382–3
Seagull, The (Chekhov) 330
Segal, Bernardo 241
Seidman and Son (Moll) 280
Selby, Hubert, Jnr 192
Sell, Christian 367
Semi-Detached (Turner) 264–5
Seneca 51, 116
Seven Arrows 340
Seven Deadly Sins 307
Seventh Veil, The (Box and Box) 234
Shakespeare, William 1, 2, 28, 48, 62, 64, 93, 109, 112, 123, 159, 177, 179, 190, 209, 214, 216, 221, 222, 228, 238, 239, 251, 275, 282, 295, 296, 298, 301, 302, 359, 384, 390
Shaul, Liz 175, 181
Shaw, George Bernard 69, 113, 284
Shaw, Robert 260, 261
Shaw, Vincent 177, 230, 231, 244
Shepard, Sam 69
Shepherd, Mrs (at W. Bill) 162, 163
Sher, Tony 337, 363, 364, 365, 372, 373, 376, 378, 379, 380, 383, 387
Sheriff of Fractured Jaw, The (film) 224
Shivas, Mark 7–8, 66
Shivas, Mr (English teacher) 7–8, 11
Shmidt, Estella 367
Simon, Neil 98
Six Day War 127, 291–2, 293
Skiathos 327
Skyros 314, 327
Sleep, Wayne 60
Smart and Weston menswear 161
Smith, Roger 153

Snowdon, Lord *see* Armstrong-Jones
Soho Market, London 241
Southend, Essex 48
Spain 303–4
Speilberg, Mrs 93
Spohr, Will 121
Spriggs, Elizabeth 245
Stabb, Dinah 108, 298
Stallone, Sylvester 333–4
Stamford Hill, London xi, 12, 13, 15, 25, 29, 30–31, 33, 34, 35, 42, 43, 48, 65, 66, 70, 133, 134, 149, 151, 161, 178, 203, 252–3
Stamford Hill Boys' Club, London 12, 15, 33, 133
Stamford House, Shepherds Bush, London 138
Stamp, Terence 113, 114, 274
Stander, Lionel 276
Stanislavski (Konstantin Sergeivitch Alexeyev) 109
Stanley, Kim 263
Stanton, Barry 19, 20–21, 328, 368, 379
Stanyon, Bryan 178
Steele, Barbara 338
Stephen D (based on Joyce) 286
Stephens, Robert 184, 188
Stepmother, The 234
Stevens, Roger 241, 386
Storey, David 125
Strasberg, Lee 97
Stratford East 187, 231, 270, 272, 274, 276
Streetcar Named Desire, A (Williams) 176, 222, 266, 267, 352
Strindberg, August 315, 316, 320
Strong, Roy 307
Stuart, Bill 307, 309, 310, 328, 372
Sturm und Drang 392
Summerfield, Diana 154
Sunday Times 274, 302, 346, 362, 371, 372, 385
Super Cinema 44, 45
Sutherland, Donald 260

Tanner, Stella 70
Tanner, Tony 179, 180
Taste of Honey, A (Delaney) 231

Tea and Sympathy 234
Teatro della Pergola, Florence 280
Tel Aviv 127, 364
Tell-Tale Heart, The (Poe) 354
Tenerife 351–2
Terry, Dame Ellen 207
Thatcherism 373, 375
The Place theatre 300, 302
Théâtre du Rond-Point, Paris 95
Theatre and its Double, The (Artaud) 182
Theatre Royal, Brighton 227
Theatre Royal, Drury Lane, London 216
Theatre Royal, Stratford East 270
Thieves' Carnival, The (Anouilh) 180
This Sporting Life (film) 125
Thompson, David 270, 271, 272, 276
Time magazine 69
Time of Your Life, The (Saroyan) 22
Time Out 3, 296, 301, 321, 327, 359, 362
Times, The 126, 318, 386
'Tis Pity She's a Whore (Ford) 222–3, 311, 312
Titus Andronicus (Shakespeare) 29, 307, 308
Toller, Ernst 188, 222
Tottenham 31, 43
Tottenham Lido 14
Tottenham Royal (a Mecca dance hall) 31, 34, 37, 38–9, 41, 47, 68, 134, 136
Traverse Theatre, Edinburgh 20, 48–9, 50, 268
Treasure Island 243
Treblinka 74
Trial, The (Kafka) 76–7; *see also under* Berkoff, Steven
Trier 168
Troxy Cinema, Poplar 7
Tsarfati, Asher 110, 128
Tucker, Chris 337
Turner, David 264
Tushingham, Rita 188
Twelfth Night (Shakespeare) 292
Twigg, Mrs (of Buxton) 231
Tynan, Kathleen 274
Tynan, Kenneth 188, 219, 242, 274–5
Tyzack, Maggie 284

Ubu Roi (Jarry) 109
Ulysses in Nightown (Barkentin) 341
Unexpected Guest, The (Christie) 234, 388
Unity Theatre, King's Cross, London 235, 236
Ustinov, Peter 240

Valentine, Dicky 16
Van Gogh, Vincent 210, 390
Vakhtangov, Evgeny 98
Variorum (Shakespeare) 228
Vaudeville Theatre, Strand, London 269, 270, 272
Velázquez, Diego de Silva y 363
Victorian Comedy, A 112
Vienna 95, 336, 337, 376
Vienna International Festival 309, 328, 329, 336
View From the Bridge, A (Miller) 225–6, 232, 233, 234
Village Voice 325

W. Bill, South Molton Street, London 162–3
Wailing Wall, Jerusalem 100, 102
Waiting for Godot (Beckett) 271
Wajda, Andrzej 243, 376
Walken, Chris 1, 371
Walpole, Hugh 235
Wanamaker, Sam 230
War and Peace (Tolstoy) 263, 264
War and Remembrance (television programme) 335
Ward, Eliza 289–90, 301, 316, 318
Wardle, Irving 3, 126, 318, 388
Warner, David 245
Warner, Deborah 95, 348
Warner, John 285
Warner, Marina 3
Webber-Douglas Academy of Dramatic Art 54, 55, 110–16, 120–22, 223–6, 274, 290, 296, 297, 308, 339, 363, 378
Wedekind, Frank 185
Wednesday Play series (BBC television) 259
Weill, Kurt 254
Weldon, Duncan 280, 281
Welles, Orson 116, 185, 208, 243, 269, 270

Wesker, Arnold 110, 184, 188–9, 242, 243
West Side Story (Berstein, Laurents and Sondheim) 241, 386
Westhaven 269
White, Michael 223
Whitechapel, London 25, 26, 210, 335
Whitman, Walt 390
Who's Afraid of Virginia Woolf (Albee) 269–70, 284
Widmark, Richard 151
Wiesbaden 166, 168–72, 182, 189, 195, 199, 235
Wild One, The (film) 151
Wilde, Jimmy 6, 211
Wilde, Oscar 134, 176, 210, 221, 267, 354, 358–61
Wilder, Thornton 180
Williams, Clifford 245
Williams, Robin 363
Williams, Steve 308, 309, 310, 311, 312, 313
Williams, Tennessee 113, 194, 222, 241–2, 290, 325–6, 390
Williamson, Nicol 108, 125, 176, 274, 280
Willis, Kathleen 231
Wilson, Pilton 231
Wind in the Willows, The (Bennett) 387
Windmill Theatre, London 16
Wingham, Walter 231, 233
Winter Garden, Drury Lane, London 219–20, 226
Wise, Barry 34–5, 36, 37, 139, 149, 203
Wood, Colin 316–17, 320, 326
Woodvine, John 223
World Theatre season 218, 295
Worshipful Company of Grocers 8
Worth, Irene 371
Wouk, Herman 337
Wreford, Edgar 285
Write Me a Murder (Knott) 222, 249, 388
Wyndham's Theatre, Charing Cross Road, London 3, 4
Wyngarde, Peter 223, 345

Yeats, W. B. 210
Yiddish Theatre, London 356
Yiddish Theatre, New York 241
YMCA, Tottenham Court Road,
    London 21, 27, 28, 212, 243, 247,
    300, 305
Young Elizabeth, The (Dowling and
    Letton) 114
Young Vic 254

Zanzibar Club 59–60, 61, 63
Zohar, Uri 124–5, 126, 128–9, 130
Zoo Story (Albee) 270–76, 280, 284,
    285, 314–15, 318–19, 326